HOLISTIC LONDON

The London Guide to Mind, Body & Spirit

Kate Brady
Mike Considine

Brainwave • London

Acknowledgements

Book reviews

Brian Wade of Changes Bookshop for reviews in the Psychotherapy section
David Redstone and staff at Watkins Bookshop for reviews in Body and Spirit section

Writers

Will Parfitt for the section on Qabalah
Richard Mowbray for the section on Primal Integration

Anecdote writers

Gill Stow, Karin Grey, Malcolm Stern, Sabine Kurjo McNeil, Alex Read, Anne Turner, David Templar, Christine Davidson, Sue Anne Deakin, Andy Hilton, Sue Owen, Imogen Fox, Mary Fee, Maureen Kennedy.

Production team

Danielle Juving, Gill Stow, Karin Grey, Ofra Anker.

Other help

Thanks also to: The Institute of Complementary Medicine, Malcolm Stern, William Bloom, Stephanie Collins and Guy Dauncey for information; Tony Day for emergency computer counselling.

Disclaimer

While every effort has been made to provide accurate information, the publishers do not assume and hereby disclaim any liability to any party for loss or damage caused by errors or omissions in this book.

Inclusion in this book is not intended in any way as a recommendation or ensorsement of individuals, organisations or therapies and is not an indication of the quality of therapy, medicine or instruction given by any of the individuals or organisations included.

Further copies of this book

These can be obtained from Brainwave, BCM Raft, London WC1N 3XX. Please send £7.95 plus £1 post and packing (UK only).

Published by Brainwave
BCM Raft
London WC1N 3XX

© BRAINWAVE 1990

Printed in Great Britain by
BPCC Wheatons Ltd, Exeter

Cover illustration by Bodel Rikys

ISBN 0 9513347 1 9

Published May 1990

Line illustrations froma selection of Dover Publications Inc, New York, copyright free books.

Like to write about *your* experiences?

We are looking for anecdotes and stories about readers' experiences of psychotherapy, alternative medicine, spiritual approaches and aspects of holistic health and growth, for the next edition.

If you would like to contribute, send your stories to us as at **Holistic London, BCM Raft, London WC1N 3XX**. Stories should be a maximum of 350 words long, and names of real people or organisations should be omittted or changed. You will be credited in the book (though you may retain anonymity if you wish) and receive a free copy of the edition in which your story is published.

Looking forward to hearing from you!

Like to be listed in the next edition?

Inclusion in the listings of *Holistic London* is free. If you would like your centre or organisation to be included in the next edition of Holisic London, or know of a centre or organisation which you think would like to be included, please fill in the form below, and send to **Holistic London, Brainwave, BCM Raft, London WC1N 3XX.** We will send you details of how to be listed when preparing the next edition.

— —

Please send the organisation below details about how to be listed in the next edition of *Holistic London.*

Name of contact in organisation_____

Organisation_____

Address _____

_____

Telephone number_____

Type of organisation (e.g. psychotherapy or natural therapies centre, spiritual group etc)

_____

Any other comments_____

_____

PSYCHOTHERAPY

Introduction

What is Psychotherapy? 1 • The Difference between Psychotherapy and Counselling 1• The Difference between Psychology and Psychotherapy 2• Approaches to Psychotherapy 2• The Varieties of Psychotherapy 3• Does Psychotherapy Work? 4• Styles of the Therapist 4• Who Should have Psychotherapy? 4• How to Choose a Particular Psychotherapy 5• How to Choose a Therapist 5• Individual Therapy Versus Group Therapy 6• Does the Sex of the Therapist Matter? 8• Too Old for Therapy? 8• Cost 8• What the Different Centres are Like 8

Training in Psychotherapy

Why Train in Psychotherapy? 9• Which School of Psychotherapy to Train In? 9• The Training Programmes 9• Accreditation and 1992 11• Can I Get Work When Trained? 12•Entry Requirements 12• Cost of Training 12

The Psychotherapies

Other Psychotherapies 76-77

Adlerian Psychotherapy • Anti-smoking Therapy • Bereavement Counselling • Biosynthesis • Child Psychotherapy • Creativity Counselling • Dream Therapy • Eating Problem Counselling • Enlightenment Intensives • Hakomi Method • Inter-cultural Therapy • Journal Keeping • Life Improvement Workshops • Management Training • Mind Clearing • Past Life Therapy • Regression Therapy • Resonance Therapy • Video Therapy

Other Trainings 78-79

Adlerian • Arts/creativity • Biodynamic Psychology • Child Psychotherapy • Enlightenment Intensives • Mind Clearing

Eclectic or Special Trainings 79-80

BODY THERAPIES

Introduction 83

Training in Body Therapies

The Body Therapies

Other Body Therapies 165-167

Other Trainings 167-168

SPIRIT

Introduction
What is Spiritual? 171 • The difference between Religion and Spirituality 171 • The Search for a New Spirituality 171• East meets west 172 • Gurus and spiritual teachers 173 • Cults 173 • Different types of Groups 174 • What they do 174 • Spiritual Groups in London 176 • Spirituality versus Psychology 176 • The 'New Age' 177

Meditation 181
The Traditions
Buddhism 185• Christianity 187• Hinduism 189• Paganism 191• Qabalah 192• Shamanism 193 • Spiritualism 197 • Sufism 198

Modern Teachers 199
Other Groups 203

RESOURCES

Communication 209
Bookshops • Libraries • Publishers and Distributors • Films • Magazines and Publications • Networks

Education 224
Recognised Academic Courses • Adult Education Classes

Products 226
Air Purifiers • Aromatherapy Oils • Back Products • Biofeedback Machines • Biorhythm Charts • Birthing Pools • Clothes and Shoes • Crystals • Friendship Agencies • Daylight Bulbs • Home Acupuncture • Futons • Games • Herbs and Herbal Remedies • Homoeopathic Pharmacies • Ionisers • Jewellery • Juicers • Martial Arts Suppliers • Massage Aids • Miscellaneous • Natural Birth Control • Organic Wines • Pollution Control • Posters • Recruitment • Tapes - Personal Development • Tapes - Music • Tapes - Relaxation • Videos • Water Filters

Services 243
Ethically Sound Investments • Rooms For Hire

Food 247
Macrobiotics • Vegetarianism and Veganism • Vegetarian Resaurants

London Getaway 253
Residential Workshops • Holidays • Residential Communities • Residential Health Centres • Retreats

Events 262
Discos And Dances • Lectures • Exhibitions • Galleries And Museums • Radio Counselling • Other Events

Help 264
Organisations For Specific Problems • Useful Organisations

LIST OF CENTRES 271

INTRODUCTION TO PSYCHOTHERAPY

What is Psychotherapy?
Psychotherapy is a term used to denote a variety of methods in dealing with emotional problems. There are many different types of psychotherapy, and each of these therapies may differ considerably from one another. What they all have in common is they all try to help the client in changing. In each of their own ways they will enable the client to better understand his or her self, feelings and relationships with others and help to explore new ways of behaving. It may involve the client re-enacting old conflicts within the therapy but with a resulting different outcome so that the client finds new ways of dealing and resolving those conflicts. Most of the therapies can be seen as a teaching in the art of therapy so that when the client leaves the therapy he or she will be able to continue his or her own analysis.

In general usage the word psychotherapy is confined to what goes on between a therapist and a client, though this limited definition leaves out self-help and help that can be offered by lay people - and the magnitude of this help should not be underestimated. The advantage of seeing a therapist is that the client will have the space to deal with his or her concerns with someone who has an armoury of strategies in helping.

The Difference between Psychotherapy and Counselling
Counselling used within this book refers to psychotherapeutic counselling rather than other types of counselling such as career or financial counselling. A caption on an Oxfam billboard advertisement many years ago read 'Give a man a fish and you feed him for a day. Teach a man to fish and you feed him for a lifetime'. Analogously counselling is usually an approach which helps the client with a problem, whereas psychotherapy is aimed at helping the client to help himself with his own problems. After receiving psychotherapy the client should be able to manage the daily tasks of living without getting tied up in destructive or mundane patterns of behaviour or negative feelings. Counselling is usually much shorter and involves less personal change on the part of the client. Counselling usually revolves around a specific problem while psychotherapy may not do so. However, having said that, there is still a great overlap between counselling and psychotherapy.

1

PSYCHOTHERAPY

The Difference between Psychology and Psychotherapy

Psychology is the study of human behaviour. It is primarily a science. The domain of psychology is large and covers such things as perception, intelligence, conditioning, the nervous system, the behaviour of people in groups, to name but a few. Psychotherapy is only one aspect of psychology. Psychologists enter the jobs market within a specialised field, either as industrial psychologists, educational psychologists, experimental psychologists, social psychologists or clinical psychologists. Clinical psychologists have more experience of psychotherapy than their fellows as they apply their knowledge of psychology to dealing with emotional and behavioural problems. They work in different settings throughout the National Health Service, especially in mental hospitals and institutions for people with a mental handicap. Psychotherapists, on the whole, have much more varied backgrounds. Whilst some are clinical psychologists, others are psychiatrists and social workers, and there are many who have a teaching and management background.

Approaches to Psychotherapy

There are four main approaches to psychotherapy: psychoanalytic, humanistic, cognitive and behavioural. The psychoanalytic approach developed by Sigmund Freud explains behaviour in terms of the interplay between the conscious and unconscious mind of an individual. Freud believed that innate instincts, especially the sex and aggressive instincts, are often disapproved of in our society and are driven out of the individual's awareness, but remain in the unconscious affecting behaviour. Glimpses of the unconscious are to be had from dreams, slips of the tongue, mannerisms, some symptoms of mental illness and some artistic endeavours. Most psychoanalysts prefer to speak in terms of levels of awareness rather than a conscious-unconscious divide.

The second approach is humanistic or phenomenological. The ideas of the humanistic psychologists are similar to, and draw upon, the writings of the existentialists. Emphasis is placed on how individuals subjectively experience the world, and what sense they make of it. The humanistic psychologists are concerned with the inner life of the individual and how they experience themselves and others. They are interested in concepts of self-esteem, feelings, authenticity, self awareness and consciousness.

Thirdly there is the cognitive approach. This approach argues that we are constantly processing information in selective and organised ways, such as when planning and solving problems. We make sense of the world using particular views and assumptions which have been conditioned by our previous experience. By consciously adopting another point of view, we can change our behaviour.

Fourthly there is the behavioural approach, sometimes known as Stimulus/ Response Psychology. This approach is based on 'learning theory' which grew from experiments with animals. Behaviourists emphasise how the environment 'conditions' people to behave in certain ways and that people modify their behaviour to suit the surroundings. Punishment and reward are the stick and the carrot for this process. For instance if a child is punished for succeeding and rewarded for failing then the child will learn to fail; or we might say the child has been conditioned to fail. Since behaviour was learned, behaviourists argue that undesirable behaviour could be unlearned and be replaced by more desirable forms of behaviour.

The Varieties of Psychotherapy
Most therapists practise one of the four approaches (or a combination of these approaches) described above. There are however, literally hundreds of different types or 'schools ' of psychotherapy which come under the four basic approaches. Each of these schools has its own theories about why people behave the way they do and on how to treat emotional problems. These different types of psychotherapy may differ dramatically from one another, even though the desired aims of the therapies may well be the same.

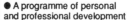

In this book we describe the major schools of psychotherapy, enabling the reader to steer through the minefield. The less well known psychotherapies are catalogued at the end of this section.

Does Psychotherapy Work?

Nobody knows if any one psychotherapy is better than another. This is partly because a great deal of research has yet to be carried out before any satisfactory conclusions can be drawn, and partly because the effectiveness of psychotherapy depends on the particular set of circumstances of the client and upon the unique quality of any therapeutic relationship. This is one reason why therapists tend to draw upon other psychotherapeutic approaches in their work. A transactional analysis therapist, for instance, may, at times use a psychoanalytic approach, or some technique he or she has borrowed from another school of psychotherapy.

Styles of the Therapist

The label of therapist gives herself may well not describe what he or she does. Two gestalt therapists, for instance, may operate in completely different ways. One may tend to ask the group to try out lots of exercises, whereas the other may not do this at all. The one therapist may be very warm and protective of the group members whereas the other may be cold and reserved. This is partly due to the character of the therapist, but it is also because no psychotherapeutic approach can ever fully determine a therapist's behaviour.

Who Should have Psychotherapy?

Most people can benefit from psychotherapy. Some people are put off therapy because they think it is just for people who are mad, or that it is an admission of weakness and of not being able to cope, or that it is something that New Yorkers spend a great deal of time and money having without ever really getting anywhere. Therapy is usually intended both as a way of healing and a method of personal growth. It is meant to help those with conflicts and problems, as well as those who are simply dissatisfied with themselves and their lives, who feel blank, bored or want more out of themselves and their relationships. Sometimes people in this last category feel drawn to psychotherapy, but worry that if they go to see a therapist, he or she will think they are 'malingering' because they are not desperate or in crisis. In fact many therapies concentrate a great deal on the idea of growth, and that therapy is too good to be limited just to those whose problems severely restrict their lives.

The most important thing is perhaps that you make the choice to do it. While this is not irrevocable, and leaves room for experimentation, it is important that you do not feel pushed into doing it by someone else, or that you know it would be a good idea but do not really feel very enthusiastic. If you do not feel it is your decision then you may just feel resentful so that the whole process may not work for you. Sometimes people who are doing therapy may try and push partners, friends or relatives into therapy because they want them to change. Unfortunately this kind of pressure can turn the decision into a kind of power struggle, and make it very difficult for the person considering therapy to feel that they can make the decision of their own free will.

How to Choose a Particular Psychotherapy
This book explains many of the different psychotherapies on offer. If any particular approach appeals to you, further reading will give you more information, though this will be theoretical. To get an experience of therapy, many of the centres listed run weekend workshops which will enable you to get a taste of the therapy in action in a group setting. If you want to get an idea of what a particular approach is like in one to one sessions, then introductory sessions with a psychotherapist who uses the approach might be indicated.

How to Choose a Therapist
The title 'psychotherapist' is not regulated by law and at present in this country there is no licencing procedure. This means that anyone can set themselves up as a psychotherapist, even if they have no formal training in psychotherapy. So it is possible that you might choose a therapist who has not undergone adequate training. However, having said that, in our experience those therapists who are poor at their job don't last long in the marketplace, and soon retire.

If you have decided that a particular therapy appeals to you then there are a number of ways of finding a psychotherapist. Look up that therapy in this book and you will find the organisations that practice them listed, together with training organisations. It is suggested that you contact one of the training organisations if one is listed. They usually keep a register of practitioners they have trained and will be able to refer you to one. Training organisations are a reliable way of finding a therapist because they are likely to recommed only those who they think have reached a certain standard, and who and subscribe to their code of ethics. If no training organisation is listed, then choose one of the centres which practice the therapy and contact them. They are listed under the description of the therapy. It's worth asking either the training organisation or centre to send you a brochure of what they offer. This will enable you to browse through their literature before making any commitment.

If you do not know which type of therapy you want and you do not feel you can make that decision then you can contact an umbrella organisation, such as the *Association for Humanistic Psychology Practitioners (AHPP), the British Psychoanalytic Society (BPS)* or the *British Association for Counselling (BAC)*. All are listed at the back of this book with some details about them.

Having found a psychotherapist, it is advisable to have a few introductory sessions before embarking on a long-term commitment. It is important to find a therapist with whom you can have a good working relationship. Carl Rogers, a well-known figure in the field of counselling and psychotherapy, suggests that clients gain positive benefits from psychotherapy if the therapist is perceived by the client to be warm and caring, authentic and honest, and understanding of the way the client sees the world. If you perceive your therapist to have these qualities, and if you are learning about yourself in the therapy, then he or she may be the right therapist for you.

Individual Therapy Versus Group Therapy

Individual psychotherapy is the most common form of psychotherapy. The advantage of this type of approach is that the client and the therapist can focus on the client's particular problems for the entire session. Individual therapy also has the advantage that confidential information can be discussed without fear of public criticism. It is also useful in that the client has the opportunity to develop a close relationship with one person. This might be useful if the client has had difficulty in forming close relationships and finds the idea of groups frightening.

In individual therapy the client and therapist usually meet at least once a week for one hour. Some therapists prefer to work to the golden 50 minute hour, others may work for up to two hours. Often therapists insist on meeting for more than once a week and for psychoanalysis five times a week is the norm. Many therapists work outside of normal office hours to accommodate their clients.

The advantage of group therapy is that it allows others to give feedback on one person's behaviour, rather than the solitary feedback offered by the therapist in individual therapy. The therapist sees how you are interacting with other members of the group rather than simply listening to your reports. It may be that the therapist and the group members can offer some observations on your behaviour with others of which you may have been unaware. A further advantage of group therapy is that it enables you to understand how others may have similar problems and difficulties as yourself and so feel less alone.

Group therapy is usually conducted in small groups of between four and fourteen members with one psychotherapist present, though there are a number of exceptions to this. There may be more than one therapist; for instance in couple therapy the norm is two therapists. Sometimes the groups can be larger, and 'large group therapy' as it is called can involve over one hundred people in one group (the Introductory Course at the The Institute of Group Analysis runs a group of one hundred and forty members) though such large groups in therapy are rare.

The timeframe for the group may vary considerably between different groups and different therapies. The two most frequent formats are weekend workshops or once weekly evening workshops. Some of the other variations include meeting throughout the day for one, two, three or four weeks (these are usually residential and are sometimes known as intensives); 24 and 48 hour marathons (the members stay together for all of this period and get little sleep); meeting in the early morning

before normal working hours; twice weekly evening groups; a combination of the aforementioned. Some people prefer to live in therapeutic communities where the boundary between therapy and everyday life can be blurred.

Does the Sex of the Therapist Matter?

Generally the sex of the therapist does not matter. Many people have difficulty in communicating with people of one or other gender. In this case they may find it too difficult to develop a relationship of trust with a therapist of this gender, and in this case it might be best to choose a therapist of the sex with which they feel more comfortable. For example if a woman is scared of men it might be best if she chooses a female therapist, or if a man is angry at women he might do better choosing a male therapist. However it may not necessarily be the opposite sex which the client finds difficult. The individual might, after some therapy, switch to a therapist of the more problematic sex to work through any unresolved issues to do with that gender.

Too Old for Therapy?

Undergoing therapy requires that you be open to change and open to new feelings and experiences. This openness to what is new and novel in understanding oneself is not related to chronological age.

Cost

Psychotherapy is expensive, but the rates may vary enormously from practitioner to practitioner. Usually the more experienced a practitioner is the more he or she will charge. But don't think that if you pay more you will automatically get a better practitioner. It is best to hunt around for value for money. Some therapists offer discounts for the low waged.

What the Different Centres are Like

Psychotherapy centres can vary from a therapist working from a room at his or her own house to a bevy of practitioners and associated administrative staff accommodated in a six storey purpose-built block. The usual set-up is a handful of practitioners who have banded together to form a practice, and use a room in one of their houses, or hire rooms in a building in which to practise. It is therefore advisable if you are not familiar with the centre to ring beforehand to make an appointment rather than turn up on the doorstep. Do not be disconcerted if the centre does not turn out to be a prestigious building. The cost of running a prestigious building may well be reflected in the fees that are charged. What is important is the quality and training of the therapist.

TRAINING IN PSYCHOTHERAPY

Why Train in Psychotherapy?

Helping other people can be very rewarding. Training as a psychotherapist means that you will have the opportunity to work on your own growth and use what you have learnt to help others undergoing the same process. Some practical advantages of working as a therapist are that you are your own boss, you can earn a decent living, and, having trained, you may also be able to apply your skills in some other setting, such as education or social work. However, the work of a psychotherapist can also be very stressful. Sometimes it is hard to cut off emotionally from clients outside working hours. It may well not turn out to pay as well as you think it will. You may even end up finding that you cannot get enough clients to support yourself. You may need to work outside of the normal nine to five office hours, and this may well bite into your social life. Are you sure you want to do it?

Which School of Psychotherapy to Train In?

Before you apply for training in any psychotherapy you should have some experience of that psychotherapy yourself. In fact many training organisations make this a requirement. Rather than embark on a training programme for a therapy you have been involved in, it might be best to sample different psychotherapies before training, just to be sure that you are making the right decision.

The Training Programmes

A training programme should include (1) opportunity for the trainee to work on own personal material (2) observation of practitioners at work with their clients/groups (3) adequate supervision when a trainee begins to see clients/groups (4) personal experience of being a participant in a group if training is in group work, or of being a client in one to one sessions if the training is in individual therapy. A training programme in psychotherapy is usually at least three years long. Most are conducted on a part-time basis, utilising evenings and weekends, so that it is possible to hold a full-time job at the same time. It is best to be wary of trainings that are only short in duration. Whilst they may be called a 'training' they will not be able to offer you a full programme which will equip you for this profession. Trainings in counselling are usually shorter than therapy training.

However, bear in mind that these training programmes have not been independently assessed. This means that any graduation certificates or diplomas they award on completion of the training may, in the end, be recognised only by the institute itself. The value of the training rests upon whether or not the therapeutic community as a whole find the institute to be reputable. If you know someone who is a psychologist, therapist, psychiatrist, social worker, counsellor or psychiatric nurse, they may be able to advise you about the reputation of the training institute.

Accreditation and 1992

At present there is no licencing procedure for counsellors or psychotherapists in this country. Many therapists have invested a lot of money in training, in the knowledge and fear that future legislation may exclude them from practising. Many potential trainees are wondering whether to invest their money in training for similar reasons. What is the story so far, and what advice can be offered, bearing in mind that the European Economic Community will be dropping its internal trade barriers in 1992?

In Holland and Italy only psychiatrists and clinical psychologists are allowed to practise psychotherapy. After 1992 this will mean that psychotherapists from Italy and Holland will be able to come to the UK to practise but many British psychotherapists will not be able to practise there, as many British psychotherapists are not clinical psychologists or psychiatrists. If more EEC countries adopt Holland and Italy's approach this will eventually mean British psychotherapists will be at a disadvantage and the UK will be forced into opting to go the way of allowing only graduates with relevant degrees to practise psychotherapy. It may take five to ten years for this to happen, though it could be sooner.

In Britain a move towards some form of regulation for psychotherapy began with the formation of a federation of psychotherapy training organisations, the *Rugby Conference,* to talk about this issue. It has recently changed its name to the *U.K. Standing Conference on Psychotherapy (UKSCP* - address at the back of the book). Their aim is to accredit trainings in psychotherapy by a process of self-regulatory monitoring of each other's training programmes, and to accredit the therapists who have trained with those organisations. It looks as if they are still a couple of years away from being able to answer potential trainees' questions about whether particular training organisations are accredited by them. If you are a psychotherapist and are worried about your future status you might keep in touch with and support the *UKSCP.* They will be at the *European Conference on Psychotherapy* in Amsterdam on 15th Dec 1990 (you can contact the *UKSCP* for times of future conferences) where issues involved in psychotherapy regulation will be discussed, and they will be hoping to influence the EEC on British therapists' interests. However, even if the *UKSCP* is successful with its self monitoring programme there is no guarantee that the government will not bring in legislation requiring a relevent degree to practice therapy.

The situation for counselling is different than for therapy. The *British Association for Counselling (BAC* - an independent charity, address at the back of the book) has recently started accrediting organisations which offer a training in counselling. They are able to tell potential trainee counsellors which organisations they accredit, but they are still some way off from processing all the trainings in the UK. The *British Psychological Society* has recently introduced a Diploma in Counselling Psychology which is likely to become a standard in the field of counselling.

PSYCHOTHERAPY

Can I get Work When Trained?
Few psychotherapists are employed within the NHS, though there are many health service professionals who practice psychotherapy. The majority of psychotherapists work in the private sector and are thus self employed. Working for oneself can be perilous as one is at the mercy of market forces. Should the market be saturated with psychotherapists at any one time then there are less clients to go round and psychotherapists trying to set up a practice will find it especially difficult. Before you embark on a training programme you should be thinking about how you will get your clients when you have finished. Will the training institute supply you with clients? Will they supply you with enough clients? It is important that they will support you when you are initially setting up a practice, as this is a most difficult time. You should discuss these points with them. There are quite a few therapists now barely scratching out a living from the few clients they have on their books. Very few training institutes equip their trainees with knowledge of business practices, something every successful psychotherapist operating in the private sector must know.

Entry Requirements
Most centres do not require that you hold a degree to be accepted for training. Many of the centre organisers believe that a degree is not a good indicator of what makes a good therapist. There is no general agreement as to what makes a good therapist. Different institutes have their own criteria, based on their own idea of what qualities are needed in a therapist. Some prefer you to be medically trained, other centres think this might work against you. Some prefer you to be somewhat crazy (so that you will have some idea of mental suffering), some others want the opposite.We indicate wherever possible the basic entry requirements of each training centre.

Cost of Training
Training is expensive and in some cases may run into five figures. There are not only fees for the course, but there may also be hidden costs, such as supervision fees and own required psychotherapy, which may be considerable and far in excess of the training fees. For instance if you are required to undergo personal therapy three times a week then this could amount to £3000 per year alone. We have tried to include all of these costs wherever possible. Do not forget to include VAT at 15% in your calculations when determining the total cost of training.

THE PSYCHOTHERAPIES

Art Therapy

People know intuitively that self expression is a way of healing oneself, whether it is through drawing, dancing, sculpting or building. Art therapy is one such means of seeking release and of understanding oneself. Its usefulness is not only for emotional release. An art therapist, through interpreting the meaning of the symbols produced, hopes to come to some understanding of the client, and to enable the client to make fresh discoveries about life and self.

The process of drawing, painting or modelling can help the client to objectify or detach themselves from feelings or problems that may seem otherwise too overwhelming to deal with. The contents of the unconscious can become visible in a very immediate way, and this method often by-passes the censoring process with which we obscure feelings and thoughts which disturb us.

Therapists of different persuasions use the medium of art. Their approach will differ depending on their school of thought. Art therapy is widely used in the humanistic psychologies, where there is more emphasis on interpretation by the client of his or her own productions. They may be interpreted in a Freudian or Jungian way if the art therapist subscribes to either of these frameworks.

Within the health service it is used mainly in psychiatric hospitals and day centres. It is especially effective with severely disturbed people who find it difficult to express their feelings verbally.

It may be used by psychotherapists practising within the NHS, or by specifically trained Art Therapists.

PSYCHOTHERAPY

READING

Art As Therapy *by Dalley, T. (eds) RKP £5.95*. Subtitled 'An Introduction to the Use of Art as a Therapeutic Technique', this is a collection of articles by practitioners of various backgrounds showing the many ways art therapy is used. It covers work both inside institutions and outside in growth oriented situations. **The Inward Journey; Art as Therapy** *by Keyes, M. Open Court 1984, £9.50*. Based around Jungian and Gestalt approaches, this is a practical handbook, full of strategies using sculpture, painting, mandalas, music and myth, providing a useful insight into how art therapy can work for the individual.

CENTRES OFFERING ART THERAPY

Art from Within, British Association for Social Psychiatry W1, Creative Arts Workshops N8, Highbury Centre N5, Imprint SW19, Person-Centred Art Therapy Centre NW11, Playspace NW1, Resonance SW17, St James Centre for Health and Healing W1, Studio 8 (Bristol), Women's Therapy Centre N7.

TRAININGS IN ART THERAPY

Goldsmiths' College *Title of Training* 1) Diploma in Art Therapy 2) M.A. in Art Therapy 3) Diploma in Group Therapy *Duration* 1) Two years part-time or one year full-time. 2) Two years part-time. 3) Three years part-time. *Entry requirements* For the art therapy courses, non art graduates need to demonstrate a long standing commitment to practise in the visual arts. 1) Degree in Art or Design or other approved subject. 2) Should be a qualified art therapist or other professional with a commitment to the theoretical development of art therapy. 3) Degree or professional qualification. *Fees* 1) For a unsponsored student £304 p.a. part-time, £607 p.a. full time. 2) For a unsponsored student £595 p.a. part-time, £1890 p.a. full time. 3) £750 p.a. part-time.

Assertion Training

Assertion training, which is sometimes known as assertiveness training, aims to help the client gain specific social skills in expressing feelings, thoughts, wishes and behaviours which allow her or him to stand up for their rights in particular situations. Because the focus is on particular change in behaviours, behaviour therapy has contributed much to this field, although humanistic psychology has also had its part to play.

The procedure of assertion training can be mapped under three headings. Firstly there is skills training, where verbal and non-verbal behaviours are taught and practised. This is mostly done in role play, where a situation requiring assertion is rehearsed and acted out. For example, a situation of returning faulty goods to a store may be enacted. The client is instructed on how to go about getting satisfaction, and the stage is set for the client to act as the irate customer with other members of the group playing the part of shopkeeper, manager and so on. Emphasis is placed on the difference between acting assertively and appearing aggressive. Homework may also be given and clients may be asked to keep a journal. Clients may be asked to assert themselves in situations outside the group and to report back on their endeavours.

Secondly, methods of reducing anxiety are taught. This may take the form of relaxation exercises, or of desensitisation. Desensitisation as used in assertion training is the process of learning to handle one's anxiety by taking the assertive role in easy stages, perhaps initially by fantasising about it and then taking on an easy assertiveness task, so that in this way the anxiety does not overwhelm. To some extent anxiety is reduced when a role play is satisfactorily completed.

Thirdly, values and beliefs about the rights of the individual in society are examined. This is particularly the case for groups within society such as women, children and ethnic minorities. The effects of social conditioning and the part it plays in people's perceptions of their own rights is considered.

In London there is a wealth of adult education classes on this subject. Consult Floodlight for a list of venues.

READING

A Woman in Your Own Right *by Dickson, A. Quartet 1982 £4.95.* Assertion is often confused with aggression. In this book the author dispels this myth and presents a full programme for developing a more fulfilling life by standing up for yourself. She deals with assertive approaches to sexuality, the workplace, money, personal criticism and more. Although aimed at women, the ideas are usable by men and she has used the techniques in mixed sex situations. **Your Perfect Right; A Guide to Assertive Living** *by Alberti, R & Emmons, I. Impact Publications 1970 (revised 1989) £6.95.* The original book on assertion training and still one of the most comprehensive. It's written as a workbook to read and work through, using the exercises and practice situations. These are related to how one can incorporate the ideas into one's life.

CENTRES OFFERING ASSERTION TRAINING

Brunel Management Programme (Uxbridge), Human Potential Resource Group (Surrey), Maitri (Hants), Playspace NW1, Skills with People N5, Westminster Pastoral Foundation W8, Women's Therapy Centre N7, Centre for Stress Management SE3, Life Directions W1, Minster Centre NW2, Psychotherapy for Individuals, Couples & Groups N10, Redwood Women's Training Association, South Camden Women's Centre WC1, Women Unlimited SW16, Women's Therapy Centre N7.

Astrological Counselling

In astrological counselling the positions of the planets are believed to indicate the character and functioning of the individual's psyche.

The astrological counsellor will draw up the client's 'birth chart', which is a symbolic diagram of the positions of the planets at the time of birth. Through the interpretations of the chart the counsellor hopes to provide the client with insights into his or her own psychology. Events in the client's life may also be assessed by comparison between the position of planets at birth and their present position or at a time of major life events. Through interpretation of the symbolism of these, the counsellor aims to determine what psychological forces are at work and may suggest what action, if any, the client should take. The birthchart of the client may also be compared with a birthchart of a partner, to throw light on the workings of the relationship.

Astrological counselling can be distinguished from other forms of astrological birth chart interpretation because it focuses on issues broached by psychotherapy (such as how the 'shadow' of mother affects present relationships with men) rather than on character traits (such as being overgenerous). It attempts to find meaning and reveal patterns in life events rather than attempting to predict future events. The astrological counsellor will not only interpret, but also allow the client's own response to the material to emerge and become part of the counselling relationship.

Much astrological counselling has been influenced by the psychology of C G Jung (see Jungian Analysis in this section), who was interested in astrology, stating that it was 'the summation of all the psychological knowledge of antiquity'.

All but one of the research studies undertaken to confirm a connection between the planets and an individual's psyche have failed. This does not mean that astrological counselling does not work, but suggests the factors for therapeutic change lie outside that explained by its theory - though the same could be said for some other therapies.

CENTRES OFFERING ASTROLOGICAL COUNSELLING

Astro-Psychotherapeutic Practice W3, Centre for Psychological Astrology NW3, Cheirological Society W6, Healing Fields Practice N7, Reiki Centre NW3.

Autogenic Training

Autogenic training is a procedure which has many elements in common with biofeedback, relaxation training, hypnotherapy and some types of stress management, but at the same time adds some new elements of its own. It helps to induce a particular hypnotic state which is somewhere between full consciousness and sleep, and in which one has greater access to the unconscious. In this state repressed material can be accessed and then used for creative problem solving, or positive affirmations can be implanted in the unconscious. Once the technique is learned from the therapist it can be practised on one's own.

At the turn of the century Oscar Vokt found that his patients could hypnotise themselves once they had been initially hypnotised by him, and were then able to use this new found method to relieve stress and induce relaxation. A few years later H. Schultz developed a series of formulaes to help patients to enter this state quickly.

The particular hypnotic state is induced by passive concentration. The client is asked to concentrate either on the breathing process, on differences between the right and left side of the body or on tensions within the body and to repeat such statements as 'I am calm and quiet'. The client is then given exercises inducing warmth and heaviness in various parts of the body. Once the client has reached a particular stage in the training, which may take many months and which may require practice several times a day, he is then given visual exercises, such as recalling incidents from the past, or recalling the face of someone known in vivid detail. If a pleasant incident is recalled it can be 'anchored' by crossing finger and thumb, so that in the future crossing finger and thumb can induce the pleasant feelings associated with the incident.

Unwanted behaviour patterns are changed when the client is open, in the hypnotic state, to ways of being and acting which are different from his or her normal stereotyped responses. The origins of the feelings associated with the behaviour pattern may also be explored. Self affirmations such as 'I am a loving and valuable person' are often used, especially to finish the session.

Autogenic training would seem best suited to those who have difficulty relaxing and who suffer from physical ailments induced by tension, such as headaches, ulcers, high blood pressure and colitis.

READING

Autogenic Therapy *by Luthe, W & Schultz, J. (Gruer & Stratton 1969).* These are the original manuals produced by the originators of the method, unfortunately out of print (and massively expensive when they were available). There are no easily available books on the subject, but is is worth checking out **The Silva Mind Control Method** *by Silva, H. (Grafton £3.99)* as he incorporated much autogenics into his work.

CENTRES OFFERING AUTOGENIC TRAINING

Centre for Autogenic Training W1, Ealing Holistic Centre for Homoeopath and Autogenic Training W13, Hampton Healing Centre, Hampton Holistic Centre for Homoeopath and Autogenic Training (Middlesex), Neal's Yard Therapy Rooms WC2.

PSYCHOTHERAPY

Bioenergetics

Bioenergetics is a body-oriented psychotherapy. The term was introduced by Alexander Lowen who evolved this particular therapy based on the initial insights and theories of Wilhelm Reich. Lowen, an American, was analysed by Reich, and he developed Reich's work in two ways. He modified and evolved Reich's approach into his own particular school of therapy. He also wrote lucidly on the mind/body relationship, avoiding the psychoanalytic jargon which abounded in Reich's writings, and made it accessible to a larger number of people.

Much of the theory is based on Reich's original formulation that the body, mind and feelings are interrelated. The body reflects the person's character. A particular configuration of tensions within the body reflects the psychological make-up of the person. It is possible to diagnose someone's emotional constraints from looking at the tensions in their body, how they hold themselves and how they move.

By working on areas of tension within the body it is possible to contact some underlying feelings. For example, if a client grinds his or her teeth at night and complains about difficulty expressing anger, the therapist may massage or knead the jaw muscles and surrounding area which is likely to provoke this underlying rage.

Much of the therapy is taken up by doing exercises which release chronically tense muscles. Lowen was creative in inventing such exercises. Attention is paid to respiration, frozen chests, locked pelvises, tensions in the throat, feeling sick (clients are often asked to vomit rather than suppress this feeling). Lowen paid particular attention to the legs which he saw as important in terms of balance and contact with the ground and introduced the concept of grounding. Unlike Reich who worked from the head down, Lowen believed in working from the feet up. Both stressed the central role of breathing.

Bioenergetics is best done as individual therapy, where the therapist can give the client individual attention. When it is practised in groups it usually follows one of the following formats or a mixture of each: the therapist works with one individual at a time, the rest of the group learn by observing; participants pair up and help each other with a bioenergetic exercise; each participant does an exercise on his or her own with the therapist doing rounds to make sure they are getting the most from the exercise.

Many people find bioenergetics bewildering at first because they are not used to the connections between bodily tensions and feelings.

You may be asked to remove much of your clothing. Clients are often asked to wear swimwear or leotards.

READING

Bioenergetics *by Lowen. A. Penguin 1975 £4.95.* Lowen developed his approach out of his work with Wilhelm Reich, and this book is his attempt to put his theories into a usable form for the interested lay reader. Bioenergetics is a study of the human personality through the energy processes of the body, and this book is a good place to start. You may also look for his book of exercises **Way to Vibrant Health** *Harper & Row, 1977, £7.95.* **Lifestreams; An Introduction to Biosynthesis** *by Boadella, A. Routledge and Kegan Paul 1987, £6.50.* Boadella, an English therapist, also worked with Reich and has developed a different approach to bodywork, bringing insights from Lowen and other Reichian influenced therapists, such as Stanley Keleman, whose books **Your Body Speaks Its Mind** and **Living Your Dying** both *by Center Press* are also worth reading.

CENTRES OFFERING BIOENERGETICS

Bioenergetic Training Association for Great Britain/Bioenergetic Associates. NW3, Bodyspace EC1, Chiron W5, Human Potential Resource Group (Surrey), Maitri (Hants), Open Centre EC1, Spectrum N4, Women's Therapy Centre N7.

TRAINING IN BIOENERGETICS

Bioenergetic Training Association for Great Britain/Bioenergetic Associates. *Title of Training* Body Oriented Psychotherapy in an Analytical Setting: Training for Practitioners. *Duration* Five years; four training blocks of four days per annum plus seminars, group process workshops, supervision and individual therapy. *Entry requirements* Previous experience in individual and group psychotherapy; current client load; references from therapist and/or supervisor. Fees £1,000 per annum payable in instalments plus residential costs, individual therapy and individual supervision. *Comments* Late entry into current training programme possible up to December 1990; next training programme likely to start 1992.

Biofeedback

Biofeedback training uses electronic gadgetry to feed back information about specific internal physiological states to the person using it. It is claimed that specific physiological states correspond to certain types of mental activity. For instance, a change in skin resistance from low to high and an increase in finger temperature corresponds to the person feeling more relaxed. These changes are signalled to the user by changes in sound tone or lights from the machine. Thus by using a small electronic box a person is able to monitor his or her particular level of relaxation. Further, from being able to monitor one's level of relaxation, it can be used to learn how to change one's own physiological responses and hence change how one feels.

Learning how to relax is one of the uses of biofeedback training, though it is not confined to this. It can be used to prevent and control stress related diseases, or to monitor changes in states of consciousness. After much research, Maxwell Cade, who pioneered biofeedback training in this country, was able to plot the significance of brainwave activity against states of consciousness. Alpha, beta and theta brainwave patterns correspond respectively to the state of consciousness one enters when meditating, to normal everyday consciousness and to the state of consciousness one enters when hypnotised.

The purpose of feedback training is to accelerate the process of learning how to relax, or how to meditate, or to know when one is in a hypnotic state. It is not intended that people should become hooked on the use of the machine to enter any particular mental state. The idea is that after training one becomes independent of the machine. It thus makes sense to take a course and use a machine rather than purchasing one for oneself, though it is possible to buy one. They range from under £100 for a relaxation meter to over £2500 for the 'Mind Mirror' (a brainwave monitor) developed by Maxwell Cade and Geoffrey Blundell.

READING
The Awakened Mind *by Cade, M. and Coxhead, N., Element 1987.* Subtitled *Biofeedback and the Development of Higher States of Awareness,* this book combines an outline of the principles of biofeedback regulation with the authors' exploration of its combination with meditation techniques to achieve a 'maximal mind-body awareness' leading to higher levels of consciousness. Another book worth seeking out is **Beyond Biofeedback** *by E and A. Green, Knoll 1989,* two of the originators of biofeedback techniques.

CENTRES OFFERING BIOFEEDBACK
Acumedic Centre NW1, Audio Limited W12, Centre for Stress Management SE3, Neal's Yard Therapy Rooms WC2.

Client-centred therapy

This is sometimes called Rogerian counselling or therapy after its founder Carl Rogers. His theory, method, and research has had a profound effect on the world of counselling.

Client-centered therapy is both an attitude on the part of the therapist which affects the style of intervention, and a particular way of behaving with the client. The therapist is trained to listen in an empathetic way and respond to the client by reflecting back to the client his or her own thoughts and feelings.

Client-centered therapy is phenomenological in its orientation. This means that the way the client perceives the world is seen as valid. The therapist will not impose any interpretations on the client's behaviour or invalidate the way the client sees himself or herself.

Rogers states that if a therapist possesses three qualities then the client will benefit. Firstly if the therapist has the quality of empathy and the client perceives this then the client will find the therapy beneficial. Empathy is the ability to put oneself in the shoes of the client, to understand the way the client sees the world and to be able to see it through his or her eyes. It is not enough that the therapist is empathetic but this quality must be perceived by the client. An essential skill for an empathetic counsellor is listening.

Secondly the therapist must be real. He or she must be genuine. It is essential that the client does not receive 'double messages' such as the therapist saying 'Yes of course I don't mind you talking about homosexuality' whilst crossing legs and going red in the face. This requires that the therapist must have undergone therapy, as being real requires understanding oneself. It means an ability to listen and be open to oneself.

Thirdly if the therapist can show a non-possessive warmth towards the client, prizing the client in a non-threatening way, then the client will feel valued and supported.

Client-centered therapy is practised on a one to one basis and in groups. Most trainings in counselling study the Rogerian approach. See 'Counselling' section.

READING
The Carl Rogers Reader *by Rogers, C. Constable 1990, £8.95.* This is a new title, a sort of 'portable Carl Rogers'. It covers all the main areas and ideas in his work. For a more in depth view, read **Client Centred Therapy** *£8.95* or his more popular **On Becoming a Person** *£7.95* both published by *Constable.* **Person Centred Counselling in Action** *Mearns, D. & Thorne, B. PBK 1988, £8.95.* Part of an excellent series, this book gives the background theory of Rogers' ideas and gives guidelines as to how these are used in therapy. The major themes, Empathy, Unconditional Positive Regard and others are explored in depth.

CENTRES OFFERING CLIENT-CENTRED COUNSELLING
Eigenwelt London NW3, Lifespace NW5.

Co-counselling

Co-counselling does not involve a professionally trained therapist. Two lay people meet to counsel each other for a set time. One assumes the role of client and talks to the other person, whose role is as a counsellor. When the allotted time is up they then switch roles and continue in a similar way.

This is a very simple idea, which was initially formulated by Harvey Jackins under the banner Re-evaluation Counselling. Courses were set up by him for people to receive guidance and training in these techniques. An emphasis was placed on learning how to practice the therapy without without hurting or damaging one another.

The client is in charge and determines what he or she wants to talk about, for how long and how much he or she wants the counsellor to intervene. The counsellor's job is mainly to listen and pay attention to the client. Validation of the client's experience by the counsellor is seen as crucial, and this is imparted by the counsellor paying attention to the client and sticking with the material the client produces.

Repeating key phrases the client uses, and contradicting self-deprecatory statements are two of the few intervention techniques the counsellor uses.

Harvey Jackins set up the main organisation in America, and one of the main organisation in this country is Co-counselling International which is a break-away from the former.

Intending co-counsellors participate in a 40 hour training course, and after the training join a network where they can meet prospective partners, and practise co-counselling. They usually meet once a week with the same partner for two hours, until they both decide to terminate the arrangement. They can then choose another partner.

This method has two advantages. Firstly it is cheap. After paying for the initial training course only a small fee is required to be on the network list. Secondly the two people remain on an equal level, and much of what seems mysterious in therapy intervention becomes obvious when playing the part of the counsellor.

There are many adult education classes in this subject. Refer to Floodlight.

READING

Fundamentals of Co-counselling Manual *by Jackins, H. National Island Publications 1982, £4.50* This is the basic 'textbook' of Re-evaluation Co-counselling as used on training workshops. It is an explicit guide to the method. **How To Change Yourself and Your World** *by Evison, R. Co-counselling Phoenix 1985, £4.95.* An English produced manual by people who broke away from the Jackins' Re-evaluation Counselling Network. Brings in many more (acknowledged) ideas from other therapies for use in the co-counselling situation.

CENTRES OFFERING CO-COUNSELLING

Human Potential Resource Group (Surrey), Humanistic Psychology at LSE WC2, London Co-counselling Community NW3.

TRAINING ON CO-COUNSELLING

London Co-counselling Community *Title of Training* Co-counselling Training *Duration* 40 hours (either once a week or over weekends) *Entry requirements* None *Fees* Payment is always based on ability to pay. £40-£80. *Comments* Training courses are run periodically. Contact the centre for information. The course is run by Co-counselling International (London). They do a further skills course for those wishing to progress further. Once trained on this course all two-way and group counselling sessions are free and you are free as a member to attend various workshops (day or residential) very cheaply. Must be able to give another person full attention without own distress disrupting the session.

Counselling

Counselling is not a particular form of therapy. We have included it in this section because of the many centres which offer counselling. The term covers a wide area of approaches, ranging from simple advice giving to something which is indistinguishable from psychotherapy.

Counselling can be used to denote consultation and advice giving on a particular subject, as in Careers Guidance Counselling. Someone like a student counsellor may deal with practical problems like the late arrival of a grant cheque, or may give full blown psychotherapy. The Samaritans give telephone counselling to people who are in acute distress, and it is intended not so much to be an in depth exploration of someone's problems, but to provide whatever support, comfort and advice is needed to get someone through a crisis.

PSYCHOTHERAPY

Counselling as a therapy is often associated with the client-centred therapy of Carl Rogers (see client-centred therapy section). The reflective technique evolved by Rogers, where the client's statements are not analysed but simply reflected back or rephrased, is often used by counsellors to help the client clarify issues. The focus of the counselling usually revolves around a specific issue or problem, such as sexual behaviour, financial situation or family crisis.

A few practitioners of alternative and complementary medicine also incorporate counselling into their approach. Many of the natural health centres offer counselling as well as body therapies. Because the term is so broad, it is as well to ask what kind of approach you will actually be getting, and what kind of training the counsellor has had.

The **British Association for Counselling** situated in Rugby is a large body which may help you with any questions about counselling and provide you with a practitioner in your area.

READING

The Counselling Handbook *by Quilliam, S & Grove-Stephenson, I., Thorsons 1989 £5.95.* A recent book (Mar '90) aimed at clients and potential clients of counselling. It is a well researched, easy to read guide to most of the different styles/ approaches available and where to find them. One of its strengths is the discussions included with both therapists and clients, which may ease one's apprehensions before taking the plunge. **Handbook of Counselling in Great Britain** *by Dryden, W. et al (Eds), Routledge 1989 £15.* A large and expensive book produced in conjunction with the British Association for Counselling. Gives an outline of the major situations where counselling is used and the major themes that can be covered. Less expensive is you are considering being counselled is the pamphlet **Counselling and Psychotherapy... Is it for me?** *by Hetty Einzig* for the British Association for Counselling, a brief 30 page introduction to what to expect.

CENTRES OFFERING COUNSELLING

Barnes Physiotherapy Clinic SW13, Bennet and Luck Natural Health Centre N1, Bodywise E2, Brackenbury Natural Health Centre W6, British Association for Counselling Register, British Association for Counselling (North London Branch) Register, British Association for Counselling (South London Branch) (Register), Centre for Counselling and Psychotherapy Education W11, Centre for Stress Management SE3, Chelsea Pastoral Foundation SW3, City Health Centre EC1, Clapham Common Clinic SW4, Clissold Park Natural Health Centre N16, Counselling in North London N11, Dancing on the Path SE22, Ealing Holistic Centre for Homoeopath and Autogenic Training W13, Eigenwelt London NW3, Equilibrium Therapy Centre SW18, Hampton Holistic Centre for Homoeopath and Autogenic Training (Middlesex), Healing Workshops, Highbury Centre N5, Hillside Practice NW5, Homoeopathic Health Clinic Kenton, Human Potential Resource Group (Surrey), Hypnotherapy/Psychotherapy Practice SW6, Identity Counselling Service W2, Inner Abilities SW10, Isis Centre for Holistic Health N17, Living Centre SW20, Mill Hill Health Care NW7, Moving Line Counselling and Therapy (Throughout London), Natural Healing Centre E7, Natural Healing Centre (Middlesex), Natureworks W1, North London Counselling Practice NW7, Nutribiotics Edgware, Primrose Healing Centre NW1, Refuah Shelaymah Natural Health Centre N16, Resonance SW17, School of the Dancing Dragon, Serpent Institute W12, Shirley Goldstein Holistic Therapies NW1, Skills with People N5, South London Natural Health Centre SW4, St James Centre for Health and Healing W1, St. Marylebone Healing and Counselling Centre NW1, Sunra SW12, Welbeck Counselling Service W1, Wellspring Clinic SW6, Westminster Natural Health Centre SW1, Westminster Pastoral Foundation W8, Wimbledon Clinic of Natural Medicine SW19, Women's Natural Health Centre NW5, Wood Street Clinic Barnet.

TRAINING IN COUNSELLING

CAER (Centre For Alternative Education And Research) *Title of Training* Royal Society of Arts Counselling Skills In The Development of Learning. *Duration* Five x 3-day residentials and an introductory weekend. *Entry requirements* Previous experience of guidance or counselling. *Fees* Organisations £840, Individuals £660, YTS/ET £520.

Centre for Counselling and Psychotherapy Education *Title of Training* (1) Fundamentals of Counselling and Psychotherapy. (2) Diploma in Counselling and Psychotherapy. *Duration* (1) One year part-time (Certificate course) (2) Four years part-time (Diploma course). *Entry requirements* (1) By Interview. (2) Must have been in therapy for at least one year, plus one year part-time counselling training. *Fees* (1) £600. (2) £750 per year excluding personal psychotherapy. *Comments* Holistic approach to counselling and psychotherapy which includes the spiritual dimension. Weekend workshops and short-term groups open to the public.

Spectrum *Title of Training* 1) Foundation course in counselling skills. *Duration*

Foundation course is half a day per week for 1 year, plus 2 three-day groups. *Fees* £375 per term.

Westminster Pastoral Foundation *Title of Training* Diploma Course in Advanced Psychodynamic Counselling. Refer to organisers for details.

Couple Therapy

Couple therapy is applicable to all couples, married or unmarried, homosexual or heterosexual, however long the partners have been together.

The couple are seen together so that both sides of any relationship conflict can be appreciated. However if it is impossible for both partners to be present, either because one partner does not want to be involved in therapy, or because the partner 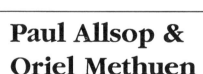 seeking therapy does not feel they can discuss their feelings with their partner at first, then one partner can go along on their own. The therapist will then discuss with the client whether he or she wants to include the other partner at any stage.

Different areas will be covered in the course of therapy depending on what the problems are. Often conflict may be caused because the partners do not know how to communicate with each other, and misunderstandings may have escalated. The therapist can help the couple to develop ways of expressing their feelings without blaming each other. Sometimes there may be more specific problems, such as an unsatisfactory sex life, and in this case if the difficulties are not just due to a more general difficulty in communicating, these can be dealt with (see Sex Therapy section). Sometimes there may be a need for individual work if one or both partners have personal issues which need to be explored. Sometimes the issues may involve quite a practical solution, for instance if one partner needs to find a means of self-expression outside the relationship such as study or work, the therapy can be used to explore the possibilities.

In some cases it may be that the couple discover that they do not want to stay together. The therapist can then help them to negotiate a separation which is satisfactory in emotional terms. If there are children involved, the therapist may suggest that they become included in the sessions so that they can participate in this process. RELATE (formerly Marriage Guidance) gives free counselling to couples.

READING

Couples in Counselling *by Gough, T. (Dartman, Longman & Todd 1989). £6.95* Most therapy approaches can be, and are used for work with couples. What is useful about this book is its down to earth appraisal of the issues that may be causing problems in a relationship, to either or both partners, and the ways that they can be worked on.

CENTRES OFFERING COUPLE THERAPY

Association for Analytic and Bodymind Therapy and Training N10, Association for Marriage Enrichment Residentals throughout the UK, Centre for Counselling and Psychotherapy Education W11, Chiron W5, Equilibrium Therapy Centre SW18, Hampstead Healing Centre NW3, Hillside Practice NW5, Holistic Yoga Centre Milton Keynes, London Institute for the Study of Human Sexuality SW5, Metanoia W5, Minster Centre NW2, North London Centre for Group Therapy N14, North London Counselling Practice NW7, Resonance SW17, Spectrum N4, Human Potential Resource Group (Surrey), Spectrum N4, Tavistock Clinic NW3, Westminster Pastoral Foundation W8.

Dance Therapy

Dance therapy aims to release the natural flow of bodily expression which is unique to each individual. Movement is a way of communicating from direct physical experience which children use quite naturally. In growing up, we are often taught to restrict this joyful and expressive movement. Dance therapy concentrates on spontaneous, individual movements which proceed from the dancer's experience rather than on learning formal dance patterns.

Tribal societies have long used dance as a way of expressing feelings, of accomplishing the transition to other states of consciousness (for instance the trance state), and for connecting to their community and environment in a way which has meaning, often through the mythic significance of the dance. In Europe over the centuries since medieval times, dance has become more and more formalised, until the appearance of Isadora Duncan at the turn of the century with her free form, emotive dancing which shocked many of her straight-laced contemporaries.

Rudolph Laban, a German psychotherapist was the first to incorporate dance into his treatment of patients between the wars. Marian Chace, an American dance therapist, developed another form of dance therapy when she was asked to work with patients in a mental hospital, after psychiatrists there had been impressed by the improvements in patients who attended her dance classes privately.

Dance therapists differ widely in their approach. Usually therapy takes place in a group. First the participants are asked to do warming up exercises, and some material to be developed in the course of the class may emerge at this stage. Music may be played, but this is not necessarily the case. The therapist may reflect the dancer by mirroring his or her movements, drawing attention to particular gestures, or inviting the dancer to find words for the emerging feelings or connect more fully to them. Interaction between the group as a whole may also be encouraged. In some dance therapy classes the emphasis may be less on 'therapy' and more on 'creativity' where the dancers are encouraged to find their own style of dance to express their uniqueness.

Dance therapy can also be used in a Jungian framework. Here movement functions as a bridge to the unconscious mind. The movements, once developed and repeated, may come to embody symbols or mythological themes, which will then be discussed by therapist and client.

Dance therapy can be used in a wide variety of situations. It is useful for people who are unable to speak about their feelings, such as autistic children or psychotics. Those who suffer from physical symptoms related to stress or other emotional difficulties can also benefit, as well as those who are suffering from immobilising organic diseases such as Parkinson's disease or a stroke. It is also useful for people who tend to intellectualise too much.

READING

The Mastery of Movement *by Laban, R. Northcote House 1980, £8.95.* This is Laban's classic book on human movement, using his approach to explore the inner motivation of movement and its expression in emotion, intellect and values/meanings. Another book worth looking at is **Personality Assessment Through Movement** *by Marion North Northcote Press 1989.*

CENTRES OFFERING DANCE THERAPY

5 to Midnight (some workshops in London), Creative Arts and Therapy Consultants N16, Dancing on the Path SE22, Open Gate (various locations in London), Playspace NW1.

Encounter

Social convention dictates that we restrain ourselves. There are many times when we have to suppress certain feelings for social reasons, but we are also imprisoned by our own neurotic constraints. Whether the suppression is due to real external constraints or whether it is due to a neurotic withholding is something an encounter group tries to find out.

Will Schutz pioneered the 'open encounter', the version of the encounter group which was the most successful in this country, and which grew at a phenomenal rate in the late sixties and reached the height of its popularity in the early seventies.

Schutz would follow the energy in the group at any one moment. For instance if a member was tapping his foot he would ask him to exaggerate it and get in touch with what this impulse was about. If the person were to say he felt impatient with someone in the group and would like to kick him into action, Schutz would have him kick a cushion and get more in touch with this feeling and to express this pent up emotion. Where this would lead to would depend on many factors. It might be that many of the group also have this feeling towards the same person, but held back from saying for one reason or another. It might be that the impulse was a frustration at his own feeling of getting nowhere, which would be further therapeutic grist for the mill. As more physical movement is required than in most other therapy groups, participants sit on cushions rather than on chairs so that they are not in any way obstructed.

Encounter groups give people permission to cut through social convention and politeness and openly encourage the expression of feeling and honesty. Rather than talking about feelings the encounter group encourages one to express the feeling. If you were to say you would like to hug a particular person in the group, you might be asked to go ahead and do it.

There are two other types of encounter groups, neither of which are as common as the 'open encounter'. Carl Rogers pioneered a form of encounter where he encouraged a more honest engagement between members and tried to induce an atmosphere of empathy, regard for the other members and genuineness in relating. It is called 'basic encounter'. Chuck Dederick pioneered the 'Synanon encounter' specifically for drug abusers. Members were asked to focus on one person and verbally attack him or her. Members would take it in turn to be target. The aim of this 'shock therapy' was to wake them up from an habitual lifestyle.

Encounter is practised in groups. Often the setting is residential. It may be a two, three or five day workshop. They have been known to go on for a month. If it is described as a 'marathon encounter', this means you are likely to get little sleep for the duration of the workshop. In this country the 'marathon encounter' usually lasts between twenty four and forty eight hours.

PSYCHOTHERAPY

READING

Joy. . . 20 Years Later *by Schutz, W. Ten Speed Press, 1989, £7.95*. This is a revised edition of Schutz's original text on the principles and practice of his ideas. Although not so specific to the actual workings of an encounter group as his other book **Elements of Encounter** (long out of print, and never widely available in the UK), it nevertheless gives a good grounding in the encounter approach and what to expect. **Theories and Practise of Group Psychotherapy** *by Yalom, I. Harper and Row, 1987, hardback £17.95*. The chapters on Encounter and T-Groups (the origins of Encounter) in this book are excellent introductions to the method. The whole book is recommended to anyone who wants to look at the many and various 'human potential' approaches to group work.

CENTRES OFFERING ENCOUNTER

Human Potential Resource Group (Surrey), Open Centre EC1, Resonance (Milton Keynes), Spectrum N4.

❝ Johnny (name changed) was a central character in an encounter/gestalt group that I participated in over six months. The group was held in 1973 at Quaesitor, a large 'growth' centre in leafy Willesden. Johnny was from Glasgow and was fond of recounting stories of his violent background. One such story was that when he felt depressed he would go out on to the street and beat up the first person he came across. Apparently this eased his own internal pain. Over a period of a few months he had punched me twice in the group and I was outraged that he had got away with this. He was not banned from the group, but instead gained a lot of support from other group members who felt sorry for him because of his troubled upbringing. I figured that the group members supported him mainly from fear, lest their own noses got punched, rather than for any altruistic reasons. Johnny loved to be in the limelight in the group, which was much resented by the other members who felt cast into the shadows. One day the group decided to cope with Johnny's 'attention seeking' by ignoring him. After about an hour Johnny could cope with this no more. He let out a big 'Ahhhhh', picked up a stool (used for bioenergetic work) by its legs, and threw it through the closed windows. They were large bay windows which had been specially double-glazed so that the sounds made in the group room would not percolate out into the street. It made an thunderous crash, and a small crowd appeared to view the spectacle. After this incident Johnny was still not banned, but instead was given the attention he sought.

I must add that this particular group was untypical of therapy groups in general. Since then I have participated in many encounter/gestalt groups and consider this one to be an isolated yet disturbing experience. **❞**

Mike Considine

Existential Psychotherapy

Existential psychotherapy can be considered more an approach than a therapy in the normal sense of the term, as it is against techniques and weak on a classification of intervention strategies on the part of the therapist. Indeed, the training of an existential therapist is quite different from that followed by trainees in many other psychotherapies. The trainee existential psychotherapist is expected to become steeped not only in psychological theory, but in the philosophy of existentialism. Most of all, she is encouraged in taking a particular attitude towards herself, towards others and towards life itself. To this end the trainee undergoes a form of apprentiship with a supervisor who acts as a guide. The training therefore bears more resemblance to the guru/student relationship found in oriental religions than it does to western psychotherapy.

To understand existential psychotherapy it is necessary to know something about its philosophical underpinning. The work of the existentialists such as Heidegger, Boss, Sarte, Kierkegaard, Nietzsche and Husserl provided the philosophical movement upon which existential psychotherapy is based. Existentialism focuses on the 'givens of existence', such as being, death, alienation, authenticity, suffering, responsibility in choosing and meaning. These themes were also echoed by clients in psychotherapy and soon the the philosophy of existentialism percolated into the psychotherapeutic arena. Existential psychotherapy grew to occupy a place of its own, with its own style of expression.

In this country, the psychiatrist Ronald Laing became famous in the 1960s for his existentialist approach in working with schizophrenics. He placed importance on understanding the subjective world of the client and attacked the swiftness of psychiatry in objectively labelling the so-called psychotic. He saw madness as an authentic experience which is in itself a healing process, through which one could journey and emerge on the other side. Laing set up the Philadelphia Association in London from which the break-away organisation, the Arbours Association was formed. This organisation turned private houses into therapeutic communities where the previously labelled schizophrenics were allowed to express their madness.

READING
Existential Counselling in Practice *by Van Deurzen-Smith, E., Sage 1988.* The first practical book written in the UK on this form of therapy. Quite readable for a book on a subject which many find intellectually difficult. She weaves the philosophy, and practice of the approach into an interesting framework. A heavier tome is *Yalom's Existential Psychotherapy, Harper and Rowe £17.95*, but for anyone intrested in the flavour of the existential approach, try reading any of R.D. Laing's works, all published by Penguin.

CENTRES OFFERING EXISTENTIAL PSYCHOTHERAPY
Eigenwelt London NW3, Philadelphia Association NW3, South London Network for Counselling and Psychotherapy (various locations in South London).

Family Therapy
There are number of different schools of family therapy, but most follow a systems theory approach whilst drawing on different therapeutic models such as psychoanalytic psychotherapy, gestalt, transactional analysis, client-centred therapy, behavioural methods and psychodrama for some of their intervention tactics.

The focus is not on the individual family member. If any one individual suffers symptoms within the family, such as a child suffering from 'school phobia', this is considered a symptom of the family, and the family must be treated as a whole. It may be that the child will not go to school because of the distant relationship that has developed between the parents, and consequently the child feels it needs to support the mother.

The aim is to discover how the behaviour of members within the family perpetuates the symptom, and to change the relationship between the members so that the symptom disappears. Emphasis is placed not on why the family is behaving the way it is, but on what present behaviour is causing the symptom.

Therapy may be carried out with one or two therapists working with the family. It is usually brief because of the difficulty often involved in bringing the whole family together at one time. Sessions are usually at least six in number.

Usually the family will go the therapist/s place of work, but sometimes the therapist/s will go to the family's home to undertake therapy or will make at least one attempt to go to the home of the family to see how they behave in their surroundings.

Family therapy is often suggested to families where one of the children has a problem, for instance a young child with a school problem or an unruly teenager.

READING
Peoplemaking *by Satir, V. Science & Behaviour 1972, £6.95.* This was the first book to bring the benefits of the insights gained from family therapy to the general public. It's an easy read that brings many of the problems of family life into sharp focus, and has been generally hailed for its healing potential. Another similar title that is worth looking at is **Families and How to Survive Them** *by Cleese, J. & Skynner, R.,* one of the principle developers of Family Therapy in the UK. **Family Therapy in Britain** *by Street, E & Dryden, W. Open University Press 1988, £12.50.* Another manual containing articles on the major approaches to Family Therapy in use in the UK, by many of the leading practitioners in their fields.

CENTRES OFFERING FAMILY THERAPY
British Association for Social Psychiatry W1, Camden Psychotherapy Unit WC1, Gale Centre for Creative Therapy (Essex), Institute of Family Therapy W1, Metanoia W5, North London Centre for Group Therapy N14, Tavistock Clinic NW3, Westminster Pastoral Foundation W8.

TRAINING IN FAMILY THERAPY
Institute of Family Therapy *Title of Training* 1) Introductory course in Family and Marital Therapy. 2) Part I, Training in Family Therapy 3) M. Sc in Family Therapy 4) Advanced Clinical Training in Family Therapy. 5) Introductory Course in Alcohol

and Substance Abuse and the Family. *Duration* 1) One year part-time 2) One year part-time 3) Two years part-time 4) Two years part-time 5) Twenty weeks part-time *Entry requirements* See training prospectus available from the Training Dept at above address. *Fees* 1) £495 per annum payable in termly instalments. 2) £575 per annum payable in termly instalments. 3) £1,950 per annum 4) £1,750 per annum 5) £265 per course, payable in two instalments.

Tavistock Clinic *Title of Training* Programme of Training in Child and Family and Adolescent Psychiatry *Duration* Four years full time. *Fees* £1450 per annum if UK or EEC. £3350 for overseas trainees. *Comments* trainees are required to have personal psychotherapy at least three times a week at their own expense.

Feminist Therapy

Feminist therapy is an attitudinal approach to the practice of therapy. It was founded by women who observed sexism and patriarchal values on the part of therapist and client which became reinforced within the therapy. Women found they were being undermined in their determination to grow when confronted with a sexist male therapist. They also found that some of the assumptions of traditional psychotherapy were based on social values which subtly affected the therapeutic encounter, whether the therapist was male or female.

Feminist therapy began at a grass roots level, and through consciousness raising groups, rape crisis work and work with battered women there has emerged a therapy with a clear philosophy.

Three common issues emerge in the therapy of women: anger, self-nurturance and autonomy or power. Women tend to turn their anger inwards rather than outwards. In feminist therapy the client is helped to be more expressive and to direct the anger to where it belongs. Women tend to have devoted themselves to others at the expense of themselves, and a consequence of this can be depression. In feminist therapy they are asked to take care of their of own needs too. To gain autonomy women are asked to expand the options they allow themselves and are helped to confront the role restrictions society places on them, at home and at work.

Susie Orbach and Luise Eichenbaum founded the Women's Therapy Centre in London.

While feminist therapy is not exclusive to women, men have not opted for it. Virtually all the clients are women, and all of the therapists are. However, some male therapists have begun to explore the theme of men's socialisation and are reaching for new definitions of masculinity.

A feminist therapist may incorporate gestalt, client-centred therapy or T.A. into the therapy, but the essential ingredient is the emphasis that is placed on the individual worth of the client, and on her socialisation. Issues frequently dealt with are body image, eating problems, self-care and sexuality.

READING

What Do Women Want *by Eichenbaum, L. & Orbach, S. Fontana 1983, £3.50.* The authors are pioneers of the Feminist Therapy approach, and are co-founders of the Women's Therapy Centre. This book explores the many issues that women have to come to terms with to fulfull their own emotional needs. A book for men as well. **Feminist Counselling in Action** *by Chaplin, J. Sage 1988, £8.95.* Written for counsellors and therapists to understand a feminist approach, it is also useful for people who may be drawn to the approach. Further readings can be found in **In Our Experience; Workshops at the Women's Therapy Centre** *by Krzowski, S. & Land, P. (Eds) Womens Press £6.95.*

CENTRES OFFERING FEMINIST THERAPY

CAER (Centre For Alternative Education And Research) (Cornwall), Communication and Counselling Foundation (courses held in London), Gestalt Studio NW5, Hidden Strengths NW5, Human Potential Resource Group (Surrey), London Institute for the Study of Human Sexuality SW5, Minster Centre NW2, Pellin Centre SW8, Psychotherapy Workshops for Women (North and West London), Redwood Women's Training Association, Serpent Institute W12, Spectrum N4, Women Unlimited SW16, Women's Therapy Centre N7.

TRAININGS IN FEMINIST THERAPY

Women's Therapy Centre *Title of Training* Working with women - a psychodynamic approach. *Duration* 1 year, 1 evening per week. *Entry requirements* For women who have some professional training, and have some psychodynamic input into their work with women. *Fees* Apply to organisers. *Comments* Training workshops for people working as social workers, health care services workers, psychotherapists and those in the voluntary sector. Includes working with women with eating problems, incest survivors, including the black experience, groupwork etc.

Gestalt Therapy

Fritz Perls was a Freudian trained psychoanalyst who became disenchanted with the practice of psychoanalysis. He was analysed by Reich for whom he expresses much affection and by whom gestalt thinking was heavily influenced. He set up the South African Institute of Psychoanalysis and then later went to America where, with his wife Laura Perls, he evolved gestalt therapy. In the sixties he introduced gestalt therapy to Esalen, California, the first growth centre. Rather than paying attention to why clients behaved the way they did as was common in psychoanalysis, he paid attention to what they did and how they behaved. He helped them become more aware of what their behaviour meant to them and what it signified to others. Thus gestalt therapy pays attention to the non-verbal more than the verbal. This does not

PSYCHOTHERAPY

❝ I came to London at 19 to study for a degree in Electronics. My life was in front of me and the thought of moving to the big capital thrilled me. I had not anticipated being lonely when I came to London as I thought of it as the big city where I was certain to make some friends amongst the millions of people living there. I knew that I had difficulty relating to people. I was shy but wanted so much to enjoy my life with other people. After three years I realised that something was wrong. I had few friends and I related to them in superficial ways. I found it especially difficult to make friends with women. I became very distressed at the thought of the rest of my life continuing in the same way. I decided I needed some help. The thought of seeing a psychiatrist appalled me as I did not consider myself to be mentally ill. Nevertheless I went to my GP and insisted on seeing a psychiatrist. After a six week wait I had an appointment to visit one at a hospital in Mile End. I climbed the stairs to the top floor where the psychiatrist shook my hand and led me into a room where there were a group of about fifteen students with clip boards sitting in a semi-circle facing two empty chairs, one of which he beckoned me to be seated in. He seated himself in the other chair and asked me if I minded the students observing the session. Can you imagine how I felt! I had come to get help with difficulty in being open and expressing who I was, and here I was being asked to talk about my life and problems in front of a group of strangers. I was enraged though I kept my feelings to myself (I sat on my feelings in those days). I told him there was nothing wrong with me (I wanted to get out of that situation as soon as possible, I could not bear being watched by those others). He said I had been wasting his time and I agreed with him. He then escorted me out. I remember we were on the top floor and I looked for a window to jump out of. I had a delicious fantasy of how foolish he would look in front of his students if someone he had just diagnosed as a timewaster took a suicide leap from his hospital window. Fortunately I realised it was a too high a price to pay and found my way home.

After several months of depression I saw an ad in Time Out classified for a Gestalt group and signed myself up. This was 1972 and it was the first Gestalt workshop in England. It proved to be the answer I had been looking for. I learned how my shyness was an expression of fear of the hostility towards me I imagined I saw in other peoples eyes. I learned how to make contact. It was not easy. In fact it was often painful. But it was also wonderful. It was such a release to be able to talk in a genuine way to others and not to feel so anxious. I remember writing then that 'it blew my mind into outer space and that I wanted to become a therapist and blow other peoples minds into outer space'. I did later become a gestalt therapist. ❞

Mike Considine

66 Barry told me he used gestalt and another psychotherapy (I forget now which one). There was a mattress and cushion in the room, but - no other furniture. He stated categorically that 'ANYTHING goes in this room, except violence towards me'. My thoughts drifted immediately to sex - he was quite attractive. However the first session consisted of me sitting on the mattress (shoes off), and him sitting on the floor (shoes off). We talked about my childhood and I wanted to cry with frustration and anger, aimed primarily against my brother. Barry then picked up a large cushion and invited me to punch it as if it were my brother. At this point I toppled over and dissolved into helpless laughter. Barry looked extremely hurt. He got his own back in the next session by us sitting in silence for a whole hour, me waiting for him to 'begin' and him waiting for me to start. I didn't begin and didn't go back. 99

Gill Stow

mean that people talk less in Gestalt groups, but that the focus of concern of the therapist is much more on the bodily messages than in more orthodox psychotherapies.

Another theme that Perls stressed was responsibility. He insisted clients take responsibility for themselves. If someone would say 'It feels good when you say that' he would ask them to rephrase it as 'I feel good when you say that', thus enabling them to become more in touch with their own feelings.

Talking to the 'empty chair' is the hallmark of gestalt therapy. If for instance you had not expressed your feelings to someone close to you, such as your mother, you may be asked to imagine her sitting in an empty chair, and to say the things you wished you had said to her. You may be then asked to switch chairs and to sit in the chair you imagined her sitting in, and pretend to be her responding to you. Thus a dialogue might ensue between yourself and what you imagine your mother would say to you. This unrehearsed dramatisation of how you see your relationship with your mother is likely to provide the group members and the therapist with a detailed and revealing story. The use of the 'empty chair' is not limited to being filled with persons. Parts of oneself can be placed there as well. For example, if you are the type of person who constantly criticises yourself, you may be asked to put the critical side of yourself in the empty chair and to have a dialogue with that side of yourself. Such a public display of the contents of one's own psyche, engenders strong emotional bonds between the group members and can produce an intense emotional atmosphere.

People who could most benefit from this type of therapy are those who feel they have difficulty expressing their feelings, those who feel stuck, those who feel cut off from others and those who would like feedback on how people see them.

READING

Gestalt Therapy *by Perls, F, Goodman, P and Hefferline, R. Souvenir Press, 1974, £7.95.* The original work describing the theory of Gestalt therapy. Good to explore its basis thoroughly, but many people find it a difficult 'read'. Probably more accessible is his later book **The Gestalt Approach & Eye-Witness to Therapy.** *(S & B, £8.95).* This was originally published as two books, the first being a last revision of his theoretical ideas, the second , transcripts of some of his films giving an insight into Perls 'live'. **The Red Book of Gestalt by Houston** *G. Rochester Foundation 1982 £3.50.* A delightful little book, self published and illustrated by line drawings, giving a simple, but not simplistic, introduction to how Gestalt Therapy works, both in group and individual settings.

CENTRES OFFERING GESTALT THERAPY

Association for Analytic and Bodymind Therapy and Training N10, Chiron W5, Gestalt Centre London EC1, Gestalt Therapy in West London W3, Holwell Centre for Psychodrama and Sociodrama (Devon), Human Potential Resource Group (Surrey), Oasis N2, Open Centre EC1, Playspace NW1, Spectrum N4, Women's Therapy Centre N7, CAER (Centre For Alternative Education And Research) (Cornwall), Chiron W5, Gestalt Studio NW5, Hillside Practice NW5, Humanistic Psychology at LSE WC2, Jeyrani Health Centre E18, Lifespace NW5, Metanoia W5, Minster Centre NW2, Natural Medicine Centre (Bromley), New Cross Natural Therapy Centre SE14, Pellin Centre SW8, Person-Centred Art Therapy Centre NW11, Psychotherapy for Individuals, Couples & Groups N10, Resonance, Resonance SW17, South London Network for Counselling and Psychotherapy (Various locations in South London), Spectrum N4.

TRAININGS IN GESTALT THERAPY

Gestalt Centre London *Title of Training* (1) Basic Gestalt Training (2) Practitioner Training *Duration* 1) Three to four years. Twelve weekly evenings plus two weekends per term. 2) Additional two years to the above, usually full-time. *Entry requirements* Experience of gestalt necessary. Other than that the course can take a trainee from scratch to psychotherapy practitioner. *Fees* Course fees are £390 per term plus individual therapy fees. *Comments* The course operates a unique termly system that allows each person to progress at his/her own work rate. Since it is both a personal and professional training, the therapy, theory and practice are interlinked.
Metanoia *Title of Training* Gestalt Psychotherapy Diploma Training *Duration* Three years. Modular basis of between one to eight five day workshops per year. *Entry requirements* Completion of introduction course on the fundamentals of Gestalt (held three times a year) or its equivalent. *Fees* £160 per workshop. *Comments* requires personal psychotherapy for the duration of the training. Some

bursaries available.

Pellin Centre *Title of Training* Pellin counselling/Gestalt Training Course *Duration* Three years part-time, one year basic, two years advanced. *Entry requirements* Should be in helping professions or wishing to find work with people. *Fees* £700-£800 per year. *Comments* They do in-depth interviews and ask for a reference.

Group-oriented Therapy

By group-oriented therapy we mean therapy where the group process is deemed to be important and worthy of analysis, and where the dynamics of the group compose part of the therapy, so that it becomes therapy of the group and by the group. Although no firm line can be drawn here, because many psychotherapies would argue that the dynamics of the group are important, the crucial thing is that the dynamics of the group take up a central role in the therapy and that historically the origins of the therapy evolved around group processes. In London the three major schools have different theoretical origins.

The 'group analytic' approach was developed by S.H. Foulkes. It was developed not only as a way of applying psychoanalytic knowledge to group practice, but takes into account factors specific to groups. In this type of group the therapist, or 'conductor' as they prefer to be called, may remain in the background much of the time, but can at times be much more active. The free floating group discussion is to group analytic therapy what free association is to psychoanalysis. Eight people (four men and four women) is seen as the optimum number for this type of group. Therapy is usually twice a week, one and half hours for each session.

The Tavistock approach to group work was developed by W. Bion. Bion (a Kleinian analyst) saw much of what went on in groups as issues over leadership. The therapist or 'consultant' usually stays in the background and offers interpretations about what is going on in the group. Groups can go on intensively for a week and are affectionately known as 'Tavi' groups.

The humanistic approach offers 'T-groups', sometimes referred to as sensitivity training groups. These groups meet residentially, often for a week. The focus is on the 'here and now' activity of the group and feedback and self-expression are a prime concern. The leader reflects, for instance, on how the group conducts itself, and the leader will focus not on 'what' decisions the group took but 'how' it went about deciding and which roles people took up in this decision making.

All of the above approaches are useful in learning both about how groups function and about your contribution to the group process. For those who feel they would like to know more about groups or for those who work in groups and need to understand more of group processes, all can be recommended, but remember that the style of each of the above schools are quite different from each other.

GROUP ORIENTED THERAPY

READING

Group Therapy in Britain *by Aveline, M. & Dryden, W. (Eds). Open University Press 1988, £12.50* A manual, giving theoretical background and practical usage of the major approaches to group therapy. Another book worth looking at is by Yalom, reviewed in the 'Encounter' section. **Once Upon A Group** *by Kindred, M. Self published 1987, £3.00* A light hearted look at what can be quite a heavy subject. In it, the author draws out, in basic lay language, the themes and issues that can be dealt with in any of the group therapies practised today.

CENTRES OFFERING GROUP-ORIENTED PSYCHOTHERAPY

Gale Centre for Creative Therapy (Essex), Group Relations Training Association Usually in North of England, Human Potential Resource Group (Surrey), Institute of Group Analysis NW3, Minster Centre NW2, North London Centre for Group

❝ I participated on an 'intensive' psychotherapy group in the seventies, which comprised a series of weekend workshops over six months with visiting groups leaders. The group was dominated by the women. They did most of the talking and took most of the decisions about what we should do as a group. My perception was that the women partly maintained control by putting the men down and I resented this. So when we had a visiting male group-oriented leader, I complained to him about this and I explained how I felt impotent in the group. He suggested the following exercise: he would go to the toilet and wait there for me to fetch him; he would *only* leave the toilet if I personally came to bring him back. The theory behind this, he said, was that he was giving me his power; it was up to the group to persuade me to bring him back so that the weekend workshop could continue; I therefore would be able to regain my potency and hold my head high once more. Upon that he dissappeared from the room and went down to the basement where the toilet was located (in retrospect I think that he needed to go to the toilet anyway and was killing two birds with one stone with this exercise). To my surprise the women sat and talked to themselves and completely ignored me. I maintained my composure knowing full well that sooner or later one of them would crack and would have to ask the favour of me. I felt gleeful of this opportunity to be in command. After about half an hour one woman turned to me and asked me to fetch our group leader to which I said 'No'. The women again resumed chatting to each other and ignoring me. After another half hour my thoughts turned to our beloved leader pent up in the loo, so I decided to go down and tell him what had transpired since he had left. No sooner had I tapped on the loo door than he shot out, but I pushed him back inside saying that the women had not even tried to persuade me to let him out, and I explained to him that I was paying him a visit rather than arranging his release. He was downcast at this, and told me to tell the women to hurry up. I went back to the group and sat there another half hour before giving up and rescuing him. **❞**

Mike Considine

Therapy N14, Playspace NW1, Skills with People N5, Tavistock Clinic NW3, Will (Workshop Institute for Living Learning) W9.

TRAININGS IN GROUP-ORIENTED PSYCHOTHERAPY

Goldsmiths' College *Title of Training* Diploma in Group Therapy *Duration* Three years part-time. *Entry requirements* Degree or professional qualification. *Fees* £750 p.a. part-time.

Human Potential Resource Group *Title of Training* Facilitator Styles Course *Duration* Two years part-time. Approx 60 days in each year including regular meetings, one day per week & 3 weekend workshops each term, plus 2 x 5 day workshops per year. *Entry requirements* For those in the teaching/training professions. The course is a balance of theoretical with experiential and practical work. *Fees* Approx £400 per term.

Institute of Group Analysis *Title of Training* 1) Introductory General Course in Group Work 2)Qualifying Course in Group Work *Duration* 1) One academic year, Thurs 4.30-7.30. 2) At least three years. *Entry requirements* 1) None specified. 2)Must have completed the General Course in Group Work. Degree with some knowledge of the field. *Fees* 1) £485 2)Selection procedure fee: £65 Twice weekly group analysis: £1464 per annum Theoretical and supervision seminars: £1,095 per annum Professional indemnity insurance: £45 *Comments* 1) Small and large group experience. 2) Training takes the form of twice weekly personal group analysis (each session lasts one and half hour). Theory and supervision.

Tavistock Clinic *Title of Training* Training in Group Work For details of training apply to the Clinic.

Westminster Pastoral Foundation *Title of Training* (1) Certificate in Groupwork in Community and Organisational Settings. (2) Diploma in Group Counselling. *Comments* Refer to organisers for details.

Hypnotherapy

There are as many types of hypnotherapy as there are practitioners. They may have different aims, but they do share one characteristic. All begin with the therapist guiding the client into an hypnotic state. The client is simply required to respond positively to the direction of the therapist. Once in this state, what happens next will depend on the aims of the therapy and the background and training of the therapist.

Hypnotherapy tends to be symptom oriented. It offers help for tension, smoking, pain relief, obesity, psychosomatic ailments and phobias - the list is extensive. Some hypnotherapists claim to be able to uncover repressed material from the unconscious. Indeed, Freud gave hypnosis respectability when he got results from using it on his early clients, but later abandoned it when he found it induced idealisation of the analyst and when its effects proved to be transient. He replaced it with *free association* within psychoanalysis which would seem to have been the kiss of death to hypnosis as a treatment tool. Nevertheless the use of hypnosis it seems has grown unabated, but the type of therapy that it is offered within, as was mentioned earlier, varies a great deal from practitioner to practitioner. It may be the therapist will simply impose a counter suggestion upon the client such as 'when you leave here you will want to smoke less', or he or she may want to explore some of the client's unwanted feelings and will perhaps encourage the client to explore the physical manifestations of the feelings.

Usually a contract is agreed between therapist and client before hypnosis begins about what the aims of the therapy are and what suggestions will be given to the client. The therapist cannot make you do anything against your will in hypnosis, or make you do anything that is outside your normal code of ethics.

READING
Hypnosis *by Waxman, D. Unwin 1981, £3.95* Subtitled 'A Guide for Patients', this

❝ Several years ago I visited a hypnotherapist because I was severely depressed, tense and my general health was suffering. I went down to 7 stone in weight. Things had been brought to a head by an unfortunate incident at work. I could see no meaning in life and had no interests. The hypnotherapist told me that he was Jungian psychologist and he thought he could help me. He said that he took the whole man into consideration.

He recommended that I take vitamin B12 and have a tonic consisting of 1/4 pint of sherry, 1/4 pint of evaporated milk and an egg all beaten up together. I soon put on weight and felt stronger.

Through hypnosis he helped me to relax, I found his voice very soothing and calming. He taught me self hypnosis for relaxation which I find very useful.

Through auto suggestion he used the word 'metaphysical', a word which I was not familiar with. Since treatment, a whole new world has opened up for me. Through studying metaphysical subjects such as philosophy, yoga, the after-life, psychology, spiritual healing, the works of Jung, Fromm and Laing, I have found a completely new outlook on life, something which has helped me greatly. I found that as I studied one subject, it led to another.

I feel that this was really the root of my depression not something that could have been dealt with by antidepressants alone. I consider that I have benefitted greatly from this treatment and I feel that it has expanded my mind considerably. **❞**

Christine Davidson

is a thorough introduction to the history, development, and practice of classical hypnosis. Its one flaw is its heavy bias against non-medical practitioners. Another introductory book is **Hypnotherapy, is it for you?** *by Sleet, R., Element 198).* **Hypnotherapy; A Modern Approach** *by Golden, W. et al. Pergamon 1988, £7.50* Another book for practitioners, which can be of use to interested or potential clients. The authors use many of the 'newer' approaches to hypnosis, for example the non-directive approach developed from the work of Milton Erikson, who is now acknowledged as the greatest hypnotherapist of our time.

CENTRES OFFERING HYPNOTHERAPY

Academy and Professional Hypnotherapy Association (Cockfosters) and W1, Acupuncture and Osteopathy Clinic SW1, Anerley Natural Health Clinic SE20, Association for Analytic and Bodymind Therapy and Training N10, Barbican Natural Health Centre EC1, Bexleyheath Natural Health Clinic KENT, Body Clinic NW11, Body-Mind Health Private Clinic N8, British Hypnosis Research (courses in London), British Hypnotherapy Association W1, British Society of Hypnotherapists (1950) (register), Capital Hypnotherapy Centre W6, Centre for Past Life Therapy and Research Woodford Green, Centre for Stress Management SE3, Chessington Hypnotherapy Clinic Chessington, Ealing Holistic Centre for Homoeopath and

Autogenic Training W13, Edgware Centre for Natural Health Edgware, Equilibrium Therapy Centre SW18, Falcons SW11, Hampton Holistic Centre for Homoeopath and Autogenic Training (Middlesex), Hayes Hypnotherapy Centre, Highbury Centre N5, Hypnoanalysis Centre W1, Hypnocare W9, Hypnotherapy Training Centre SE28, Hypnotherapy/Psychotherapy Practice SW6, International NLP Training Various locations, Jeyrani Health Centre E18, Lifecare, Living Centre SW20, London Centre for Clinical Hypnotherapy WC1, London Society for Ericksonian Psychotherapy and Hypnosis (West Sussex), McCarthy Westwood Consultants SW11, Natural Healing Centre E7, Natural Medicine Centre (Bromley), Natureworks W1, Neal's Yard Therapy Rooms WC2, New Life Lodge N4, Primrose Healing Centre NW1, School of Hypnosis and Advanced Psychotherapy N4, Sheila Revell Centre SW16, South London Hypnotherapy Association (Bromley), South London Natural Health Centre SW4, UK Training College of Hypnotherapy and Counselling W2, Wholeness E18, Wimbledon Clinic of Natural Medicine SW19, Wood Street Clinic Barnet.

TRAININGS IN HYPNOTHERAPY

British Hypnosis Research *Title of Training* Diploma in Ericksonian Hypnosis, Psychotherapy and NLP. *Duration* One year, part time. Two level training: practitioner level and advanced level. Each level involves 6 weekends, 12 supervision days and 20 evenings. *Entry requirements* 1) Professional qualification in one of the caring professions. 2) A first degree as evidence of academic achievement. 3) Experience or employment in an area related to the subject matter of the course. *Fees* £950 + VAT for each level, payable in advance (loan facilities also available). *Comments* Skills based training held at St Ann's Hospital, London. Emphasis is placed on supervising each student whilst they work with actual patients. (Volunteer patients are supplied by BHR).

Hypnotherapy Training Centre *Title of Training* Hypnotherapy Training Centre Training Course *Duration* 6-12 months + one year supervision part-time. *Entry requirements Fees* £220 + £10 per tutorial. *Comments* At least 190 hours of written and taped tuition and 8 days of workshops and seminars.

School of Hypnosis and Advanced Psychotherapy *Title of Training* Dip.THP (diploma in therapeutic hypnosis and psychotherapy) *Duration* 14 weekends (168 hours) spread over 12/18 months, followed by one year's clinical supervision via the professional society. *Entry requirements* Usual university entrance requirements; mature candidates without formal qualification and background in the caring professions will need to demonstrate their ability and commitment to undertake the courses. *Fees* Part I £365, part II £292, part III £65. *Comments* No classes held at address, for enquiries only in writing or by telephone. Interviews by appointment.

UK Training College of Hypnotherapy and Counselling *Title of Training* (1) Foundation Course in Hypnotherapy and Counselling (2) Diploma Course in

Hypnotherapy and Counselling. *Duration* (1) On year part-time (120 classroom training hours). (2) A further 240 classroom training hours part-time weekends or evenings. *Entry requirements* (1) Applicants must be at least 23 years of age. Good general standard of education. Interview given. For (2), applicants must have successfully completed (1).

Jungian Analysis

Analytical psychology is the more common name given to the psychotherapeutic approach founded by Carl Jung. Although Jung initially agreed with Freud's formulation of the unconscious he later came to view the unconscious in wider and more transpersonal terms. For Freud, the patient's history was detailed in the unconscious mind, and through the process of free association would yield up its secrets, secrets which had been buried during childhood, when natural desires and social demands came into conflict. Thus for Freud the unconscious was a chronicle of traumatic events and a repository of repressed infantile fantasies. Jung, however, came to a quite different view. He saw the content of the unconscious not just in Freud's terms, but also as something which reflected the history of the human species and the cosmic order. He called this particular unconscious the 'collective unconscious'.

The conscious and unconscious mind are seen as

complementing and interacting with one another. The individual is seen as striving towards integration of these two aspects, and he called this process 'individuation'. Manifestations of the collective unconscious are to be found in dreams, symbolic language and fantasies. By exploring the meaning of these manifestations one can come to a deeper understanding of oneself. For instance, the 'archetypes' (such as the 'wise old man') which according to Jung, are part of the collective unconscious, could be known through understanding the symbols of one's dreams. Another central theme of Jung is the relationship between the 'masculine' ('animus') and 'feminine' ('anima') abilities within each of us. In this sense he was a pioneer of present day understanding of sexuality.

Jung advocated the 'eyeball to eyeball' encounter, where both analyst and client sit upright facing each other. Rather than focussing on the past he was more inclined to focus on the present and the future.

Two schools predominate in London. Firstly there is the classical school which has stuck closely to Jung's original writings. Then there is the Society of Analytical Psychology which while still working within a Jungian framework has assimilated the work of others on early childhood development.

READING
Memories, Dreams and Reflections *by Jung, C. Fontana 1963, £6.99* Jung's autobiography, full of insights into his life and the development of his ideas. A good place to start to explore Jungian analysis. **Practical Jung** *by Wilmer, H. Chiron 1987, £9.95* Subtitled 'The Nuts and Bolts of Jungian Psychotherapy', this is a fun, but seriously researched look at how Jungian Therapy works. Illustrated with cartoon-type line drawings. A more classical approach can be found in *Fordhams, M.* **Jungian Psychotherapy** *(Wiley 1978, £9.95)*

CENTRES OFFERING JUNGIAN ANALYSIS
Abraxas W2, Association of Jungian Analysts NW3, Astro-Psychotherapeutic Practice W3, Biodynamic Psychotherapy and Teaching W3, Float Experience SW11, Guild of Pastoral Psychology SW20, Hillside Practice NW5, Human Potential Resource Group (Surrey), Imprint SW19, Society of Analytical Psychology NW3.

TRAININGS IN JUNGIAN ANALYSIS
Association of Jungian Analysts Refer to organisers for details of training programme.
Society of Analytical Psychology *Title of Training* Training in Adult Analysis. *Duration* Three years part-time. Two evenings per week and own analysis 4 times a week. *Entry requirements* Candidates must have a degree or professional qualification (e.g. Social Work or Counselling). If the degree held has not included substantial study of psychology evidence of own study in this area required. Some clinical experience of patients also required. Candidates must be under 50 years of age. *Fees* Refer to organisers.

Kleinian Analysis

The work of Melanie Klein has had a major influence on the British Psychoanalytical school of thought. She lived and worked in London from 1926 onwards evolving theories of personality development which were to lead her to the creation of a variation of the treatment style advocated by Freud. Though she accepted the common themes of psychoanalytic theory, such as the importance of the unconscious and the influence of early childhood upbringing on the later life of the individual, she also focused on some hithero unexplored areas of early development. She is most well known for her contributions towards understanding psychic development in the first two years of life and the emphasis she placed on aggression. Her focus was on the oral stage of development whereas Freud had devoted more attention to later stages of development.

She believed that the child in the first few months of life cannot make a clear distinction between himself as a separate entity and the world he inhabits. The child at this stage experiences the world in terms of what is pleasurable and what is unpleasurable. For instance he experiences the mothers breast, a warm cot, being picked up and held as good, and feeling hungry or feeling cold as bad. The two prime emotions that the baby feels as a response to these good and bad experiences are warmth and anger respectively (Klein uses the terms love and hate). The infant may fluctuate between these two prime emotions rapidly as he does not have a developed sense of time or sequence of events. This rapidity of fluctuation can be observed when an infant in rage through hunger suddenly changes to feeling warmth and love towards the mother when fed. The mother is not only the object of these warm feelings but is also, in the child's mind, the object of rage when the child has unpleasurable experiences, and to the child she is then the bad mother. After a few months the child comes to realise that it is experiencing both rage and love towards his mother whom he can then see as a separate person from himself. The interplay between these two powerful emotions towards the same person sets up conflicts in the child which he has to deal with. Klein believed that the resolution of this conflict and the primitive way in which the child perceives the world lay the foundations for defences and for transference.

So how does the theory affect the practice of Kleinian analysis? Transference interpretations are likely early on in the therapy whereas in Freudian analysis they are usually allowed to develop before being interpreted. This transference tends to be focused on interpreting good or bad feelings that are directed towards the analyst to help the client realise that these feelings may be repetitions of earlier feelings towards the good and bad mother.

The couch is used. There may be a chair so that the client can have a choice of seating, though he may prefer not to sit facing as this may impede fantasy life.

The Kleinian approach would seem best suited to those who have a sympathy with the above ideas, who feel pent up with negative feelings, have difficulty making contact with others, who may feel anxious or who find it difficult to love others and be loved.

READING

Selected Melanie Klein *by Mitchell, J. (Ed). Penguin 1986, £5.99* An excellent collection of Klein's work with analysis and comment by Juliet Mitchell. Shows the development of her ideas and how therapy works. **My Kleinian Home** *by Herman, N. Free Association Books 1988, £9.95* An account of the author's journey through four therapies, ending with a full Kleinian analysis. Moving and enlightening.

CENTRES OFFERING KLEINIAN ANALYSIS

Tavistock Clinic NW3.

Men's Therapy

Historically, men only therapy groups evolved initially as a response to the Women's Movement in the early 1970s. Groups such as *Achilles' Heel* and *Red Therapy* attempted to link left wing and feminist politics with therapy.

The rationale behind men's therapy is that men may find it easier to talk about issues such as misogyny or sexuality honestly in an all men group. Exponents of these groups see men as relying largely on women for their emotional support. In a men's therapy group they may be able to become less competitive with other men, and develop deeper friendships with them. Through this process they may become less dependent on women for emotional support, and more able to give them emotional support when necessary. The aim is to develop less polarisation in relationships into 'opposite sex' roles and characteristics. This is seen as not only benefitting the men involved by releasing them from a narrow 'masculine' role, but also their relationships with partners, children and others.

Men leading men's groups may employ a variety of methods and approaches. Some may explicitly explore the theme of masculinity. In some groups, the political or social effects of men's therapy may be seen as the most important effects of the work, while in others are more focussed on individual, psychological change, though these two aspects are seen as inseparable in practice.

CENTRES OFFERING MEN"S THERAPY

Astro-Psychotherapeutic Practice W3, Brothers SE14, CAER (Cornwall), Man To Man NW3.

Brothers

Embodying the Masculine

A programme of workshops for the spiritual empowerment of man

For inclusion on the Brothers mailing list please send your name and address to: David Findlay, 207 Waller Road, London SE14 5LX

❝ It wasn't the idea of walking along a narrow pole 45 feet up in the pine trees with no visible means of support. Or even spending two nights out alone in the wilderness. What was bothering me about this six day training programme was the *running*. A two mile run was not my idea of how to begin the day, especially a day of intensive emotional and spiritual angst and inner turmoil. The whole idea took me back to school, aged 11, slithering through muddy country lanes while Mr Wrench, the games master, ran backwards in front of me shouting 'Look at me, I can run faster than you, and I'm going backwards!'

After twenty minutes of gentle meditation in the misty morning light, things didn't look so bad. The start of the run was almost ethereal. Then, about two thirds of the way up the mountain, I met Bruce Surely on his way down.

Bruce is a tall, wiry Texan who looks as though he runs up and down mountains every day before cleaning his teeth. The moment he flashed past, I felt my legs turn to lead.

I walked along, listening to the inner dialogue 'what a competitive, macho, creepy, driven character...that is the kind of man who just can't stop proving himself...boy, am I glad I'm not like that'.

Until I heard the voice of one of my teachers 'And what, David, does it cost you to think this way?

I decided to go through the steps of the forgiveness exercise we practised the previous day. I was definitely getting off on hating Bruce Surely. And the cost to me was - the very thing I was hating him for! All my energy was being consumed in a competition that went on all the time, with any man who I thought was doing 'better' than me.

I resolved to ask for his forgiveness. 'Forgive me, Bruce!' And the strength came back into my body, as if someone had turned the lights back on.

They say you become what you hate. I just never realised that it could happen so quickly! ❞

David Templar

Music Therapy and Voice Therapy

Music has been used for healing purposes for many centuries. Culturally it is used to unify groups, for relaxation, stimulation or to evoke a particular mood or response. It evokes feelings, and is also a powerful means of expressing feelings and communicating non-verbally. It can promote a feeling of bonding and closeness in a one to one therapeutic relationship or within a group. Music can provide a safe context through which feelings which otherwise might seem unacceptable can be expressed, acknowledged and subsequently understood. Like the other creative arts, it can provide an objective framework through which the individual can bring to light perhaps hitherto hidden aspects of his or her experience, and reflect on them objectively within this framework.

Though the use of music in a therapeutic way is usually expressive - it involves playing an instrument or singing (voice therapy), it may also involve listening to music.

Music therapy has wide applications. It can be used to help those with mental or physical handicaps develop skills and satisfying means of expression. It is also useful in developing self confidence and concentration, releasing feelings and increasing vitality.

CENTRES OFFERING MUSIC THERAPY
Mu Sum Ba W12, Nordoff-Robbins Music Therapy Centre W11.

CENTRES OFFERING VOICE THERAPY
Highbury Centre N5, Inner Sound and Voice Workshops (various locations in London), Open Gate (various locations in London), Playspace NW1, Primrose Healing Centre NW1, Redwood Women's Training Association, Sound Health SE8.

TRAINING
Nordoff-Robbins Music Therapy Centre *Title of Training* Diploma Course in Nordoff-Robbins Music Therapy. *Duration* Apply to organisers for details.

66Most of my therapy has been a rather haphazard process over several years, through various workshops and series of individual sessions. Through this I have gradually lowered my anxiety level by giving up the search for 'what I should be doing' (the internatised parental demand for success) and learnt to accept the ordinary person that I am.

Along the way I discovered some fascinating ways through primal work, in which my langauge reflected by birth trauma, e.g. "I feel under pressure", "I don't know which way to go", "I'm going round and round in circles", "I can't make any headway". This knowledge has made my tendency to struggle in life less frightening and more predictable without altering the underlying pattern.

My major breakthrough was unexpected and inexplicable. At the time I was stuck in a mediocre job, having decided to give up the search for a better job or retraining. I had been married for three years after a longer period of living together, and had been unable to conceive sucessfully, having had one miscarriage at three months. My situation could aptly be described by any of the phases above.

I attended a workshop given by a lady from California specialising in Artistic Counselling, called Margret Elson. However, as I was administrator and host of the event, I did not go with much anticipation of personal gain. My usual pattern in workshops was to avoid the limelight by giving way to more assertive types, but Margret insisted that each participant have a fair turn. The workshop topic was 'Overcoming blocks in creativity'. Margret had an uncanny ability to discover the problem in a few moments of conversation. Participants wanted to lose their stage fright in singing or playing, or to lose their writer's block etc. In each case Margret devised an exercise in performance, using the group as a sympathetic audience.

I too had had these kind of difficulties and spoke about the tension which had prevented me playing the violin well, and the rigid way in which I had been taught the piano, each year replacing one set of pieces with the ones for the next exam, all learnt by rote, never developing the ability to sight read from new pieces. The exercise Margret devised for me was a pretend performance, crashing about the keyboard at will, with no regard for the actual notes being played. This I did with due ceremony. The lack of prohibition struck a deep chord in me, the tears flowed, the audience applauded and my performance ended. I never bothered much about the piano or violin afterwards, but nine months later my daughter was born. 99

Mary Fee

Neuro-linguistic Programming

In the early seventies Neuro-Linguistic Programming (NLP) was developed by Richard Bandler, John Grinder, Leslie Cameron-Bandler, Judith DeLozier and Robert Dilts. In 1975 and 1976 Richard Bandler and John Grinder were the co-authors of The Structure of Magic I and The Structure of Magic II, which are still considered to be the definitive books on NLP. They claimed to have isolated important factors which underlie the work of well known therapists. These factors were seen to be common to the three therapists they studied. The three therapists were Fritz Perls, Virginia Satir and Milton Erikson.

Rather than pay attention to the therapists' notion of how therapeutic change occurred Grinder and Bandler noted patterns in the communication in these different therapist/client relationships and from these drew the conclusion that these patterns were the 'magic' ingredient that elevated these practitioners above the rest. In this sense a parallel can be drawn with Carl Rogers' thesis that it is not so much the particular technique or theory the therapist uses that brings about psychotherapeutic change, but the underlying attitudes of the therapist, even if he or she is unaware of having these attitudes.

They believed that each client should be approached differently. Therefore, they gave microscopic attention to how the client acted and looked, and from these signs could identify mechanisms of perceptions for each person. For example they were able to deduce whether or not a person was using visual recall rather than auditory recall from noting shifts in pupil size, breathing, direction of gaze and head movements. The therapist can then communicate to the other person in the appropriate mode, thus inducing rapport.

NLP is a technique based therapy used mainly in a group setting. As a client you will not only be the recipient of these techniques but will, by participation, learn some of these skills for yourself. Some of the techniques are mirroring and matching, and reframing, pacing, V/K disassociation and anchoring. An emphasis is on 'accessing' an 'anchor', that is, recalling good experiences and using them as resources for the future. This is done by superimposing good feelings from a past event onto a situation that has unpleasant feelings, so that the unpleasant feelings become less potent.

READING

Frogs into Princes *by Bandler, R. & Grinder, J. Real People Press 1978, £6.95.* This was a first book on NLP and in a burgeoning literature, it still stands as probably the nearest one can come to 'experiencing' NLP in a book. It is edited transcripts of weekend workshops and it covers all the basics of the subject with live interaction between the authors (as workshop leaders) and the participants. **What is NLP?** *Eric Robbie, Self-Published 1989, £2.95.* A small pamphlet, actually an extended version of the author's article in 'Innovative Therapies in Britain' (Eds Dryden & Rowan, Open Univ. Press), which gives a concise history of NLP, a good exposition of its theoretical background, and examples of how it works in practice. It is also written in 'English', rather than 'American'. Available from specialist bookshops.

CENTRES OFFERING NEURO-LINGUISTIC PROGRAMMING
Association for Neuro-Linguistic Programming N16, British Hypnosis Research (courses in London), City Health Centre EC1, Fulham Clinic SW6, Human Potential Resource Group (Surrey), International NLP Training Various locations, Lifecare, Natureworks W1, New Cross Natural Therapy Centre SE14, School of Hypnosis and Advanced Psychotherapy N4, Wholeness E18.

TRAININGS IN NEURO-LINGUISTIC PROGRAMMING
British Hypnosis Research *Title of Training* Diploma in Ericksonian Hypnosis, Psychotherapy and NLP. *Duration* One year, part time. Two level training: practitioner level and advanced level. Each level involves 6 weekends, 12 supervision days and 20 evenings. *Entry requirements* 1) Professional qualification in one of the caring professions. 2) A first degree as evidence of academic achievement. 3) Experience or employment in an area related to the subject matter of the course. Fees £950 + VAT for each level, payable in advance. (Loan facilities also available). *Comments* Skill based training held at St Ann's Hospital, London. Emphasis is placed on supervising each students whilst they work with actual patients. (Volunteer patients are supplied by BHR).

John Seymour Associates *Title of Training* NLP Diploma *Duration* Eight weekends (one a month) *Entry requirements* Must have completed their introductory weekend. *Fees* £75 + VAT per weekend. 10% discount if whole amount for course is paid in advance. Concessions available. *Comments* All courses are held in Bristol. There will be opportunities for further training.

NLP Training Program *Title of Training* Neuro-linguistic Programming Practitioner Certification Training. *Duration* One year part time (7 weekends) + one evening per week for 20 weeks. *Entry requirements Fees* £900 (including VAT) + £75 testing and certification fee.

Personal Construct Therapy
George Kelly proposed this theory of personality and a method of treatment in 1955. Though it has gained a major foothold in academic circles and now ranks as a major theory of personality, it has not been widely used as a form of treatment.

PERSONAL CONSTRUCT THERAPY

According to Kelly we all have a personal construct system. 'Construct' because we construe people, events and situations. 'Personal' because we construe in a highly personal way, and 'system' because the constructs are related to each other in a particular order or system.

Whist PCT draws on a number of other therapies for techniques it also claims a number of techniques of its own, namely enactment, self-characterisation, fixed role therapy and repertory grid analysis.

Enactment is used on a one-to-one basis, and is an informal role play technique. A situation is elaborated and the therapist and client act out the situation. The aim of this is to allow the client a fresh and detached view of a familiar situation.

The client may be asked to write a biography of him or herself as if written by a good friend. This is analysed by the therapist and is used as an evaluation technique in establishing the client's self image. This technique is known as self-characterisation.

The fixed-role technique is rather novel. Once the therapist has a picture of how the client sees him or herself and the world, a fictional character is created by the therapist. This fictional character views the world in in a way which is quite different, though not opposite, from the way the client does. The client is then presented with a description of this fictional character and is asked to pretend to be this person for at least a week. The aim of this is for the client to note how others react to the new character, and from this the client will review his or her own construct system.

The repertory grid technique may involve filling out a questionnaire that asks for ways the client pictures his or her world. It is then used for further analysis.

Personal Construct Therapy can also be practised in a group. George Kelly saw a group as a vehicle for its members to elaborate their construct system. By being a member of a group one has the opportunity of seeing how others see you and one can gain a new perspective on how people relate to each other.

Fay Fransella has pioneered work on PCT with stutterers at the Royal Free Hospital.

READING
Theory of Personality *by Kelly, G. Norton 1955 (63), £5.95.* This book consists of the first three chapters of Kelly's major work **The Psychology of Personal Constructs**, and gives the basic background and theory to Personal Construct Psychology. Another book to look for is **Inquiring Man** *by Bannister, D. & Fransella, F. (Croom-Helm 1986).*

CENTRES OFFERING PERSONAL CONTRUCT THERAPY
Centre for Personal Construct Psychology SW1.

TRAININGS IN PERSONAL CONSTRUCT THERAPY
Centre for Personal Construct Psychology Refer to Organisers for details.

Postural Integration

Similar to Rolfing (see the section on 'Body Approaches') from which it is derived, but rather than just physical manipulation of the body, as in Rolfing, postural integration delves into the emotional issues connected with body tensions. It takes the form of a manipulation of deep tissue combined with Reichian analysis and awareness of the body through movement.

The format of the session is similar to Rolfing, ten sessions of up to two hours. The client is encouraged to focus on breathing and feelings whilst the practitioner works on the body. New physical movements are encouraged with a focus on their meaning to the client.

CENTRES OFFERING PERSONAL CONTRUCT THERAPY
Open Centre EC1, Centre for Release and Integration (Middlesex).

Primal Integration

Primal Integration is a term coined by Bill Swartley to describe the very free-form type of primal work he developed (independently of Arthur Janov - see 'Primal Therapy' below) within a growth model.

Primal Integration works with very early preverbal experiences from the womb, birth and infancy, as well as with later experiences, in an eclectic way. The emphasis is on self-direction and self-regulation and allowing spontaneous growth processes to unfold rather than employing a highly structured or directed programme. The work is frequently undertaken in groups with a minimal leader determined structure but with appropriate ground rules for safe working. Thus primal material is allowed to emerge under its own dynamic but is not directly aimed for.

There is not usually an individual intensive when commencing the work as is the case with Primal Therapy Intensives are usually on a group basis and undertaken at a later stage in the work.

Primal material is worked with through bodywork, through transference (see Psychoanalysis for a definition of 'transference'), through face to face work and a variety of other ways.

CENTRES OFFERING PRIMAL INTEGRATION
Open Centre EC1

Primal Therapy

Arthur Janov, the founder of primal therapy, holds that the seat of neurosis lies in the past and that the maltreatment of children, some of society's child-rearing practices, pain and lack of love in upbringing all contribute to this. Neurosis consists of pain that is warded off, and which lies deep within the person, profoundly

affecting feelings towards self and others. By re-experiencing this pain and hurt and expressing it, neurosis will dissolve.

The process of therapy is sequential. First the client is asked to submit an autobiography and history. There then follow two interviews. If the client is accepted for treatment a three week intensive process begins. During the three weeks the client is seen daily for up to three hours. After the three weeks the clients enters individual or group therapy for up to a year.

The therapy usually takes place in a room that is sound protected, with cushions and mattresses. The lighting is usually dim.

During the therapy the focus is on the client's hurt. Time is spent going over incidents of neglect or abuse. Freedom is given to physical expression of these feelings, whether it is curling up into a foetal position, screaming abuse, or sobbing with pain, while the therapist acts supportively to enable this healing of past pain.

READING

The Primal Scream *by Janov, A. Shere 1973, £4.99* Some people find the claims made by Janov in this book somewhat extravagant, but it makes compulsive reading and there can be no denying that Primal regressive therapy can be a powerful therapeutic tool. **The Primal Issue Revisited** *by S&S (Eds) in Self & Society 1987, £1.50* A special issue of the journal of Humanistic Psychology devoted to developments in primal type work. Worth seeking out to look at the wide range of practitioners working and their different approaches.

CENTRES OFFERING PRIMAL THERAPY

Association for Analytic and Bodymind Therapy and Training N10, Hillside Practice NW5, London Association of Primal Psychotherapists NW5.

TRAININGS IN PRIMAL THERAPY

London Association of Primal Psychotherapists *Title of Training* Primal Psychotherapy Training *Duration* Three years part-time, two to three evenings per week. *Entry requirements* Must have been in primal therapy at least one year and have a good academic degree. *Fees* £750 per annum payable in three instalments, plus cost of personal therapy.

Psychoanalysis

Classical full scale Freudian psychoanalysis requires the client, referred to as patient or analysand, to attend a fifty minute session with an analyst four or five times a week, for at least three years. It thus means a huge investment in time and money which is one of the reasons it is not as widely practised as psychoanalytic psychotherapy (see below).

The reasons for such prolonged and regular contact are to be found in the theory initially formulated by Freud. Two cornerstones of the theory are transference and resistance. Such prolonged contact revives feelings and impulses one originally had towards significant figures from the past (usually one's parents) which become directed towards the analyst. This is transference. Time is needed for resistances to emerge too. Resistance is the withholding from oneself and the analyst of one's psychic interior. By helping the patient to become more aware of the workings of the unconscious in transference and resistance, he or she can become free of neurotic symptoms.

The basic rule is that the analysand 'free associates', in other words says whatever comes to mind. The analyst pays attention to the emergence of transference and resistance and tries to tease them out further.

The analyst may intervene in various ways, but usually by confrontation or interpretation, for example 'you're really angry at me and you express this by being continually late', or 'you seem to feel you have been mistreated by fate and dealt an unfair hand'.

Classically, the analysand lies on the couch with the analyst sitting behind, out of sight. Usually the analysand does most of the talking.

Analysts often work early in the morning or early evening, to accommodate their clients' employment schedules.

READING
What Freud Really Said by *Stafford-Clark, D. Peng 1967, £4.50* As its title suggests, this book explains in down to earth terms the major ideas of the father of psychoanalysis. He also examines the context in which Freud developed those ideas.

CENTRES OFFERING PSYCHOANALYSIS
British Psycho-Analytical Society and The Institute of Psycho-analysis W1.

TRAININGS IN PSYCHOANALYSIS
British Psycho-Analytical Society and The Institute of Psycho-analysis
Title of Training Training in the Psycho-analysis of Adults *Duration* Minimum of four years *Entry requirements* (1) Medically qualified or undergoing medical training or (2) good university degree or its equivalent. *Fees* £60 per term approximately for the seminars. Personal psychoanalysis fees £20 per session on average. Supervision fees are the same as personal psychoanalysis fees. Comments Trainees must undergo personal psychoanalysis (five sessions per week). Seminars and supervision are provided. If the trainee does not have sufficient experience of working with psychiatric patients he/she may be required to get more experience. Loans may be provided if the student does not have sufficient funds.

PSYCHOTHERAPY

Psychoanalytic Psychotherapy

Psychoanalytic psychotherapy takes its lead from psychoanalysis. It upholds the basic psychoanalytic theory but takes into account some the realities of commitment of time and money. Unlike psychoanalysis sessions are usually only once or twice, though sometimes three times a week with a fifty minute hour.

Also, unlike psychoanalysis, patient and analyst sit upright facing each other, and the engulfing intensity of the relationship which distinguishes psychoanalysis is tempered as the patient's everyday life becomes more the currency of the transactions.

Psychoanalytic psychotherapy is a name that covers a wide range of psychotherapies that either hold to the basic Freudian theory or to one of the neo-Freudian theories. When one thinks of visiting a psychotherapist this is what most people expect to get.

READING
Introduction to Psychotherapy *by Brown, D. & Pedder, J. RKP 1979, £8.95.* Although not only on the psychoanalytic approach, this book provides a good background introduction to how psychotherapy is practised.

CENTRES OFFERING PSYCHOANALYTIC PSYCHOTHERAPY
Arbours Consultation Service N8, British Association of Psychotherapists N3, British Psycho-Analytical Society and The Institute of Psycho-analysis W1, Camden Psychotherapy Unit WC1, Centre of Integral Psychoanalysis W11, Ealing Psychotherapy Centre W3, Institute of Psychotherapy and Social Studies NW3, Lincoln Centre and Institute of Psychotherapy SW4, New Cross Natural Therapy Centre SE14, Philadelphia Association NW3, Tavistock Clinic NW3, Women's Therapy Centre N7.

PSYCHOANALYTIC PSYCHOTHERAPY

❝ I had wanted to go into therapy to 'sort out my life' for several years before I actually took the plunge and did something about it. One evening, flicking through the first edition of this book, I came across the listings for psychotherapy centres and picked one that seemed the right place for me to approach. I also obtained a letter of referral from my very unsympathetic doctor who told me that 'life is not a bowl of cherries' , who dashed off a quick letter to get me out of her surgery.

I contacted the centre which set up an initial assessment interview with a therapist. When I got there I felt fine - or so I thought. The first question put to me was 'tell me about yourself', so I rattled off factual information from my curriculum vitae. The therapist gently suggested that this was not very helpful and asked me to talk about how I felt about my life. It was like the opening of a dam. I spoke about each area in which I experienced difficulty - work, friends, family, boyfriends i.e. everything - and to my surprise could not stop sobbing. I left fifty minutes later feeling completely drained, but with a promise that a suitable therapist would be found for me, convenient for either my office or home. I specified that I would prefer to see a female.

About six weeks later I received notification of my allotted therapist and I duly went along. The first few sessions were very difficult in that I did not know what to expect, what I should talk about, or how to deal with her. I also found it hard to keep to the appointments even though she was very flexible as to the times she he would see me. I wanted either early mornings or late evenings so as not to take time off from work.

Gradually I felt I was beginning to get the hang of it and was persuaded to lie down on the couch rather than sit bolt upright in the chair opposite. Lying down means you don't have to make eye contact all the time and it is less like a social occasion. You feel more relaxed and are able to stare at the ceiling, close your eyes or say nothing for a while.

Having fixed an appoinment, one is expected to keep it, if not you are charged, unless there is a very good reason why you haven't turned up. My therapist also allows payment on a sliding scale according to how much you think you can afford - from £16 to £20 per session. I have been in therapy for nearly a year now and expect to keep going for another year or two. It's a long process and often not easy or fun, but for anyone who thinks they could benefit from it, do it! ❞

Sue Owen

TRAININGS IN PSYCHOANALYTIC PSYCHOTHERAPY
Arbours Association *Title of Training* Training Programme In Psychotherapy. *Duration* Three years. *Entry requirements* Personal maturity and academic competence. *Fees* £1,050 per year exclusive of fees for individual therapy and personal supervision. *Comments* Trainees are required to be in individual psychoanalytic psychotherapy at least three times a week for the duration of the training. Training is individual psychotherapy. Trainees are expected to complete

a six month placement in one of the Arbours therapeutic communities. All prospective students must complete at least two terms on the Associates programme before beginning the full training.

British Association of Psychotherapists *Title of Training* Training In Adult Individual Psychotherapy. *Entry requirements* University degree in medicine, psychology or social science or an equivalent professional qualification and some experience of working with disturbed people. The age limit for the Freudian section is 45 years and for the Jungian section it is 50 years. Only in exceptional will these criteria be waived. *Fees* Apply to secretary for details. *Comments* They also do brief external courses: Jungian section: 'Working with Analytical Concepts'. 10 three hour seminars for each of three terms, £185 per term. Freudian section: Psychoanalytic Aspects of Work with Individuals' . 10 one and half hour sessions for each of two terms £195 per term.

Tavistock Clinic *Title of Training* An Interdisciplinary Programme of Training in Adult Psychotherapy for Experienced Professional Workers in the Health and Social Services. *Duration* Four years full time. *Entry requirements* Must be a clinical psychologist *Fees* £1,450 per annum if UK or EEC. £3,350 for overseas trainees. *Comments* Trainees are required to have personal psychotherapy.

Psychodrama

Jacob Moreno created psychodrama. He began experimenting with the use of role playing with children as early as 1908 and evolved his method in the intervening years before his death in 1974.

Moreno felt that 'all the world's a stage'. He believed that we adopt rigid roles and act them out and so focused his work on freeing spontaneous expression through make-believe situations.

Psychodrama is psychotherapy married to the theatre. The therapist is called the director, and the client the protagonist. The client produces a scene from his or her life that is loaded with feeling - it may be getting a salary rise at work, leaving home, or whatever, and this becomes the drama that the protagonist and the other members of the group enact. The director tries to recreate the scene in all its vividness with a here and now quality.

As in the theatre the director encourages members to visualise what the surroundings are, and may point out where the imaginary door or window is and ask members to keep these in mind when dramatising the incident. The director may also use props as in theatre improvisation.

The group members do not learn lines for the characters they are playing, but feed on the descriptions given by the protagonist of how they are likely to respond in certain situations. Thus they slowly build up a picture of their assumed character, and modify it by a process of improvisation and rehearsal. The protagonist may switch roles to gain insight into another character's position. Such insight is often a revelation to the client.

If a group member does not appear to be acting out the character as the protagonist remembers him or her, the director may ask another group member to play the character.

If the group members feel the protagonist is not saying what he or she really feels in the situation, they are allowed to go up behind that person and say what they think he or she really feels. The protagonist has the option of rejecting or adopting this new thought.

Eventually a climax is reached and catharsis occurs. The cast then sit down and assimilate what transpired. Members may relate how they felt playing their particular character.

Another client may then choose to relate another incident, and so the process goes on.

READING
The Essential Moreno *by Fox, J. (Ed) Springer 1987, £14.95* Moreno was, of course, the father of Psychodrama and the editor has here made an excellent selection from his work, showing the development of his ideas and how they work in practice. **Acting In** *by Blatner, H. Springer 1976, £15.95* Blatner worked with Moreno towards the end of his life and this book has long been thought of as *the* basic textbook of psychodramatic methods. A book to look for later in 1990 is **Psychodrama: Inspiration and Technique** *by Holmes, P. & Karp, M. (Routledge £14.99)*, a collection of articles by twelve psychodramatists who have developed beyond the ideas of Moreno.

CENTRES OFFERING PSYCHODRAMA
Bodyspace EC1, Eigenwelt London NW3, Gale Centre for Creative Therapy (Essex), Holwell Centre for Psychodrama and Sociodrama (Devon), Minster Centre NW2, Open Centre EC1, Playspace NW1, Spectrum N4.

Psychosynthesis

Psychosynthesis is sometimes called a 'transpersonal' psychology. It is one of the psychologies which emphasise the importance of the spiritual dimension, and of developing higher levels of consciousness and self actualisation.

Its founder was Roberto Assagioli who was trained in psychoanalysis but became dissatisfied with Freud's preoccupation with the 'basement' of the psyche - with repressed feelings and neurosis. While acknowledging the importance of bringing to light these feelings for psychological health, Assagioli felt that there was also a 'higher' unconscious as well as the 'lower' unconscious. The 'higher' unconscious is the source of inspiration, imagination and 'peak' experiences - experiences of unity or joy which transcend the individual's sense of themselves as a separate, isolated unit. Assagioli studied Indian philosophy and religion and sought to marry western psychology which emphasises the importance of the individual and the personality, with eastern mysticism's concern with higher levels of consciousness.

In psychosynthesis the psyche is seen as being made up of many different parts; our body, feelings and mind; the different roles we play in life which are all part of our overall personality but which may seem in conflict; and our experience of the depths and heights of the psyche. The process of psychosynthesis is to synthesise these often seemingly different and even contradictory parts. What unites all these elements is the self, a conscious experience of ourselves which is not identified with any one part, but which can observe and direct awareness of them.

Assagioli also emphasised the importance of what he called the 'will'. By this he did not mean will in the sense of will power, but our ability to make choices and to mould our selves and lives which is based on a deep experience of our own individuality.

Psychosynthesis therapists may use a variety of techniques. They may ask you to engage in an inner dialogue with particular parts of yourself, or lead you through a guided fantasy to clarify your feelings about a particular issue. They may encourage you to draw or paint from material which arises in the course of therapy. Therapists also draw on techniques used in other therapies such as gestalt and psychodrama. While the basic theory has been applied as a kind of psychotherapy, it also has applications in education, medicine and religion.

READING
Psychosynthesis; A Collection of Basic Writings *by Assagioli, R, Thorsons 1976.* In this book, Assagioli outlines his theory, and its difference to the other psychotherapies. He then describes the techniques that are used. A very full explanation but some people find it quite a difficult read. **What We May Be** *by Ferruci, P., Thorsons 1982.* Ferruci was originally a students of Assagioli, and later his collaborator. This book is a manual of self help exercises in psychosynthesis. It's well laid out and as such is easy to read and use.

CENTRES OFFERING PSYCHOSYNTHESIS
Art from Within, Brothers SE14, Communication and Counselling Foundation (courses held in London), Cortijo Romero (Spain), Highbury Centre N5, Humanistic Psychology at LSE WC2, Institute of Psychosynthesis NW7, Living Qabalah SE22, Moving Line Counselling and Therapy (throughout London), North London Counselling Service N5, Psychosynthesis and Education Trust SW9, Re-Vision NW2.

TRAININGS IN PSYCHOSYNTHESIS
Communication and Counselling Foundation *Title of Training* 1) Professional Training in Psychosynthesis and Counselling Skills and Attitudes. 2) Psychosynthesis and counselling Skills and Attitudes for Professionals. *Duration* 1) Three years part-time 2) Two years part-time. *Entry requirements* 1) Completion of The Psychology of Transition programme and substantial personal growth work. 2) Suitable for

Using the tools of psychosynthesis in creative painting and writing

66 I have a painting before me, conceived from an emotional side of me. It allows me to see how a part of me is and can be. This 'can be' is often held in shadow but when revealed shows new possibilities and passions.

I permit myself to see my thoughts of design, of making something which gives shape, form, and rhythm; allows colour and shade of how I feel. I am mindful that I have accepted to draw, to move my had across the page, quite freely. My body willingly accepts and holds itself steady, a receptacle, but it allows the intent of my purpose to spill out as milk form the jug.

And as I look someone fights to shut my eyes. It is my mind furtively searching his cold cabinets to reject this change in my body. He is vain and arrogant, greedy for success and control of his making. Here he is forced to be a silent observer of these new characters who have for long stood in his shadow.

In the painting these characters appear exuberant, excited, engaged and passionate. They are modestly arrayed and I experience them in my body. It is not difficult for me to gladden as they rise from the paper for here they lend hope. I would lift the twists of colour, the volumes of shape, and dance to their music.

He, my mind, is tempted to join in to take rest from his high throne. To lay off his judge's ermine and jewels and welcome these modest strangers into his palace. The king is saddened at his years of self-imposed exile, remembers the scars he bore in battles never won, and sees now these new friends could help him to be a kinder, wiser king. **99**

Maureen Kennedy

those who are currently working in a chosen field who want to enhance their own skills through this course. Substantial personal growth work is also a prerequisite. Applicants may be required to complete The Psychology of Transition course. *Fees* Apply to organisers.

Institute of Psychosynthesis *Title of Training* Diploma in Psychosynthesis Psychotherapy. *Duration* 4 years part-time. 9 weekends, 1 week residential, plus some evenings, plus personal therapy, per annum. *Entry requirements* Completion of prerequisite course Fundamentals of Psychosynthesis. *Fees* £1,500 per annum.

Psychosynthesis and Education Trust *Title of Training* Professional Training Programme: Counselling and Psychotherapy Diploma Course. *Duration* 3 Years part-time (evenings and weekends). *Entry requirements* Relevant degree or sufficient life experience. *Fees* Apply to organisers for details. *Comments* Professional training is recognised by the British Association for Counselling.

Re-Vision *Title of Training* (1) Psychosynthesis Counselling Training. (2) Advanced training in psychosynthesis therapy and group leadership. *Duration* (1) Two and a half years part-time. First year and a half courses held over weekends plus some intensive residential courses. Final year one weekday over three 10-week terms plus some extra requirements. (2) Two years part time, one day a week (total 30 weeks), plus 3-4 day intensive. Courses may also be taken individually. *Entry requirements*

(1) Preference is given to applicants in the caring professions. Those who have successfully qualified will be eligible for the Advanced Training Programme. (2) Must be professionally qualified counsellor or therapist. *Fees* (1) Details on request. (2) Approximately £800 per annum plus VAT.

Rebirthing

Rebirthing is the process of reliving one's own birth and of coming to terms with the original experience. It is therefore a regression technique. Frederick Le Boyer, a leading exponent of natural birth, has suggested that birth can be painful for the baby and that this might affect the baby's outlook on the world. If it was harsh then the person might grow up to view the world in a negative way. Rebirthers argue that if one can regress to the initial birth and live it through, one can change negative thoughts and attitudes.

There are two different types of rebirthing in this country. One was founded by Leonard Orr on the West Coast of America in the 1970s and the other was developed by Frank Lake.

Orr rebirthing involves using a breathing exercise. The therapist and client occupy a quiet room and pillow and blankets may be used to cover the client if necessary. The client is asked to lie down and breathe in and out in a regular way without pausing. A contract is made beforehand about how long this will continue. Usually it is for an hour or until the client experiences a breathing release, which is the eventual aim of rebirthing.

An Orr rebirther also employs 'affirmations'. These are sentences which are repeated by the client such as 'Every breath I take, increases my aliveness' or 'I feel much love for people'. They affirm how the client would like to feel or be, and are intended to counteract negative attitudes.

Sometimes clients are asked to be reborn in water, as this is closer to the original experience of birth. A bath is usually used for this, and so that the client can remain submerged, he or she may be asked to use a snorkel.

The other type of rebirthing is usually done in a group. One member chooses to be reborn. The other members physically assemble themselves into a simulated womb around the member who lies on the floor in a foetal position. Cushions are liberally employed and are used as buffers between the group 'womb' and the 'foetus'. Gradually the members apply increasing pressure (usually by sitting on or pressing against the 'foetus') which simulates the growth of the foetus in the contained environment. The 'foetus' decides (usually when overcome with claustrophobia) to get out from the enclosing walls and makes its way out of an opening. This is a physically demanding exercise.

Both of these techniques are quite different so make sure you know which one you have signed up for.

READING

Rebirthing: The Science of Enjoying All of Your Life, *Laut, P., Trinity 1983*. An excellent manual of rebirthing techniques as originated by Leonard Orr. It shows how it works, how sessions may proceed and gives affirmations to further the growth process. **Clinical Theology** *by Lake, F., (Dartman, Longman & Todd). 1980.* This is Lake's major work on his approach, a fusion of theological, analytical / psychodynamic, and existential ideas. It doesn't give a clear outline of how his approach is used. His ideas are more usually defined as being 'Primal Integration'. There have been two special issues of **Self & Society** which cover this approach, 'Birth and Rebirth' and 'Voices from the Past', both of which may be available from specialist shops or direct from Self & Society.

CENTRES OFFERING REBIRTHING

CAER (Centre For Alternative Education And Research) (Cornwall), Primrose Healing Centre NW1, Rebirthing Centre SW18, Resonance SW17, Sunra SW12.

66 When I did rebirthing I did not regress to my actual birth. I initially found the breathing very difficult to get into, but when I did grasp it, I had some amazing physical experiences - tingling in my chest, arms and hands - the vibration was so strong that I felt I was purring! On my second attempt sorrows welled up. I actually felt acute physical pain in my left arm and it seemed immobile.

Rebirthing was an interesting experience (I thought it would be terrifying) and coupled as it was with affirmation work, was also a positive one. 99

Karin Grey

66 One of my flatmates who was a new age junkie was constantly trying out his latest new found therapy. He had recently discovered rebirthing and would practice it in the bath. He would lock himself in for at least an hour in the bathroom and submerge himself in the bath water and use a snorkel to aid his breathing. My other flatmate was an architect who worked at home. He hated his work though and would drop his work to visit the toilet where he spent much of his time there reading. I remember how I resented each of them enjoying their 'therapy' while I waited to use the shared facilities. 99

Relaxation Training

Relaxation training is a method of inducing in the client the relaxation response. The relaxation response was identified by Wallace and Benson as a decrease in blood pressure, respiratory and heart rate and an increase in alpha and theta brainwaves and skin resistance. These physiological changes correspond to a state of calm and well being. There are a variety of approaches which bring about the relaxation response, such as biofeedback, autogenic training, hypnosis, tai chi, yoga and some forms of meditation, all of which are covered elsewhere in this book. There is another method, however, which is to systematically tense and let go of various muscles in the body to achieve a state of reduced tension, which is the main focus here. This method of progressive relaxation was developed by Jacobson.

Relaxation training takes place in quiet surroundings with the client in a rested position. The client is asked to focus on relaxing the muscles one by one. Usually starting from the feet first the client is asked to tense a foot and then relax it, and to notice the difference between the foot when it is tense and when it is relaxed. This tensing and relaxing is done systematically throughout the muscles of the body. At times the client will be directed to focus on parts that have been tensed and relaxed, such as the right hand side of the body and asked how this compares with the left hand side of the body which has not yet undergone the process. By comparing differences the client is helped to gain awareness of muscular tension and how to relax all of the muscles throughout the body. The client may be asked to practise at home and supplied with an instruction led audio tape as an aid.

Relaxation training was incorporated into behaviour therapy when Joseph Wolpe adopted it to help hypertense people relax. It has also been used for helping people suffering from anxiety. On its own, the relaxation response will help reduce anxiety, but will not effectively help in situations which provoke anxiety unless it is used within a programme of desensitisation or another psychotherapy.

Relaxation training is something that can be learned quite quickly so that one can practise it on one's own. It is possible to learn from audio tapes alone and there are an abundance of such tapes on the market.

As mentioned above, there are many techniques for inducing the relaxation response, relaxation training being only one of them. It does not suit everyone and there are a significant number of people who find, for one reason or another, that they cannot learn the relaxation response. Some people even have an aversion to it, and are therefore advised to try a different approach entirely.

Courses offering relaxation may provide one of the approaches listed above or the one focused on here, or a combination of these.

READING

The Relaxation Response *by Benson, H., Fontana 1977 £2.95.* A description of relaxation response discovered by the author, and an outline of techniques and exercises to develop it for oneself. **You Must Relax** *by Jacobson, E., Unwin 1975, £3.95.* A popular introduction to his work, outlining the dangers of tension and its effects on oneself and society, followed by a 'manual' of techniques in Progressive Relaxation.

CENTRES OFFERING RELAXATION TRAINING

Audio Limited W12, Equilibrium Therapy Centre SW18, Natureworks W1, Oasis N2, St James Centre for Health and Healing W1.

Sex Therapy

This is a short term therapy designed to help couples who are suffering from a range of sexual difficulties including premature ejaculation, impotency, vaginismus (an involuntary spasm of the vaginal muscles which makes penetration impossible), non-ejaculation and orgasmic problems. As it is a therapy for couples it could be considered part of family or couple therapy with a specific issue in focus, though due to the work of Masters and Johnson it has grown into a therapy in its own right.

Usually, though not always, a male and female therapist work with the couple. The couple are asked to give their medical history so that any organic reasons for the sexual problem can be eliminated. After some discussion about the nature of the problem the couple are asked to follow homework assignments. The first stage is often an exercise called 'sensate focus' where the couple are asked to touch each other and to communicate to each other how it feels and what is, or is not, pleasurable. They are asked to abstain from sexual intercourse and genital and breast touching is usually forbidden. In the second stage breast and genital touching is allowed but intercourse and orgasm are not. The path of the third stage depends on the presenting problem. For instance, if the couple is a heterosexual one and impotence is the problem, the woman is taught how to manipulate the penis in specific ways and she is instructed to insert the penis into the vagina, thus relieving the man of the responsibility. However, many sex therapists nowadays do not adhere any more to such a 'performance orientated' programme, and find it more important to help couples relieve the pressures that are caused by the performance orientation in their sex lives.

It is not necessary to go along with a partner at first to receive sex therapy. Some people prefer to go on their own to build up confidence before they talk with their partner.

For sex therapy to be effective the couple should still be able to communicate with each other and it works best if there is a specific behavioural problem with sex, such as one of those listed above. In fact there can be a great deal of overlap between sex, couple and family therapy. There may be other attitudes, problems or conflicts at the root of the difficulties and in this case couple or family therapy might be more suitable. If there is still love between the couple and a mutual desire to work on the problem then sex therapy has a good success rate.

READING

Sex Therapy in Britain *by Cole M. and Dryden, W. (Eds),* Another textbook giving articles by leading practitioners on various approaches to, and themes in, sex therapy. Quite a heavy read. Before taking the plunge into therapy, you may want to look at the many self-help books on the market, for instance, **Treat Youself to Sex** *by Brown and Faulder, Penguin 1977* or **Sex Problems; Questions and Answers** *by Cole and Dryden, Optima 1989.*

CENTRES OFFERING SEX THERAPY

London Institute for the Study of Human Sexuality SW5, Neal's Yard Therapy Rooms WC2, North London Counselling Practice NW7, Redwood Women's Training Association, Spectrum N4, Welbeck Counselling Service W1, Women's Therapy Centre N7.

TRAININGS IN SEX THERAPY

London Institute for the Study of Human Sexuality *Title of Training* Training to Certificate and Diploma Level. Course takes the form of 5 modules: (1) Basic counselling skills (2) Human sexuality (3) AIDS counselling (4) Sex education (5) Sex therapy. Certificate is awarded on satisfactory completion of (1). *Fees* Basic counselling skills £600. Human sexuality £600. Integrative sex therapy £900. Sex education - composite fee AIDS counselling £200

Stress Management

Two researchers, Rosenman and Friedman, found that people could be divided into two categories which they called 'A' and 'B'. 'Type A' people tend to suffer from hurry-up sickness; they are aggressive, have difficulty relaxing, have few friends and tend to be workaholics. 'Type B' have opposite characteristics. 'Type A' people have a tendency to develop hypertension, heart problems, stomach aches, ulcers, diabetes and alcoholism. It is the 'Type A' person who may want to consider participating in a stress management programme.

The treatment programme is holistic and many techniques such as hypnosis, biofeedback, behaviour therapy and massage are combined with information on diet and exercise. It also employs 'cognitive restructuring' which is a means of teaching clients new ways of interpreting what they themselves and others do or say. These individual and often habitual interpretations are an important aspect of the 'stress response' in that they determine a person's stress related behaviour.

Practitioners vary in the emphasis they place on the above treatments. Some stress physical exercise above all else and some see cognitive restructuring as more important, so it is worth seeing details of the programme before opting for this type of therapy to see if it suits your needs.

Many stress management consultants teach clients to hypnotise themselves. Some practitioners use relaxation audio tapes and will sell these to you. If biofeedback is taught then technical equipment to monitor physiological activity may to be used to help clients relax more (see Biofeedback).

Stress management is practised in group settings. Programmes tend to be short and deliver a package of treatments for managing stress. For those who wish to delve more deeply into their own psyche and their relationships with others, some of the other therapies mentioned in this book might be preferable.

READING
Stress Management *by Charlesworth, E., Cogi 1989.* Of the many stress books available, this is one of the most comprehensive. The authors look at what stress is physiologically and gives exercises using most relaxation techniques, including progressive relaxation, imagery and visualisation, autogenics and diet. **Guide to Stress Reduction** *by Mason, L.J., Cel. Arts 1985.* A nicely presented collection of stress reduction techniques. Less comprehensive than the above but probably easier to use.

CENTRES OFFERING STRESS MANAGEMENT
Acumedic Centre NW1, Brunel Management Programme (Uxbridge), C.H.I Clinic SW6, CAER (Centre For Alternative Education And Research) (Cornwall), Centre for Stress Management SE3, Falcons SW11, Hampton Healing Centre, Health Management NW3, Human Potential Resource Group (Surrey), Jeyrani Health Centre E18, Life Directions W1, Lifecare, McCarthy Westwood Consultants SW11, Minster Centre NW2, Natureworks W1, Primrose Healing Centre NW1, Skills with People N5, St James Centre for Health and Healing W1, Welbeck Counselling Service W1, Women's Therapy Centre N7.

Transactional Analysis

Eric Berne, a Canadian psychoanalyst was the founder of transactional analysis or T.A. as it is also known. As its name indicates, transactional analysis concerns itself with the analysis of transactions, a transaction being a unit of communication. In 1964 Berne wrote the bestseller *Games People Play*, which describes particular ways in which people relate to each other, which he calls 'games'. These are habitual and often destructive ways of relating with titles like 'Kick Me', 'Wooden Leg' and 'Yes

- But'. In his follow-on book, *What Do You Say After You Say Hello?* he develops his original ideas and posits that we live our lives in terms of a 'script'. A script is a life plan which we live out from decisions made in childhood, decisions which we still act upon although we have forgotten about them.

Through learning about the theory of games and scripts it then becomes possible to use these as a map to understand one's own history and one's present way of relating to others.

Part of the initial sessions of most T.A. groups is educational. Clients are taught the language and theory, which is subsequently put to use when analysing a member's behaviour in a group. For example a client may be provoking others in the group to become angry, whilst denying any responsibility for this. The therapist may interpret this behaviour as a game of 'Kick Me', a masochistic game of manipulating others into a persecutory role, so that the 'victim' can cry 'why does it always happen to me'. Further analysis might follow as to why certain people chose to take on the persecutory role.

T.A. provides a set of theories with which clients can see life and relational patterns more clearly. Once understood, the original decisions upon which these patterns are based can be changed, and as a result of this, the client's behaviour can then become more appropriate.

T.A. provides a palatable and often amusing jargon. Unlike most therapies which keep the theoretical jargon out of the consulting room, T.A. employs it as part of the process of understanding.

READING

What Do You Say After You Say Hello? *by Berne, E., Corgi 1975.* Probably a better place to start looking at Berne's ideas than **Games People Play.** It oulines the principles of TA and covers many of the developments of his ideas including the 'script theory'. **TA Today** *by Stewart, I. and Joines, V., Lifespace 1986.* Subtitled *A New Introduction to T.A.*, this is a comprehensive textbook of the theory and practice of T.A. It's widely recommended to clients by most TA practitioners and is the obvious place to go to understand how T.A. could work for you.

CENTRES OFFERING TRANSACTIONAL ANALYSIS

Heron Training Workshops (various locations), Lifespace NW5, Metanoia W5, Minster Centre NW2, Open Centre EC1.

TRAININGS IN TRANSACTIONAL ANALYSIS

Metanoia *Title of Training* Training in Transactional Analysis and Integrated Psychotherapy. *Duration* Four years. Ten weekends per year. *Fees* £600 per annum. *Comments* Require personal psychotherapy for the duration of the training. Some bursaries available.

Transpersonal Psychotherapy

The term 'transpersonal psychotherapy' covers a wide area, and can be used to describe Jung's analytical psychology and psychosynthesis (qv). It emphasises the spiritual aspect of people's experience, and the search for meaning. It has its roots in both eastern and western religious traditions on the one hand, and in Abraham Maslow's work on peak experience and the psychology of what he called 'self actualising' people on the other.

A key concept in transpersonal psychology is the belief that the central organising principle of the individual's life is the 'self'. The 'self' goes beyond the personal sense of I or ego, and is seen to include this personal sense with an awareness of the collective and universal. This self is also sometimes called 'soul' in transpersonal therapy. The self is seen to unit the different parts of the personality in an experience of wholeness.

TRANSPERSONAL PSYCHOTHERAPY

Myth and archetypes are used to connect the individual with the collective and historical search of the human race for meaning. Crises are not seen as 'illness' or even 'problems' but rather as part of the process of the individual becoming more aware. Dreamwork, symbols, guided imagery or fantasy, meditation are used in sessions, as well as more extroverted methods of gestalt dialoguing with empty chairs, dialogue between the client and a part of themselves. The therapist may also make use of the 'Chakras' model. The chakras are the eight energy centres of the body according to Indian philosophy, which are situated at various points from the base of the spine to the top of the head. Work here may include for instance visualising an energy blockage at a particular chakra, and exploring what it means in terms of the client's life. Astrology may also be used to clarify the life events of the client.

CENTRES OFFERING TRANSPERSONAL PSYCHOLOGY
Humanistic Psychology at LSE WC2, Studio E NW6.

PSYCHOTHERAPY

OTHER PSYCHOTHERAPIES

ADLERIAN PSYCHOTHERAPY
Adlerian Society for Individual Psychology SE7.

ANTI-SMOKING THERAPY
Capital Hypnotherapy Centre W6, Redwood Women's Training Association.

BEREAVEMENT COUNSELLING
British Association for Social Psychiatry W1, Friends of Shanti Nilaya UK, Psychotherapy for Individuals, Couples & Groups N10, Westminster Pastoral Foundation W8.

BIOSYNTHESIS
Minster Centre NW2.

CHILD PSYCHOTHERAPY
Anna Freud Centre NW3, British Association of Psychotherapists N3, Children's Hours Trust N7.

CREATIVITY COUNSELLING
Actors Institute EC1 (Samurai and Mastery Programme), Arts Psychology Consultants SW5, Cortijo Romero (Spain), Creative Arts Workshops N8, DMA UK Technologies for Creating N19, Human Potential Resource Group (Surrey), Open Gate (courses held in London), Playworld (New Malden), Resonance SW17, Skills with People N5.

DREAM THERAPY
Abraxas W2, Highbury Centre N5, Imprint SW19, Playspace NW1.

EATING PROBLEM COUNSELLING
Equilibrium Therapy Centre SW18, Women's Therapy Centre N7.

ENLIGHTENMENT INTENSIVES
Holistic Yoga Centre (Milton Keynes), Maitri (Hants).

HAKOMI METHOD
Hakomi Institute W4, Iris E3,

INTER-CULTURAL THERAPY
Nafsiyat Inter-Cultural Therapy Centre N4,

JOURNAL KEEPING
Humanistic Psychology at LSE

LIFE IMPROVEMENT WORKSHOPS
Insight Seminars W2, Life Training Centre W2, Natale Insitute (London), Universal Training (various locations), Workshops with a Difference (Twickenham).

MANAGEMENT TRAINING
Argo Human Resource Consultants N5, Brunel Management Programme (Uxbridge), Heron Training Workshops (various locations), Human Potential Resource Group (Surrey), Life Directions W1,

MIND CLEARING
Holistic Yoga Centre (Milton Keynes), Sunra SW12.

PAST LIFE THERAPY
Centre for Past Life Therapy and Research (Woodford Green).

REGRESSION THERAPY
Bexleyheath Natural Health Clinic KENT.

RESONANCE THERAPY
CAER (Centre For Alternative Education And Research) (Cornwall), Maitri (Hants), Open Gate (courses held in London).

VIDEO THERAPY
Video Therapy WC1

OTHER TRAININGS

The following list of trainings are included here because either the range of therapies they draw upon for the training is very broad and therefore will not fit into any one particular category, or because the training is one which we have not covered in the list of major therapies explained.

ADLERIAN
Adlerian Society for Individual Psychology *Title of Training* Certificate and diploma in Adlerian counselling. *Duration* Certificate 2 years part-time (evenings and weekends). Diploma one year part-time under supervision. *Entry requirements* None for the certificate. For diploma, must have certificate. *Fees* Current minimum fees £140 for members of the Adlerian Society, £170 for non-members.

ARTS/CREATIVITY
Creative Arts and Therapy Consultants *Title of Training* Diploma in the Therapeutic and Educational Application of the Arts. *Duration* One year part-time. One day a week plus six weekends (300 hours). *Entry requirements* 2 'A' Levels; agreement to undergo personal therapy throughout the course; have worked or are presently working within education, a helping profession or the arts; have sufficient maturity and life experience to cope with course material. *Fees* £1200 pa. Comments The course is ideally suited to those already working in a counselling, therapy or education, who wish to work with the arts in ways which enhance personal growth. The course is run at Regent's College, London.

Living Art Training *Title of Training* The Living Art Training *Duration* One year part-time of twelve weekends and a week in the country. *Entry requirements* Application can only be made after taking a living art seminar weekend, and having a private interview. *Fees* £1,950 + VAT. Payment in three equal instalments of £650 + VAT. *Comments* No art experience necessary.

THE ADLERIAN SOCIETY FOR INDIVIDUAL PSYCHOLOGY

ADLER called his system Individual Psychology, "individual" because he saw each human being as a unity of body, mind and spirit within a social environment attracted by his/her own self-chosen goals rather than driven by instinctual urges. "Meanings are not determined by situations but we determine ourselves by the meaning we give to the situation" - Adler.

Alderian counsellors endeavour to help by encouragement and strengthening rather than correction so that a positive use of inferiority feelings can be established in coping with the three life tasks as defined by Adler: Occupation; Friendship/Society; Love/Sex/Intimacy.

The Society is active in many parts of Great Britain. Counsellors, group facilitators and speakers dealing with all aspects of human relationships are available.

Training courses in theory and practice of individual and family counselling, as well as experiential workshops, are held on a regular basis. Our Counselling Centre in Swiss Cottage is open on Monday evenings from 7.00-9.00pm.
The Adlerian Society For Individual Psychology, 161 Charlton Church Lane, London SE7 7AA.
Tel: 081-858-1767 or 081-858-7299.

OTHER TRAININGS

BIODYNAMIC PSYCHOLOGY
Institute of Biodynamic Psychology and Psychotherapy *Title of Training* Certificate in Biodynamic Psychology and Psychotherapy *Duration* 1) Four years part-time, one weekend a month, one full day per week. Five day seminars in spring and summer holidays each year. *Entry requirements* All professional and academic qualifications acknowledged. Good general basic education and/or life experience essential. Experience of biodynamic therapy and/or oather therapeutic approaches an advantage. All applicants interviewed and considered. *Fees* £2,100 per aanum, £2,000 if paid in advance, otherwise payable by instalments.

CHILD PSYCHOTHERAPY
Anna Freud Centre *Title of Training* Training in the Psychoanalysis and psychotherapy of children and young people. *Duration* 4-5 years, first three years full-time. *Entry requirements* One of: Degree in psychology or equivalent (e.g. sociology, social anthropology); post-graduate diploma or higher degree in psychology, social work etc. *and* previous experience of working with children, and preferably some experience of residential care of children. Applicants of 40 or over accepted only in exceptional circumstances. *Fees* Tuition fees are waived because students contribute to services of the centre. Personal analysis five times a week at minimum of £15 per session, and supervision of one session weekly in second year rising to 4 or 5 sessions weekly in latter three years of training (£12 per session). *Comments* Admission is by written application and two interviews.

ENLIGHTENMENT INTENSIVES
Holistic Yoga Centre *Title of Training* Enlightenment Intensive Masters Training Duration 10 days residential (plus previous participation in Enlightenment Intensives). *Entry requirements* At least one 3-day Enlightenment Intensive, preferably a 14-day EI. *Fees* £325 (£75 deposit, balance payable at start of course). *Comments* Study of two 250 page manuals has to be completed prior to the course.

MIND CLEARING
Holistic Yoga Centre 1) Basic Mindclearing Training 3) Advanced Mindclearing Training *Duration* 1) and 2) 2-3 months weekday evening and 3-5 day residential. *Entry requirements* 1) at least 30 hours of mindclearing in one to one sessions. 2) At least 50 hours of mindclearing in one to one sessions. *Fees* 1) £475 all inclusive. 2) £425 all inclusive. *Comments* 1) and 2) Study of three substantial manuals must be completed by end of course.

ECLECTIC OR SPECIAL TRAININGS
Association for Analytic and Bodymind Therapy and Training *Title of Training* Diploma Training in Modern Therapeutic Methods. *Duration* 2 years: one evening per week, weekend larger group training, six-day intensive training, residential in Cornwall. *Entry requirements* Must have completed 2-year (minimum)

therapy to satisfaction of both therapist and client, or be in ongoing therapy, or be willing to run therapy concurrently with course. Degree and advantage, but not essential. *Fees* £290 per term, payable before each term begins. *Comments* Training groups is kept small and intimate (maximum 10). Includes interpretation of group dynamics, gestalt therapy, hypnotherapy, relaxation techniques, therapeutic holding, regression therapy etc.

CAER (Centre For Alternative Education And Research) *Title of Training* Institute for the Development of Human Potential Diploma in Humanistic Psychology *Duration* 2 years, part-time. *Entry requirements* Apply for details.

Chiron *Title of Training* Training in Holistic Psychotherapy. *Duration* Three years part-time, approx eleven hours per week. Entry requirements None specified. *Fees* Refer to organisers. *Comments* Programme consists of body-centred psychotherapy, biodynamic massage, gestalt and 'charge therapy'.

Institute of Psychotherapy and Social Studies *Title of Training* Diploma in Psychotherapy (Analytic and Humanistic). *Duration* Three years, two days a week and individual therapy twice a week. *Entry requirements* Degree or equiva lent. Some professional experience. Two hundred hours of growth work. Emotional stability and maturity. Ethical life. Reading of literature. *Fees* £1300 pa. (payable in instalments) plus individual therapy fees. *Comments* Special interest in social context.

Lincoln Centre and Institute of Psychotherapy *Title of Training* Training in Psychotherapy *Duration* Five years *Entry requirements* Medical or relevant degree or in exceptional circumstances a qualification in one of the helping professions. *Fees* £720 per annum.

Minster Centre *Title of Training* Course in Psychotherapy. *Duration* Three years part-time. *Entry requirements* None specified. *Fees* £1000 per annum *Comments* Training includes a wide variety of approaches.

Philadelphia Association *Title of Training* 1) Study programme in Social Phenomenology. 2) Training in Individual Psychotherapy and Community Therapy. *Duration* 1) Minimum of one term (one night/week). Three terms per year. 2) Min three years, open ended. (one night per week plus therapy plus supervision. *Entry requirements* a) None b) Completed three terms of study programme; must have been in own therapy for at least a year; relevant experience of working with disturbed/distressed people. *Fees* 1) £120 per term. 2) £150 per term plus therapy plus supervision fees.

Serpent Institute *Title of Training* (1) Diploma course in counselling (2) Diploma course in psychotherapy. *Duration* (1) Two years (2) Three years. *Entry requirements* Acceptance for the course is based on the applicant's readiness and own self development as well as ability and commitment. *Fees* £1,000 per year. Comments Theoretical framework is Goddess spirituality - the valuing of the feminine principle within everyone. Training is for both sexes, with some single sex opportunities within it.

INTRODUCTION TO BODY THERAPIES

It could be said that in the twentieth century western world we have a curious and often paradoxical relationship with our bodies. While many are no longer dependent on hard manual labour to earn their living, most of us spend our working lives sitting in offices using only our heads or performing repetitive manual tasks which impose a strain on the body, while the rest of our way of life also offers little in the way of creative physical expression. Cars and public transport, while greatly convenient have obviated the need to walk anywhere. In the big cities, especially London, we usually live crammed together and have little more than the prospect of a Sunday afternoon walk in the park with the hundreds of other people looking for a dose of nature in the urban jungle.

Though a modern city lifestyle seems to offer little opportunity for us to express natural physical energy, paradoxically our culture also seems to be very concerned with the body in some ways. We are surrounded with images of fitness and beauty on billboards, TV and in films giving impressions of how our bodies ought to look. The 99% of us whose bodies don't measure up to this fantasy ideal may end up feeling self-conscious or dissatisfied with our physique. This pressure to focus on how the body looks from the outside can also leave us out of touch with how it feels from inside and from an immediate experience of our physical self expressing itself in its own unique way.

Western philosophy has tended to see mind and body as separate and science too has played its part in fostering the idea that our bodies are somehow different from our real selves. Modern medicine tends to treat the body in this way and on the whole deals with it as a machine, replacing defective parts if they malfunction, or readjusting the body with drugs and other chemicals, sometimes without much sense that the physical level might be connected with other levels of experience - emotional, mental or spiritual.

We have a long life expectancy now in the modern west, due largely to improved sanitation and nutrition. But we still fear the spectre of disease as much as ever. Perhaps more because most people living in this secular, semi-atheistic culture have little belief in the prospect of an after-life. So with little prospect of a hereafter, most people are even more anxious to conserve the life they have in the here now. Modern medicine has made advances particularly in the areas of surgery, vaccination and medicines. However, we are becoming increasingly dependant on modern medicine and drugs to cure quite common or relatively minor complaints. Modern drug therapy can be like using a hammer to crack a nut. By over-using this powerful method of disease control, we are in danger of upsetting the natural powers which the body has to cure itself. The more we rely on intervention from outside, the more we are in danger of losing our own innate power to heal ourselves, and others.

Alternative and Complementary Medicine
Not all the therapies and practices dealt with in the 'Body' section of this book come under the banner of 'Alternative Medicine'. For instance, the Alexander technique is an educational method which seeks to teach people to use their bodies in a more natural way, and to regain a freedom of movement which may have been lost. Similarly tai chi, which is a system of physical movements, is very much part of a wider philosophical and spiritual system and outlook. The title 'Body' is intended as very broad, and we have used it to include all approaches - therapeutic, educational and inspirational - which encompass the whole person through the medium of the body.

In the ever-growing field of holistic health there is still a lot of debate about what these much used words such as 'holistic', 'alternative medicine', 'complimentary medicine' and 'natural therapies' mean, and different people define them in different ways. Most practitioners feel that their therapy is not 'alternative' to conventional medicine in the sense that it is a case of 'either-or' - either you go for traditional treatment or you go to a homoeopath - but rather that it broadens the patient's choice about how to get treatment.

The term 'complementary' is now being used more to stress that these natural therapies can be used alongside conventional medicine. 'Complementary' can also be used in the sense that different natural therapies may be needed to treat one patient and therefore complement each other. Sometimes these complementary therapies are referred to as 'natural' therapies because on the whole they aim to work by co-operating with natural processes, rather than trying to override them as conventional medicine often does.

'Holistic' too seems to be a word which has as many meanings as there are different people using it. One possible definition is that it is an approach which takes into account the whole person, and the whole range of their experience; physical, mental, emotional and spiritual within their whole environment; physical, social and personal.

The Holistic Approach

The holistic approach to health does not just treat symptoms in order to 'get rid' of them. It tries to treat the underlying causes of the symptoms, which may be found in considering the patient's history, lifestyle, relationships, temperament and his or her whole outlook on life. Within the holistic framework, disease is not seen as a matter of chance, or as an affliction which comes purely from outside the body, but more as the whole organism's attempt to reach once again a state of harmony and equilibrium with itself and its environment. An illness, especially a chronic one, can be the body's way of drawing attention to the fact that something needs to change in the sufferer's lifestyle, that he or she may need something they are not getting, that some part of him or her self which was previously unacknowledged is seeking recognition, or it can even be part of an overall point of spiritual crisis or growth, part of a reorientation of life purpose.

An experienced holistic practitioner will look at particular symptoms in any of these contexts as appropriate. The holistic approach stresses the responsibility the individual has for his or her own health and well-being. This may mean taking active steps to change the things which cause illness where it is possible. This is not to say that the patient is in some way to blame for his or her malaise, but that we have the power to cure ourselves, or at least to change our attitude to our disease. Alternative medicine offers the opportunity to co-operate with the processes by which the body heals itself.

The core of the holistic approach is that it sees all aspects of the human being as connected and interrelated: body, mind, emotions and spirit.

Diagnosis

Most people turn to complementary medicine when conventional medicine has failed to cure them, or offers no treatment. It is often stubborn, chronic conditions such as backache, migraines, asthma, menstrual problems, insomnia, arthritis or chronic indigestion with which the practitioner is presented.

Alternative therapies have their own methods of diagnosis - an acupuncturist will take your pulses, an osteopath will examine your spine, and a shiatsu practitioner will feel your abdomen. There are also specific forms of alternative diagnosis which you may want to try if you want more information. Iridology examines the eyes for signs of physical weakness and Kirlian photography shows the electrical field round the body and in this way detects early signs of illness. These alternative diagnostic methods can be most useful in helping people to develop a more positive and balanced attitude towards their bodies, thus preventing illnesses.

Most forms of diagnosis in complementary therapies are non-invasive; they do not probe into the body but are carried out by observing the signs given by the body.

Choosing a Particular Therapy

So how to choose the approach which will be most effective for you? It is easy to feel bemused by all the therapies on offer. Most people choose either by having someone who practises a particular therapy recommended to them by a friend, or by reading something about a therapy and feeling attracted to that particular approach. With the descriptions of the therapies in this book, we offer some guidelines about the kinds of ailment they may deal with best. However, it is by no means obvious that if you have a bad back you should visit an osteopath, although this may be a good start. Your pain in the back could also be due to other physical or psychological problems.

Reading about the different therapies can give you a good lead. Then, follow your instincts. If you feel interested in a particular therapy or don't like the sound of another you probably do have a real sense of what might or might not be helpful for you. It must also be stressed that if you have not already done so, you should always consult your doctor if you have any troublesome symptoms, just to be sure that your complaint is not one which would be better treated by modern medicine. You may also think of discussing any alternative treatment with your doctor, who is hopefully understanding and not totally dismissive of alternative medicine. There are some contra-indications for particular natural therapies. For instance, shiatsu is not recommended for people with cancer, because the stimulation of the metabolism can spread the cancer cells throughout the body. In pregnancy care should be taken with some of the therapies listed here. Once again, your doctor can help here, and the complementary therapy practitioner needs to be informed of the full details of your condition.

Some of the centres listed in this book which offer more than one therapy give advice on which one would be most effective. Practitioners should tell you if they think that their form of therapy is not appropriate for your symptoms, or may even suggest another form. However, it must be stressed that what works for one person will not necessarily work for another, even if they have the same complaint. Some are now offering consultations specifically to help people choose.

Finding the Right Practitioner

At present there is no law in the U.K. which stipulates that a practitioner of alternative therapies must have reached an agreed standard and must be registered. Complete quackery is not so much the problem - there are probably few people with no qualifications who set themselves up to treat people. However, although a

Brackenbury
Natural Health Centre

30 Brackenbury Road, London W6 0BA
Telephone: 081-741 9264

ACUPUNCTURE   ALEXANDER TECHNIQUE
AROMATHERAPY   BATES EYE METHOD
BIODYNAMIC MASSAGE
DIETARY THERAPY   HERBALISM
HOMOEOPATHY   HYPNOTHERAPY
NATUROPATHY   OSTEOPATHY
PSYCHOTHERAPY   REFLEXOLOGY
SHIATSU   THERAPEUTIC MASSAGE
ALLERGY TESTING

WHICH THERAPY?
For help or advice in choosing the most appropriate therapy please telephone, or write, or call in at the Centre. Leaflets and books are available and it is always possible to talk to a practitioner.

APPOINTMENTS
Reception open ....9.00-6.00 MON-FRI
Appointments available.9.00-9.00 MON-FRI
9.00-1.00 SAT

ALL THE PRACTITIONERS ARE FULLY
QUALIFIED AND EXPERIENCED IN
THEIR FIELD.

practitioner may seem to be qualified, there is little way of knowing whether their qualification has demanded that they undertake the necessary study and experience to make them effective. In this sense, letters after the name are no guarantee of good service!

For osteopaths, medical herbalists and chiropractors there are registers compiled by governing bodies, and you can write off for registers of members to be sure of getting a well-qualified practitioner. If in doubt about practitioners of other therapies it may be as well to ask about their training - how long it was, how intensive, how much experience they had and also if they are insured, so that if anything does go wrong, at least you have the chance of a successful comeback.

There is of course also the question of rapport. It is important that you trust the practitioner and feel able to talk to him or her. If you feel uncomfortable with a therapist and this fails to change, it might be best to try another one who you feel more able to get on with. You might also like to consider whether the sex of the practitioner matters to you. Some people find it easier to talk about their health problems with someone of the same sex, and some with members of the opposite sex. Again, follow your gut feeling in this, and don't be afraid to ask for the practitioner you want.

Length and cost of treatment

There is no way of saying how long you may have to persevere with any particular treatment. This all depends on the kind of illness you have, the seriousness of the condition, how long you have had it, whether and how well you may be able to change any of the conditions which may be contributing to it and many other factors. If you are worried about how long it make take (and consequently how much you may have to pay) ask the practitioner after the initial session if they can give you any idea of how many sessions you will need. Few practitioners are so hard up for patients that they will string out a treatment longer than necessary. Similarly, if at any time you feel you are getting nowhere and want to try another therapy, talk with the practitioner about it. They may also be able to throw some light on a new approach, or be able to explain why the treatment does not seem to be having the desired effect.

Cost too is variable, depending on the experience of the practitioner, and sometimes where he or she practises. Initial consultations usually cost more and last longer for homoeopathy, acupuncture and osteopathy because the practitioner will have to take some time to make the diagnosis. A few practitioners will give discounts for the unwaged. Some training institutes of body therapies such as massage and Alexander technique offer sessions given by trainees at a cheap rate. Homoeopathy is available on the National Health Service at the Royal Homoeopathic Hospital, and there are some homoeopathic GPs, though many of these work in the private sector and therefore charge for treatment. While finding the money for the cost of these treatments may be quite a problem for the low waged, we include details of centres which do offer lower rates for cases of hardship.

What the Centres are Like

Centres vary enormously. Some are really people's homes where perhaps a couple of people practice. Others may be rented rooms, and some are large, permanent buildings which may include restaurants and bookshops. Appointments are always necessary, although some centres run an emergency service or acute clinic. Even if they do, it is advisable to ring beforehand. Some centres have secretaries or receptionists who are always by the telephone to take your call, others make do with an answerphone.

Finding Practitioners Outside the Centres

If for any reason you want to find a practitioner who does not work in a centre there are several ways in which this can be done. Some training institutes or governing bodies provide registers of qualified practitioners. We list these after each therapy with 'register' after their name, rather than a postcode. In this way you can at least be sure that the therapist is qualified. You can telephone the training institute in question and ask them about the length and thoroughness of their training before you ask for the register. Some practitioners are listed in the local Yellow Pages. Local health food shops, community centres, specialist bookshops or wholefood restaurants sometimes have practitioners' cards on noticeboards, though you may have to check their qualifications for yourself in this case. There are also some directories available which list practitioners who advertise in them.

Another way of finding a practitioner is to apply to the Institute of Complementary Medicine, who run a referral service for the general public and the British Register of Complementary Practitioners, which is now recognised by the government. They can give you the names of practitioners of a particular therapy in your area. However they are not allowed to recommend a particular therapy for a particular complaint.

SCHOOL OF COMPLEMENTARY MEDICINE

STRUCTURE	ENERGY	PHYSICAL THERAPIES	CHINESE ACUPUNCTURE
PSYCHOSOMATIC	BIOCHEMISTRY	PSYCHOSOMATIC MEDICINE	NUTRITION HERBALISM

The School of Complementary Medicine offers a specially designed Course for people who want to be professional practitioners. The Course provides training, to practitioner standard, in a selected range of therapies: Chinese Acupuncture, Shiatsu, Acupressure, Swedish Massage, Reflexology, Cranial Osteopathy, Herbalism, Nutrition, Bach Remedies, Counselling and Psychosomatic Medicine, with Exercise, Anatomy, Physiology, Pathology - and more. **Students learn to practise and combine all these therapies.**

The School works with a truly Complementary Teaching-Learning-Practising Model which enables us to work with more healing skills in less time.

The Course is for sixty-four weekends in three and a half years, starting each February. There are free introducotry meetings to explain Complementary Medicine, help people to choose a course in this field and describe the SCM Course. These meetings are held from September to January.

The SCM also teaches a one year evening course (thirty-three evenings) for people who want to heal their family and friends. This course is a simplified version of the Practitioner Course, with an emphasis on the development of intuition. This course also starts in February.

For details of either course, please contact:
Peter Stanton,
9 Sharpleshall Street,
Primrose Hill,
London NW1 8YN.
Telephone number 071 586 1263.
Please include your day and/or evening telephone number. We make a point of contacting interested people personally.

SCM

TRAINING IN BODY THERAPIES

Why Train?

Alternative and Complementary Medicine is a growing concern. The number of people who are consulting practitioners of the natural therapies is increasing every year. At the moment, there are hardly enough practitioners to meet this demand, and most good practitioners are extremely busy. Healing people in this way can of course be tremendously satisfying, and it is also a great responsibility. The training can be long and expensive, but most people who really feel motivated to undertake a course find the time and money in some way.

Before you start training, it is helpful to decide what level of skill you want in your chosen therapy. There are three different levels of expertise.

(1) Awareness of the principles, and to a certain extent the practice of a particular therapy, to a level where one can practice it on oneself. The degree to which one can do this depends very much on the therapy in question. For instance, Bach flower remedies can be self-applied very successfully, but osteopathy is not suitable for self-treatment.

(2) Application of the principles and practice to friends and relatives. This requires more skill and training, and though it may give a great deal of satisfaction, will probably not involve any financial reward.

(3) Treatment of members of the public. To do this, a practitioner needs insurance and preferably the protection of a governing body, if there is one for their particular therapy.

It is a good idea to ask yourself what level of training you really want. You may decide that (1) is a good place to start, and to that end you may then choose a less intensive, introductory course. If you want to train to treat the general public, then this is a much more serious undertaking. It is certainly makes sense to find out as much as you possibly can about the therapy you are thinking of training in. It is not unknown for people to discover at the end of a three year course that they do not want to practice that therapy.

Finding the Right Course

There are many different courses around, and they vary a great deal in terms of time commitment, teaching methods and cost. What constitutes a satisfactory course varies enormously from therapy to therapy. Before enrolling for any course, it is advisable to shop around and this will give you an idea of what the norm is for training in your chosen therapy. A shorter, cheaper course may seem more attractive in some ways than a lengthy intensive course, but it may not provide you with the skills and experience you need to practice successfully and well. Though it is difficult to make hard and fast rules because different therapies require different levels of knowledge and experience, there are some guidelines when looking at trainings.

(1) How long has the training institute been established? What kind of experience do the teachers have?

(2) On completion of training, will you be eligible for membership of a professional association which has its own register, code of ethics and disciplinary procedures? Homoeopathy, acupuncture, chiropractic, osteopathy, naturopathy, medical herbalism, reflexology, Alexander technique, polarity therapy and aromatherapy all have professional bodies to which qualified practitioners may belong. With other therapies this is not the case however, and so this criterion cannot be applied.

(3) How much home study is required? How much clinical training will you get? Will you receive thorough tuition in the philosophy and theory of the discipline? There should be a good deal of all of these elements.

(4) What kind of teaching facilities does the training institute have?

(5) Is the personal development of the trainee taken into account? To be able to help other people some measure of self knowledge and stability is necessary.

(6) For courses in homoeopathy, chiropractic, acupuncture and medical herbalism there should be a great deal of time devoted to the study of anatomy and physiology.

(7) Look carefully at the amount of tuition time given. It may seem that the course is long and takes place over a year or two, but if it is taught over weekends at six monthly intervals the actual time you are going to get being taught may be very little.

The Institute of Complementary Medicine offers a list of courses which they think provide a satisfactory training to those thinking of studying a particular therapy. Of course, if you simply want to learn about a therapy out of interest, or to practise on your family and friends in a modest way, the correspondence course or low time commitment course may be just what you want. However, if you are intending to treat the public the above are important considerations.

Entry Requirements
Once again, entry requirements vary enormously from college to college and therapy to therapy. For some courses, notably some of those in homoeopathy and acupuncture, training in orthodox medicine is required. Some require that applicants are medical doctors, or at least that they have been trained in nursing, or in one of the paramedical professions. For courses in reflexology, aromatherapy, massage and Alexander technique there are often no formal educational requirements, and the personal qualities and suitability of the applicant will form the basis for selection.

In general to become an effective practitioner in a natural therapy, you will need a genuine desire to help people, a certain amount of sensitivity and a lot of stamina to cope with the physical and emotional demands of healing.

Getting Clients
Some professional bodies place the same restrictions on advertising as those which govern medical doctors. However, to offset this these bodies will usually have a register of qualified practitioners which is sent out to enquirers. Many people starting out choose to work at a centre through which they can get clients more easily. However, practitioners of natural therapies are in great demand, especially those where the training is long and intensive.

Future Legislation Governing Practitioners - 1992
In some countries, practitioners of alternative and complementary medicine must be medical doctors. In some, such as France, even such things as herbal medicines and some dietry supplements can only be obtained on prescription. In Britain at the moment there are no such laws which means that we have been able to benefit from the proliferation of these therapies. However, an EEC directive has been issued to get Britain more in line with the rest of Europe when the 'single market' comes into force in 1992. This may not mean that our legislation has to be the same, but there is a possibility that the very restrictive standards which apply in some European countries could also be adopted here. Those who oppose such standards in Britain point out that most training courses in homoeopathy for doctors consist of a few weekends, whereas a lay practitioner usually has to study for three or four years. Thus though a medical doctor may know a great deal about orthodox medicine, the lay practitioner has by far the greater knowledge of homoeopathy.

On the positive side, the next ten years may see more standardisation in training courses, and a system of accreditation developing. As yet there is some doubt about who is going to be doing the accreditation, and whether it will be a government body or a body formed of those within the Alternative and Complementary medical professions. The latter would of course be more acceptable to practitioners.

It is difficult to predict how this will affect things. However, in the light of the reorganisation of these professions, it certainly makes sense for the intending trainee to be especially careful about the kind of training course he or she opts for.

Future legslation could have a very far reaching effect on the availability of complementary therapies. A recent piece of legislation has already lumped together manufacturers of herbal products with producers of orthodox drugs, making them liable for a yearly licensing fee. The size of this licensing fee is beyong the means of most small manufacturers and may put some of them out of business. The effect of this for the public will be that many herbal preparations will no longer be available to them.

If you would like to protect complementary medicine in this country, write to your MP and European MP to demand the continued right to purchase and receive complementary therapies and medicines from the same sources they are currently available (e.g. health food shops and private practice).

Useful Contacts

Institute for Complementary Medicine, *21 Portland Place, London W1N 3AF. (071) 636 9543.* Referral service for the public to complementary pracitioners, and network of public information points around the country. Advice on trainings to those thinking of training.

British Holistic Medical Association, *179 Gloucester Place, London NW1 6DX (071) 262 5299.* Membership/networking organisation for those interested in promoting holistic approaches to health care. Produce quarterly newsletter and professional journal, organise conferences and workshops. Produce self-help books and tapes and general information about holistic medicine, available mail order. Send SAE for full details. Members receive the qrtly 36-page newsletter Holistic Health, get discounts on self-help tapes, books and events and details of regional group activities. Membership for different categories: health care professional, health care student, and open membership for the public. Sliding scale from £15-£45 depending on income.

Holistic Health Concessions Register, *36 Broadway Market, Hackney, London E8 4QJ (071) 254 1158.* List of 250 qualified practitioners offering complementary therapies/psychotherapy at reduced fees for the low waged. Ring for details or write enclosing SAE because they are completely unfunded and can't afford to pay for stamps. Have worked with Angel Drug Project to make complementary therapies available to drug users. Lowest £5, and some practitioners will work free with people who are HIV positive or have AIDS.

94

THE BODY APPROACHES

Acupuncture

Acupuncture is the ancient Chinese healing art which, at least until recently, was the standard form of medical treatment in China. How the system was discovered is unknown, but one theory is that as far back as the stone age healers noticed that small areas of the skin at certain points on the body became sensitive when a particular organ was affected by illness. These areas indicate the acupuncture points of which there are about 800. The points are linked together by their association with a particular organ or function and form pathways or meridians as they are called, through which the life energy or ch'i flows.

The ch'i energy is made up of two forces, *Yang* and *Yin* energy. Yang corresponds to the masculine, positive, active principle and Yin to the feminine, negative, receptive principle. Good health is maintained while these two forces are balanced, and while the energy is flowing freely through the meridians.

The art of the acupuncturist is to restore any imbalances in energy and to unblock the pathways by stimulating the points along them where there may be a blockage. This is done in one of three ways. Usually very fine needles made of silver or stainless steel are inserted a little way into the skin. The needles may be just left there to have their effect, or they may be stimulated by the acupuncturist who may twirl them or push them gently in and out of the point. Sometimes moxa (dried mugwort, a pleasantly aromatic plant) may be burnt over the point, and this is a popular form of self-treatment practised in some countries. Thirdly the points may be massaged or gently scratched with the fingers.

When you visit an acupuncturist for a treatment, he or she will first take a case history of your complaint and will try to build up a picture of any imbalances in energy by asking you about such things as your food preferences, your reactions to heat and cold, and your emotional reactions in certain circumstances. Then they will take your pulses. Although these are taken at the wrist as they are by any ordinary doctor, the acupuncture pulses are a more complex and subtle aid to diagnosis than the one recognised by western medicine. There are six pulses on each wrist, and these are felt with three fingers by the acupuncturist, who will note the quality and relative strength of each one. Having made the diagnosis in this way, the needles will be inserted.

The idea of having needles stuck into your skin may be very alarming, especially if it brings back memories of injections and innoculations! But there is usually no pain involved in the treatment because the needles are very fine and inserted very lightly, usually only a little way into the skin. The needles are sterilised, but since the advent of AIDS many acupuncturists are making extra sure of hygiene by using

BODY THERAPIES

❝ I had never had any experience of alternative medicine before, but several of my friends were visiting this acupuncturist and reporting fantastic results. I had had a chronic problem with inflamed gums for years, so I thought this would give me something to go along with.

I felt quite excited about my foray into the esoteric world of Chinese medicine, though I was worried that the needles would hurt. The visit certainly lived up to expectations. The acupucturist worked from home and led me into a dark room with a massage table in it. Then she asked me some questions about my complaint, and some more about how I reacted to certain situations, which didn't seem to me to have anything at all to do with my gums. The she asked me when my birthday was and worked out something in her head which she wrote down in a kind of diagram. She told me that I was mostly wood and not much metal - or was it the other way round? - at any rate it didn't make much sense.

Then she told me to lie on the couch, and she held my wrists and seemed to be tapping them very slowly and gently with her fingers. I wondered if this was some sort of massage; it was very soothing anyway. When she eventually got out the needles, she stuck one in my knee and another in my foot, and this certainly seemed like a long way from my gums.

After lying there for what seemed like half an hour she took the needles out. To my surprise I felt incredibly relaxed, so much so that I could hardly get up. This was most unusual since I tend to be rather hyperactive. My acupuncturist solemnly instructed me to eat miso (a Japanese food made out of matured soyabeans). I walked out feeling dazed but calm.

Despite the evident after-treatment effects, after a course of treatments my gums weren't that much better. But two things did change dramatically. I always used to be picky about food, and I never ate breakfast. However, during my treatment I started to develop a much better appetite, and starting eating much more, though I didn't put on any weight. Another effect was that my periods became much heavier. Though my gums didn't get any better, I felt like I became a heartier person, and these effects have lasted in the years subsequently ❞

Alex Read

disposable needles.

The treatment may last from 20 minutes to an hour. After a treatment some people feel relaxed, some elated or as if they are walking on air. Occasionally you may feel worse before you feel better. You will probably need to go for treatment once or twice a week for chronic ailments, and more often for an acute illness. Acupuncture is also very effective if used preventatively. Traditionally, a treatment at the turn of the season will keep your energy balanced and maintain good health.

The effectiveness of acupuncture in relieving pain has been shown rather dramatically by stories of major operations carried out in China using only skillfully applied needles for anaesthesia. These are rather special cases, but acupuncture can be used effectively for relief of less acute pain. While acupuncture can theoretically cure any reversible disease it is best when there is no actual damage to organs or tissues, and especially for chronic conditions which conventional medicine cannot deal with. Complaints such as headaches, toothache and inflamed gums, colds and asthma, digestive disorders, menstrual disorders, obesity, rheumatism and 'nervous' problems can all benefit from treatment.

READING

Alternative Health - Acupuncture *by Dr Michael Nightingale, MacDonald £3.95*. This consumer's guide to acupuncture concentrates on the actual treatment itself seen from the patient's viewpoint. It answers practical questions about acupuncture as well as providing background information about this popular therapy. The author tries to dispel the concerns of first time patients. **Traditional Acupuncture - the Law of the Five Elements** *by Diane Connelly, Centre for Traditional Acupuncture £9.99*. Diane Connelly is a qualified acupuncturist and author. This book is primarily intended for students of the discipline. It is also useful for the interested lay person. This book has been popular for the depth and seriousness with which it approaches its subject.

BODY THERAPIES

CENTRES OFFERING ACUPUNCTURE

Acumedic Centre NW1, Acupuncture and Osteopathy Clinic SW1, Acupuncture Clinic E17, Acupuncture Clinic of North London N13, All Healing Clinic NW5, Anerley Natural Health Clinic SE20, Association for Systematic Kinesiology, Barbican Natural Health Centre EC1, Bennet and Luck Natural Health Centre N1, Better Health Centre NW3, Bexleyheath Natural Health Clinic (Kent), Body Clinic NW11, Body-Mind Health Private Clinic N8, Bodywise E2, Brackenbury Natural Health Centre W6, British Acupuncture Association and Register SW1, British College of Acupuncture WC1, Camden Osteopathic and Natural Health Practice NW5, Chinese Clinic W1, Chung San Acupuncture School W2, City Health Centre EC1, Clapham Common Clinic SW4, Clinic of Alternative Therapies E18, Clissold Park Natural Health Centre N16, East-West Clinic of Natural Healing Middlesex, Edgware Centre for Natural Health (Edgware), Edmonton Acupuncture Clinic N9, Equilibrium Therapy Centre SW18, European Shiatsu School W8, Faculty of Traditional Chinese Medicine of the UK W5, Fook Sang Acupuncture and Chinese Herbal Practitioners Training College UK NW11, Forty Hill Natural Therapy Centre Enfield, Fulham Clinic SW6, Haelen Centre N8, Hale Clinic W1, Hampton Healing Centre, Hong Tao Acupuncture and Natural Health Clinic Pinner, Insight Care Complementary Health Clinic N1, Isis Centre for Holistic Health N17, Jeyrani Health Centre E18, Lever Clinic W1, Lever Clinic Middx, Lifeworks NW5, Meridians Clinic W1, Natural Healing Centre E7, Natural Healing Centre Middlesex, Natural Medicine Centre Bromley, Nature Cure Clinic W1, Natureworks W1, Neal's Yard Therapy Rooms WC2, New Cross Natural Therapy Centre SE14, Nine Needles Health Care Centre Richmond, Primrose Healing Centre NW1, Private Health Centre E7, Private Polyclinic E7, Putney Natural Therapy Clinic SW15, Sayer Clinic W1, W8, WC2, W4, South London Natural Health Centre SW4, St James Centre for Health and Healing W1, Sunra SW12, Wellspring Clinic SW6, Westminster Natural Health Centre SW1, Wholistic Health Centre (Croydon), Wimbledon Clinic of Natural Medicine SW19, Women's Natural Health Centre NW5, Wood Street Clinic (Barnet).

TRAINING IN ACUPUNCTURE

British College of Acupuncture *Title of Training* Postgraduate Training in Acupuncture. *Duration* Three years. *Entry requirements* Applicants should be registered members of one of a number of professions, e.g. doctor, osteopath, naturopath, chiropractor, dental surgeon, vetinary surgeon, physiotherapist, nurse. *Fees* First year £600, second year £900, third year £1,000

Chung San Acupuncture School *Title of Training* (1) Training in acupuncture (2) Training in Chinese herbal medicine. *Duration* (1) Three years part time, weekends. (2) 2 years part time. *Entry requirements* (1) Must have 'A' levels in science subjects. (2) Must have Chinese medical background (e.g. qualification in acupuncture). *Fees* (1) £100 enrolment, £1,900 study fee for whole course. (2) £100 plus £1,300 for whole course.

ACUPUNCTURE

College of Traditional Chinese Acupuncture *Title of Training* Training in Acupuncture *Duration* Three years part-time. Fourteen weekend sessions per year in the first two years. You work under supervision in the final year. *Fees* £1516 per annum.

Faculty of Traditional Chinese Medicine of the UK *Title of Training* Refer to Organisers.

Fook Sang Acupuncture and Chinese Herbal Practitioners Training College UK *Title of Training* Acupuncture and Chinese Herbal Practitioners Training (including training in traditional diagnosis). *Duration* Three years. Weekend attendance. October start. *Entry requirements* Preferably degree level or vocational training. Minimum 'A' level standard. Mature students must show enthusiasm and desire to learn. *Fees* Year 1 £950, year 2 £800, year 3 £700. Payable instalments. *Comments* Successful graduates eligible for membership of Acupuncture Practitioners Association and Hong Kong Chinese Acupuncture Association.

```
┌─────────────────────────────────┐
│          FOOK SANG              │
│  ACUPUNCTURE AND CHINESE HERBAL │
│  PRACTITIONERS TRAINING COLLEGE UK │
│                                 │
```

590 Wokingham Road Earley, Reading Berks. RG6 2HN Tel: (0734) 665454

1037B Finchley Road, Golders Green London NW11 7ES Tel: (081) 455 5508

Our College provides a unique opportunity to acquire correct training in Chinese Acupuncture and Herbal Medicine emphasising the importance of Traditional Diagnostic skills.

Our intensive training combines practical experience, traditional techniques and modern scientific understanding enabling future practice with full confidence. Membership for graduates. Close links with China.

Courses: Weekends by Chinese Practitioners.

Write to: The Registrar, 1037B Finchley Road, Golders Green, London NW11 7ES
or telephone: (081) 455 5508/(0734) 665454

CONSULTANTS

Prof W.W. Lai (Rector Chinese College of Acupuncture, H.K.), Dr K.L. Tsui (Principal Tsui Tze Chun Medical Research Unit, H.K.), Prof C.G. Xin (Guang Dong Province Hospital), Prof W. Chia (Jiang Xi Medical College of TCM), Prof H.C. Liu (Jiang Xi Medical College), Dr C.G. Zhen (Jiang Xi Province Hospital), Dr K.S. Fu (Sha He Hospital, Guang Dong), Dr Y.K. Cheung (Guang Dong workers Hospital), Dr W.T. Sheng (Guang Dong Workers Hospital), The People's Republic of China.
Hon Member: E. Robertson D.O. Acupuncture.

International College of Oriental Medicine *Title of Training* Acupuncture Course *Duration* Three years full-time, fourth year part-time. *Entry requirements* Minimum of 2 'A' levels preferred, but will consider serious applicants individually. *Fees* £2800 per annum approximately. *Comments* As a full time course, this attracts local authority grants.

London School of Acupuncture and Traditional Chinese Medicine *Title of Training* Diploma Course in Traditional Chinese Medicine *Duration* Three years part-time, 27 weekends per year. *Entry requirements* 2 'A' levels or equivalent in experience. Applicants should be aged 21 years or over. Fees £2,000 per annum, payable quarterly. *Comments* Course requires 12-15 hours of home study per week. Basics of western medicine taught to those without a background in it.

Nine Needles Health Care Centre *Title of Training* (1) One year evening course in Shiatsu (2) 3 year course in

99

Oriental Medicine including acupuncture, shiatsu, moxibustion, etc. *Fees*(1) £1,410 or £1,100 on lump payment. (2) First and third years as above, second year £2,800 or £2,500 on lump payment.

Aikido

Aikido is a Japanese martial art developed by Morihei Uyeshiba who popularised the art after the Second World War. He felt that the object of a martial art should not be to win, but to promote harmony and co-operation, a message which was as sorely needed in the post world war world as it is today.

The word comes from 'ai' which means 'union', 'ki' which is 'life force' and 'do' which means road or way. The object of aikido is to achieve harmony and union with the life energy which is in and around all of us. Power is not a matter of physical strength, but comes from strengthening and deepening the connection with this life force. As with tai chi chuan, the expert does not exert his or her strength over the opponent, but uses the attacker's own force for defence. The student must learn that winning itself is not important, and a contest between two practitioners is not so much a fight to the death as a dance in which there is a high degree of co-operation.

Although aikido can be an effective method of self-defence, responsibility is taken for not inflicting unnecessary harm on the attacker. The method should have given the practitioner sufficient skill and awareness to make it unnecessary for them to use the same kind of brute tactics as the aggressor. Strength comes from concentration and awareness, and for this reason aikido is a spiritual discipline as well as a form of self defence. In becoming more in tune with the 'ki' or life energy, one also becomes more centred or rooted in the 'hara'. The 'hara' is the physical centre of gravity in the body and is located about two inches below the navel. It is also the symbolic centre of the top and bottom halves of the body, a point where the physical and mental spheres meet.

Aikido is usually taught in classes of about 20 people. Tuition is given in the 'dojo'

or practice hall, a word which also means the hall where Zen monks practise meditation. Teachers have their own approach to discipline in the dojo; some are stricter than others and require a certain etiquette to be maintained inside. Keeping a formal etiquette is in itself a kind of discipline which is seen to reinforce the discipline involved in learning a martial art. A class usually lasts about an hour, and there is a uniform of jacket, belt and baggy trousers. As with most martial arts beginners move up through a series of 'gradings' or examinations to attain higher levels of proficiency. Because the emphasis is on developing inner strength, there is no need to be physically strong to practice Aikido.

READING

Aikido: The Way of Harmony *by John Stevens, Shambhala £12.95.* This definitive, profusely illustrated book covers the essential elements of the philosophy and practice of Aikido, the Japanese martial art that has been embraced by modern psychology and many western bodywork therapies. Useful to beginners and experienced practitioners, with descriptions and photographs of the main Aikido techniques and interesting insights into the history of Aikido and the life of its founder, Uyeshiba Morihei. Written by one of the main western Aikido teachers in Japan, under the direction of one of the founder's ealiest students.

CENTRES OFFERING AIKIDO

Apply to Martial Arts Commission for list of approved, local clubs, British Ki Aikido Association.

Alexander Technique

Named after the creator, Australian F. Matthias Alexander, the Alexander technique is the application of a subtle guidance by a practitioner in the movement of the client. Alexander practitioners call themselves 'teachers' and their clients 'students'. They aim to re-educate the students by enabling them to 'unlearn' their habitual poor habits of movement.

Observing a teacher and student at work, it looks as if very little is happening. Imagine a typical scene: the teacher seems to spend much time holding the back of the student's head with one hand and jaw of the student with another, and guiding the student gently out of a chair, little by little, then sitting him or her down again. What is happening is that the student is learning by being taken slowly through a simple movement, in this case standing up. When the student is about to fall into a poor use of the body, the teacher will stop them and make them aware of what they are doing. The teacher will lead the student through these movements time and time again until the student learns a new way of moving and the misuse disappears.

The student may be asked to take up other positions such as as 'the monkey' (standing like a monkey), or asked to lie down on a table whereupon the teacher may lift and gently rotate the arms and move the legs.

At about the seventh session many people experience a feeling of walking on air. As the sessions continue they may report more energy and an ease in physical mobility.

Many of the students are actors or musicians. Musicians practise it because they are prone to bad posture huddled over their instruments and actors because they need to claim more versatility in their movements.

Some people notice alterations in the structure of their body, such as the disappearance of stoops and the hollow back. Some people claim to notice little difference.

The usual arrangement for lessons is three times a week for the first two weeks, twice a week for the next five weeks and once a week thereafter until about thirty visits have occurred. There are enormous variations upon the figures just quoted, mainly depending on the progress of the student. Students are asked to dress in loose clothing.

Each lesson lasts for half an hour. Many teachers practise outside of normal working hours. Alexander technique is also sometimes taught in week long intensives.

READING

Body Learning *by Michael Gelb Aurum Press £5.95*. The approach to learning and the techniques outlined in Body Learning can transform your life if you read and practise the methods outlined in this extremely well illustrated introduction to the Alexander Technique. **Art of Changing** *by Glen Park, Ashgrove Book £9.50 Cassette £6.95*. This book takes a deeper look at the Alexander technique introducing the basic exercises to aid personal growth and transformation, and deal with physical and mental stress. Glen Park then develops this study to encompass the way in which the emotional and spiritual dimensions may be developed with reference to Alexander's system of working. The cassette is a useful adjunct to the book helping the student to work through the exercises and combine them with awareness of the chakra centres.

CENTRES OFFERING ALEXANDER TECHNIQUE

Alexander Teaching Centre EC1, Bloomsbury Alexander Centre WC1, Bodywise E2, Brackenbury Natural Health Centre W6, CAER (Centre For Alternative Education And Research) (Cornwall), City Health Centre EC1, Clapham Common

Clinic SW4, Constructive Teaching Centre W11, Edgware Centre for Natural Health (Edgware), Hale Clinic W1, Highbury Centre N5, Institute of Holistic Therapies SW6, Living Centre SW20, Natural Healing Centre E7, Neal's Yard Therapy Rooms WC2, New Cross Natural Therapy Centre SE14, Primrose Healing Centre NW1, Society of Students of Holistic Health (courses held in London), South Camden Women's Centre WC1, South London Natural Health Centre SW4, West London Buddhist Centre W11, Westminster Natural Health Centre SW1, Wimbledon Clinic of Natural Medicine SW19, Wood Street Clinic (Barnet).

TRAININGS IN ALEXANDER TECHNIQUE
Apply to the **Society of Teachers of the Alexander Technique**. They have a list of the training schools in London. The waiting list at all of these centres is typically longer than four years.

Allergy Therapy

It has been accepted for a long time now that pollen can cause an allergic reaction called hayfever which can spoil the sufferer's enjoyment of summer. It was not until recently however that research carried out by a London hospital convinced the medical profession that common foods could also cause a wide range of physical and mental symptoms in some people. Formerly such symptoms might have gone unrecognised and been treated by painkillers or tranquillisers.

An allergic reaction takes place when the body reacts to a substance which has been eaten, inhaled or in contact with the body in some other way, as if it were harmful, even though the substance is not in any way a threat to the organism. The immune system rejects the substance, and in its attempts to do so causes allergic symptoms. White flour, dairy products and food additives are often the culprits in food allergy.

Allergy can be involved in ill health in different ways. Sometimes the patient's symptoms, which can range from headaches, digestive problems, depression, palpitations and arthritic pains, are due to the allergy alone, and by not eating the food which causes the allergic reaction the symptoms are cured. Sometimes allergy is implicated in a particular illness, and helps to aggravate the symptoms. This is more controversial, and research has not been at all conclusive. An example of this was the claim that schizophrenia could be precipitated by food allergy. While this is debatable, it is certainly true that if the immune system is weakened by allergy, it may be less able to contend with any other disturbance which is present in the body.

The increase in environmental pollutants such a car fumes, industrial waste and pesticides has also had its part to play in causing ill health. These substances can be harmful, and the body's reaction may represent a response to a genuine threat, rather than being a strictly allergic reaction. Dr Peter Mansfield and Dr Jean Monro have investigated the effects of chemicals in the environment on chemically sensitive children. Although it is a moot point whether reactions to these substances are allergic or simply intolerant, allergy therapy can still be used here to identify the possible source of the patient's symptoms.

There are various methods used to diagnose an allergy. The patient may be put on a very restricted diet of foods which are usually non-allergenic. Then other foods will be reintroduced into the diet one by one, and the reactions of the patient to each food are charted. Another method is the 'scratch test' where the surface of the skin is lightly scratched and different substances are applied to it. Any irritation or inflammation may be an indication of an allergic reaction. A variant of this test is the introduction of the substances by injection into the skin and noting any skin reactions. The cytotoxic blood test uses a sample of blood to which the suspected allergens are introduced, and the effects monitored. Analysis of hair will show the long term effects of allergy, although it will not show recent developments. Applied kinesiology can be used to test muscle strength in the presence of a potential allergen.

Once the cause has been found, the foods or substances which cause the allergy can be eliminated from the diet or environment. One form of treatment offered by some therapists is the 'neutralising dose'. If the allergen is greatly diluted to the level of a homoeopathic potency and injected, the body will build up a resistance to the substance and be able to tolerate it again. However, to many people it may seem easier just to stop eating what the body rejects.

For information about allergy, contact Action Against Allergy.

READING

Food Allergy and Intolerance *by Jonathan Brostoff and Linda Gamlin, Bloomsbury Publishing £4.99.* This explains comprehensively and simply how certain foods can cause problems for some people and how by identifying and eliminating the culprits they can improve their health. Includes chapters on chemical sensitivity, the mind and body connection and problems in childhood. Also links common ailments with food allergies and details elimination diets to be followed. **Arthritis - The Allergy Connection** *by John Mansfield, Thorsons £4.99.* Dr. Mansfield explores a revolutionary new approach to alleviating one of the most crippling diseases known. He describes effective ways of dealing with the way in which food allergy may affect the development of arthritis including desensitization and avoidance of stimulants. His ideas are reinforced by the results of clinical trials and scientific evidence.

CENTRES OFFERING ALLERGY THERAPY

Bayswater Allergy Clinic W2, Bexleyheath Natural Health Clinic (Kent), Institute for Complementary Medicine W1, Natural Healing Centre Middlesex, Oasis N2, South London Natural Health Centre SW4, Wimbledon Clinic of Natural Medicine SW19,

Alternative and Orthodox Medicine Clinic NW1, Barbican Natural Health Centre EC1, Brackenbury Natural Health Centre W6, Breakspear Hospital, Clinics Health International SW6, Food and Chemical Allergy Clinic (Croydon), Holistic Health Consultancy SW1, Institute of Allergy Therapists, International Colon Hydrotherapy Foundation W9, Living Centre SW20, Natural Healing Centre E7, Natural Healing Centre (Middlesex), Natural Health Clinic (Harrow), Natureworks W1, Wimbledon Clinic of Natural Medicine SW19.

Applied Kinesiology / Touch for Health

Applied Kinesiology is a manipulative therapy. It involves testing muscles with the hands for any signs of weakness, which if present may show a disturbance in the fuctioning of an organ. In this way, it is useful as a diagnostic technique. Kinesiologists are particularly interested in this weakness if it occurs in a set of muscles on only one side of the body, for this indicates an imbalance which, they believe, can be the first stage in the development of a particular health problem.

The technique was first developed by Dr George Goodheart, an American chiropractor. He linked his discoveries about muscular weakness with oriental medical ideas of energy flow through the body in 'meridians' (see 'Acupuncture'). Through the meridians, the muscles are linked to particular organs. Whatever underlying problem is revealed by the muscle tests, it is usually treated by working on the reflexes to strengthen the muscles, massaging meridians and in some cases by diet.

Applied kinesiology is often used to diagnose food allergies. Muscles are tested before and after the ingestion of foods suspected of causing allergy. If the muscles are weaker a few seconds after the patient has chewed the suspected food, this indicates the presence of an allergy.

The difference between Applied Kinesiology and Touch for Health is that the former is used by professionals for diagnosis and treatment of patients, while Touch for Health is taught to the general public as a self-help technique for preventative health care.

TRAININGS IN APPLIED KINESIOLOGY
Academy of Systematic Kinesiology *Title of Training* Basic Kinesiology, certificate and diploma courses in Kinesiology. *Duration* From basic weekend classes to 1 or 2 years part-time, 8 weekends plus one eight

day course. *Entry Requirements* Suitability assessed through screening for personality, ethical approach and integrity. *Fees* £80 per weekend, £500 advanced communications week long course, £1250 certificate course. Comments Leaflets, books, videos, tape recordings.

Aromatherapy

Aromatherapy is a treatment method which uses essential oils extracted from flowers, plants, trees or spices. These are massaged into the body, inhaled, sprinkled in baths or in some cases ingested.

Aromatic substances were used in healing throughout the ancient world, notably by the Egyptians who buried jars of frankinsense and myrrh alongside their pharohs in their tombs, and who used the same perfumes for both medical and cosmetic effect. Proponents of aromatherapy have to this day developed the art for purposes as diverse as the healing of wounds, treating skin cancer and banishing wrinkles.

The essential oils used in aromatherapy are highly concentrated and have to be extracted from large quantities of the mother plant. They are expensive to buy and need to be stored carefully in the right conditions and temperature, and these factors place some limitation on the popular use of aromatherapy. The oils are absorbed into the body through the skin. Although it is not known how aromatherapy works, since research has shown that if a drug is administered in this way its effects may be different from those it produces if it is taken orally, it may be that it is the method of application used in aromatherapy which enables the therapeutic effect of the oils.

The practitioner will decide on the essential oils which will be most efficacious for the client. Sometimes diagnosis is made using radiesthesia. This technique uses a pendulum - a small object such as a ring or a bead used as a weight and attached to a length of string or thread about a foot long. The therapist then asks questions, either about the health of the patient, or about what particular remedy is indicated and the pendulum responds with a 'yes' or 'no' answer.

Having selected the appropriate oil the aromatherapist will probably want to spend some time preparing the skin because diet, pollution and make-up have dulled the receptivity of the modern skin. Inhalation is used for the treatment of head and lung complaints. About six to ten treatments may be required, although beneficial effects may be felt earlier.

As might be expected, aromatherapy is most effective used in the treatment of the skin, in healing wounds and burns, and

AROMATHERAPY

treating shingles, acne and conditions related to stress. The massage with which the oils are applied adds to the therapeutic effect of the treatment.

READING

Practical Aromatherapy *by Shirley Price Thorsons £3.50*. A simple explanation of all aspects of aromatherapy and how it can be used to good effect as a self-help therapy. Included is an illustrated section on aromatherapy massage techniques and also how to blend pure essential oils for different purposes. Suitable for the lay person and practitioner alike. **Aromatherapy, An A-Z** *by Patricia Davies, C.W. Daniel £9.95*. This book provides the answers to such questions as: 'can I combine aromatherapy with other therapies or even conventional medicine? Which oil could help my skin? How are essential oils obtained from plants?' This popular book is a suitable reference work for students and practitioners of aromatherapy.

CENTRES OFFERING AROMATHERAPY

International Federation of Aromatherapists (register), Acupuncture Clinic E17, Aromatherapy Associates SW6, Aromatherapy Training Centre SW16, Barbican Natural Health Centre EC1, Bennet and Luck Natural Health Centre N1, Bexleyheath Natural Health Clinic (Kent), Bluestone Clinic NW1, Body Clinic NW11, Bodyworks Natural Therapies (client's home or workplace), Brackenbury Natural Health Centre W6, Bretforton Hall W2, Chessington Hypnotherapy Clinic Chessington, Clapham Common Clinic SW4, Clissold Park Natural Health Centre N16, College of Natural Therapies, European Shiatsu School W8, Falcons SW11, Fulham Clinic SW6, Guild of Aromatherapy Practitioners SW19, Hendon Natural Health Clinic, Institute of Clinical Aromatherapy SE6, Institute of Traditional Herbal Medicine and Aromatherapy W8, Jeyrani Health Centre E18, Lifecare, Lifeworks NW5, Living Centre SW20, McCarthy Westwood Consultants SW11, Micheline Arcier Aromatherapy SW1, Natural Healing

KOBASHI — discover for yourself the therapeutic qualities of these PURE ESSENTIAL OILS. Select from our carefully chosen range for:—
* aromatherapy
* bathing
* body perfume
* natural room fragrance

Use with confidence that these are the best; and with pleasure in their remarkable properties of healing towards body and mind.

Attractively packaged — the ideal gift.

All our products are produced & tested without cruelty to animals.

BODYCARE,
50 High St., Ide, Exeter
Devon Ex2 9RW ✆ **0392 - 217628**

Please enclose a S.A.E. for literature. Products available at independent health & whole food outlets.

107

BODY THERAPIES

Centre E7, Natural Medicine Centre Bromley, Natureworks W1, Neal's Yard Therapy Rooms WC2, Primrose Healing Centre NW1, Putney Natural Therapy Clinic SW15, Resonance SW17, Shirley Goldstein Holistic Therapies NW1, Society of Students of Holistic Health Courses held in London, South Camden Women's Centre WC1, South London Natural Health Centre SW4, Sunra SW12, Therapy Made Unique, Wellspring Clinic SW6, West London School of Therapeutic Massage and Reflexology W11, Westminster Natural Health Centre SW1, Wholistic Health Centre (Croydon), Wimbledon Clinic of Natural Medicine SW19, Wood Street Clinic Barnet, Ziva Belic Aromatherapy International School W5.

TRAININGS IN AROMATHERAPY

Aromatherapy Associates *Title of Training* (1) Foundation Course (2) Advanced Course *Duration* (1) Ten days full time. (2) Vary *Entry requirements* (1) Knowledge of massage and anatomy and physiology. (2) Must have done the Foundation course. *Fees* (1) £610 incl VAT. (2) Varies. *Comments* Course is accredited by the International Federation of Aromatherapists and upon successful completion of the course, graduates are entitled to apply for membership of the IFA.

Institute of Clinical Aromatherapy *Title of Training* (1) Clinical Aromatherapy (2) Advanced Essential Oils Course. *Duration* (1) 6-8 days (2) 6 days. *Entry requirements* (1) Applicants must have qualified in either the course in anatomy and physiology given by the College of Natural Therapies or in a recognised course elsewhere. *Fees* (1) £379.50 (including VAT). (2) £97.75 (including VAT). *Comments* Also run Aromatherapy for the Qualified Beauty Therapist Certificate course.

Jeyrani Health Centre *Title of Training* Scientific Aromatherapy *Duration* Three part course of long weekends. *Entry requirements* Preferably for already qualified aromatherapists. *Fees* £675.

London School of Herbology and Aromatherapy *Title of Training* (1) Herbal Medicine/Medical Aromatherapy Diploma Course. (2) Aromatherapy Massage Course. *Duration* (1) 3 years part-time (500 hours). (2) 9 months part-time (100 hours). *Entry Requirements* None: students are trained in all aspects of required knowledge. *Fees* (1) £1,000 per annum. (2) £575 for whole training. *Comments* Training in both Chinese traditional approach, and western medical approach. Both courses include clinical practice.

Micheline Arcier Aromatherapy *Title of Training* Aromatherapy Diploma Course. *Duration* 8 days over two long weekends. *Entry requirements* Qualified in anatomy, physiology, face and body massage with 2 years practical experience. *Fees* £460 including VAT.

Shirley Price Aromatherapy *Title of Training* Aromatherapy training courses including diploma standard with reflexology techniques. Basic massage course, anatomy and physiology correspondence course, diploma course, 4 post-diploma courses. *Duration* Diploma course in two parts, 3-9 months depending on qualifications already held in anatomy and physiology and basic massage. *Entry* *requirements* For diploma course, students must have a recognised qualification in basic massage and anatomy and physiology. *Fees* Basic course £165 + VAT, Diploma course parts 1 and 2 (5 days each) £250 + VAT each. Post diploma courses £100-£195 + VAT depending on subject. *Comments* Accredited school of the International Federation of Aromatherapists. Courses held at venues throughout the UK including London.

Ziva Belic Aromatherapy International School *Title of Training* Three part course (1) Basic Aromatherapy, (2) Aromatherapy and Illness, (3) Aromatherapy and Beauty. *Duration* Weekends. *Entry requirements* None. *Fees* 1 weekend: £80, 3 weekends: £225, 6 weekends £750.

Ayurvedic Medicine

Ayurveda (which means 'science of life') is the traditional medicine of India which has been practised for over two and a half thousand years. It is based on texts which, among other things, describe operative techniques, how infection can be transmitted during surgery and even describes the body as being composed of cells long before Western medicine had made such important discoveries.

According to this system of medicine there are five elements (doshas) - earth, air, fire, water and ether. There are also three basic qualities of energy - rajas (active), ramas (passive) and sattva (unifying, wise). It is the correct balance of these, constantly changing with environmental conditions, which constitutes health.

Diagnosis involves observing the quality of 32 pulses, taking a personal history, considering astrological information and observing the condition of the body. Treatment can by with herbs, exercises, diet, breathing techniques, massage, urine treatment, yogic cleansing techniques or surgery.

Ayurvedic medicine is the main form of medicine available to people living in India. The training is long and thorough, and involves some knowledge of western medicine.

Unani medicine is an offshoot of Ayurveda, and includes ideas based on Greek and Arab sources. Siddha medicine is another form which has incorporated the use of minerals for treatment.

CENTRES OFFERING AYURVEDIC MEDICINE

Association of Ayurvedic Practitioners NW11, Private Polyclinic E7.

Bach Flower Remedies

These are herbal remedies derived from the flowers of plants. They are prescribed to treat the underlying negative emotional states which are seen as the cause of disease.

This system was devised by Dr Edward Bach, a doctor who practised at the beginning of this century. Working first as a pathologist and bacteriologist he found that different diseases seemed to be linked to the different temperaments of his patients, and classified these character types into seven categories which can be recognised by a predominant emotional state. These states are: fear, uncertainty or indecision, lack of interest in the present, despondency and despair, over concern for the welfare of others, loneliness and over-sensitivity. While he saw each type as possessing positive qualities which could be developed, it is the characteristic negative emotions of each which become apparent in illness.

Each category is further sub-divided for the prescription of the various flower remedies, so that for instance under the heading of 'over-sensitivity' there are four remedies: Agrimony for anxiety and mental torment hidden under a brave face; Centaury for weak will and a 'doormat tendency'; Walnut for major life changes and Holly for jealousy and suspicion.

There are no 'official' practitioners of Bach flower remedies. There are a very few doctors who will prescribe them. Since they are completely safe most people who use them will select a remedy for themselves by self diagnosis, using the Handbook of Bach Flower Remedies which is available from the Edward Bach Healing Centre and some health food shops; and the remedies themselves are available from these two sources. Bach himself discovered the remedies by intuition, often working himself into the same state of mind for which a remedy was required and, walking among the flowers and plants growing locally, he would feel drawn to the one which offered some relief. Prescribing the appropriate remedy for yourself can also be done in this intuitive way, especially since it can be difficult to decide among the long list of mental symptoms described in the handbook which ones are really at the root of your condition. To do this some people use radiesthesia - dowsing with a pendulum (q.v.).

An invaluable item for the first aid kit is 'Rescue Remedy' which is a mixture of five of the flower remedies and can be used after a shock, or in any emotional crisis. To take the remedies, put two or three drops in a glass of water or fruit juice.

More information about Bach Flower Remedies can be obtained from the **Dr Edward Bach Centre.**

READING
A Guide to the Bach Flower Remedies *by Julian Barnard C.W. Daniel £1.50.* A thorough and straightforward guide to the remedies in pocket size for instant reference. **Bach Flower Therapy** *by Mechthild Scheffer, Thorsons £6.99.* This is the most popular of the Bach Flower books and has a chapter on each of the remedies and also describes how to choose the right remedy. It is suitable for practitioner's reference but clear and simple enough to be of benefit to the layman.

BATES TRAINING / BIODYNAMIC MASSAGE

CENTRES OFFERING BACH FLOWER REMEDIES

Bexleyheath Natural Health Clinic (Kent), Brackenbury Natural Health Centre W6, Hampton Holistic Centre for Homoeopathy and Autogenic Training (Middlesex), Healing Fields Practice N7, McCarthy Westwood Consultants SW11, Mill Hill Health Care NW7, Natural Healing Centre (Middlesex), Neal's Yard Therapy Rooms WC2, Primrose Healing Centre NW1, Sheila Revell Centre SW16, Bennet and Luck Natural Health Centre N1, Brackenbury Natural Health Centre W6, Ealing Holistic Centre for Homoeopath and Autogenic Training W13, Hampstead Healing Centre NW3, Holistic Health Consultancy SW1, Nutribiotics Edgware, Orpheus Centre W14, Primrose Healing Centre NW1, Shirley Goldstein Holistic Therapies NW1, Therapy Made Unique, Wholistic Health Centre (Croydon).

Bates Eyesight Training

This is a natural method of eyesight improvement through eye exercises. It was devised by Dr William H Bates, an eye specialist who gave up orthodox methods in order to find a more satisfactory way of treating bad eyesight. He published his bestseller, *Better Eyesight Without Glasses*, detailing these exercises in 1919. Various exercises are recommended. 'Palming' involves covering the eyes with the palms of the hands for 10 minutes at a time, two or three times a day. This excludes all light and relaxes the eyes. 'Shifting and swinging' involve deliberatly imitating the natural minute and constant shifting movements of the eyes around an object, or objects. 'Splashing' involves splashing the eyes with hot and cold water repeatedly morning and night. Bates believed blinking reguarly - once or twice every ten seconds - was also of great importance. He also recommended remembering colours or beautiful scenes while 'palming', because he found this improved vision in actuality. A practitioner of the Bates eyesight training will give these and other exercises to be practised every day.

Aldous Huxley, who as a young man could hardly see to read, is perhaps the most famous of those who have been helped by this method, as he explains in his book, *The Art of Seeing*.

CENTRES OFFERING BATES EYESIGHT TRAINING

Bates Association of G.B. (register), Brackenbury Natural Health Centre W6.

Biodynamic Massage and Psychology

Biodynamic massage and biodynamic psychology were formulated by Gerda Boyesen, a Norweigan psychologist, physiotherapist and Reichian analyst. As in Reich's psychology, Biodynamics works on the premise that the mind and body function together in any emotional process, and that shocks, traumas and continually repressed feelings can build up chronic physical and psychological blocks. This is especially true if during childhood the growing child did not feel in a safe enough environment to be able to express its feelings. The modern world too tends to exacerbate these feelings of insecurity and stress, and the body may be holding itself in a permanent state of alert and tension.

Boyesen, through her work as a physiotherapist, found that blocked energy builds up in the form of fluids trapped between muscles and nerves. Her unique contribution to Reichian therapy was that she found that in massaging the patient to disperse this build up of fluids, the intestine was activated in a spontaneous peristaltic movement. This movement was not to eliminate foods, but rather a kind of psychic clearing process which occurs when emotion is allowed to follow its natural process of expression. This she likened to the concept in Chinese medicine that every organ has two functions. One function is physical, and one is esoteric or 'meaningful'. According to Boyesen, the meaningful function of the intestine is to digest stress.

The cornerstone of the theory and practice of biodynamic massage is that the healthy organism has the power to express and resolve, to digest all emotional traumas and shocks once the body has ceased to armour itself in patterns of chronic tension and blocks.

The therapist works using a stethoscope to listen to the noises inside the abdomen. There are many different sounds made by the intestines and the therapist is guided by these which are not just the sound of food being digested, but responses to the massage. The sounds mean that the therapist has been able to set free the emotional energy that has become trapped in a particular part of the body. The therapist may massage any part of the body. If enough energy is being released in a 'biodynamic updrift' the therapist may stop the massage, and instead encourage the client to tune in to his or her own 'stimuli from within'. These may take the form of memories, emotions, physical movements or expansive breathing.

Biodynamic massage is helpful in the treatment of migraines, high blood

---

INSTITUTE OF BIODYNAMIC PSYCHOLOGY AND PSYCHOTHERAPY
EALING

CERTIFICATE IN BIODYNAMIC MASSAGE METHODS AND BIODYNAMIC PHYSIATRY
• A Two Year Course leading to Associated Professional Membership of the Institute PLUS a One Year Post-Graduate Supervision Course leading to the Practising Certificate in Biodynamic Physiatry. (See also 'Body Therapy' and 'Psychotherapy' Section.)

BIODYNAMIC MASSAGE COURSES FOR BEGINNERS
• monthly lectures and demonstrations at Ealing Town Hall
• weekend workshops - Saturday and Sunday, 10.00am-6.00pm.
• short courses - a series of four weekends, as above

BIODYNAMIC MASSAGE COURSES FOR PRACTITIONERS IN ALTERNATIVE AND COMPLEMENTARY MEDICINE AND ALL HEALTH CARE PROFESSIONALS
• Basic and Advanced Courses - a series of six weekends in each course to learn and apply biodynamic skills and methods in your own profession.

Please apply in the first instance to IBPP, 23 High Street, The Green, Ealing, London W5 5DF. Tel 081 567 6677.

BIODYNAMIC MASSAGE

pressure, digestive problems and muscular pain as well as stress, anxiety and depression. It helps to maintain good health and brings about a greater sense of aliveness.

CENTRES OFFERING BIODYNAMIC MASSAGE
Association of Biodynamic Psychotherapists (register), Biodynamic Clinic W5, Biodynamic Psychotherapy and Teaching W3, Brackenbury Natural Health Centre W6, Chiron W5, Gerda Boyesen Centre for Biodynamic Psychology and Psychotherapy W3, Hidden Strengths NW5, Highbury Centre N5, Hillside Practice NW5, Neal's Yard Therapy Rooms WC2, New Life Lodge N4, Psychotherapy Workshops for Women (North and West London), Westminster Natural Health Centre SW1.

TRAININGS IN BIODYNAMIC MASSAGE AND PSYCHOLOGY
Gerda Boyesen Centre for Biodynamic Psychology and Psychotherapy *Title of Training* (1) Two Year Certificate Course in Biodynamic Psysiatry. (2) Two Year Advanced Training Course in Biodynamic Psychology and Psychotherapy. *Duration* (1) Two years (2) Two years. *Entry Requirements* None specified for (1). For (2) completion of (1). *Fees* £1410 per annum. Individual sessions at £15.
Institute of Biodynamic Psychology and Psychotherapy *Title of Training* (1) Certificate in Biodynamic Massage Methods and Biodynamic Physiatry (Basic Methods). (2) Certificate in Biodynamic Psychotherapy (Advanced Course). (3) Certificate in Biodynamic Psychology and Psychotherapy *Duration* (1) Two years part-time, one weekend per month, one full day per week, five day seminars in spring and summer holidays. One year post-graduate clinical practice and supervision leading to Practicing Certificate and Register of Practitioners. (2) Two years part-time. One weekend per month, one day per week during three ten week terms. Five day seminars in spring and summer holidays. (3) Four years part-time, one weekend a month, one full day per week. Five day seminars in spring and summer holidays each year. Entry requirements (1) All professional and academic qualifications acknowledged. Good general basic education and/or life experience essential. Experience of biodynamic therapy and/or other therapeutic approaches an advantage. All applicants interviewed and considered. (2) Certificate in Biodynamic Massage Methods and Biodynamic Physiatry. (3) All professional and academic qualifications acknowledged. Good general basic education and/or life experience essential. Experience of biodynamic therapy and/or other therapeutic approaches an advantage. All applicants interviewed and considered. *Fees* (1) £2100 per annum. If paid in advance £2000, or each term £700 or monthly standing orders of £210 x 10 months. (2) £2100 per annum. If paid in advance £2000, or each term £700, or monthly standing orders of £210 x 10 months. (3) £2100 per annum. If paid in advance £2000, or each term £700, or monthly standing orders of £210 x 10 months. *Comments* 1, 2 & (3) Regular Biodynamic Psychotherapy sessions during training compulsory (exclusive of *fees*).

Chiropractic

Chiropractic is a method which uses manipulation of the joints and especially the spine by the hands to restore and maintain health.

The system was devised by Dr Daniel David Palmer at the turn of the century when he cured his janitor of deafness by manipulating his spine. Although there are obvious similarities between chiropractic and osteopathy, the main differences lie in the slightly different styles of manipulation used, and that chiropractors are more likely to use X-rays and orthodox physiological tests such as blood samples and neurological examination for diagnosis. Like osteopathy it is based on the idea that displacement of the vertebrae causes disease, but while traditional chiropractic theory states that these impair the functioning of the nervous system, osteopaths maintain that the resultant disease is caused by impaired circulation.

The chiropractor will take a detailed medical history and make a physical examination, possibly using the tests outlined above. He or she will also feel the spine and joints with their hands to locate tissue changes and assess the range of mobility present. Then the appropriate manipulation is carried out. This takes the form of twists and pulls with the chiropractor and patient in a number of different positions.

A chiropractor should have undergone an intensive 4 year training at a recognised college. Conditions which respond well to chiropractic are not surprisingly low back pain, slipped discs, sciatica, headaches, migraines, digestive disorders and even asthma. Some cases of arthritis may be suitable and respond to treatment.

CENTRES OFFERING CHIROPRACTIC

British Chiropractic Association SW1, Chiropractic Advancement Association (register), Chiropractic Clinic W8, Hale Clinic W1, Hampton Healing Centre, Hendon Natural Health Clinic, Institute of Pure Chiropractic, Napier Chiropractic Clinic NW11, Neal's Yard Therapy Rooms WC2, Sayer Clinic W1, W8, WC2, W4, South London Natural Health Centre SW4, Teleos Clinic W1, Wellspring Clinic SW6, Westminster Natural Health Centre SW1, Wood Street Clinic Barnet.

TRAINING IN CHIROPRACTIC

Anglo-European College of Chiropractic *Title of Training* Bsc. Chiropractic (CNAA). *Duration* Fours year full time *Entry requirements* 3 'A' levels or equivalent or over 23 years of age (consideration is given to each individual case). Must have some chemistry qualification/background. *Fees* £4140 pa. *Comments* Qualifies you to practice as a chiropractor in most parts of the world.

Colonic Irrigation

Sometimes also called colonic hydrotherapy, colonic irrigation is the cleansing of the large intestine (or bowel) by passing water through and out of it via the rectum.

COLONIC IRRIGATION

❝ There are an amazing number of ways to get treatment. Should you go herbal? Or risk life, limb and sanity with conventional medicines? There will be small help from your orthodox doctor should you decide to go for 'fringe' medicine. He sees patients requiring other types of treatment in the same light that the commandant of Colditz saw escapees.

The Wise Woman will need to retain her wits if she is to tight rope walk between the vast gulf of conventional and alternative methods. If it's the body that needs a little help do try to resist the urge to make your own herbal concoctions unless you are very sussed about what you are doing. You run the risk of giving yourself a bad case of the wretched retching should you mistake the herb or spice. Never, never if you have to call the doctor tell him you were trying to cure yourself. Merely tell him you made a mistake putting the salad together. The penalty for admitting to your G.P. that you have been tampering with nature will be enemas and an edifying lecture on what a silly little girl you have been. If you live in the country it will be a lot easier to find yourself a herbalist or witch doctor. Country folk have less inhibitions about using old granny Moles' receipes that have cured everything from the plague to rabies since time began.

Even the fittest of us have our off days, so it's wise to know what kind of treatment we can expect when we lurch towards our nearest psychotherapist's surgery. Choosing is no light matter. Too handsome and you won't want to see him with a bad case of depression; too ugly he may make you fell worse. A woman doctor may or may not be the answer. Always interview your therapist's receptionist, just strike up a causal conversation and it won't take you long to discover if:

"Doctor is a very, very busy person and certainly hasn't time to waste on patients" or "Doctor is tied up a lot of the time". This means the consulting rooms are permanently closed as the doctor is using the couch for other types of practice. "Doctor is permanently attached to a maximum security unit for the hopelessly bewildered", means that Doctor is, in fact, an inmate.

Remember to take a good look at your surroundings, early giveaways of things amiss include stuffed birds, particularly if there's a raven on display. Any pieces of strange equipment, black boxes, couches with straps? Is there a family retainer crouched in the corner with a moving hump? Any or all of these things mean you should be prepared to decamp unless of course you are a Sun reporter, in which case pack a cross. Always be prepared to interview your doctor. Does he ever go out during the day? Does your perfume 'scent of wild garlic' make him feel faint? Does he salivate when he looks at your neck? All these things are little signs of future problems. **❞**

Sue Anne Deakin

The function of the colon is to extract minerals, nutrients and excess water from food after is has passed, partly digested, out of the stomach and small intestine. Food is moved through the intestine by means of regular muscular contractions (called 'peristalsis') towards the rectum from which it is excreted. However, bad diet, stress, emotional trauma or the side-effects of medicines and drugs can interfere both with this movement, and with the colon's ability to absorb and it can become blocked

115

with toxic waste matter. This not only further interferes with digestion, but is also believed to fester and release poisonous substances into the blood stream. These eventually reach and affect the vital organs, and this, according to the theory of colonics, is the cause of bad health.the aim of colonic irrigation is to unblock the colon and flush out the toxins so that it is restored to healthy functioning.

A series of four to eight colonic irrigations is usually suggested for new clients. A sterile speculum is placed in the rectum, and then a small tube through which water flows into the colon. The water is extracted through a separate tube, and the contents on the colon can be watched through a transparent window as they come out.

The process itself is not unpleasant. The recipient's lower half is kept covered throughout so that they do not feel undignified or embarrassed. The temperature and pressure of water is monitored by the practitioner, and hot and cold water may be alternated to stimulate the bowel. It should take about half and hour.

Immediately afterwards, recipients may need to open their bowels. Bacteria which normally lives in the gut and which is important to the digestion of food is replaced with an implant.

With the initial course of treatment, the practitioner may recommend a change of diet, or the taking of a particular dietary supplement to maintain the healthy functioning of the colon. Treatments are often taken two to four times a year.

While in trained hands, colonic irrigation is safe, in the hands of untrained people it can be dangerous and should *never* be attempted at home. The Colonic International Association has a list of trained practitioners.

READING

Tissue Cleansing through Bowel Management *by Bernard Jensen, Bernard Jensen £4.95.* Includes chapters on imbalances of the intestine and the benefits of colonic cleansing. Describes specific methods of cleansing and detoxification using

---

COLON HEALTH

Nutritional and colonic health advisory service

(071) 286 1592
(071) 289 7000

supplements, colonic irrigation and diet. The book also offers insights into connection between mind and body and inner cleanliness. **The Colon Health Handbook** *by Robert Gray, Emerald Publishing £5.50.* This book is written by a nutrition counsellor and covers the use of supplements, bran and psyllium husks to strip the inside of the colon of waste materials. The methods are clearly explained and also included are notes on iris diagnosis to follow the progress of benefits gained from following the plan.

CENTRES OFFERING COLONIC IRRIGATION
Brackenbury Natural Health Centre W6, Colonic International Association (register), Hampton Healing Centre, International Colon Hydrotherapy Foundation W9, Lifeworks NW5, Refuah Shelaymah Natural Health Centre N16, South London Natural Health Centre SW4, Wellspring Clinic SW6, Wholeness E18, Wimbledon Clinic of Natural Medicine SW19.

TRAINING IN COLONIC IRRIGATION
Colonic International Association *Duration* 1 weekend and 3 day extended weekend.

Crystal/Gem Therapy
This is the therapeutic use of semi-precious and precious stones in a number of different ways.

Gemstones have been used for healing, or revered as having special powers through the ages. The Chinese have used jade to treat kidney and bladder complaints for at least 5,000 years. The American Indians were given personal stones at birth which had special powers and significance. These would be carried around in pouches worn on the owners' body.

Each variety of stone is believed to have specific therapeutic properties, though the same stone can have different effects on different people. Quartz and amethyst crystals are both used for general healing and are believed to magnify healing energies so that they become more effective, whether transmitted by some mechanical means or by a human being. The crystals or gems can be worn, carried and used as an adjunct to massage, or sometimes to focus thoughts and wishes for healing.

They can also be used in conjunction with colour therapy, using a crystal light box. This is a box with a light inside it and a hole on the outside covered with different coloured filters or gels through which the light is projected. Crystals are placed on the filter to intensify the energy of the light emitted.

Electro-crystal therapy has also been developed. This involves the transmission of different pulses of high frequency electromagnetic energy through crystals and onto the part of the body which needs to be treated. Gem elixirs are another way in which the healing energy of crystals and gems are believed to be absorbed.

Many people like to have crystals in their homes, because they feel they have a positive effect on the atmosphere. Prices for these 'domestic' crystals can range from 50p for a very small one, to five thousand pounds for a very large cluster.

READING

The Healing Power of Crystals *by Magda Palmer, Arrow £3.99.* In this book the author reveals how we can forge a link through crystals and gems to the energies of the solar system and lists a number of stones appropriate to each birthsign. Also included are the particular healing properties of specific stones and the ailments most susceptible to crystal healing. **The Power of Gems and Crystals** *by Soozi Holbeche, Piatkus £7.95.* This charming book, now in paperback, is written by one of Britain's pioneers in crystal healing. The book is packed with the most interesting historical facts and illustrated exercises. It also offers information on dowsing and healing. Just about everything you would want to know about gems and crystals.

CENTRES OFFERING CRYSTAL/GEM HEALING

Crystal Connection NW1, Crystal Research Foundation, Natureworks W1, Nutribiotics (Edgware), Orpheus Centre W14, School of Electro-Crystal Therapy (Ruislip), Wholistic Health and Life Extension (Hampton).

Colour Therapy

Colour therapy is the use of colour or coloured light for therapeutic purposes.

On the most basic level most people are aware that if the rooms they live in are painted different colours they will have a different affect on their moods. Research has shown that blue light lowers blood pressure and has a calming effect while red light puts blood pressure up and excites the nervous system. It has also been shown that some forms of depression may be due to the light deprivation we suffer either during winter, or in offices where there are only fluorescent lights. Daylight bulbs have been invented to correct this deficiency.

COLOUR THERAPY

The use of colour as an aid to healing is a very subtle art, and the whole spectrum of colours is used. Colour therapists may diagnose what colour someone needs by noting what colours they like and dislike, or by looking at them to see what colour their 'aura' is, or by taking a medical history. The diagnosis of exactly what colours someone lacks is a complex matter, and self-treatment is not as easy as one might think.

There a many ways in which the colour may be administered. The colour therapist may advise you to eat certain foods which have the desired colour, or ask you to drink water which has been placed in coloured containers and exposed to sunlight, or you may be bathed in coloured light. Some colour therapists concentrate on colour in clothes, and help you to discover which colours are best for you to wear because they suit your physique and temperament.

Colour therapy is perhaps best used as a supplement to other forms of treatment, and has been used for a variety of complaints, from physical disorders to depression and anxiety states. Colour visualisation can also be used as a method of self help.

The Luscher Colour Test, devised by Dr Max Luscher is a personality test which can be self administered. Here, colour preferences are used to uncover psychological make up, and this is an interesting way to find out how colour reflects one's personality.

READING
Healing Through Colour *by Theo Gimbel, C.W. Daniel £7.95.* A complete book on colour therapy. The author explains the historical background to the use of colour and the use of healing in the ancient temples. In addition the modern approach to colour is discussed in detail including uses in decoration, clothing, stage illumination and as a supplementary therapy in medical work. **The Healing Power of Colour** *by Magda Palmer, Thorsons/Aquarian £3.99.* This book examines what colour does to us, how it can be used in magic and dream interpretation and how we can use it to improve our behaviour and our health. It will help you to gain an expanded understanding of the nature of colour and how it can be used to enhance your life.

CENTRES OFFERING COLOUR THERAPY
Aetherius Society SW6, All Healing Clinic NW5, Association of Colour Therapists N10, Brackenbury Natural Health Centre W6, Bretforton Hall W2, Hygeia Studios, International Association of Colour Healers SW14, Living Colour NW3, Natureworks W1, Neal's Yard Therapy Rooms WC2, Orpheus Centre W14, South London Natural Health Centre SW4.

TRAININGS IN COLOUR THERAPY

Hygeia Studios *Title* (1) Certificate Course (2) Advanced Course. Duration (1) 6 foundation courses, fully residential weekends. (2) 2 week residential course. *Fees* Apply to organisers. Comments Students must submit a 2,000 essay after each weekend, and a dissertation of 6,000 to enter the Advanced course. On passing three examinations, students are given the Certificate of Colour Therapy. On receipt of 12 case studies, the college will endorse certificate, and students are eligible to apply to me mebers of British Register of Complementary Medical Practitioners.

Living Colour *Title of Training* Training Diploma Course. *Duration* Twenty weekends over two years. *Entry requirements* Completion of Foundation Colour Courses. *Fees* £2000 incl. VAT for the whole course. Bursaries available. Comments The course is stepped so that you can graduate from colour awareness to being a colour counsellor.

Feldenkrais Method

In the Feldenkrais method gentle sequences of movement are taught so that students can learn how to reorganise patterns of action.

Moshe Feldenkrais was a Russian born Jew who escaped to England in 1940 from Nazi occupied France where he was working as an atomic physicist. When a knee injury prevented him from playing football he started to explore the dynamics of movement in the human body.

As with the Alexander technique much of the work involves letting go of ways of moving and holding the body which are habitual and restrictive. The process of re-learning freer movement is facilitated by slow exercises which should involve no strain or pain at all. They resemble the ways in which babies and young children learn to move. To release the 'pupil' from the pressure of gravity which puts added strain on the body, the lessons are at first carried out lying on the floor. By becoming more relaxed and more aware of how the individual body moves, the pupil has more freedom to choose a range of movements.

The Feldenkrais method is taught in two ways. 'awareness through movement' is taught in classes with a teacher verbally leading the class through a lesson. 'Functional integration' is a term used for an individual session where the teacher will guide the pupil's body through touch and gentle manipulation. These individual sessions are especially useful for those with disabilities or painful injuries.

The benefits of the method are not confined to the body. Feldenkrais felt that physical movement and posture can have a profound effect on the mind and emotions. The body not only reflects mental and emotional states but can also in turn affect them. Feldenkrais felt that by changing negative physical patterns the state of mind that produced them could be changed too.

Anyone can benefit from the Feldenkrais method. It has been used with those who have disabilities, including stroke patients and children with cerebral palsy and stiffness or injuries. The gentleness of the method makes it particularly suitable in such cases. People whose professions involve skillful, expressive movement such as dancers, singers, actors and athletes can also benefit.

CENTRES OFFERING THE FELDENKRAIS METHOD
Bodywise E2, Feldenkrais Method NW3, Feldenkrais Method EC1, Open Centre EC1, Playspace NW1, South London Natural Health Centre SW4.

TRAININGS IN THE FELDENKRAIS METHOD
Feldenkrais Method *Title of Training* Professional Training Programme. *Duration* Four years part-time. *Entry requirements* None specified. *Fees* £2,000 per eight weeks full-time per year. *Comments* Training in segments of 3-5 weeks.

Floatation Tank Therapy

A floatation tank is a bath or pool containing a concentrated saline solution of about a foot's depth, enclosed in a sound proof and light proof capsule or cubicle. The water is maintained at body temperature, and supports the body because the high concentration of Epsom salts makes the water extremly buoyant, and prevents the crinkling of the skin normally caused by prolonged immersion in water.

Floating in such an environment, where stimulation of the senses is reduced to a minimum, promotes relaxation. Some studies have shown that floating can lower blood pressure and reduce levels of stress-related biochemicals in the body. It can also help to alleviate pain, because it stimulates production by the body of endorphins - hormones which act to reduce pain.

Before floating it is necessary to wash or shower the whole body and shampoo the hair, so that body oils are not deposited in the pool. Vaseline should be applied to any wounds or scratches because the saline solution can sting on contact with breaks in the skin, although it is perfectly safe and can even promote healing. Floaters are also instructed not to touch their eyes during floating, because the water will sting these also, though once again it will not harm them. Once floating in the water on his or her back, the floater should be able to choose whether to be in total darkness, or whether to have a low level of light for reassurance. Those who suffer from claustraphobia are usually able to keep the door of the tank ajar, and the floater is able to leave the tank at any time, simply by opening the door. During the float, many floaters report feeling able to let go of tensions and anxiety, a sense of relaxation and peacefulness, and the sensation of being cosy. After the float it is common for this sense of relaxation to endure. Floats can last from fifty minutes to two hours.

One benefit of floating is that while other relaxation methods require effort to relax, floating is passive and may be an easier way to relax for those who find other methods such as meditation or biofeedback more difficult.

Floating is can also be used as an aid to learning. Audio or visual tapes can be played to the floater while in the tank, and this can accelerate learning. Some people choose to listen to subliminal tapes to bring about therapeutic change.

CENTRES OFFERING FLOATATION TANK THERAPY
Float Centre NW8, Float Experience SW11, Ki Kai Shiatsu Centre N17, Resonance SW17, South London Natural Health Centre SW4.

66 I found floating very disappointing. It's supposed to take you to a different mental plane, but I felt totally bound to the physical plane. When the music was switched off, I felt very lonely and isolated. Then I got bored so I splashed around from side to side of the tank. My neck got quite sore, but you're told beforehand that this may happen and told to cradle your neck with your joined hands. I think enjoyment of a float is very mood-dependent, and I was told it does get better on subsequent sessions. However, I did feel very relaxed and calm *afterwards.*99
Karin Grey

DEPRESSED, RUN DOWN, HAD ENOUGH?
THEN TRY FLOATING

Floating is essential for those living a hectic lifestyle. In between a competitive job, working at a good relationship, raising children and just trying to keep up, there is little or no time left over for ourselves. Unless we take time for ourselves, and reflect, regenerate, and rejuvenate, day to day events become too much and our bodies flood the blood stream with stress-causing chemicals. These make us tense, depressed, anxious, irritable, sometimes unable to sleep and more than often finds us turning to alcohol and drugs to try to alleviate those symptoms. These factors lead to a lowering of productivity, and an inability to concentrate, with a general feeling of being tired, apathetic and fighting against the tide, just not able to give our best.

Floating doesn't change your life style for you; but it can certainly lower those chemicals that cause stress, help you work harder and with more enthusiasm, put a kick back in your step and make life a far more enjoyable experience. So begin this "New Age - The 90's" in a calm, controlled, stress-free state of mind.

LIFE WAS NEVER MEANT TO BE A STRUGGLE, AND NOW IT DOESN'T HAVE TO BE.

FOR MORE DETAILS ON HOW AND WHERE TO FLOAT CONTACT:
THE FLOAT CENTRE
20 BLENHEIM TERRACE
ST JOHNS WOOD,
LONDON NW8. 071-328-7276

BODY THERAPIES

❝ I had my first float at a time when my work was very stressful an intensive. I really believed that nothing, but nothing could make me relax. But even before I got into the tank, the whole feeling of being in a cosy, warm environment and being really looked after by the people running the tank set me up with a sense of being nurtured and safe. When I first got into the tank I became aware of how tense I really was. I though 'It's no good, nothing's going to work, the only thing that's going to relax me is a month on a tropical beach'. But then - it must have been about half an hour into the float - I started to have this sensation of slipping, very gently and slowly, into what seemed like an ocean of calm.

When the music started to signal the end of the float, I didn't want to get out - it seemed like miles to the door of the floatroom, and like I was moving in slow motion. Apparently it took me half and hour to get ready and reappear - it seemed like five minutes to me! The effects lasted for several days afterwards. I felt really as if I'd been mentally 'cleaned out', much more awake and calm.**❞**

Anne Turner

LE PLAN

LE PLAN INTERNATIONAL HEALING SCHOOL
Two year professional training in 4 fortnights. Subjects include: Distant healing; Self healing; Earth healing; Anatomy and Physiology; Myths & Symbols; Use of ritual; Lucid dreams for Healing; Death & Dying; Body language; Group dynamics; Chakras; Meditation.

LE PLAN SEMINARS
Fortnightly courses by well-known leaders on New Age Teachings such as healing, earth energies, Transpersonal psychology etc.

Prospectus of Healing School or brochure of seminars, please write to Lorna St Aubyn, 10 Irene Road, London SW6 4AL.

THE ULTIMATE IN FLOATATION ENVIRONMENTS
Float effortlessly into the deepest states of relaxation
Stimulate your creativity and your learning
and meditative potentials
De-stress profoundly

Member of the Floatation Tanks Association of U.K.
The Ocean Floatroom may be purchased for private or
business use call 071 720 9506
For individual Float sessions call 071 720 8817

124

Healing

Though the technique of the 'laying on of hands' is in practice the same for many healers who see themselves as mediums for a healing force, there is often a great difference in the way they see their role in this process, and experience the force or energy itself.

This kind of healing has a long history in the Christian tradition and some spiritual healers believe that it is the power of God working through them which brings about a cure. Another kind of spiritual healer would best be described as a spiritualist healer, and believes that this power is mediated by a spirit guide or guides. Some healers are secular in their approach and do not regard their power as divine in origin, but more as a natural manifestation of their own, or universal psychic energies. However individual healers may see it, healing is usually seen as involving the transmission of energy in some form from the healer to his or her client.

A session with a healer may or may not involve them physically laying hands on you. Some work off the body, and all follow their intuition in treating each individual patient. Subjects report feeling heat or cold under the healer's hand, or pins and needles, or tingling sensations, but everyone's reactions will be different. Some people feel better immediately, others may need repeated treatments. Sessions will probably last about 30 minutes. Some spiritual healers offer 'absent healing' where healing thoughts are 'sent' to the person wishing to be healed, without any physical contact being made. Some healers have extended their work and use guided imagery and visualisation, counselling and a variety of other techniques.

Reputable healers stress that there are few 'miracle cures', and much depends for a permanent improvement of the condition on the patient's attitude and efforts to get well.

Although some healers are ambivalent about charging for their work, particularly if they feel that their ability to heal is a gift, and as such something which in turn needs to be given to others, they have to eat and pay overheads like anyone else. Some may ask for a donation rather than a fixed fee, which can be a little confusing to the client, but does offer him or her the opportunity to make their own evaluation of the treatment. Healers are now allowed to visit patients in some hospitals, at patients' request, especially those who are gravely ill.

READING

The Seven Levels of Healing *by Lilla Bek and Philippa Pullar, Rider £5.99.* The two authors describe how healing capacities can be trained and developed by applying an understanding of the seven levels of energy to the process of healing, by training and forms of self-discipline including meditation, visualisation an relaxation. **Peace, Love and Healing** *by Bernie Siegel, Rider £6.99.* This new book by the author of Love, Medicine and Miracles teaches how to be receptive to the messages the mind gives the body through dreams and symbols. Supported by inspiring stores of patients who have achieved remissions and miraculous cures, Dr. Siegel shows how love, hope, joy and peace of mind have strong physiological effects just as powerful as those of depression and despair.

CENTRES OFFERING HEALING

Aetherius Society SW6, Awakenings W9, Better Health Centre NW3, Chalice Foundation NW1, College of Psychic Studies SW7, Confederation of Healing Organisations, Hampstead Healing Centre NW3, Harry Edwards Spiritual Healing Sanctuary, Healing Centre NW6, Healing Workshops, Hypnocare W9, Isis Centre for Holistic Health N17, Lifeworks NW5, National Federation of Spiritual Healers (Middlesex), Natureworks W1, Neal's Yard Therapy Rooms WC2, Primrose Healing Centre NW1, Raphael Clinic NW6, School of T'ai-chi Ch'uan - Centre for Healing WC1, School of the Dancing Dragon, Shirley Goldstein Holistic Therapies NW1, South Camden Women's Centre WC1, Spiritualist Association of Great Britain SW1, St James Centre for Health and Healing W1, White Eagle Lodge W8, Women's Natural Health Centre NW5.

TRAININGS IN HEALING

Le Plan Seminars/International Healing School *Title of Training* Healing Training. *Duration* Four two week residential courses in France *Entry requirements* Application plus personal interview. *Fees* £525 for each of the four parts of the course. *Comments* Course covers a wide variety of subjects, including chakras, auras, counselling, guided imagery, crystals, colour healing, use of ritual, meditation and professional and personal issues involved in healing.

National Federation of Spiritual Healers: *Details* Apply to organisers.

School of the Dancing Dragon *Title of Training* Healer Training Course *Duration* One weekend a month over a year. *Entry requirements* None. *Fees* £450 approximately.

Herbalism

The use of herbal remedies to cure disease must be one of the oldest and most widespread of medical arts, and formed the basis of much of modern pharmacology. But while modern drugs which derive from plants are made by separating out the 'active' ingredient and concentrating it, herbal remedies use the whole plant. Supporters of herbal medicine say that the natural chemical balance present in the entire plant means that its effects on the body are in turn more balanced, and so the side effects caused by many modern drugs are avoided.

A herbalist may follow the western tradition and use herbs from this country and Europe, or he or she may be a Chinese herbalist and use traditional Chinese herbs.

A herbalist is not usually medically trained, though they should have undergone a training course lasting a few years. As with homoeopathy, the herbalist will take a detailed medical history and perhaps focus particularly on your diet to see whether you may be suffering from any allergies. However, unlike homoeopathic treatment, the remedies are usually prescribed for a particular complaint, rather than through building up a picture of your personality and symptoms.

Herbs are prescribed in different forms. They can be taken as an infusion, and prepared in a similar way to tea. Sometimes they need to be boiled for quite a long time. Some herbs are prescribed in tinctures, where they are suspended in alcohol, and they can also be prepared as lotions, tablets, liquids, poultices and suppositories. Often a combination of different herbs is prescribed, so that if one herb does not effect a cure, another might.

Many people take herbal remedies as a method of self-help. If you do, you can go to a specialist herbal shop (see below in the 'Resources' section) to ask advice, though it is possible to find out which herbs work for you by trial and error. Treating yourself involves infusing the plants as tea, and of course pre-prepared herbal remedies for such things as insomnia, stress and menstrual pain are available at chemist shops. One word of warning - some herbs can be toxic, especially if taken in large quantities, so if experimenting with a new herb, it is best to take advice.

READING

The Holistic Herbal *by David Hoffmann, Element £8.95.* Illustrated with original line drawings and photographs, this book places herbs in the context of Gaia, the living earth, and offers a practical, comprehensive look at the use of herbs. It includes a detailed look at the systems of the body; circulation, respiration, digestion and nervous systems. There are sections on herb gathering, preparation and herbal chemistry. As well as being a complete traditional herbal, this is a fascinating practical guide for maintaining a healthy body and soul. **Complete Herbal Handbook for the Dog and Cat** *Juliette de Bairâcli Levy, Faber & Faber £4.95.* One of a series of herbals by this author covering herbal treatment for different types of patient. Cats and dogs respond well to natural medicine and this book, divided into three parts, concentrates first on the care and rearing of young animals, secondly on the use of herbs to cure disease. The third part is a general section focusing on disease prevention.

CENTRES OFFERING HERBALISM

National Institute of Medical Herbalists (Register), Acumedic Centre NW1, Acupuncture Clinic E17, African Herbs Ltd Houslow East, Anerley Natural Health Clinic SE20, Brackenbury Natural Health Centre W6, C.H.I Clinic SW6, Chinese Clinic W1, City Health Centre EC1, Clinic of Herbal Medicine SW12, Clinics Health International SW6, Clissold Park Natural Health Centre N16, East-West Clinic of Natural Healing Middlesex, Edgware Centre for Natural Health Edgware, European Shiatsu School NW3, European Shiatsu School W5, European Shiatsu School W8, Fook Sang Acupuncture and Chinese Herbal Practitioners Training College UK NW11, General Council and Register of Consultant Herbalists, Haelen Centre N8, Hale Clinic W1, Herb Society SW1, Holistic Health Consultancy SW1, Marigold Treatment Centre Middlesex, Natural Healing Centre (Middlesex), Natural Medicine Centre (Bromley), Natureworks W1, Neal's Yard Therapy Rooms WC2, New Cross Natural Therapy Centre SE14, Nutribiotics Edgware, Primrose Healing Centre NW1, Private Polyclinic E7, Putney Natural Therapy Clinic SW15, Refuah Shelaymah Natural Health Centre N16, South Camden Women's Centre WC1, South London Natural Health Centre SW4, St James Centre for Health and Healing W1, Thames & Ganges Trading Co W1, Westminster Natural Health Centre SW1, Women's Natural Health Centre NW5, Wood Street Clinic Barnet.

TRAININGS IN HERBALISM
Fook Sang Acupuncture and Chinese Herbal Practitioners Training College UK *Title of Training* Acupuncture and Chinese Herbal Practitioners Training (including training in traditional diagnosis). *Duration* Three years. Weekend attendance. October start. *Entry requirements* Preferably degree level or vocational training. Minimum A level standard. Mature students must show enthusiasm and desire to learn. *Fees* Year 1 £950, year 2 £800, year 3 £700, payable in instalments. *Comments* Successful graduates eligible for membership of Acupuncture Practitioners Association and Hong Kong Chinese Acupuncture Association.
Herbs Hands Healing *Title of Training* (1) Natural Health Course (2) Master Herbalist (3) Doctorate in Herbal Medicine. *Duration* Residential weekends and fortnights plus home study. *Entry requirements* for (2), completion of (1).
London School of Herbology and Aromatherapy *Title of Training* Herbal Medicine/Medical Aromatherapy Diploma Course. *Duration* 3 years part-time (500 hours). *Entry Requirements* None: students are trained in all aspects of required knowledge. *Fees* £1,000 per annum. Comments Training in both Chinese traditional approach, and western medical approach. Course includes clinical practice.
School of Herbal Medicine *Title of Training* (1) One year course in herbal medicine (2) Four year tutorial course in herbal medicine (3) Full time course in herbal medicine (4) Specially structured course. *Duration* (1) 1 year (correspondence) (2) 4 years part-time (3) 4 years, 3 days a week. (4) 1 year (correspondence) *Entry requirements* (1) None (2) Intending students should have good educational background, with qualifications in relevant subjects including English language, chemistry and biology 'O' levels. Preliminary courses available for those with insufficient qualifications. (3) 2 'O' levels, preferably 2 'A' levels, or equivalents, in biological sciences and chemistry. (4) Course for professionals such as GPs and Osteopaths. *Fees* Vary - apply to organisers.

Homoeopathy

Homoeopathy is a system of medicine which is based on the idea that an illness which produces certain symptoms can be cured by a substance or drug which produces the same symptoms.

Homoeopathic remedies are substances which have been diluted sometimes up to tens of thousands of times. In their undiluted form they would produce similar symptoms to those for which they are prescribed. While conventional medicine treats with drugs which produce contrary, suppressive effects (for instance aspirin to suppress a temperature), homoeopathy follows the treatment of like by like. A simple parallel can be drawn to illustrate this contrast: if one had cold feet, one could either plunge them into hot water which would alleviate the feeling of cold for a while, or put them in cold water which might make them feel colder at first, but would then stimulate the circulation so that the body would be working to heat itself up. In the same way, the homoeopathic remedy, by aggravating the symptoms very minutely, stimulates the body's own defences or 'vital force'. The concept is also similar to that of innoculation.

Critics of homoeopathy claim that the substances are so highly diluted (sometimes as if one were putting one drop of a liquid into the Baltic sea) that the original cannot be found in the remedy. Supporters claim that even highly diluted remedies still contain the energy of the substance, though they cannot be detected by existing chemical methods.

The founder of this system was Samuel Hahnemann, a German doctor who practised in the early 19th century. He tested hundreds of drugs on healthy volunteers or 'provers' as he called them (some of whom must have been dedicated since many of the substances produced unpleasant symptoms) and catalogued the effects they had. Since many of the drugs were poisons, when Hahnemann prescribed them for his patients he tried diluting them as much as possible, and through this he discovered that in fact the more he diluted them, the stronger they became in their curative effects.

Diagnosis in homoeopathy has to be made very carefully and precisely to find the right remedy not only for the disease, but also for the individual patient. On visiting a homoeopathic doctor, he or she will take a detailed history, not just about your complaint, but also about the sort of person you are, your likes and dislikes and your physical and emotional temperament. He or she will take important events in your life into consideration and your family's medical history. For this reason the initial consultation is usually the longest.

When the remedy has been prescribed the homoeopath will tell you when and how to take it. The remedies have to be stored and taken carefully to preserve their properties. Since conventional drugs work in a way which is directly contrary to the way in which homoeopathic remedies take effect, you may decide to stop taking ordinary medicines, although it is worth discussing this with your homoeopath if this will be difficult. Some homoeopaths also recommend that you do not drink coffee, eat sweets or consume peppermint around the time you take the remedy, but this varies with the practitioner. Homoeopathic remedies can be used to treat most reversible illnesses. On the whole they are not suitable for diseases requiring surgery, though dedicated homoeopaths would probably disagree. Useful to have around the house is the 'homoeopathic first aid kit' since all the remedies are safe enough to be self-administered. Homoeopathy has even be used with success on animals.

READING

Everybody's Guide to Homoeopathic Medicines *by Stephen Cummings and Dana Ullman Gollancz £4.95.* The authors explain in clear terms how to treat yourself and your family with safe and effective remedies. Learn about 'casetaking' and how to prescribe for ailments such as colds, digestive problems, headaches and cystitis. Remedies for first aid use are also described as well as instructions for when it is necessary to seek outside help. The book begins with a brief outline of the fundamental ideas behind homoeopathy. **The Science of Homoeopathy** *by George Vithoulkas Thorsons £7.99.* Written by one of the world's leading homoeopaths, this work outlines both theory and practice of homoeopathy. The clear, concise language, inclusion of case histories, references and illustrations make it an excellent reference work for physicians and an informative introduction for the lay reader.

CENTRES OFFERING HOMOEOPATHY

British Homoeopathic Association (register), Homoeopathic Trust (register of GPs), UK Homoeopathic Medical Association (register), Acumedic Centre NW1, Acupuncture Clinic E17, Aetherius Society SW6, Anerley Natural Health Clinic SE20, Barbican Natural Health Centre EC1, Bennet and Luck Natural Health Centre N1, Better Health Centre NW3, Bexleyheath Natural Health Clinic (Kent), Body-Mind Health Private Clinic N8, Bodywise E2, Brackenbury Natural Health Centre W6, Camden Osteopathic and Natural Health Practice NW5, City Health Centre EC1, Clapham Common Clinic SW4, Clinic of Alternative Therapies E18, Clissold Park Natural Health Centre N16, Ealing Holistic Centre for Homoeopath and Autogenic Training W13, European Shiatsu School NW3, European Shiatsu School W8, Faculty of Homoeopathy WC1, Fulham Clinic SW6, Haelen Centre N8, Hahnemann College of Homoeopathy E13, Hale Clinic W1, Hampton Holistic Centre for Homoeopathy and Autogenic Training (Middlesex), Hillside Practice NW5, Holistic Health Consultancy SW1, Homoeopathic Development Foundation Ltd W1, Homoeopathic Health Centre E13, Homoeopathic Health Clinic Kenton, Insight Care Complementary Health Clinic N1, Lavender Hill Homoeopathic Centre SW11, Lewisham Homoeopathic Clinic SE13, Lifeworks NW5, Living Centre SW20, London College

BODY THERAPIES

of Classical Homoeopathy SE1, Melissa Morant Centre NW3, Natural Healing Centre (Middlesex), Natural Healing Centre E7, Natural Health Clinic Harrow, Natural Medicine Centre (Bromley), Natureworks W1, Neal's Yard Therapy Rooms WC2, New Cross Natural Therapy Centre SE14, Nutribiotics (Edgware), Primrose Healing Centre NW1, Private Health Centre E7, Private Polyclinic E7, Putney Natural Therapy Clinic SW15, Royal London Homoeopathic Hospital WC1, Sayer Clinic W1, Society of Students of Holistic Health (courses held in London), South Camden Women's Centre WC1, South London Natural Health Centre SW4, Spectrum N4, St James Centre for Health and Healing W1, Sunra SW12, Teleos Clinic W1, Therapy Made Unique, W4, W8, WC2, West London School of Therapeutic Massage and Reflexology W11, Westminster Natural Health Centre SW1, Wimbledon Clinic of Natural Medicine SW19, Wood Street Clinic Barnet.

TRAININGS IN HOMOEOPATHY

College of Homoeopathy *Title of Training* Professional Course in Homoeopathy. *Duration* Part-time course: one weekend per month over min 4 years. Full-time course: three days per week over min 3 years. *Entry requirements* Education to 'A' level standard and above. (Specific subjects not required). Students should usually be over 21 years. Mature students without 'A' levels but with relevant experience considered. *Fees* Part time: £800 + VAT p.a. Full-time: £2,400 + VAT p.a.

Faculty of Homoeopathy *Title of Training* Postgraduate Training in Homoeopathy *Entry requirements* Applicants must be qualified MB or BS (Batchelor of Medicine or Surgery). *Comments* Refer to organisers for details

Hahnemann College of Homoeopathy *Title of Training* (1) Beginners course (2) Paramedics course (3) Postgraduate. *Duration* Generally courses are two weekends a month, but a combination of full time and part time study is possible. (1) 3 years, (2) 2 years, (3) 1 year. *Entry requirements* (1) Four GCE passes which must include one 'A' level in a science subject. (2) Must be qualified, registered

---

London School of Homœopathy
provides a four year, part time, professional training course, leading to a recognised qualification. The course comprises monthly weekend seminars, guided home study and supervised clinical training. Tuition is by experienced and qualified teachers and practitioners.

for prospectus contact: The Registrar (MBS)
23, Sarum Avenue, Melksham, Wilts.SN12 6BN or

❝I had developed a dry barking cough. The doctor gave me a ten day course of antibiotics, then, when that failed, he gave me a course of different treatment. There was no change so he sent me to the chest hospital where they examined my chest, said it was clear and sent me to a specialist. He X-rayed my head, noted my sinuses were blocked causing draining onto my throat, hence the cough. He suggested washing out my sinuses. No thanks! Well OK, 'we can dry them out' - by shining an infra-red beam into them four times a week. This was tedious and lengthy and gave some relief, but in the wet weather they filled up again. The doctor suggested a hot, dry climate. So I took a holiday in Greece and they healed completely.

When I got back to England they filled up even worse than before and the cough was unbearable. The doctor put me on a course of decongestants. This worked for a time, but as soon as the weather changed, the sinuses would fill up and the cough return. I suffered this for four years.

Eventually I went to a homoeopath, who gave me a single dose of pulsatilla. I developed a streaming cold which lasted eight days and several boxes of tissues. At the end my ears popped, my hearing improved and my cough vanished. **❞**

Gill Stow

paramedical practitioner with sufficient knowledge of anatomy, physiology and diagnosis. (3) Applicants must be qualified homoeopathic practitioners from abroad or from recognised institutes. *Fees* (1) £700 per year. (2) £1,400, for two years. (3) £700, including a non-refundable admission fee of £100. Examination £40.

London School of Homoeopathy *Title of Training* Refer to organisers for details of training.

Iridology

Iridology is a method of diagnosis in which the eyes, especially the iris, indicate the physical and psychological condition of the patient. Iridologists claim that the whole body is reflected in the eye, because this is where the entire nervous system comes to the surface.

Dr Bernard Jensen, in developing this technique, has mapped the iris and correlated different segments with parts of the body. If a segment has an unusual colour or markings, or is flecked, this is an indication that the corresponding part is not not functioning properly. As a diagnostic technique, Iridologists claim that not only past disorders can be recognised, but tendencies towards disease in the future can be spotted and remedied before developing. The eyes are also examined for their condition: bright or dull, coarse or fine.

Iridologists may employ a magnifying glass to examine the eyes, or take photographs and make slides from which a diagnosis can be made.

Iridology can be used as a diagnostic aid in conjunction with any other therapy.

READING

Iridology - Personality and Health Analysis through the Iris *by Dorothy Hall, Angus & Robertson £4.95.* Dorothy Hall, an experienced practitioner, introduces the way to use this diagnostic technique by detailing how to recognise the signs shown in the iris. Using this book you can attempt to find your own pattern of good health and well-being, a pattern as distinct as a fingerprint for each one of us. **The Science and Practice of Iridology** *by Bernard Jensen, Bernard Jensen £20.00.* The classic textbook for serious students of iridology. The colour photographs clearly illustrate the diagnostic techniques and the comprehensive text aids the development of skills in the student's powers of diagnosis. There is also a second volume of this work which is in even greater detail and costs approximately £80.

CENTRES OFFERING IRIDOLOGY
National Council and Register of Iridologists (register), British School of Iridology, City Health Centre EC1, Community Health Foundation EC1, European Shiatsu School SW5, Holistic Health Consultancy SW1, Insight Care Complementary Health Clinic N1, Institute of Holistic Therapies SW6, Neal's Yard Therapy Rooms WC2, Wholistic Health Centre Croydon.

TRAININGS IN IRIDOLOGY
British School of Iridology Apply to organisers for details.
College of Opthalmic Somatology *Title of Training* Diploma Course and Advanced Course in Opthalmic Somatology. *Duration* (1) Diploma: 1 year part-time. One day per month plus 15 hours home study per week. (2) Advanced Course: part-time. One seminar per quarter (3 years) plus research, thesis and 15 hours home study per week. *Entry requirements* Assessed on individual merit. *Fees* (1) Diploma: £1,200 payable in 3 instalments. (2) Advanced: £400 per year. Comments The course is aimed at homoeopaths and students of homoeopathy.

Kirlian Photography

This is high-frequency photography used to produce a photograph of the 'aura' of energy around the body, and from this some people believe that diagnosis of illness can be made, whether manifest or latent.

It was discovered by Semyon and Valentina Kirlian, from the Kuban in the Soviet Union. They found that photographs made using this technique would show differences in the energy field of healthy and diseased subjects.

A Kirlian photograph is usually taken using the two hands of the subject. A furry or hairy effect can be observed in the photographs, following the outline of the palm and fingers. This is believed to be the energy emitted from the hand. However, while in strictly controlled conditions Kirlian photography can be used to diagnose certain illnesses, in normal conditions the photograph can be affected by many extraneous factors such as the condition of the film, humidity of the air and so on. It is also not at all clear whether a Kirlian picture can accurately diagnose *potential* illness, as some enthusiasts claim.

CENTRES OFFERING KIRLIAN PHOTOGRAPHY
London Natural Health Clinic W8, Resonance SW17.

Massage

Massage is a way of working on the soft tissues, the muscles and skin, to relieve tension held in the body. There are many different massage techniques and individual practitioners may use or have been influenced by different body therapies like shiatsu, rolfing, physiotherapy or hand healing. Some masseurs (masculine) or masseuses (feminine) may rely very much on a technique, and others may use 'intuitive' massage. In 'intuitive' massage the practitioner is guided by the way the client's body feels to apply basic techniques where they are most needed - in areas where there is a build-up of tension.

A masseur/se might come to the home of the client if they are elderly or bedridden, but usually the client will visit them in their home or a health centre. Some work with the client lying on the floor but most will use a massage table. The room should be kept very warm or the cold will make the recipient of the massage tense up. The masseur/se will use oil to help their hands move smoothly over the skin and will use a variety of strokes, such as kneading, rubbing, pummelling, circling, or stroking using fingertips, thumbs or the whole hand. You may not realise how tense your muscles are until the masseur/se begins to touch them, because tension gives rise not only to feelings of pain or stiffness, but sometimes shows itself just in numbness.

Individual practitioners have different ideas on pain. A few feel that a certain amount of pain in necessary if the massage is to be effective in releasing tension. Most would feel that while working on areas which have become very tense can give

rise to a feeling of discomfort, they would be careful to keep this to a minimum. While a muscle may be sore to the touch, there is also a feeling of relief which usually overrides any discomfort. Individual clients have different tastes too; some prefer a vigorous massage while others may want something more soothing. The most important thing as a client is to feel that you can discuss this with the masseur/se and they will be responsive to your needs.

Having a massage is a pleasant experience. It is a way of being nurtured, it is relaxing and, in releasing energy which has become stored up in tension, it can also be invigorating. Massage is useful as part of a programme for combating stress.

Self-massage is also possible, although it is not as effective as being massaged by someone else. Relieving a friend's stiff neck can be a very satisfying way of giving and receiving physical contact - something which can be neglected. Most people can learn how to do the basic strokes and there are many weekend courses for beginners who want to learn to use massage on family and friends. The centres listed below may offer individual massage, courses for those who want to learn to give massage or both.

READING
The Massage Book *by George Downing, Penguin £5.99.* This well known simple manual of massage has been recently republished, a testament to its popularity. Massage is an art of healing and a powerful means of communicating without words. In order to convey the full range and effect of the art, the author outlines its wider philosophy and its links with oriental cults. Included are chapters on meditation, zone therapy and massage for lovers. **The Book of Massage** *by Lucinda Lidell, Ebury Press £7.95.* A classic guide to the relaxing and healing skills of the hands. It is beautifully illustrated with drawings and photographs and includes step-by-step instructions with authoritative advice on all aspects. This book teaches the effects of the power of human touch.

CENTRES OFFERING MASSAGE
All Healing Clinic NW5, Association for Systematic Kinesiology , Bennet and Luck Natural Health Centre N1, Bluestone Clinic NW1, Body Clinic NW11, Bodywise E2, Bodyworks Natural Therapies (client's home/ workplace), Brackenbury Natural Health Centre W6, Bretforton Hall W2, CAER (Centre For Alternative Education And Research) (Cornwall), Centre for Massage and Movement Studies SW2, Chalice Foundation NW1, Chiron W5,

The Centre for Massage and Movement Studies

THE EYERMAN TECHNIQUE

Massage with Movement

Workshops with Ken Eyerman

A blend of Shiatsu, Polarity Therapy, breathing techniques, energy awareness and Feldenkrais method. Certificate Courses starting in the Autumn in Central London.

For details of these and other courses send SAE to

Ken Eyerman
c/o Natureworks
16 Balderton Street, London W1
or ring 081-888 1735 or
Worthing (0903) 204893

MASSAGE

Churchill Centre W1, City Health Centre EC1, Clapham Common Clinic SW4, Clare Maxwell Hudson NW2, Community Health Foundation EC1, Edgware Centre for Natural Health Edgware, Food and Chemical Allergy Clinic Croydon, Fulham Clinic SW6, Gerda Boyesen Centre for Biodynamic Psychology and Psychotherapy W3, Haelen Centre N8, Hale Clinic W1, Hampstead Healing Centre NW3, Health Management NW3, Hendon Natural Health Clinic , Highbury Centre N5, Institute of Holistic Therapies SW6, Isis Centre for Holistic Health N17, Lifeworks NW5, Living Centre SW20, Maitri (Hants), Mehta Method of Therapeutic Head Massage , Meridians Clinic W1, Napier Chiropractic Clinic NW11, Natural Healing Centre E7, Natural Medicine Centre (Bromley), Nature Cure Clinic W1, Natureworks W1, Neal's Yard Therapy Rooms WC2, New Cross Natural Therapy Centre SE14, New Life Lodge N4, Open Centre EC1, Primrose Healing Centre NW1, Private Health Centre E7, Private Polyclinic E7, Putney Natural Therapy Clinic SW15, Raphael Clinic NW6, Resonance SW17, Sayer Clinic W1, W8, WC2, W4, School of the Dancing Dragon , Shirley Goldstein Holistic Therapies NW1, Sivananda Yoga Vedanta Centre W11, South London Natural Health Centre SW4, Sunra SW12, Wellspring Clinic SW6, West London Buddhist Centre W11, West London School of Therapeutic Massage and Reflexology W11, West London School of Therapeutic Massage and Reflexology W11, Westminster Natural Health Centre SW1, Wimbledon Clinic of Natural Medicine SW19, Women's Therapy Centre N7, Wood Street Clinic (Barnet).

TRAININGS IN MASSAGE
Centre for Massage and Movement Studies *Title of Training* The Eyerman technique training in massage. *Duration* 3-year diploma course. 6 weekends a year plus 6 practical days per year. *Entry requirements* None for first year of diploma course, but for 2nd and 3rd years must have completed first year. *Fees* £375 per year. *Comments* Eyerman technique is a synthesis of massage and movement utilising techniques from eastern and western massage forms. Also weekend workshops.

Churchill Centre *Title of Training* Advanced massage course. Churchill Centre Certificate in Health Care and Relaxation with Massage. *Duration* Basic training three weekends for ITEC certificate. Advanced course two weekends *Entry requirements* None specified *Fees* approximately £50 to £60 per weekend

Clare Maxwell Hudson *Title of Training* Introductory through to advanced techniques including basic massage, reflexology, shiatsu, sports massage, facials, etc. ITEC. *Duration* Vary. *Fees* Vary depending on length of course. Weekend £115 including VAT.

School of the Dancing Dragon *Title of Training* Basic Massage Course *Duration* Four weekends and four evenings. *Entry requirements* None. *Fees* £275 *Comments* Also introductory massage courses plus psychic development. Advanced massage training also.

Shirley Goldstein Holistic Therapies *Title of Training* Holistic Massage Diploma Course. *Duration* 3 weekends. *Fees* £195.

South London Natural Health Centre (Academy of Natural Health) *Title of Training* Holistic massage courses, from introductory to practitioner level, leading to ITEC and AMP qualifications. *Duration* For practitioner level, 5 weekends plus homework, case studies etc, or 12 evenings plus 2 weekends. *Entry requirements* Must do introductory weekend or evening. *Fees* £55-60 per weekend or £240 for 12 evenings.

Sunra *Duration* Five half days (20 hours). Refer to organisers for details.

West London School of Therapeutic Massage and Reflexology *Title of Training* Training in massage, anatomy and physiology, reflex zone therapy and sports therapy. ITEC. *Duration* Various. *Entry requirements* None specified *Fees* Apply to organisers.

Metamorphic Technique

Metamorphic technique was originally developed from foot reflexology by Robert St John, but evolved into a completely different therapy. Rather than positing that each area of the foot corresponds to a part of the body, metamorphic techique is based on the idea that the foot from toe to heel corresponds to the pre-natal period from conception to birth. This is also seen to correspond to the spine from base to head. By massaging the foot it is believed that physical and psychological traumas incurred in the womb can be healed. For it is in the nine months of gestation, according to the theory of metamorphic technique, that all our mental, physical, emotional and spiritual patterns and responses are set.

Each foot is massaged for about half an hour, generally starting at the toe and working on the arch of the foot, down to the heel. The practitioner may also work on the hands and the back of the head.

Though it was originally devised to help handicapped children, it is a gentle technique which can be used by anyone.

BODY THERAPIES

CENTRES OFFERING METAMORPHIC TECHNIQUE
Jeyrani Health Centre E18, Metamorphic Association (register), New Cross Natural Therapy Centre SE14.

Natural Birth Control

There are various methods of natural birth control, but they all work on the theory that the fertile period in a woman's menstrual cycle can be worked out, either on certain principals, or by observing signs and changes in the body. During this time, the couple can either abstain from penetrative sex or use barrier methods of birth control (e.g. condom or diaphragm with spermicide). Couples wanting to conceive can also use them to indicate when it's likely, and, according to some theories (still unproven) can try to determine the sex of their child by making love just before ovulation (for a girl) or just after ovulation (for a boy).

Natural birth control doesn't involve taking substances or putting devices into the body, nor does it have the side effects sometimes associated with orthodox methods of birth control. However, they do require a degree of commitment by both the woman and her partner if they are to be effective. Though perhaps somewhat time consuming, natural birth control methods may provide a woman with the opportunity to get to know her own body and natural cycles more, to share responsibility for contraception and for both partners to communicate more with each other about sex. A combination of methods outlined below should be used, and *it is very important to get an expert in natural birth control to teach you.* Contacts for this are listed at the end of this section.

In general with all these methods you are more likely to avoid conceiving if you have unprotected intercourse only in the time after ovulation (a woman's fertile time) up to the next period, than if you have unprotected sex in the time after a period up to ovulation. They are only suitable for those in a long-term, monogamous relationship since they offer no protection against AIDS and sexually transmitted diseases.

Mucus Method

This involves observing the changes in quality and quantity of the mucus in the vagina throughout the menstrual cycle.

During menstruation this mucus (called 'cervical mucus') can't be observed easily, so these are not necessarily safe days. After menstruation, there may be a couple of days of no mucus, and a sensation of dryness in the vagina (however, if yours is a short cycle, you may have mucus straight away). Then the mucus will start to become more profuse, starting off whitish or yellowish, thick and tacky and becoming clearer, more slippery and stringy like raw egg white (you can stretch a strand of it between two fingers). These changes start about five days before ovulation and on the most fertile days you may have a sensation of slippery wetness and lubrication. Unprotected intercourse should be avoided from the first time you

140

see or feel the mucus until four days after the slippery, wet sensation has gone. After this, the mucus will resume a whitish, yellowish, cloudy appearance and tacky consistency. A properly trained natural family planning teacher will enable you to learn the difference between these different kinds of mucus.

Basal Body Temperature

Just before ovulation, a woman's temperature drops slightly, and after ovulation it rises. By taking your temperature every day at the same time on waking with a basal fertility thermometer which can measure minute temperature changes, you can tell when you have ovulated. When you have recorded a temperature for three days in a row which is higher than all the previous six days the fertile time is over. Charts can be obtained from the Family Planning Association to note these temperature changes.

Because many things affect body temperature (even taking aspirin), expert help

is needed to interpret the chart. This method by itself does not predict which are the infertile days before ovulation.

Calendar method

This should only be used as a cross-check with the above two methods. Before using this, you need to keep a chart of your periods for at least 6 consecutive cycles. Work out the number of days in the shortest cycle and subtract 19 - this gives you the probable first fertile and therefore unsafe day after the first day of your period. Then work out the number of days in the longest cycle and subtract 10 - this gives the probable last day of the fertile time after which it is safer to have sex again. If your cycle changes you will need to alter your calculations.

Astrological birth control

This method cannot be recommended unless you are happy to get pregnant, since there is no proof at all that it works! The fertile time, according to this method is when the sun and moon are the same distance apart in degrees as they were when the woman was born. This happens once every twenty nine and a half day lunar cycle. It is calculated with an ephemeris (an astrological table of the planets' positions).

Centres offering Natural Birth Control

Natural Family Planning Teachers (register).

Naturopathy

Fundamental to the practice of naturopathy is the idea that if provided with favourable conditions, nature itself can heal the body. Illness is a result of toxins accumulating in the system and symptoms of disease are the attempts of the body to throw off these harmful waste products. We need only co-operate with this process to establish and maintain good health because nature itself is always striving for the good of the organism. While animals are in tune with this and will instinctively fast or eat foods which contain medicinal substances when they are ill, human beings, according to Naturopathy, have lost contact with this instinct for health.

Naturopaths use different methods to restore the body to a natural state. Fasting is an important way of clearing out the substances which cause disease, and maintaining a healthy, natural diet afterwards consolidates the benefits gained from fasting. Naturopaths often use osteopathy (q.v.) as well, and hydrotherapy which is treatment with water such as the taking of hot and cold baths or showers, taking spa waters and so on.

Naturopathy is essentially a self-help therapy. Though the naturopath can prescribe a regime which will suit the individual, it requires work on the part of the patient to stick to it. While fasting can have unpleasant side-effects at first, naturopaths stress that these are the results of the body throwing off harmful waste

BODY THERAPIES

and are part of the healing process. The fast may not be total, fruit juice or fruit may be recommended, and the naturopath will take into account your age and disposition when advising you of how to go about it. He or she may suggest ways to ease in and out of the fast so that the exercise is not too much of a shock to the system. Diets may be rigourous at first, but once the system becomes sensitive to what it really needs, healthy eating becomes more instinctive.

Naturopathy emphasises the importance of maintaining good health by eating well and exercising rather than taking action when symptoms develop and a cure is harder to achieve. Increasingly orthodox medicine is also now emphasising that prevention is better than cure.

READING
Natural Therapeutics *by Henry Lindlahr and Jocelyn Probyn* Volume 1 Philosophy of Natural Therapeutics *£12.00* Volume 2 Practice of Natural Therapeutics *£8.95*. Volume 3 Dietetics *£6.50* Volume 4 Iridiagnosis *£8.75*. These four volumes are concerned with laying down the general principles of natural therapeutics and go on to give guidance and directions on the application and combination of the methods which can be used to prevent disease, promote health and help to bring about cure.

CENTRES OFFERING NATUROPATHY
British Naturopathic and Osteopathic Association (register), General Council and Register of Osteopaths (register), Acupuncture Clinic E17, Barbican Natural Health Centre EC1, Bennet and Luck Natural Health Centre N1, Body Clinic NW11, Bodywise E2, Brackenbury Natural Health Centre W6, British College of Naturopathy and Osteopathy NW3, Camden Osteopathic and Natural Health Practice NW5, Edgware Centre for Natural Health Edgware, Forty Hill Natural Therapy Centre Enfield, Hale Clinic W1, Hocroft Clinic NW2, Holistic Health Consultancy SW1, Lifeworks NW5, Nature Cure Clinic W1, Natureworks W1, Neal's Yard Therapy Rooms WC2, Primrose Healing Centre NW1, Putney Natural Therapy Clinic SW15, South London Natural Health Centre SW4, Tibbi-Naturopathic Medical Foundation SW11, Westminster Natural Health Centre SW1.

TRAININGS IN NATUROPATHY
British College of Naturopathy and Osteopathy *Title of Training* Diploma Course in Osteopathy and Naturopathy *Duration* 4 years full time.

144

Entry requirements Two 'A' Levels (preferably including a biological science and chemistry) plus minimum 2 GCE/GCSE 'O' level passes (including at least 1 of English Language, Physics, Maths or Science or Biological Science BTech or equivalent). *Fees* Approximately £3,400 per annum for 1990/91 entry.

Osteopathy

Osteopathy uses manipulation of the spine and joints to restore the bones, muscles, ligaments and nerves to their proper alignment and thus the patient to health.

The founder of osteopathy, Dr Andrew Taylor Still, had studied engineering as well as medicine. In developing osteopathic techniques, he approached the human body as if it fitted together like a machine, and found that disease was caused by the spinal vertebrae slipping out of position. When this happens 'lesions' appear where the muscles round the displaced vertebrae are so stressed that they pass on inaccurate information to the central nervous system, or the nerves around them become over sensitive and affect the surrounding tissue. This then affects the circulation of the blood. Since the blood was seen by Still as carrying the substances which protect us from disease, illness is then the result of blocked circulation.

On a visit to an osteopath, he or she will take your medical history, and will also be looking at the way you walk, sit and stand to see where the vertebrae may be out of alignment. Examination is also carried out with the hands, and the osteopath will feel the bones and joints. Some may also use X-rays. Treatment itself is very active and physical and may involve you in taking a variety of positions while the osteopath pulls, pushes or applies pressure to your head, arms, legs or back in a number of ways. While this may sound alarming, the treatment is usually painless. A session may last 20-30 minutes and how long you have to keep going back for depends on the severity of the problem. However, since most osteopaths are inundated with patients, they are unlikely to need to prolong your treatment

unnecessarily for their own benefit! Sometimes the osteopath may give exercises to be done at home as a back up to the treatment sessions.

Osteopaths are rarely medically qualified, but should have undergone a thorough training of at least three years and be able to recognise medical conditions which lie outside their field of practice. Since osteopathy is one of the best organised therapies of the complementary medicines it is easy to get registers of qualified practitioners.

People usually go to osteopaths for 'bad backs'. and it is of course a good treatment for this ubiquitous complaint as well as for migraines and painful joints. The treatment was evolved to have a wide ranging application and can be helpful with other less obviously suitable complaints.

READING

Osteopathy - is it for you? *by Chris Belshaw, Element £5.95.* A simple worded guide to osteopathy for the patient which includes explanations of the technical terms. It explains how this manual therapy can influence the physiological mechanisms in the body that lead to healing and freedom from pain.

CENTRES OFFERING OSTEOPATHY

British Naturopathic and Osteopathic Association (register), General Council and Register of Osteopaths (register), Independent Register of Manipulative Therapists (register), Acupuncture and Osteopathy Clinic SW1, Acupuncture Clinic E17, Anerley Natural Health Clinic SE20, Barbican Natural Health Centre EC1, Bennet and Luck Natural Health Centre N1, Better Health Centre NW3, Bluestone Clinic NW1, Body Clinic NW11, Bodywise E2, Bodyworks Natural Therapies (client's home/workplace), Brackenbury Natural Health Centre W6, British and European Osteopathic Association (Middlesex), British College of Naturopathy and Osteopathy NW3, British Osteopathic Association NW1, Camden Osteopathic and Natural Health Practice NW5, City Health Centre EC1, Clapham Common Clinic SW4, Clissold Park Natural Health Centre N16, College of Osteopaths Education Trust (Surrey), Cranial Osteopathy and Structural Therapy NW3, Creative and Healing Arts W11, Edgware Centre for Natural Health Edgware, Equilibrium Therapy Centre SW18, European Shiatsu School W11, European Shiatsu School W8, Haelen Centre N8, Hale Clinic W1, Hocroft Clinic NW2, Isis Centre for Holistic Health N17, Jeyrani Health Centre E18, Lever Clinic W1, Lever Clinic Middx, Lifeworks NW5, Living Centre SW20, London College of Osteopathic

CRANIO-SACRAL THERAPY

Complete courses in an exceptionally gentle yet extremely powerful therapy

SUMMER COURSE	August 4th-8th 1990
TWO YEAR COURSE	Starting November 3rd/4th
WINTER COURSE	January 1991

For full details contact:
**Society for the Study of Holistic Health
160 Upper Fant Road, Maidstone, Kent
ME16 8DJ
Telephone (0622) 729231**

OSTEOPATHY

Medicine NW1, Mehta Method of Therapeutic Head Massage, Natural Healing Centre E7, Nature Cure Clinic W1, Natureworks W1, Neal's Yard Therapy Rooms WC2, New Cross Natural Therapy Centre SE14, Primrose Healing Centre NW1, Private Health Centre E7, Private Polyclinic E7, Putney Natural Therapy Clinic SW15, Refuah Shelaymah Natural Health Centre N16, Sayer Clinic W1, W8, WC2, W4, Society of Students of Holistic Health (courses held in London), South London Natural Health Centre SW4, St James Centre for Health and Healing W1, Sunra SW12, Wellspring Clinic SW6, Westminster Natural Health Centre SW1, Wholistic Health Centre Croydon, Wimbledon Clinic of Natural Medicine SW19, Women's Natural Health Centre NW5, Wood Street Clinic Barnet.

TRAININGS IN OSTEOPATHY

Andrew Still College of Osteopathy *Title of Training* Diploma in Osteopathy. *Duration* 5 years part time, weekends. *Entry requirements* Minimum of 5 GCEs, 2 of which should be 'A' levels, preferably in a science subject. For mature students with sufficient experience these may be waived. *Fees* £750 per year, 1989-90.

British College of Naturopathy and Osteopathy *Title of Training* Diploma Course in Osteopathy and Naturopathy *Duration* 4 years full time. *Entry requirements* Two 'A' Levels preferably (including a biological science and chemistry) plus minimum 2 GCE/GCSE 'O' level passes (including at least 1 of English Language, Physics, Maths or Science or Biological Science BTech or equivalent). *Fees* Approximately £3,400 per annum for 1990/91 entry.

British School of Osteopathy *Title of Training* BSc in Osteopathy *Duration* 4 years full-time. *Entry requirements* 2 science 'A' levels, preferably biology and chemistry. Will consider applicants without requirements, subject to interview. *Fees* For current academic year, first year fees £4,250. Since this is an academic course discretionary awards may be available from local authorities. *Comments* Write to the Registrar for further details.

College of Osteopaths Education Trust *Title of Training* Diploma in Osteopathy *Duration* 6 years part-time mostly weekends. *Entry requirements* 'A' Levels but for suitable applicants without these an Osteopathic Science Preparatory Course is available (six weekends). *Fees* Refer to organisers

London College of Osteopathic Medicine *Title of Training* Membership course MLCOM. *Duration* Thirteen months of 3 days per week. *Entry requirements* (1) Registered medical practitioner (2) 6 years at least post qualification (3) Must pass entry examination. *Fees* £2,000 for 13 months.

London School of Osteopathy *Title of Training* Diploma Course in Osteopathy *Duration* 5 years part-time (18 weekends per yr). *Entry requirements* 3 'A' levels in science subjects. *Fees* £1,750 payable by monthly bankers order. *Comments* Exceptions to the above entry requirements may be made in the case of mature students.

BODY THERAPIES

Polarity Therapy

In polarity therapy the body is seen as a made up of the universal energy which forms both the material and spiritual universe. It uses a variety of techniques including manipulation, stretching postures, and adjustment of diet to remove blocks in the flow of this energy through the body and to bring about the state of balance and health.

Randolph Stone, its originator, studied osteopathy, naturopathy and chiropractic and spent the last ten years of his life in India with his spiritual teacher.

He saw the body as having five energy centres which correspond to the elements of earth, water, fire, air and ether (ether is the fifth of five elements which according to Indian philosophical systems make up the universe). Specific exercises of 'polarity yoga' are prescribed to release and harmonise the energy of these centres, which may have become blocked through early emotional traumas, bad living habits or environmental influences. It is important that the energy is not only released, but also balanced between centres. The body's energies are seen as flowing in polarity between positive and negative poles. Good health is achieved when this flow reaches a point of equilibrium called 'neutral'.

Most of the work in polarity therapy is manipulation to balance the energies. This is sometimes done by the therapist by placing each hand on different parts of the body to facilitate the flow of energy between them. The body can be massaged in a clockwise or anti-clockwise direction or on the right or left side as is appropriate to the energy pattern of the recipient. Three types of pressure can be applied: positive, which makes the energy move, negative, which unblocks energy and can involve deep work on tissues, and neutral which is soothing. The therapist may also discuss the feelings which arise in the course of treatment, and any problems the client has.

The nutritional approach in polarity therapy usually begins with a cleansing programme. Natural, cleansing foods are eaten to purify and strengthen the body's own resources by expelling toxins from the system. Different foods are then reintroduced into the diet and monitored for the effects they have on the client's mental and physical well-being. Then a healthy eating programme is worked out for the individual client which will help to maintain this state of balance and health for life.

Polarity therapy requires some effort on the part of the client to change habits which are harmful, and for him or her to work on their own using the postures. Stone himself stressed that the achievement and maintenance of good health requires that we make this effort. It also asks for a positive attitude and willingness on the part of the client to change.

READING
The Polarity Process *by Franklyn Sills, Element £8.95.* This is a detailed explanation

of how the theory of 'universal energy' can be understood and applied. Based on Dr. Randolph Stone's work in facilitating the free flow of life's finer energies. Franklyn Sills also provides a study guide to Dr. Stone's original writings, offering a new clarity to the subject. **Your Healing Hands** *by Richard Gordon, Wingbow £9.95.* This introduction to Polarity Therapy is well written and clearly illustrated and provides a practical hands-on approach to the therapeutic touch and natural healing. The book reinforces the feeling more than the intellect for those who want to practise polarity.

CENTRES OFFERING POLARITY THERAPY
Polarity Therapy Association (register), Brackenbury Natural Health Centre W6, Highbury Centre N5, Jeyrani Health Centre E18, Maitri (Hants), Natural Healing Centre E7, Neal's Yard Therapy Rooms WC2, New Cross Natural Therapy Centre SE14, Primrose Healing Centre NW1, Refuah Shelaymah Natural Health Centre N16, Shirley Goldstein Holistic Therapies NW1.

TRAININGS IN POLARITY THERAPY
Polarity Therapy Education Trust: Apply to organisers for details.

Radionics

Radionics (in some cases known as radiesthesia or psionic medicine) is diagnosis and treatment which is carried out at a distance using particular instruments to aid the healer's own psychic faculties.

The principle involved is similar to dowsing, where a stick held by the dowser will twitch to show the hidden presence of water, oil or minerals underground, or can be used to find missing articles or persons. In radionics, a pendulum (a weight on the end of a lenght of thread) is often used. After getting the patient to fill in a detailed questionnaire, a 'witness' - a drop of blood on a piece of blotting paper or a lock of hair - is taken. This 'witness' is believed to act as a link between the practitioner and the patient. Diagnosis can then be carried out in a number of ways. The practitioner may ask questions about the patient's condition and the pendulum will indicate either a positive or negative answer depending on the way it swings. The pendulum may be used over diagrams of the body, to indicate which parts need treatment, and further questions will indicate how severely affected these parts are and what has caused them to malfunction. The pendulum may be used with special charts to show, on a scale of 0-100, how well or how feebly an organ is working. Practitioners vary in how much equipment they use; some prefer to use only a pendulum, while others may use boxes with dials, and an array of electronic equipment.

Once diagnosis has been made, a similar process is used to find the right treatment. Once again, different practitioners may use different methods, so that a wide range of treatments, and methods of 'transmitting' them to the patient may be used. Some will simply write and recommend that patients take a particular remedy or course of treament. Others may perform a kind of 'distant healing', by focussing on the patient and their particular complaint mentally.

Radiesthesia's beginnings were fraught with difficulty, largely because of the hostility of the medical establishment towards what they saw as 'quackery'. It was developed by a distinguished American neurologist, Dr Albert Abrahams. At the beginning of this century, Abrahams made a curious discovery while using the standard medical technique 'percussion' - tapping the body of a patient to determine the condition in the internal organs. He found that if the patient was facing west, the same sound would be given consistently by patients suffering the same disease, as long as they were tapped in the same area. Developing this, Abrahams then found that if a healthy person held a sample of blood from a diseased person, the sound given when he tapped them was characteristic of the disease suffered by the owner of the blood. Believing that the reaction was caused by electromagnetic force, he devised and marketed a box device to measure resistances from the patient's sample. However, results from 'the box' as it was called, were not always consistent, and it was even banned in some states in America. Ruth Drown, a Californian chiropractor in the 1930s developed her own kind of box and was prosecuted by the Food and Drug Adminstration. The pioneer of Radionics in the UK, George de la Warr narrowly escaped prosecution by someone who had bought his version of 'the box' .

The problem for exponents of radionics had been that they believed that the force involved was electromagnetic and could be measured under test conditions. In fact, results of such tests tended to be patchy except in one notable case. In 1924 a committee was set up to investigate a British version of the box, headed by Sir Thomas Horder. A Scottish homoeopath was asked to identify substances using the box, and to the surprise of the committee his results were almost completely correct.

Radionic theory is now less concerned with electromagnet energy exclusively, but sees all life forms as part of and affected by a common field of energy which includes, in its grossest form, electromagnetic energy. It is by influencing this field that the healing is performed.

Radionics can be used for any condition, mainly because it does not interfere with any other form of treatment. It is best perhaps with chronic, mysterious complaints which conventional medicine has failed to diagnose. It is also frequently used by those with terminal illness to ease pain and provide psychic support. It is also used in agriculture to increase crop yields, and animals respond well to radionic treatment.

READING

Spiritual Dowsing *by Sig Lonegren, Gothic Image £4.95.* This is a book for all who approach dowsing in a spirit of openness and sincerity. A new and dynamic

❝ In the mid 1970s, I spent six months with a totally blocked nose. I had just become interested in things alternative, but at first I tried various doctors' prescriptions, but it soon became obvious that nothing I did was making the slightest difference to my condition.

I then beat a path to the door of every type of complementary practitioner - homoeopath, acupuncturist, naturopath, iridologist and psychotherapist - that I could think of. Nothing seemed to shift the condition and I resigned myself to the fact that breathing was going to continue to bother me for the forseeable future.

Some months later, I was visiting a friend in Devon, who remarked on my bunged up condition and suggested I went to see an elderly pendulum diagnostician who lived close by. With some scepticism, I went to see the lady who sat me down and asked me to point my finger down a page where many types of alternative treatments were listed. When my finger pointed at the word 'osteopathy' the pendulum she was holding began to circle dramatically. She then turned to another page where a picture of the spine was portrayed and the same process took place. At the first vertebrae (the axis) the pendulum again took off and I was told to go and see an osteopath she recommended.

When I went, the osteopath cradled my head in her hands and gave it a sharp jerk. At that second, my nose cleared and the problem never recurred. **❞**

Malcolm Stern

approach which makes explicit the link between this ancient art and inner growth. The approach is extremely practical, guiding the beginner into both usage and philosophy, empowering the reader to take personal responsibility in his or her action in dowsing either the earth's energies or for healing. **Radionics and the Subtle Anatomy of Man** *by David Tansley C.W. Daniel £2.95.* David Tansley believes that the time is ripe for radionics to bear witness to an energy field of a more subtle nature and to this end wrote an examination of the wider influences of radionic energy with regard to the probability of underlying force fields which may affect the health of the physical form.

CENTRES OFFERING RADIONICS OR RADIESTHESIA
International Federation for Radionics, Keith Mason School of Radionics (Salisbury), Keys College of Radionics, Mill Hill Heath Care NW7, Natural Healing Centre (Middlesex), Wellspring Clinic SW6.

TRAINING IN RADIONICS
Keith Mason School of Radionics *Title of Training* Intensive course in Radionics for healthcare professionals. *Duration* 3 days. *Entry requirements* Short courses for professional practitioner. *Fees* On application. *Comments* Courses held in Salisbury.

Reflexology

This is a technique in which particular areas on the soles and sides of the feet are seen to correspond to the organs of the body. These are massaged to promote the health of the organs. Reflexology can also be used as a diagnostic tool.

Reflexology is an art the origins of which stretch back to ancient China. It was Dr William Fitzgerald, an Ear, Nose and Throat specialist interested in acupuncture who started using it in the West. His ideas were developed and exported to the United States by Eunice D Ingham whose book, Stories the Feet Can Tell, was published in 1932.

Treatment is carried out with the patient lying bare footed on a couch. The reflexologist will feel for tiny lumps under the surface of the skin which are believed to be crystalline deposits. The place on the foot where these are found indicates which organ is not functioning properly. For instance, the big toe corresponds to the top of the head and brain, and various parts of the heel to the bladder, sciatic nerve and sexual organs. The reflexologist will massage these spots which can be surprisingly sensitive when touched, so it is not uncommon to feel some pain. Most people feel the discomfort is worth it to achieve the therapeutic results, and at least the very sensitivity of the spot convinces patients that the reflexologist is really 'onto' something. Treatments continue until the spot is no longer sensitive. A session may last from 15 to 45 minutes and a course of treatment a few weeks.

READING

Reflexology Today by Doreen Bayly, Thorsons £3.99. A well loved introduction to the practice of reflexology which is one of the most pleasant of all holistic therapies. This book is valuable for student and layman alike and includes charts of the feet and the body zones. **Better Health with Foot Reflexology** by Dwight Byers, Ingham Publishing £10.95. This book combines the use of both hand and foot reflexology and is the most accurate and complete guide to the subject. It has become the standard reference for the International Institute of Reflexology and is extensively illustrated with methods of treatment as well as the organs of the body and other functions. **Holistic Reflexology** *by Avi Grinberg Thorsons £20.00.* An authoritative and detailed fully illustrated guide designed to meet the need for in depth treatment. Mainly for therapists and their students, including case histories and the understanding of holistic treatment of patients. New and highly recommended.

CENTRES OFFERING REFLEXOLOGY
Association of Reflexologists (register), British Reflexology Centre (register), All Healing Clinic NW5, Aromatherapy Training Centre SW16, Bennet and Luck Natural Health Centre N1, Better Health Centre NW3, Bodywise E2, Bodyworks Natural Therapies (client's home/workplace), Brackenbury Natural Health Centre W6, British School - Reflex Zone Therapy of the Feet (Ann Lett Ltd) (Wembley Park), British School of Reflexology (Essex), Churchill Centre W1, Community Health Foundation EC1, Falcons SW11, Food and Chemical Allergy Clinic Croydon, Forty Hill Natural Therapy Centre Enfield, Hampstead Healing Centre NW3, Hendon Natural Health Clinic, Institute of Holistic Therapies SW6, Jeyrani Health Centre E18, Lifecare, Lifeworks NW5, Living Centre SW20, Meridians Clinic W1, Mill Hill Health Care NW7, Natural Healing Centre E7, Natural Healing Centre (Middlesex), Natural Medicine Centre (Bromley), Natureworks W1, Neal's Yard Therapy Rooms WC2, New Cross Natural Therapy Centre SE14, Primrose Healing Centre NW1, Private Health Centre E7, Putney Natural Therapy Clinic SW15, Resonance SW17, Sayer Clinic W1, W8, WC2, W4, South London Natural Health Centre SW4, Sunra SW12, Therapy Made Unique, Wellspring Clinic SW6, West London School of Therapeutic Massage and Reflexology W11, Westminster Natural Health Centre SW1, Wimbledon Clinic of Natural Medicine SW19, Women's Natural Health Centre NW5, Wood Street Clinic (Barnet).

TRAININGS IN REFLEXOLOGY
Bayly School of Reflexology *Title of Training* Introductory and advanced courses in reflexology leading to certificate. *Duration* Attendance at two weekends, spaced a minimum of two months apart. Minimum of 2 months interval before examination can be taken. *Entry requirements* None. *Fees* Introductory course £74.75, advanced course £69, examination £34.40. *Comments* Regular courses held in central London and regional venues. School is official teaching body the British School of Reflexology.

66 After the first reflexology session I ever had, I walked away feeling more 'grounded' than I have ever felt - as if I understood that word for the first time. It was a reflexologist who correctly pinpointed the cause of a long-standing back complaint I had. So impressed was I, I later became a reflexologist myself! 99
Karin Grey

British School - Reflex Zone Therapy of the Feet (Ann Lett Ltd) *Title of Training* (1) Introductory and (2) Advanced Training in Reflex Zone Therapy of the Feet. (3) Midwives course (4) Reflex Zone Therapy of the Nervous System. *Duration* Courses are three days each. *Entry requirements* Applicants should have previous medical training, or training in nursing, physiotherapy, midwifery, acupuncture, osteopathy or naturopathy. *Fees* £125 per course.

British School of Reflexology *Title of Training* Reflexology training courses. *Duration* 8 months part-time. *Entry requirements* None at present, but shortly by questionnaire/interview. *Fees* £525

Churchill Centre *Title of Training* Basic and advanced trainings in Foot Reflexology. *Duration* Basic training two weekends or four days. Advanced training is two weekends. *Entry requirements* None specified. *Fees* approximately £50 to £60 per weekend.

Clare Maxwell Hudson *Title of Training* Introductory through to advanced techniques including basic massage, reflexology, shiatsu, sports massage, facials, etc. ITEC. *Duration* Vary. *Entry requirements Fees* Vary depending on length of course. Weekend £115 including VAT.

Crane School of Reflexology *Title of Training* Training in Reflexology. *Duration* Four weekends bi-monthly plus 100 hours home study. *Entry requirements* None. *Fees* £495 including VAT. *Comments* Venues around the country. Phone for details of London venue.

Reflexology Centre *Title of Training* Basic and advanced course in reflexology. *Duration* Weekend courses. Details on request.

West London School of Therapeutic Massage and Reflexology *Title of Training* Training in massage, anatomy and physiology, reflex zone therapy and sports therapy. ITEC. *Duration* Various. *Entry requirements* None specified. *Fees* Apply to organisers.

Rolfing

Rolfing is a technique evolved by Ida Rolf, which is also sometimes called structural integration. It seeks to realign the body by manipulation of the connective tissue.

A useful rule of thumb in looking at body alignment is that the body should show a symmetry between the right side and the left, looking face on. Looking side on, one should be able to draw a straight line from the bottom of the ear to the ankles which should pass through the middle of the shoulders and middle of the hips. If the body is not in alignment extra energy is needed to maintain equilibrium. For instance if the head is protruding forward (sticking one's neck out) then the muscles in the back of the neck must work at holding the head in position. Whereas if the head is sitting centrally, balanced directly over the spine, little energy is needed to hold it in place. Thus if one's body is out of alignment, one is using more energy when simply standing than if the body were not out of alignment.

154

The purpose of Hellerwork is to provide the individual with a sound foundation for good health by structurally realigning the body and freeing it from stored stress while at the same time offering an education in movement principles that will help maintain and improve this balance once achieved.

Each session combines three elements;

bodywork
verbal dialogue
& movement
education

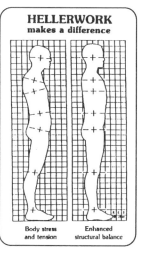

HELLERWORK
makes a difference

Body stress
and tension

Enhanced
structural balance

Hellerwork differs from other forms of bodywork in that it focuses on the individual's total growth and well-being. The goal is not only to produce physical results but to educate and empower clients to grow, change and continue the process of growth for themselves.

Hellerwork is an awareness training on how to have one's body be a source of energy and vitality and how to incorporate ease and joy of movement into one's daily life.

To book private session of Hellerwork, or for information about training, contact your nearest practitioner:-

Rose-Marie Amoroso
The Natural Healing Centre
165 Capel Road
London E7
Tel: 081-478 3942 (day)
081-539 3923 (eve)

Gordon Glass   *Also*   The Hale Clinic
7 Pagoda Avenue   7 Park Crescent
Richmond,   London W1
Surrey TW9   Tel: 071-631 0156
Tel: 081-948 0755   071-637 3377

Wendy Helyar
35 Devonport
Radnor Place, London W2
Tel: 071-402 8613

Jeannette Tuppen
Rocklands, Boreham Lane
Hailsham, East Sussex BN27
Tel: 0323-83 2633

David Dene
Vorderstadt 25
6370 Kitebuhel, Tirol, Austria
Tel: 010-43-5356 71582

Roger Golten
The Peak
Hyatt Carlton Tower
Cadogan Place
London SW1
Tel: 071-235 5411

Terry Petersen
Cutlers Squash and Gym Club
9 Devonshire Square
London EC2
Tel: 071-626 3161 (day)

BODY THERAPIES

The experience of being rolfed is like having a very deep and sometimes painful massage. The rolfer uses not only his or her hands but elbows too.

There are a standard ten sessions of one hour duration. Each session builds on the last one and works on a different part of the body. Some rolfers take before and after photos to keep a record of the changes that happen and let you have duplicates.

Fritz Perls the founder of gestalt therapy swore it helped him reduce the pain of angina. However, like the Alexander technique, it is not a treatment for any particular disorder, but a system aimed at prevention.

In this country, rolfing usually comes under the umbrella of 'structural bodywork' which includes other techniques such as structural integration.

READING

The Power of Balance *by Brian Fahey, Metamorphous Press £13.95.* Dr. Fahey is a fine worker in the interdisciplinary effort to enhance mutual co-operation between rolfing, medicine and chiropractic. This book reflects his comprehensive philosophy and provides dynamic information for all health professionals concerned

❝ My sixth to tenth rolfing session took place in winter, (1972 I think), in Toronto, Canada. Snow had just begun to fall as I reached the Rolfer's consulting room.

I had previously had five Rolfing sessions at Esalen in California and knew full well how painful it was. I had heard rumours that there was a groundswell within the Rolfing Institute to make an anaesthetic available to clients as many of them had complained how painful the process was, but that Ida Rolf had crushed the idea. So it was with apprehension that I now embarked on my sixth session. I am not able to recall whether that particular session was more or less painful than any of the others.

What I do remember is the difficulty I had in walking at the end of the session. The Rolfer had spent an hour working mostly on my legs and it's difficult to describe the sensation of trying to walk after having my legs pummelled for an hour. It was as if my legs were not my own. That old familiar feeling of my legs being securely anchored to the rest of my body had gone. Instead I found that I could only take a step forward by throwing out a leg in front of me and waiting for it to land, being surprised when it did so. I am convinced that I looked like one of those puppets on a string which each part of the body moving separately from any other part, and look totally unco-ordinated. I 'walked' around the room exclaiming to him about the peculiar sensation and wondering whether it was an improvement over my old way of walking.

I left in a confused state of mind wondering about the confused state of my body. By then the snow had reached about three foot deep and the task of making it home with my 'funny' legs was like climbing Mount Everest. I must have cut a pretty sight that day. ❞

Mike Considine

with improving their patients' level of well-being. **Rolfing** *by Ida Rolf, Healing Arts Press £15.15.* This is the classic text on Ida Rolf's therapy which attempts to align and balance the physical body within its gravitational field. Rolfing is a system of massage of the connective tissue which releases physical and emotional stress and leaves the patient with both physical and emotional well-being. **Rolfing** is intended for the interested but untrained lay-person as well as the professional in need of specific technical information. Well illustrated with both photographs and line drawings.

CENTRES OFFERING ROLFING
Institute of Structural Bodywork (register), Hakomi Institute W4 .

Shiatsu and Acupressure

Shiatsu is a massage technique which involves stimulating or relaxing the acupuncture points and meridians. The word shiatsu means 'finger pressure' in Japanese. It is like a form of acupuncture which does not use needles. The principle is the same: to release and balance the flow or ki (chi in Chinese) or life energy at points where it may have become blocked or over stimulated.

In Japan shiatsu is practised widely, often as a form of self help by one member of the family on another. The Chinese version is called acupressure, and in practice is virtually the same as shiatsu.

After the completion of the case history, diagnosis is usually carried out by palpation of the abdomen and observation of any abnormalities in the skin or muscles. Sometimes the practitioner may take the pulses, as in an acupuncture session (see section on acupuncture for an explanation of 'pulses'). In this way the practitioner decides which points and meridians need work to balance the energy flow. The massage itself is a mixture of general strokes over particular parts of the body to promote the harmonious flow of ki energy, and direct pressure on the acupuncture points with the fingertips or elbows. The intensity of the pressure also varies between gentle massage to a very strong pressure, but the recipient should not have to experience any more pain than is involved in the pleasurable release of tension. The practitioner may also use gentle manipulation to loosen joints and stretch the meridians, the energy pathways. A session may last from 45 minutes to an hour and a quarter.

Shiatsu helps to maintain health by toning up the body's energy, and can be used to treat a variety of complaints, such as tension, low vitality, pre-menstrual tension, lower back pains, stiffness in the neck and shoulders, digestion problems, asthma, headaches and insomnia. It can also help to promote greater emotional tranquillity. As will some other alternative therapies, there are contra-indications for some conditions.

If you know the right pressure points to use, you can practise shiatsu on yourself for first aid to relieve pain or cramps, and some people become so adept at this that they use it on trips to the dentist.

READING
Shiatzu *by Yukiko Irwin, Arkana/Penguin £7.99.* The line drawings and clear concise instructions in this book are intended to help anyone learn and use the shiatsu points to the best advantage. Aches and pains of everyday living can be relieved by this therapy at the hands of almost any sympathetic layman. **The Natural Healer's Acupressure Handbook** *by Michael Blate, Henry Holt £6.80.* This book illustrates how 'acupuncture without needles' can be used by the lay-practitioner as a alternative to aspirin and other commonly used drugs to alleviate pain and discomfort. Problems for which treatment is suggested include headaches, anxiety, nosebleeds, stagefright, cramps and exhaustion. Also included are first-aid treatments while awaiting medical attention. **Soft Tissue Manipulation** *by Leon Chaitow, Thorsons £19.95.* This is a practitioner's guide to the diagnosis and

The
EUROPEAN
SHIATSU
SCHOOL

treatment of soft tissue dysfunction and reflex activity. The book provides students with a working knowledge of the diagnostic and therapeutic use of neuro-muscular, muscle energy and strain-counterstrain techniques. It also covers systems involving reflex points and trigger points.

CENTRES OFFERING SHIATSU

Shiatsu Society (register), Acumedic Centre NW1, Acupuncture and Osteopathy Clinic SW1, Bennet and Luck Natural Health Centre N1, Bodywise E2, Bodyworks Natural Therapies (client's home/workplace), Brackenbury Natural Health Centre W6, British School of Oriental Therapy and Movement (Twickenham), British School of Shiatsu-Do EC1, City Health Centre EC1, Clare Maxwell Hudson NW2, Community Health Foundation EC1, Creative and Healing Arts W11, East-West Clinic of Natural Healing Middlesex, European Shiatsu School W11, European Shiatsu School NW3, European Shiatsu School SW5, European Shiatsu School W5, European Shiatsu School W8, Haelen Centre N8, Hillside Practice NW5, Institute of Holistic Therapies SW6, Ki Kai Shiatsu Centre N17, Living Centre SW20, Maitri (Hants), Melissa Morant Centre NW3, Natural Health Clinic Harrow, Natural Medicine Centre (Bromley), Natureworks W1, Neal's Yard Therapy Rooms WC2, Nine Needles Health Care Centre (Richmond), Primrose Healing Centre NW1, Putney Natural Therapy Clinic SW15, South London Natural Health Centre SW4, Sunra SW12, West London School of Therapeutic Massage and Reflexology W11, Westminster Natural Health Centre SW1, Wholistic Health Centre Croydon.

TRAININGS IN SHIATSU

British School of Oriental Therapy and Movement *Title of Training* (1) One Year Certificate Course in Shiatsu - Traditional Chinese Medicine and Ki-Development (Kitaiso). (2) Advanced Course in Shiatsu. *Duration* (1) One year consisting of 3 terms, 12 classes per term (Saturdays 2-6pm). *Entry requirements*

BODY THERAPIES

None specified. *Fees* Approximately £190 per term. *Comments* Study background, philosophy and aetiology of traditional Chinese medicine. Students must complete a number of ongoing treatments for practical assessment, and taught Kitaiso (a 'movement system') to facilitate student's own healing powers.

British School of Shiatsu-Do *Title of Training* (1) Beginners course in Shiatsu-Do. (2) Diploma Course in Shiatsu-Do. *Duration* (1) 99 Hours. Evening, weekend or daytime timetables. (2) Three years part-time. Evening, weekend or daytime timetables. *Entry requirements* Open to everyone. They have an equal opportunity policy covering gender, race, religion, sexual orientation. Limited access for disabled applicants. *Fees* (1) £348 + VAT (2) Refer to organisers. Instalments payable in advance. *Comments* Diploma course includes oriental diagnosis, philosophy, exercise, counselling, anatomy and physiology. Students may study a beginners course for self study/development or complete the course to practitioner level.

Clare Maxwell Hudson *Title of Training* Introductory through to advanced techniques including basic massage, reflexology, shiatsu, sports massage, facials, etc. ITEC. *Duration* Vary. *Entry requirements Fees* Vary depending on length of course. Weekend £115 including VAT. *Title of Training* Introductory through to advanced techniques including basic massage, reflexology, shiatsu, sports massage, facials, etc. ITEC. Duration Vary. *Entry requirements Fees* Vary depending on length of course. Weekend £115 including VAT.

European Shiatsu School *Title of Training* (1) Shiatsu Foundation Course (2) Shiatsu Practitioner Diploma Course *Duration* (1) Four weekends, one weekend in every three. (2) Three years part time, average one weekend in every three. *Entry requirements* No entry requirements for the Foundation course. Practitioner Diploma courses requires completion of Foundation course. *Fees* (1) £189 (2) Year 1 £483 Year 2 £728 Year 3 £728. *Comments* Branches in London, Bath, Brighton, Reading, Wiltshire, Portugal and Spain. Most of the teaching staff have paramedical qualifications, mainly chartered physiotherapists.

Healing Shiatsu Education Centre *Title of Training* Professional training course in healing-shiatsu. *Duration* 3 years part-time. Choice of format: either weekends or series of 5-day residential workshops. *Entry requirements* None, but must have done one introductory weekend. *Fees* £165 plus 15% VAT per term (3 terms per year) all inclusive of residential courses. *Comments* The training can also be undertaken purely as a form of personal development and self-healing.

Ki Kai Shiatsu Centre *Title of Training* 3 year Diploma Course in Shiatsu and Oriental Medicine. *Duration* 24 weekends spread over two and a half years. *Entry requirements* None *Fees* £405 per annum, payable by 3 post-dated cheques at commencement of course. *Comments* Also one year course (9 weekends) £405.

Nine Needles Health Care Centre *Title of Training* (1) I year evening course in Shiatsu (2) 3 year course in Oriental Medicine including acupuncture, shiatsu, moxibustion, etc. *Fees* (1) £1,410 or £1,100 on lump payment. (2) First and third years as above, second year £2,800 or £2,500 on lump payment.

Shiatsu College *Title of Training* Shiatsu training to professional standard, beginners classes and post graduate workshops. *Duration* 3 years, 12 weekends per year or 2 years, 2 days a week. *Entry requirements* Application forms considered individually. *Fees* 3 year course: £900 per annum in advance.

Tai Chi Chuan

Though tai chi is often bracketed with the martial arts, it is more akin to moving meditation. In tai chi slow, flowing movements which follow a set pattern enable practitioners to harmonise mind, body and spirit and become more deeply centred in themselves. Its applications can be as form of healing, for self-defence and as a spiritual discipline.

Legend has it that tai chi was originated by Chang Sanfeng, a thirteenth century Chinese Taoist monk, who adapted an earlier martial art form used by the monks for protection. The story goes that observing the movements animals make, Chang Sanfeng saw that they comprised of circular movements which he then formalised into a set of postures. These were then joined together and became the ritualised, dance-like movements or 'forms' of tai chi. The practice of tai chi lies within a whole spiritual and philosophical tradition which is largely Taoist, but which also incorporates some aspects of Buddhism.

The emphasis in performing the movements is not on strength or exertion, but on relaxation, concentration and balance. The knees are kept bent and movement is achieved by shifting the greater part of the body's weight slowly from one foot to the other while the hands make careful and gentle pushing and circling gestures. Attention is also paid to correct breathing. Physically the aim is to develop muscle control, fluidity and grace. After mastering the techniques and much practice, the practitioner should become one with the movements to the extent that they are no

BODY THERAPIES

longer exercising deliberate control, but letting the movements happen through them. This can occur if the practitioner has been able to open themselves up sufficiently to the chi energy, which in Chinese philosophy is the lifeforce present in everything.

As a form of self-defence the idea is that aggression can be neutralised through yielding. If one does not meet an attacker's force head on but instead gives way, the aggression will exhaust itself. Most people however do not take up tai chi primarily for self-defence, since one would probably have to be very experienced to use it successfully in this way.

Tai chi is often recommended therapeutically to those who suffer from tension and anxiety, high blood pressure and heart complaints because of its relaxing effect. It can promote and maintain good health both physically and mentally.

READING

Embrace Tiger, Return to Mountain *by Chungliang Al Huang, Celestial Arts, USA £9.95.* A popular classic first published in the USA, beautifully produced and illustrated with photographs an calligraphy. Not a martial arts manual, but a unique exploration of the basic principles. Al Huang writes: 'I remain interested less in the structure of exact positions, but more in the content and the spirit of dance in the form' and describes himself as a 'Tai Ji dancer'. **Way of Harmony: A Guide to the Soft Martial Arts** *by Howard Reid, Unwin Hyman £7.95.* Written by the producer of the 1983 BBC TV series *Way of the Warrior* this book is a practical guide to Chi Kung, Tai Chi Chuan, Hsing I and Pa Kua systems of exercises which cultivate inner strength and vital energy and increase self-knowledge. It also includes a section on oriental paths to balance: diet, breathing exercises, meditation and therapeutic techniques. The book is aimed at those who want to combine the physical skills of the martial arts with a deeper mental approach. Profusely illustrated with colour photographs and drawings. **Tai Chi for Two: the Practice of Push Hands** *by Paul Crompton Shambala £11.95.* 'Push Hands' is a basic exercise for two partners practiced by Tai Chi students. This book presents it as a means of training oneself to relax under physical and mental pressure and to improve one's interactions with others in everyday life. Includes step-by-step instructions and photographs demonstrating the movements, plus chapters on Taoist philosophy and the concept of Tai Chi energy. Paul Crompton has been teaching Tai Chi in Britain since the early 1970s.

CENTRES OFFERING TAI CHI CHUAN

Bodywise E2, British T'ai Chi Association W1, Community Health Foundation EC1, Lifeworks NW5, London School of T'Ai Chi Chuan EC1, Martial Arts Commission SE8, Mushindokai N12, School of T'ai-chi Ch'uan - Centre for Healing WC1, Spira - Self Defence for Women W12, Studio E NW6, Sunra SW12.

162

Yoga

Yoga is a means of self help towards physical and mental health. It has been practised in India for over 3000 years, and can be used as a way of relaxing and keeping fit, as well as a kind of meditation technique.

Yoga comes from a Sanskrit word meaning 'union' which has the same root as the English word 'yolk'. The aim of yoga is union with the divine, with life. Though in the west we are most familiar with the form of yoga which involves physical postures ('hatha' yoga) the word yoga is used to describe many different disciplines which can be used to develop spiritual potential. For instance, there is karma yoga which is service to others through work and bhakti yoga which is union with the divine principle through religious devotion.

There are different systems of hatha yoga teaching too. However, all involve basic postures which have names like 'Cobra', 'Praying Mantis', 'Tree' and 'Corpse' pose. The poses are designed to stretch and strengthen muscles and ligaments, and to stimulate the internal organs and circulation. Though encountering the body's stiffness can be uncomfortable at times, yoga teachers stress that there should not be too much strain involved, and one should not try to push one's body beyond its limits. The temptation to push the body into the pose, rather than relaxing into it can be strong, and can even lead to injury. For this reason it is advisable to attend a yoga class, where the teacher will be able to show you the best way to do the pose.

Hatha yoga also involves attention to the breath. Proper breathing is seen as crucial to good health and to developing mental and emotional clarity. Breathing exercises are usually part of yoga practice, and the aim is to let go of the tension, particularly in the diaphragm, which leads to tense, shallow breathing and an overall sense of restriction. After a yoga session, the practitioner should relax fully. This may also involve some sort of meditation.

The benefits of yoga are increased relaxation, greater strength and suppleness, and better posture. Yoga has also had beneficial effects in the treatment of diseases, notably high blood pressure, multiple sclerosis, arthritis, asthma, backache (but care should be taken not to strain the back), painful periods, constipation and other chronic conditions. Some places hold classes specifically for handicapped people.

READING

Book of Yoga *by the Sivananda Yoga Centre, Ebury Press £7.95.* This classic guide to yoga is clear and comprehensive, superbly illustrated with full colour photographs. There are easy to follow instructions for working into the postures and authoritative teachings covering all aspects of this timeless discipline. The book is an inspiration for beginners and experts alike. **Yoga for A New Age** *by Bob Smith and Linda Boudreau Smith, Smith Productions £9.95.* Written by two yoga teachers this copiously illustrated book examines a modern approach to the discipline of yoga. The photographs include examples of bad posture and how to correct it. The yoga

BODY THERAPIES

❝ For me nothing has been more rewarding than the regular practice of yoga. The form I practise is composed of a combination of postures *(assanas)*, breathing *(pranayama)*, meditation and a form of deep relaxation *(Yoga Nidra)*. The postures reveal and work upon all the tensions in the body, in some positions parts of my body tremble and shake, presumably releasing energy in the same way as Reichian bodywork. Practiced with consciousness, I find them deeply centering, leaving me relaxed and in control of my body. The breathing vitalises and purifies the system - this can actually be felt, and with formal meditation takes me into an extremely calm and inward place (although sometimes I can overdo it and get a headache!). Afterwards, I feel joyful, view the world with equanimity, and everything in light - literally.

I practice Nidra usually before sleeping or on waking. Its beneficial results have been scientifically proven and is enough on its own to ward off minor illness, to guarantee a beautiful sleep and stress-less morning (I find that by lunch time a top-up is required). I know that only through regular practice can I be at my best. ❞

Andy Hilton

164

courses start at beginner's level and progress to an advanced standard. Included is a chapter on working in pairs and groups and some explanation of the way yoga practice helps the muscular system.

CENTRES OFFERING YOGA
Bharatiya Vidya Bhavan (Institute of Indian Culture) W14, Bodywise E2, CAER (Centre For Alternative Education And Research) (Cornwall), Chinese Yoga Federation SW11, Creative and Healing Arts W11, Croydon Buddhist Centre (Croydon), Health Management NW3, Hillside Practice NW5, Holistic Yoga Centre Milton Keynes, Iyengar Yoga Institute W9, Jeyrani Health Centre E18, Living Centre SW20, New Cross Natural Therapy Centre SE14, Private Polyclinic E7, Satyananda Yoga Centre SW12, School of Yoga (various locations in London), Shanti Sadan W11, Sivananda Yoga Vedanta Centre W11, South London Natural Health Centre SW4, Sri Aurobindo Circle (Ashram) SW16, Sunra SW12, West London Buddhist Centre W11, Westminster Natural Health Centre SW1, White Eagle Lodge W8, Yoga Culture and Therapy Foundation WC1, Yoga Dham Middlesex, Yoga for Health Foundation (Bedfordshire).

TRAININGS IN YOGA TEACHING
Iyengar Yoga Institute *Title of Training* Teacher Training Course in Yoga. *Duration* 2 years part-time, one class per week. *Entry requirements* Candidates must have studied with a qualified Iyengar teacher for 2 years previously, have a good grounding in the basic postures, and be able to maintain headbalance for 5 minutes. *Fees* £480 for 2 year course. *Comments* In addition to the basic Yoga teaching qualification, the Institute runs courses for teachers wishing to progress and gain higher certificates.

OTHER BODY APPROACHES

ACTIVE BIRTH
Active Birth Centre NW5, Dick-Read School for Natural Birth W8, Highbury Centre N5, Splashdown Birth Pools.

ASTON PATTERNING
Institute of Structural Bodywork Various London locations, Reiki Centre NW3.

CRANIAL OSTEOPATHY
Cranial Osteopathic Association (register), Bexleyheath Natural Health Clinic (Kent), Forty Hill Natural Therapy Centre Enfield, Fulham Clinic SW6, Isis Centre for Holistic Health N17, Neal's Yard Therapy Rooms WC2, New Cross Natural Therapy Centre SE14, Society of Students of Holistic Health (courses held in London), South London Natural Health Centre SW4.

HELLERWORK
Institute of Structural Bodywork (register).

BODY THERAPIES

LASER THERAPY
Body Clinic NW11, Insight Care Complementary Health Clinic N1, Natural Healing Centre E7, Wholistic Health Centre Croydon, Wimbledon Clinic of Natural Medicine SW19.

MAGNETIC THERAPY
Natural Healing Centre E7.

NUTRITIONAL COUNSELLING/DIET THERAPY
Bayswater Allergy Clinic W2, Better Health Centre NW3, Bexleyheath Natural Health Clinic (Kent), Bluestone Clinic NW1, Community Health Foundation EC1, Hampton Holistic Centre for Homoeopath and Autogenic Training (Middlesex), Institute for Complementary Medicine W1, Institute for Optimum Nutrition SW6, McCarthy Westwood Consultants SW11, Mill Hill Health Care NW7, Nature Cure Clinic W1, Neal's Yard Therapy Rooms WC2, Primrose Healing Centre NW1, South London Natural Health Centre SW4, Westminster Natural Health Centre SW1, Association for Analytic and Bodymind Therapy and Training N10, Bennet and Luck Natural Health Centre N1, Body-Mind Health Private Clinic N8, Brackenbury Natural Health Centre W6, Chessington Hypnotherapy Clinic Chessington, Dietary Therapy Society N6, Falcons SW11, Holistic Health Consultancy SW1, Institute for Optimum Nutrition SW6, International Colon Hydrotherapy Foundation W9, Living Centre SW20, Natural Health Clinic Harrow, Nature Cure Clinic W1, Neal's Yard Therapy Rooms WC2, New Cross Natural Therapy Centre SE14, Nutribiotics Edgware, Primrose Healing Centre NW1, Putney Natural Therapy Clinic SW15, Refuah Shelaymah Natural Health Centre N16, South London Natural Health Centre SW4, Therapy Made Unique, Wholistic Health Centre (Croydon).

POSTURAL INTEGRATION
New Cross Natural Therapy Centre SE14, Open Centre EC1.

REBALANCING
Institute of Structural Bodywork (register).

REIKI
Lifeworks NW5, New Cross Natural Therapy Centre SE14, Primrose Healing Centre NW1, Radiance Education Unlimited NW3, Reiki Centre NW3.

SPAGYRIK THERAPY
Naturemed Partnership (Stroud).

TIBETAN MEDICINE
Tibet Foundation.

OTHER TRAININGS

ACTIVE BIRTH
Active Birth Centre *Title of Training* The Active Birth Teacher's Training Course. *Duration* Two years part-time and can be done largely through correspondence if you wish. Twelve study days per year. *Entry requirements* None. Mostly for women. *Fees* £395 all in. *Comments* Certificate given by the association. Intake in September of each year. Would welcome Scottish applicants!

Jeyrani Health Centre *Title of Training* Midwifery Trends for the 1990s *Duration* Six days on day release. *Entry requirements* Must be professional practising midwife with interest in natural childbirth and water births. Must produce qualification certificate. *Fees* £125 *Comments* Run by a specialist in water births at Whipps Cross hospital, and includes one day with Dr Michael Odent.

DIET THERAPY/NUTRITIONAL COUNSELLING
Centre for Nutritional Studies *Title of Training* Diploma course in nutritional counselling. *Duration* 2 years part time, both home study and attendance. *Entry requirements* Entry by interview. *Fees* £1,975 for two years.

Institute for Optimum Nutrition *Title of Training* 2 year Course for Nutritional Consultants. *Duration* 2 years, 1 evening a week, plus 1 weekend a month. (Satellite course also available for those who can't attend evenings). *Entry Requirements* None specified. *Fees* £1,497 for the whole course, payable in instalments. *Comments* Students are expected to do 12 hours per week, have clinical experience and run a three-month research project.

BODY THERAPIES

MACROBIOTICS
Community Health Foundation *Title of Training* Kushi Institute Certificate Course *Duration* Level 1: 6 weekends and 6 day intensive or 4 weeks daytime. Level 2: 4 weekends and 9 day intensive or 6 weeks daytime. Level 3: 5 weeks daytime. *Entry requirements* Ideally completed an introductory Shiatsu or cooking course. *Fees* Level 1: £645 Level 2: £845 Level 3: £745 *Comments* Emphasis is on teaching students the deeper understanding behind macrobiotics and shiatsu, along with practical skills.

ECLECTIC/SPECIAL TRAININGS
Association of General Practitioners of Natural Medicine *Title of Training* (1) Foundation Course of Comprehensive Training in Natural Medicine. (2) Post graduate Diploma Specialist Courses *Duration* (1) One year foundation course 20 hours per week. (2) Three-four year Post Graduate Diploma specialist courses - 20 hours weekly of formal study. *Entry requirements* 1 and 2: A reasonable standard of English and an aptitude for learning. All applicants will be interviewed by the Principal of the College. (2) Must be a graduates of Foundation Course or have recognized training in natural medicine. *Fees* (1) £1500 plus registration fee £30. (2) £4000 approx. Scholarships and work awards are usually available on post graduate courses. *Comments* Prospectus £1 available from the Registrar.

Association of Natural Medicines *Title of Training* Training in Acupuncture, Homoeopathy, Naturopathy, Massage, Aromatherapy, Reflexology or Hypnotherapy. *Duration* Acupuncture, Homoeopathy, Naturopathy: 4 years, part-time, one weekend a month. Massage, Aromatherapy, Reflexology, Hypnotherapy: between 3 and 9 months part-time. *Entry requirements* Acceptance by interview. *Fees* 4 year courses: £600 p.a. Short courses prices vary, approx £200. *Comments* For prospectus send £1 plus A5 size SAE to the Secretary.

School of Complementary Medicine *Title of Training* Course in Complementary Medicine. *Duration* Three and half years, part-time starting in February of each year. A total of 60 weekends for the whole course. *Entry requirements* Love of life and people, reasonably good health, average academic ability, sensitivity and compassion, some intuition, inner sense of freedom, desire to heal, some time to study, ability to apply what you know. These qualities are more important than academic qualifications. *Fees* £120 per months for 44 months (no VAT). Cranial osteopathy. *Comments* It's a course to become a general practitioner in the field of Complementary Medicine. It takes a much more holistic approach than trainings which specialise in one subject only. Subjects covered are Chinese acupuncture, shiatsu , acupressure, massage, reflexology, touch for health, kinesiotherapy, cranial osteopathy, herbalism, Bach flower remedies, nutrition, psychosomatic medicine, counselling skills, transactional analysis techniques, NLP, chi kung exercises, anatomy and physiology.

INTRODUCTION TO SPIRIT

What is Spiritual?

The word spiritual must be one of the most difficult to define in the English Language. The dictionary definition of 'spirit' alone ranges across the whole gamut of soul, ghost, animation, courage, breathing, mind and alcohol. The meaning it has for an individual tends to vary according to their particular values and beliefs. However, though the word may take different forms for different people, it is usually used to  denote whatever is of greatest, highest or deepest value for that person, and how this is expressed in their lives.

The groups included here fall under the category of spiritual because their practices and beliefs all aim to take the practitioner beyond their normal, limited sense of themselves. Specifically they aim to take people beyond their sense of themselves as separate egos or selves, isolated from other people, from the world and the universe in which we live. In some way they aim directly to facilitate contact with the 'transpersonal'; that experience of the self as being part of a greater whole, and of partaking of what is spoken of in traditional religious systems as the divine, something which exists both within and beyond time and the particular. They may seek to do this in many different ways.

The Difference between Religion and Spirituality

Religions are one way in which spirituality can be expressed. They represent a system of beliefs and practices which have become recognisable as a particular tradition. Religion and the spiritual are *not* synonymous, and spirituality can be expressed and developed in many ways outside of religion.

The Search for a New Spirituality

In many people's minds the emergence of 'alternative' spiritual movements is associated with the sixties and the search of many people at that time for deeper, more lasting values than those offered by what seemed to them to be an over-materialistic society. Disaffected with a society which seemed to be obsessed with consumerism, achievement and conformity, and with orthodox religions which appeared irrelevant and stultified, some turned to drugs, some to politics and others to religion, while some turned to all three.

The seeds of this collective change in consciousness were sown much earlier however. It was in 1893 that The League of Liberal Clergymen of Chicago, Illinois set up the World Parliament of Religions, a forum where followers of faiths from East and West could meet together and share perspectives. This assembly of Christians, Jews, Muslims, Buddhists, Hindus, Taoists, Confucians and Spiritualists led to the creation of the first centres of Hinduism, Buddhism and Islam in the U.S.

But it was not until 1965 when the U.S. government ended the restrictions on Asian immigration which had been in force for nearly fifty years that the dialogue between East and West was opened on a massive scale. Though this move was intended to allow refugees from Maoist China to take up residence in the U.S., many Asian teachers and holy men took the opportunity to make their voices heard in the heart of the West.

It was not only to the East that those in search of spiritual nourishment turned. At the same time Christianity experienced experienced a revival in the form of 'born again' sects, who sought to rekindle enthusiasm for the religion that many Americans and Europeans had grown up with. There has also been a revival in interest in western occult traditions, and pre-christian or 'pagan' belief systems. At the turn of the century groups were formed which took some of their inspiration from the esoteric Judaic Kabbalah, and in some cases this was blended with the practice of ritual magic - notoriously in the case of Aleister Crowley. Today there are still practitioners of the 'old religion', witches and warlocks, who adhere to the folk religion of Europe which went underground with the advent of Christianity, but was never quite eradicated by it. Recently too there has been a growing interest in the religious beliefs and practices of the American Indians.

East meets West

Originally it was Europeans who went out to colonise what were then thought of as the less 'civilised' countries of the east, Africa and the 'New World 'of the Americas, or to convert their people to Christianity. Subsequently a strange reversal has taken place. Now the west is benefiting from a counter-colonisation and the ideas and philosophy of these countries seem to offer many people a different perspective. It seems as if many of the attitudes and beliefs which underpin the culture and religion of these countries are not only as valid as ours, but also offer an outlook which may complement the traditional emphasis of western culture. In the west a high value tends to be placed on individual achievement and activity, on science and the intellect, and on technical ability. Broadly speaking, the outlook of eastern religion speaks more of what is collective, and stresses the importance of looking inwards, of experience rather than mental knowledge. In addition to this, 'native' or pagan religions offer a profound sense of connection with the natural world of which we are a part - a sense which we urgently need to recapture if we are to avert ecological disaster. Broadly speaking, while the west strives, the 'new religions' accept and open to what is. The influx of these new ideas perhaps offers an opportunity for a balance between these two poles.

Some people in the West have been attracted to this complementary attitude and have found it in an expansive, holistic way of being. However, perhaps there can be a danger here of rejecting western culture wholesale, which not only has a great deal of value within it, but also represents an integral part of a westerner's whole outlook and response to life.

Gurus and spiritual teachers

The guru-disciple or teacher/apprentice relationship has been important in many spiritual traditions. In the west however we tend to be sceptical about gurus and people who might be purporting to know more than we do. This scepticism may be by no means a bad thing sometimes as there are some teachers who have shown themselves to be simply more charismatic than wise. We are also very wary of leaders because while they can do great good they can also do great harm.

A common image of the guru is perhaps of an Indian swami, bearded and loinclothed who probably lives in a cave and gives forth to hundreds of faceless, adoring disciples. The whole idea seems very foreign. Most gurus are not in fact like this, and the mystique which surrounds them, not always of their own making, may obscure the wisdom they might have to offer. The only way to determine if a particular teacher has something for you is to follow your instinct about him or her.

Though the guru is in the main an eastern concept, there have been and still are western teachers in the same vein. Gurdjieff, the native Russian teacher who gathered a number of followers round him at the beginning of this century, and who is still influential, is an example.

There are also spiritual groups who do not emphasise the importance of a teacher or leader. Sometimes they take their inspiration from the writings of a teacher who is dead, or simply from a particular faith or set of beliefs.

Cults

One fear often expressed about spiritual groups is that they are cults designed to take away people's autonomy. Stories of dubious recruitment tactics and brainwashing techniques hit the headlines a few years ago. In some cases there have even been allegations of physical force being used on troublesome group members.

While some of these reports may be true, it is this kind of scandal which tends to get publicised. The groups which have operated in this kind of way represent a very small number indeed of the total. Perhas what has not been publicised as much is the very real benefits many people have derived, and satisfaction they have gained from their involvement with *bona fide* spiritual groups. If you come up against dogmatism, intolerance or authoritarianism it is to be hoped that you will recognise it, though of course this is sometimes easier with hindsight than when faced with a teacher, group or leader who seems to have it all worked out.

Different types of Groups

The groups included in this book have different beliefs and ways of organising themselves. They employ different practices and are organised differently, and some are large, some small. In some the emphasis is on community and there may even be residential communities associated with the group. In others importance may be placed on individual study and practice; in fact in some groups there are few or even no meetings at all. Some of the centres we have listed are less like groups but are individuals or organisations running courses and workshops with a strong spiritual dimension.

Another variable is the level of commitment seen as ideal by different groups. Some groups offer an alternative lifestyle to those deeply involved, and others are more informal. Some are much more closely knit as groups and others are much looser in structure. The centres range from those with residential communities, offices and commercial enterprises on the premises, to those which meet in members' own homes.

Some of these groups are religious in the traditional sense of the word. They follow a recognisable set of religious teachings such as Sufism, Buddhism, Hinduism or Christianity. Others may have a spiritual framework in the sense that they emphasise a univeral perspective and the divinity present in humanity, perhaps using traditional religious terminology, but not subscribing to to any one particular traditional religious philosophy. A group like the Theosophical Society is an example of this. Then there are others which are much more secular, and which do not have any religious context at all, but which see themselves as addressing the spiritual perspective. Enlightenment Intensives are an example of this approach.

What they do

Once again a very wide range of activities constitute the practices of spiritual groups in London.

Meditation: This came from the east and to a greater or lesser extent usually forms part of the practice of those groups which hail from the eastern tradition. However, meditation has also been practised in western traditions. In Christianity it usually takes the form of contemplation of a particular subject, though some people have also incorporated a less directed style into the traditional forms of Christian worship. Secular groups are also using meditation since it adapts itself well to a non-religious framework. More information about the different kinds of meditation is given in the section on the subject in this book.

Ritual and devotional practices: While meditation has gained a great deal of credibility with many people in the west, even some sections of the medical profession who recognise its therapeutic value, ritual is often still regarded with a great deal of suspicion. Some people find such activities weird or esoteric, and others feel uncomfortably reminded of their own religious upbringing, especially if they have rejected it. Some people fear they will be taken over in some way if they let themselves get involved in rituals. Perhaps this is because we live is a society in which the rituals have to a certain extent lost the meaning they originally had.

Weddings and funerals though they do in fact serve a useful purpose, socially, psychologically and spiritually, rarely act now as a way in which we can recognise and demonstrate the significance of important events in our lives. But ritual is an important way of focussing on feelings and values, and giving them a communal context.

Spiritually, ritual is used in this way. It serves to enable the participants to get in touch with their highest values and express these communally. It also places personal experience and emotion in the wider context of universal human experience. Many people enjoy ritual from the outset, finding that they recognise and respond to its use of the imaginative faculties. Others find they they prefer to know what is going on first before they engage.

Rituals are used by some Christian, Buddhist and Hindu groups, and in Paganism and Shamanism.

Chanting and prayer: Sound has been used in both east and west to express the spirit. The repetition of

E L E M E N T

PUBLISHERS

OF

HIGH QUALITY BOOKS

ON

PHILOSOPHY

WORLD RELIGIONS

HEALTH . PSYCHOLOGY

SELF HELP

Available from good bookshops

ELEMENT BOOKS
LONGMEAD SHAFTESBURY
DORSET SP7 8PL
☎ (0747) 51339

mantras (short phrases with spiritual significance or meaning) focuses the mind and also calls up deeper levels of energy. It can unite the physical (because singing, chanting or praying is a physical act), the emotional (because music evokes a strong emotional response) and the mental (especially if words are involved). Prayer is traditionally central in Christianity. Mantras are often used by Buddhist and Hindu groups. Music and chanting is important in the Sufi tradition.

Study: Some groups particularly emphasise study, talks and discussion. They may discuss the writings of a teacher or teachers and philosophers. They may have programmes of lectures by people on various topics. Taped lectures are becoming increasingly popular as a way in which people can make more contact with a teacher or lecturer, and absorb his or her teachings more fully by repeated listening. In some cases these methods are the only ones used by a particular group or association

Other methods: There are many other ways in which particular groups facilitate growth and communication. Some adapt therapeutic techniques, some meet together in different ways, some emphasise the importance of the arts and so on. This all points to the fact that the definition of what is spiritual is widening to include different aspects of culture.

Spiritual Groups in London

There are many spiritual groups in London practising in different ways. The decision to investigate the possibility of a spiritual path is very much a matter of instinct, of the heart. People usually become interested in a particular group because they have read something which seems to make sense to them, or because they have met someone involved in some sort of spiritual path, or because they feel attracted to a practice, like meditation or chanting. If you are drawn to this kind of search, don't be put off too soon by the vast array of groups which you may feel are not for you. As it says in the bible - 'seek, and ye shall find'!

Spirituality versus Psychology

Psychology has been called the modern religion. Freud's work exposed for the first time to much of the western world the depths of the human psyche, the inner world. What he saw there was the dark underside of experience, the unregenerated primitive instincts which had remained throughout the long process of civilisation seemingly untouched and merely pushed into unconsciousness. The resistance which Freud encountered in the course of publicising his work and ideas is a measure of how deeply his picture of human nature threatened the image of what it was to be human at the time. Yet paradoxically in many ways Freud's view echoed assumptions of the time - that man is essentially 'sinful', and his lower nature needed to be kept in check by society and religion. But while the orthodox solution was salvation by God and good works, Freud's was that knowledge of unconscious functioning through analysis would set the patient free of his or her own 'demons'.

With the development of Freud's original ideas, some psychologists and therapists have attempted to redress the balance, and in different ways have stressed that as well as hiding problems and complexes, the psyche also has hidden heights. While we may be largely unconscious of our instincts and repressed desires and hates, we are also unaware of our potential for joy and loving participation with the universe.

The question of when psychology and spirituality are similar, and when they are different is still being hotly debated as some psychologists turn to meditation and mysticism, and some gurus incorporate therapeutic techniques into their teachings. Both seek to offer practices and techniques which bring about individual growth, and both aim to free people from restrictive habitual ways of acting and being.

However, while it may often be difficult to distinguish the difference between spiritual and psychotherapeutic practice, it may be possible to distinguish different levels within both disciplines. Various theorists have suggested that it may be important to build a mature sense of one's individuality before going beyond the individual self. Some psychotherapies may concentrate more on developing a sense of 'who I am', and regard this as the limit of their work. Others have sought to include a more spiritual dimension into their work, or may have been founded on the premise that the spiritual quest is the most important one from a psychological point of view.

However, while there may be a great deal of overlap in practice, many psychologists and therapists are still quite wary of what they may see as an attempt to avoid painful feelings by going off into a cosmic 'bliss-out' in religion. Spiritual teachers too can be suspicious of therapy, feeling that it is simply equivalent to putting an elastoplast on the mortal wound of human suffering. It seems that the dialogue between psychology and spirituality has only just begun. It may take a long time for the two to settle their differences. However, in general more people are beginning to question what they see as an artificial division between what has in the past been called 'spiritual' and what has been called 'worldly'.

The 'New Age'

The last two decades has seen a growth in what has become known as 'New Age' activity and thinking. Even some sections of the media have hailed the 1990s as and era when society will turn away from the hard-edged, money-making 1980s and adopt caring, green, spiritual values.

The term 'New Age' can be used to cover a diverse number of attitudes, beliefs and activities, to the extent that it can be difficult to see what they have in common. As the name suggests, the central idea in New Age thinking is that humanity has reached a critical stage in its evolutionary development which will lead to a change in people's outlook and consciousness. New Age philosophy is characterised by various concerns:

SPIRIT

Astrology
Buddhism
Castaneda
Dhamma
Eastern Traditions
Fiction
Gurdjieff
Health
I Ching
Jung
Krishnamurti
Living Earth
Meditation
New Age
Ouspensky
Parapsychology
Qabalah
Religion
Sufism
T'ai Chi
Upanishads
Vedanta
Women's Spirituality
Yoga
Zen

FREE YOUR
MIND WITH
ARKANA

New Age Books for Mind, Body and Spirit

Saturn
A New Look at an Old Devil
LIZ GREENE
£5.99

Shadows in the Cave
Mapping the Unconscious Universe
GRAHAM DUNSTAN MARTIN
£5.99

For a free catalogue of Arkana titles please write to:
Arkana Marketing Dept, Penguin Books Ltd
27 Wrights Lane, London W8 5TZ

PUBLISHED BY PENGUIN BOOKS

NEW IN BOOKSHOPS NOW

1) The mystical nature of the universe: the fundamental reality of the universe is seen as love, and the universe is seen as ultimately benign and purposeful.

2) Global conciousness: belief in the oneness of humanity, and the importance of community and sharing.

3) Non sectarian spirituality: all religions are seen as expressions of the same vision, and great importance is placed on the individual's right to choose their own path, whether this takes a traditionally religious form or the form of secular spirituality.

4) Abundance rather than scarcity: the belief that that there are enough resources for everyone in the world both material and immaterial. 'Scarcity' mentality is seen as responsible for scarcity.

5) The importance of preserving natural environment, an ecologically sound lifestyle and a respect for nature.

6) Human potential and personal development: human beings have more potential than they realise, and are, in essence, divine. It is seen as our responsibility to develop this potential.

7) Human beings as creators of their own reality: the individual is seen as responsible for his or her own life, and as creating that reality through attitudes, thoughts, feelings etc.

8) Importance of the feminine: belief that it is necessary to redress the balance caused by over-valuing what is seen as the 'masculine' in our culture by reasserting the value of the 'feminine' and questioning the power of men.

9) 'Holistic' model in science, medicine etc: the belief that the universe is not a mechanism made up of randomly functioning parts but is a living organism which works as an indivisible whole.

In general, humanity is seen as progressing into a time of greater spirituality and world harmony.

There is much overlap between the New Age movement and the 'Human Potential' movement, which grew out of humanistic psychology in the 1960s. This is more psychotherapy and 'personal growth' oriented and less mystical in outlook, though in practice there are ideas, approaches and methodology common to both.

Critics of New Age philosophy have claimed that it concentrates too exclusively on the positive aspects of the universe, and therefore attempts to ignore, or at least deals inadequately with, the presence of suffering and evil in the world. New Agers have been criticised for being too credulous and subjective, and of attempting to dispense with reason and logic. Whatever the pros and cons of the movement, it is proving to have a steady following as evinced by the continuing popularity of New Age events.

Meditation

There are so many different kinds of meditation that it can seem hard sometimes to define what it is they all have in common. The benefits of meditation are being recognised in the west, though it is still sometimes seen as something strange or eccentric. However, it is more down to earth than going into some sort of psychedelic trance, or 'contemplating one's navel'.

Meditation is turning the attention inwards, away from all the external things which demand our attention. It involves focussing the mind, usually on one particular object or idea. In meditation the mind is cleared of all the extraneous thoughts which take up a lot of our energy, or for a little while at least our involvement with all those thoughts is suspended, so that a clearer, calmer experience of oneself is possible.

There are various ways of achieving this, depending on the particular meditation practice. Different kinds of meditation may be useful for different purposes, or temperaments. There are practices in which the meditator concentrates on the breath as it comes in and out of the body, without trying to change it in any way. This focuses the attention, and helps to bring together the awareness of mind and body. There are meditation techniques where a colour, shape or form is pictured and held in the attention. This 'visualisation' technique has been used in a very particular way to help in the treatment of illness, especially by cancer sufferers. Here the meditator will visualise his or her illness, and then see the body fighting that illness and suppressing it. Some Yogic forms of meditation involve concentrating on an actual object such as a candle or a stone, and some use a 'mantra' or phrase repeated over and over again. There are meditation practices where there is no one object of concentration at all, and the meditator just tries to sit and be aware of all the changing thoughts and feelings passing through his or her mind. This is the Zen 'sitting' meditation.

Usually these kinds of meditation are done sitting down, often cross-legged or kneeling while sitting on cushions. However, this is by no means essential if it is difficult for you to do, and they can be done sitting in a chair. However, some practices involve movement. There are 'walking meditations' where concentration is on the body as you walk, and the processes involved in moving. The 'Dynamic Meditation' practised by followers of the Bhagwan Shree Rajneesh involves very vigorous whirling and dancing movement.

MEDITATION

The benefits of meditation are just as diverse as the practices. One of the most immediate effects can be that the meditator feels more calm and relaxed. Many people take up meditation initially as a way of combating stress. It can also increase one's ability to concentrate, and helps the meditator develop a sense of a still, calm centre from which they feel more able to direct their lives creatively. It can also help to generate a greater sense of self-acceptance and warmth towards others. It can also be a way of achieving higher states of consciousness and heightened awareness.

Although there are quite a few books on the subject, as with learning any other skill, it is important to find a teacher who has experience themselves and can give you direct instruction and help. Centres which teach meditation are listed below, and will offer an explanation of their particular practices.

CENTRES OFFERING MEDITATION

Audio Limited W12, Barry Long Foundation WC1, Bharatiya Vidya Bhavan (Institute of Indian Culture) W14, Brahma Kumaris World Spiritual University NW6, British Buddhist Association W9, Buddhapadipa Temple SW19, Cortijo Romero (Spain), Croydon Buddhist Centre (Croydon), Foundation for International Spiritual Unfoldment E7, Gaia House (Devon), Healing Workshops, Humanistic Psychology at LSE WC2, Karma Kagyu Cho Khor Ling E2, Ki Kai Shiatsu Centre N17, London Buddhist Centre E2, London Dharmadhatu SW4, London Kagyu Centre E2, London Soto Zen Group NW2, London Sufi Centre W11, London Zen Society NW1, Maitri (Hants), Manjushri London Centre N4, Raphael Clinic NW6, RIGPA Fellowship NW1, Satyananda Yoga Centre SW12, School of Meditation W11, School of T'ai-chi Ch'uan - Centre for Healing WC1, Shanti Sadan W11, Sivananda Yoga Vedanta Centre W11, Sri Aurobindo Circle (Ashram) SW16, St James Centre for Health and Healing W1, Sunra SW12, Teach Yourself Meditation, Transcendental Meditation Baker Street Centre NW1, Transcendental Meditation National Office, West London Buddhist Centre W11, White Eagle Lodge W8.

SHAMBHALA
THE SACRED PATH OF THE WARRIOR
A secular path of meditation founded by
CHOGYAM TRUNGPA RIMPOCHE
The path of the warrior is both simple and profound. It provides a straightforward yet far reaching way to learn and practice meditation. Shambhala Training comprises a series of weekend courses running at 3 monthly intervals.

Contact: 17 Marius Road London SW17 7QU 081-673-6115

❝ In 1966 when I was 22, I first meditated according to 'transcendental meditation'. The amazing effect was that I fell to the floor and was unconscious because 'my mind had touched the areas which had been polluted by medicine'. I still remember vividly the spiral that I followed downwards in my imagination, barely knowing that my body did the same by falling out of the chair.

When I was 29, I remember falling in a car thinking 'this must be the end, this must be the ocean'. I woke up with a dislocated hip which gave me permanent pain for some seven years and still occasionally now, 17 years later. Doctors said that my pain was 'psychological' and as I had considered my 4 year Jungian analysis finished, I decided to study humanistic and transpersonal psychology by attending all possible workshops and training groups. You name it, I did it and got so much out of it that I have been promoting the transformation of consciousness ever since 1976.

These two stepping stones come to mind as I remember what put me on the track of 'inner directedness'. As a teenager I began to ask questions about God, eternity and life after death. Now I may still not have answers, but at least I have an understanding that satisfies my curiosity.

I would not want to have lived without any of my workshop style experiences since I healed what doctors could not heal: myself. But I wonder how such ways of thinking and living can be made more commonplace. In particular, I wonder whether this is not the social responsibility of the Church which seems to experience a splendid isolation, while the non-organised mind-body-spirit movement surely by far exceeds in numbers what bishops would like to see in parishes . . . ❞

Sabine Kurjo McNeill

❝ I had been meditating regularly for about a year. Sometimes when I meditated I felt very good, calm, relaxed or contented. Other times I just felt bored, sleepy, tense or downright angry. One time I remember I settled myself down for a good meditation session, and as I sat there I just felt more and more filled with joy and contentment - I had never known anything like it. It was as if I was overflowing with this sense of happiness, and more kept flowing into me, like waves of light. I felt too that I was radiating love to everyone in the world, I didn't have to think about it or try, but it was just shining out of me. The I had the sense of how powerful this light or love was. It seemed so powerful that suddenly I had the feeling that it didn't matter how much suffering there was in the world - and I knew there *was* a great deal of suffering - this love was somehow stronger than all that. It was as if the suffering was a flimsy veil over this powerful light and Julian of Norwich's words came into my mind: 'All shall be well, all shall be well, and all manner of thing shall be well'.

I felt the effects of this meditation very strongly for about three days afterwards. I felt uncharacteristically confident and able to perceive and relate to others. I never had another experience quite like it, inside or outside meditation, but it was a very important one and I felt gave me a valuable perspective on life. ❞

THE TRADITIONS

Buddhism

Buddhism has been dubbed 'Britain's fastest growing religion' by Arnold Toynbee. It has in fact been in existence for over 2,500 years. Its founder, the Buddha, saw suffering as central to the human condition, and his teaching concerned the ways in which people could transcend this suffering. These are the practice of an ethical lifestyle, and of meditation which then leads to insight into the nature of existence and the causes of human suffering.

Suffering is caused because according to Buddhism everything is impermanent. Human beings seek everlasting happiness by trying to hold onto what must fade or die. When this happens we experience pain, and try to avoid this pain by seeking another object of happiness in the world. Buddhist practices seek to take the practitioner beyond this cycle of holding on and running away, and to cultivate not a state of indifference, but of joyful acceptance of the impermanent nature of existence. This understanding is not intellectual but a profound experience which leads to complete freedom. This state is called 'Nirvana'.

Buddhism emphasises the importance of the individual's own growth towards greater consciousness of him or herself. The development of 'mindfulness' is an important part of much of Buddhist meditation. Mindfulness starts with awareness of oneself - of one's body, one's feelings and emotions, and one's mind - and of other people and the world around one. It develops ultimately into awareness of absolute reality.

Alongside the emphasis on individual development, concern for other people and for life - the development of compassion - is also seen as crucial. In the later developments of Buddhism especially, Nirvana is not seen simply as a neutral state

SPIRIT

of being without passion or desires, but more positively as a dynamic state of joy, contentment and compassion.

As it spread to different countries from India where it started (and from where it has now virtually died out), Buddhism adapted itself to different cultures. This gave rise to very different approaches to the original teachings. The groups listed below reflect these approaches. The Theravada tradition emphasises morality, the monastic lifestyle and the original Pali scriptures. Tibetan Buddhism is part of the 'Vajrayana' or tantric tradition which is colourful, ritualistic and emphasises psychic energy and often visualisation meditations. Zen Buddhism is perhaps the form that most people in the West have heard of through pithy Zen stories or the cryptic sayings which abound in the tradition. Zen's approach is anti-rational with an emphasis on zazen (meditation) and direct experience.

READING

What the Buddha Taught *by Walpola Rahula, Evergreen/Grove Weidenfeld £7.15.* Addressed to the 'educated and intelligent reader' and written by Dr Rahula, himself a Buddhist monk and scholar, this is a lucid and comprehensive introduction to Buddhism. The new revised and expanded edition also contains selected texts from *sutras* and the *Dhammapada*. With sixteen black and white illustrations. **The Buddhist Handbook: a Complete Guide to Buddhist Teaching and Practice** *by John Snelling, Rider £6.95.* John Snelling is the editor of the Buddhist journal *The Middle Way* and uniquely placed to offer this overview of a vast subject. This is the first basic introduction to help the newcomer orientate him or herself to the many different schools, doctrines and organisations which comprise the world of Buddhism, as well as a useful addition to the library of the practising 'western' Buddhist. **A Buddhist Bible** *by Dwight Goddard, Beacon Press U.S.A. £11.95.* First published in 1932, this is one of the books which originally stimulated western interest in Buddhism. Goddard's preface states that his collection of major texts: 'is not intended

RIGPA

founded by

Sogyal Rinpoche

Buddhist scholar and meditation master from Tibet

Regular courses held on:

Meditation
Tibetan Buddhism
Compassion
Healing
Death and Dying

Beginners are most welcome.

Details and programme from:
RIGPA, 44 St. Paul's Crescent,
London NW1 9TN
(071) 485 4342

186

to be a sourcebook for critical, literary and historical study; it is only intended to be a source of spiritual inspiration designed to awaken faith, and to develop faith into aspiration and full realisation'.

CENTRES OFFERING BUDDHISM
British Buddhist Association W9, British Shingon Buddhist Association, Buddhist Society SW1, Croydon Buddhist Centre (Croydon), Gaia House (Devon), Karma Kagyu Cho Khor Ling E2, London Buddhist Centre E2, London Dharmadhatu SW4, London Kagyu Centre E2, London Soto Zen Group NW2, London Zen Society NW1, Manjusri Institute N4, Mushindokai N12, Nichirin Shoshu of the United Kingdom (Richmond), RIGPA Fellowship NW1, Throssel Hole Priory (Northumberland), West London Buddhist Centre W11.

Christianity
Christianity is the majority and official religion of this country. Central to Christian belief is the importance of love (expressed in Christ's axiom 'love thy neighbour as thyself') which is seen as a divine attribute made manifest by god sending his son to earth to become man. This symbolises for Christians the possibility of humanity also expressing this love of god. The worship of the creator god in prayer and ritual is also central to Christian practice.

Acting in the world to help others is also stressed, and for this reason Christians have traditionally been involved in medical and charitable work, both in their native countries and abroad, often in Third World Countries.

As well as this emphasis on good works, there is also a strong mystical tradition within Christianity where solitary communion with and personal experience of, god enables the believer to become receptive to the divinity, and thus enter a deeper union with him.

Some Christian groups today seek to re-interpret the original doctrines in a way which is relevant to modern life. Christianity is rich in myth and symbol, and this has inspired many artists, writers and composers through the centuries.

READING
Meister Eckhart - The Man from whom God hid Nothing by Ursula Fleming, Fount £2.95. "God is a light shining in itself in silent stillness." These are words from the great German mystical theologian, Meister Eckhart (1260-1329). Ursula Fleming's incisive exploration into his teaching sheds light on this remarkable man who is one of the most controversial figures of Christian history. This is a selection from his writings which are as relevant today as they were six centuries ago. **A Lesson of Love: The Relevations of Julian of Norwich** Edited and translated by Fr. John-

SHANTI SADAN YOGA CENTRE

Founded in 1933 by Hari Prasad Shastri

Key Books on the Yoga of Self-Knowledge

TRAINING THE MIND THROUGH YOGA
Marjorie Waterhouse

Beauty, humour, deep wisdom and warm humanity are combined in this collection of essentially practical lectures by a Western pupil of Dr Shastri. The authority of one with personal experience is unmistakable.
"Miss Waterhouse has written a most pleasing book. There is much of good common sense for a disciple on any path." *The Middle Way*
166p paper £3.50 inc. p & p.

MEDITATION—ITS THEORY AND PRACTICE
Hari Prasad Shastri

The practice of meditation calms and strengthens the mind, and leads to the discovery of the inner source of peace, joy and inspiration. In this helpful and encouraging handbook, the theory of meditation is followed by clear details of some simpler practices, with a final section for the more advanced student.
84pp paper. £2.50 inc. p & p.

Illustrated book catalogue available on request.

MEETINGS AND COURSES

are held at Shanti Sadan during term-time on Wednesdays and Fridays at 8.00 pm., and also at other London venues. Attendance is free—contact us for details.

Shanti Sadan, 29 Chepstow Villas, Notting Hill Gate, W11 3DR. Tel. 071-727 7846

HINDUISM

Julian OJN, Darton Longman and Todd £6.95. At the age of thirty, Dame Julian of Norwich (14th Century) was granted a series of sixteen mystical revelations of the crucified Christ. She devoted the next twenty years to prayer and contemplation, and described her visions and her understanding of them in The Revelations of Divine Love, the first book written in the English language by a woman. **Original Blessing: A Primer of Creation Spirituality** by Matthew Fox, Bear & Co £8.50. Matthew Fox is a Dominican scholar and spiritual teacher, an eloquent advocate of Creation Spirituality. Original Blessing is an empowering and necessary book which leads us back to our own creativity and that deep ecstatic centre which resides beneath any fear of death.

CENTRES OFFERING CHRISTIANITY
Christian Community W6, Creation-Centred Spiritituality W1. Friends House NW1.

Hinduism

Hinduism is not a homogenous religious system in itself. It is more a collection of different ideas, schools and cults. The word 'Hindu' is Persian for Indian, and was used by outsiders to lump together all the indigenous cults and religions of the Indian sub-continent.

It is difficult to isolate any one belief or practice which all Hindus have in common. For instance, though most Hindus believe in a creator god in some way, there are some who don't. Some are vegetarian, while others will eat meat. Most accept the authority of the Veda scriptures, which have been written over the 5,000 years of Hinduism's development.

However, the struggle for personal salvation is common to all Hinduism. The spirit or true self, Atman as it is called, is present in each individual. The Atman is the god within us, and is identified with Brahman, the Absolute, the origin and cause of all that exists. Maya, or human ignorance, keeps us from understanding our real nature, and realising our identity with this ultimate principle, and so we identify more with the phenomenal, ever changing world. The soul is seen as passing through countless births because it is attached to this world of appearances. Release from the cycle of incarnation is possible when the individual reaches a full realisation that the real self is one with Brahman. This release is called moksha.

Because Brahman is seen as indefinable and unknowable, Hindus have traditionally worshipped the divine principle in more accessible forms. There are many more personal gods who are believed to be manifestations of Brahman, and who are worshipped because they are more human and act as a bridge between

189

the relative world of human experience and the Absolute or god.

There are many different schools within Hinduism. Some have a very devotional approach, some see asceticism as a path to liberation, and others emphasise the importance of working in society for the collective good. Meditation, chanting and ritual are all practices employed by Hindu groups. The practice of Yoga is central in Hinduism. This not just the Hatha Yoga we are familiar with in the West, which is the physical discipline of perfecting poses or Asanas (see 'Yoga' in Body section). Yoga means yoke or union, and it is a discipline which unites one with the universal or divine. Other forms of Yoga practised by the groups below include Bhakti Yoga, the discipline of devotion or love, Mantra Yoga, the chanting of Mantras, and Karma Yoga which is work as a spiritual practice.

In the personal struggle towards freedom, the teacher or guru is of great importance. Most modern Hindu groups centre around a teacher and their interpretation of the Hindu vision.

READING

Hinduism *by K M Sen, Penguin £4.50*. This book is an introduction to Hinduism and its sacred texts, the *Vedas*, the *Upanishads* and the *Bhagavad Gita*. Included is also a discussion of the three Hindu religious paths — the path of knowledge *(jnana)*, the path of work *(karma)* and the path of devotion *(bhakti)*. While giving insight into the caste system, the history of Hinduism and its nature and function, it also provides a look at current trends and customs and festivals. **Training the Mind through Yoga** *by M V Waterhouse, Shanti Sadan £3.00*. This collection of fourteen lectures introduces the general reader to the traditional methods of training the mind used in the spiritual science of *Adhyatma Yoga* and the 'yoga of self knowledge'. Beginning with an introduction to the *Bhagavad Gita* the lectures cover various aspects on refining the mind and emotions through discussing the stages in meditation the training of the yogi, awakening the higher consciousness and

THE CENTRE FOR PAGAN STUDIES

The Centre has been established for educational, therapeutic and spiritual purposes. It provides theoretical classes and experiential workshops in north European shamanism and ritual mythic drama. At a counselling level it aims to act as a guide to seekers through the occult labyrinth of competing wares in the esoteric marketplace. The research function of the Centre is well developed and provision can be made to people requiring a more one-to-one training after the manner of an apprentice.

Flat B, 5 Trinity Rise, London SW2. 081 671 6372

training and discipline. **Autobiography of A Yogi** by *Paramahansa Yogananda, Rider £5.95.* An authoritative introduction to the science of yoga, this book is a classic in its field, revealing the scientific foundation underlying the great religious paths of both east and west. It is an account of Yogananda's own search for truth which includes explanations of the laws governing miracles and recounts his meeting with many saints and sages throughout the world.

CENTRES OFFERING HINDUISM
Bharatiya Vidya Bhavan (Institute of Indian Culture) W14, International Society for Krishna Consciousness (ISKON) W1, Satyananda Yoga Centre SW12, Shanti Sadan W11, Sivananda Yoga Vedanta Centre W11, Sri Aurobindo Circle (Ashram) SW16.

Paganism

The word 'pagan' derives from the Latin 'pagus' which simply means an inhabitant of the countryside. However, since the fourth century AD it has been used in a derogatory sense to denote those who subscribe to a creed other than the majority religion. In former times, the word inspired fear, hatred and the zeal to convert those who, in their primitive ignorance, did not know any better.

In reality Paganism is the natural religion, the native spirituality of the country, and it has been practised in Britain ever since the end of the last Ice Age 11,000 years ago. Any indigenous cult specific to a land and its culture may be called 'pagan'. British paganism was influenced by successive waves of pagan invaders over the centuries - Celtic, Scandinavian and Teutonic. Under its umbrella can be included the Celtic Druids, the Scandinavian godi, the medieval witchcult, Renaissance hermeticism and alchemy, and paganism still survives in the succession of 'New Age' cults and sects today.

The sense of continuity in Paganism derives from the magic of place, of myth and of music. It comes from the heart rather than the head, and a central feature of it is the celebration of Mother Earth and of nature. One expression of this is in the rituals which acknowledge the year's turning. These take place ideally at ancient sites such as Stonehenge and Glastonbury, which were specifically built to harness the stellar, lunar, solar and human energies in one harmony.

Modern British paganism is a revival of the old beliefs and practices, and today in many parts of the country

FREYA ASWYNN

Author: LEAVES OF YGGDRASIL, for Runic Divination, counselling, Magic, Shamanic work, Private tuition, workshops, correspondence course, send S.A.E. to Freya Aswynn BM ASWYNN, Londn W1C 3XX phone 071-607 9695. Also Consulting & treatment rooms available in N7 for alternative practitioners from £12.50 @ day.

there are cults of the Goddess, the Wicca, Odinism and Druidism. Imported varieties of paganism have also made their impact over the last decade (e.g. the shamanism of the North American Indians). Common to all pagan cults are 'green' values - the promotion of an ecologically sound environment and the celebration of a transpersonal spirit through rite, dance, song and music. Paganism also explores the possibilities for empowering the individual through getting into a right relationship with the cosmos.

READING

Life and Times of a Modern Witch *by Janet and Stewart Farrar, Headline £2.95.* This book is written by two well known witches, as a result of a worldwide survey conducted to answer the many questions concerning their beliefs and rituals. Read this book to discover what kind of people become witches, what powers they possess, whether or not they worship Satan and a host of other things. **The Spiral Dance: A Rebirth of the Ancient Religion of the Great Goddess** *by Starhawk, Harper and Row £9.95.* A classic resource book for the women's spirituality movement, including rituals, invocations, exercises and magic. It is a brilliant overview of the growth, suppression and modern day re-emergence of witchcraft as a Goddess worshipping religion. This is a book of tools, continually in the process of renewal in response to changing times. **Wicca: the Old Religion in the New Age** *by Vivianne Crowley, Aquarian/Thorsons.* Vivianne Crowley here explains the 'way of the witch', the quest for the self, showing how wicca — rapidly regaining its former popularity — has relevance in today's world. Included are the subjects of black and white magic, nudity, the God and Goddess within, the future of witchcraft and more. Additionally there is an explanation of the relationship between Witchcraft and Jungian psychology.

CENTRES OFFERING PAGANISM

Acca and Adda WC1, Asatru Folk Runic Workshop N7, Centre for Pagan Studies SW2, House of the Goddess SW12, London Group.

Qabalah

The Qabalah (alternatively spelt Kabbalah or Cabala) is primarily based on esoteric Jewish teachings and it is at the heart of the western esoteric tradition. It is a philosophy and psychology of great theoretical and practical depth, its essential doctrine being that each individual person has the potential to realise their inner divinity and express this in all walks of life. There is evidence in the Old Testament of the existence of the Quabalah in pre-Christian times. It was not committed to writing until the Middle Ages, however, and most development has taken place in the nineteenth and twentieth centuries.

The Qabalah uses the 'Tree of Life' as a complete map of different levels of consciousness. There are may ways to use the Tree of Life. Being easy to both visualise and memorise, it can serve as guide to personal development.

The Tree of Life is composed of eleven spheres, which represent everything from the body and the physical world through to the most central, or deepest aspect of our spiritual being, the place where individuality blurs into union with all other consciousness. In learning to have practical experience of these different spheres, so the individual can add to his/her knowledge of the different parts of him/herself.

In the Qabalah, each individual is believed to have their own Tree of Life inside them which has to be directly experienced rather than believed as a matter of dogma. Just as human beings have experiences common, so there are also group or collective Trees. It can thus be seen as relevant to both the evolution of the individual, and through the individual, the whole planet.

(Will Parfitt)

READING

Kabbalah and Psychology *by Z'ev ben Shimon Halevi, Gateway* £6.95. The author examines psychology as the study of the archetypal world which hovers between Earth and Heaven. Psychology here is set against the scheme of Kabbalah which takes into account the divine origin of the human being, reincarnation, mystical experience as well as madness. The Tree of Life is studied in relation to both Freudian and Jungian psychology. **The Mystical Qabalah** *by Dion Fortune, Aquarian/Thorsons* £7.95. Of the books that Dion Fortune wrote, this one stands out as a seminal work in the development of the Qabalah and its incorporation into the Western Mystery Tradition. This is a useful reference book for those involved in the esoteric philosophy of the West and the study of the psychology of mystical experience. **The Living Qabalah: A Practical and Experiential Guide to Understanding the Tree of Life** *by Will Parfitt, Element* £8.95. Fully understood, the Qabalah offers a unique system of personal exploration and development, allowing us to examine all aspects of ourselves - our personality, soul and spirit. Using practical and experiential exercises designed for newcomer and experienced alike, this illustrated manual provides a new way of using Qabalah in daily life.

CENTRES OFFERING QUABALAH

International Order of Kabbalists SW19, Living Qabalah SE22.

Shamanism

This is found as part of the native cultures of many different societies all over the world, for instance among the Aborigines of Australia, Lapplanders, American Indians and the Bon Po priests of Tibet. Traditionally the shaman uses rhythmic

drumming and chanting, or more rarely, hallucinogenic drugs to alter consciousness and journey into 'non-ordinary reality' (as Carlos Castenada called it in his popular Don Juan shamanic books) in order to gain insight, heal the sick or make contact with guides or teachers.

It is largely the shamanism of the North American Indians which has made the most impact here, with their *sweat lodge* tradition (a sort of do-it-yourself sauna in which participants chant for long periods) and the *medicine wheel* teachings.

Ritual, mask-making and a veneration for, and co-operation with, nature are also important.

Shamanic ritual and journeying to 'non-ordinary reality' has also been taken up for psychotherapeutic purposes, notably by Stanislav Grof in his *holotropic therapy*. Grof uses various techniques to induce hallucinations in his clients, and has evolved a system of psychotherapy around their experiences.

READING

Way of the Shaman *by Michael Harner Bantam (U.S.A.) £3.60.* Written by an experienced healer and widely travelled field worker, the Way of the Shaman is the most popular guide for the beginner on the shamanic path. Clearly explained practical techniques lead us up to the the the understanding and practice of deep physical and spiritual healing, as practised by shamans everywhere. **Medicine Woman** *by Lynn Andrews, Penguin £5.99.* Neither Lynn Andrews nor Carlos Castaneda have escaped controversy in their books but the value of their accounts grows out of the potential for personal transformation they demonstrate which is available to us all. Andrews' first book describes her initiation by Agnes Whistling Elk. In later books she goes on to work with shamans and medicine people all over the world. **Shamanic Voices** *by Joan Halifax, Dutton U.S.A. £9.55.* This anthology allows shamans from as far afield as Australia, Africa and Alaska to speak for themselves about the rituals they guard and the experiences they have undergone. Their altered states of consciousness act as a bridge for those they serve between everyday life and the eternal. Dr. Halifax provides an excellent introductory essay and brief prefaces to every individual account.

CENTRES OFFERING SHAMANISM

CAER (Centre For Alternative Education And Research) (Cornwall), Eagle's Wing Centre for Contemporary Shamanism NW2, Open Gate (various locations in central London), Resonance SW17.

❝The American Indian who ran a native American shamanistic workshop I participated in looked well cast in the part of leader. When he donned his full headdress, painted his body and danced in a trance he looked as if he had been snatched straight from the Amazon and planted in our midst, which happened to be a country house in Devon.We were a newly formed tribe of twelve Westerners about to be initiated into the local religious practices of the Amazon jungle. I had not met any other members of the group before, other than one, who had been a friend for many years. I had booked that weekend to get out of London and into something different from the environment I was familiar with. I didn't realise just how different it would be.

Most of the Saturday was spent in a large room banging on a drum and chanting. I hated the chanting initially as it seemed monotonous and reminded me of singing chorus after chorus of hymns in church. Later I warmed to the chanting as I slowly got into the groove. I spent much of the day glancing at the beautiful women in the group, wondering when, if ever, I would get to talk to them. At the end of the day a 'sweat lodge' was planned and I was looking forward to this as an opportunity of talking to some of the other members of our group.

In preparation for the evening ritual we were instructed by our chief to build the sweat lodge next to a stream located on the grounds. We did this by foraging for branches which we used for the basic frame. We bent the long branches in the form of a semi-circle and put both ends into the ground. The branches were then tied together and blankets put over the frame so that it ended up igloo shaped. Inside, in the middle of the lodge, we dug a pit, to house the hot coals, which were to be used for the ritual. We then went back to the house to drink some tea (it's hard to drag the English away from their habits).

Most of our tribe had made their way down to the lodge while I lingered over a further cup of tea and made conversation with the few remaining dalliers. When I made my way down to the lodge it was turning dusk. At the bottom of the hill where the lodge lay, to my surprise, I could see the men standing naked in one group painting their bodies and the women standing fully clothed in another group. I wondered what was going on, as I had not been told that nakedness was on the agenda, nor could I fathom why the women were clothed and the men not.

I headed for the male camp and no sooner had I reached them than they started putting pressure on me to disrobe. I had nothing against going naked, but resented doing it on demand and without any mental preparation. It was my hesitancy (I think) that prompted the women to take off their clothes. At this point I took off my clothes too (how could I hold my head high as a red Indian warrior if I was afraid to do this?).

We were then instructed to dance round in a circle tapping a hand to the mouth making what seemed like common Red Indian warpath noises. As I looked around the group whilst we danced it was obvious how strange we must have appeared to any passers by (fortunately the grounds were private), and I thought 'what if my mother would see me now, what would she say'. I was very aware too, of how the extra flab round my waistline must be doing damage to my image as a virile warrior, as it wobbled when I danced, so I did my best to hold it in.

We then moved hot coals from a fire outside the lodge to the pit inside, then tumbled into the lodge. There were no lights and it was pitch black. Water was thrown on the coals and before long a strong heat developed, making me sweat profusely. We continued with the chants we had been rehearsing all day. The hot house became not only a hot house for my body, but my mind and soul also. The familiar gave way to an enveloping hypnotic overpowering rhythm. It was magical and I did not want it to end. The heat finally overcame me and I made my way to the door and was instructed to throw myself into the stream. It must have taken me five minutes in that freezing November water to cool down. I then had to go back into the lodge to heat up. We continued this chanting in the lodge for several hours and I made frequent visits to the natural splash pool. Near the end I was so exhausted that I was crawling out of the lodge on all fours to make my way to the pool. Here I was, naked, on all fours, covered in mud and paint, crawling out of a mud hut. I realised then that there was no way I could salvage my image. This in itself became a great freedom. **99**

Mike Considine

66My experiences in the framework of the Shamanistic/native American tradition have had a profound effect on my life. Through ritual, dance, teachings of the Medicine Wheels, sweatlodge and visionquest, the ancient wisdom came alive, and I contacted the 'Source' with a reality which was undeniable vivid and also unnerving. It was like the Real Thing! - a living 'therapy' rooted in nature, the earth and the body which made other therapies seem artificial, unnatural creations of our society. And it was fun!

My experiences included a mystical revelation of shamistic flying (over South America!), visionary baptism and visions of archetypical symbols which I am still trying to understand. Three workshops over a span of nine months formed the basis of a journey of initiation and for me, it was the biggest trip of my life. It is only now, two years later that I have finally made the return to earth and mundane life, but with an inner richness which is constantly manifested by psychic and sychronistic events in the external world.

As city dwellers we struggle, sometimes desperately, to create a sense of community and connectedness. Shamanism is rooted, amongst other things, in a holistic experience of community. To rewaken this was both threatening to the alienated life I have led, but deep enough to make sense and give meaning to life, even in London. **99**

Andy Hilton

Spiritualism

Spiritualism is centred round the belief of the survival of the personality after death, and that there can be communication between the living and those 'on the other side'. This communication takes place through 'mediums', or 'sensitives' as they are sometimes known, who channel the messages of the dead. The messages may take the form of words of comfort or advice to friends or relatives, and spiritualists believe that this proves that they are still in existence, but in another 'plane' or world .

Many spiritualists are also involved in spiritual healing, which involves either the laying on of hands (hand healing) or absent healing where the patient undergoes treatment at a distance (see 'Healing' in the Body section). Spiritualism in this country usually has a Christian context, although orthodox Christianity tends to regard it with suspicion.

There are a number of spiritualist churches throughout London, where services are held. These involve a service similar to a church service, but at a paticular point a medium will give messages from the 'other side' to particular members of the congregation.

Spiritualism is an organised religion, and is therefore distinct from other forms of psychism, where mediums contact what they believe are spirits in order to make predictions and/or give advice. Another example of psychism is the 'channelling' of books or philosophical or religious teachings through someone who belives themselves to be in touch with a spirit guide.

READING

The Wanderings of a Spiritualist *by Sir Arthur Conan Doyle, Ronin £5.95.* This is a personal account of spiritualism or communication with the dead by the popular writer of the Sherlock Holmes stories. It includes meetings with remarkable people, geographical accounts and political musing from a spiritualist perspective. **The Book on Mediums** *by Allan Kardec, Weiser £9.95.* Although over a century has passed since its original publication, the Book on Mediums remains the most comprehensive and basic text on spiritualism, revealing the fundamental principles of communication with the spirit world. The book contains instruction on the theory of manifestations, the meaning of communicating with the invisible world, the development of mediumship, the difficulties and the dangers that are to be encountered in the practice of spiritism. **Testimony of Light** *by Helen Greaves, C.W. Daniel £4.95.* This book describes the after death experience through the communication given to Helen Greaves by her former friend and teacher, the late Frances Banks, through telepathy across the veil. The message given in the scripts is that the death of the body is but a gentle passing to a much freer and fuller life.

CENTRES OFFERING SPIRITUALISM

Spiritualist Association of Great Britain SW1.

Sufism

Sufism originated in Persia in the sixth century AD as a reaction against what the Sufis saw as the rigidity and worldliness of orthodox Islam. After the time of Mahommed the movement became unpopular with some Muslims, who thought it heretical, and many Sufis suffered condemnation and persecution. The word itself comes from 'suf' which is Persian for the white woollen cloaks the mystics wore. The term 'sufi' is actually correctly used to describe those who have attained knowledge of the divine. An individual who is still on the path is called 'faquir', which means poor, in the sense of spiritual poverty.

Like most mystical traditions the aim of Sufism is direct experience of, and ultimately union with, God, and this is achieved through love, both of other people and of God. Sufism has been called 'the religion of the heart'. There is no dogma, nor any highly structured philosophical system which defines the beliefs of Sufism. The approach is largely devotional, and the emphasis is on intuition and feeling. It stresses the idea of equilibrium and wholeness. The human being is potentially a microcosm of the balanced unity of the universe. The ideal is not to withdraw from the world, but to bring vision and insight into the world. Achieving knowledge of God, the practitioner becomes in turn a vessel for God's knowledge to act in the world.

It is a very fluid tradition and personal communication between teacher and pupil is of central importance. The Teacher initiates the pupil into a chain of Teacher-pupil relationships, the lineage of which stretches back to Mahommed.

The Sufis have always used many different methods to develop consciousness, as the groups which exist in the West today still do. Their practices include contemplative meditation, guided visualisation, breathing exercises, music and the 'whirling' which is associated with the dervishes.

Sufism has inspired much literature. Poetry and the use of symbolism figure largely in the tradition as a means of expressing the experience of the divine. *The Rubaiyat of Omar Khayyam* is perhaps the most famous Sufi inspired text in the West, though their influence is thought to be widespread in European culture. Some claim that Gurdjieff, the Russian mystic and philosopher, was taught by Sufis.

Today Sufi groups vary a great deal. Some are still very much rooted in Islam, and others are more eclectic in their approach. Some advertise their activities while others maintain the traditional secrecy about their activities, believing that those who are truly seeking will find them.

READING
What is Sufism? *by Martin Lings, Mandala/Unwin Hyman £4.95.* An eloquent and authoritative introduction to the mystical dimension of Islam. Martin Lings writes from his own personal experience and deep understanding of Arabic culture and religion: nine concise and powerful chapters convey the essence of Sufism. **Rumi and Sufism** *by Eva de Vitray-Meyerovitch, Post-Apollo Press, U.S.A. £9.95.* A beautifully illustrated book exploring the life thought and background of one of Islam's greatest mystics, written by a French scholar who became a believer in Islam through her works on Sufism. A clear but approachable introduction to the subject, with fascinating material on the *Mevlevi* brotherhood to which he belonged. **The World of Sufi** *by Idries Shah and others, Octagon £12.50.* An anthology of writings about Sufis and their work, with contributions from many authors, including Idries Shah, Doris Lessing and Peter Brent. Chapters on the classical tradition of the Sufis; Sufi humour; Sufi spiritual practices; modern psychology and Sufism; Sufi literature; and current study materials.

CENTRES OFFERING SUFISM
London Sufi Centre W11, Nimatullahi W2.

Modern Teachers

Anthroposophical Association NW1
Rudolph Steiner, an Austrian living at the turn of the century, coined the term 'anthroposophy' (meaning awareness of one's humanity) to sum up his wide-ranging philosophy. Anthroposophy seeks to unite all of humanity's spiritual knowledge, covering the arts, science, philosphy and reilgion, and encompasses a whole social outlook emphasising the importance of human growth. Steiner applied his teaching to medicine, (see the Anthroposophical Medical Association), education (there are several Steiner Schools in the UK), science, and even agriculture where he devised a unique organic system of growing crops.

Barry Long Foundation WC1

Barry Long is an Australian, born in 1926, who lived for 20 years in London and began teaching publicly in 1983. He now teaches in Australia, New Zealand, Europe and the UK through public meetings and seminars, and through books and tapes covering various aspects of 'life and living, death and dying, love and making love, meditation and the art of being'.

There is no formal practice, but Barry Long's teaching encourages the application of greater attention and stillness to all aspects of living to bring about greater self-knowledge and love. He stresses the importance of direct experience rather than religious forms or dogma, and of realising the truth for onself, rather than relying on a guru. No groups or gatherings as such except when Barry Long gives a seminar or talk. Books and tapes available mail order only.

Christian Community   W6

Set up by Rudolph Steiner in 1922 (see Anthroposophical Society, above), the Christian Community seeks to re-affirm the spirit of Christianity. Central ideas are the importance of the resurrection as a symbol of individual growth; the inner meaning of the sacraments; reincarnation; freedom of thought. The arts and counselling are seen as an important part of spiritual practice.

Eckankar   W12

Eckankar takes its direction from Sri Harold Klemp, with the help of whom followers aim to make contact with the Light and Sound of God which is believed to purify the consciousness, and lift the individual into heavenly states. Three principles are important: firstly that the soul is eternal, secondly that travellers on the path of ECK dwell in the spiritual planes, and thirdly that the soul has no past or future, but lives in the present. ECK spiritual aides are provided to give spiritual assistance. Practice is through spiritual exercises (e.g. contemplation of the mantra 'HU', study of dreams and discourses, and service to life.

Foundation for International Spiritual Unfoldment E7
Non-denominational, non-sectarian organisation under the direction of Gururaj Ananda Yogi. Meditation is central, and spiritual practices are individually prescribed for each meditator. Spiritual unfoldment is seen as 'an unveiling of the patternings of the mind' and the dissolving away of unecessary conditionings and attachments which are believed to make us lose sight of our true divine nature or real self.

Free Daist Communion N10
Founded by Heart-Master Da Free John, a western born, living teacher. Disciples believe that he conducts the transforming power of the divine to those who relate to him in the traditional guru-devotee manner. Direct experience of the transcendental is made possible through contact with Heart-Master Da's spiritual company *(satsang yoga)* The teaching itself is about happiness - we are already happy but we don't know it because we are so involved in the self-absorbed quest for happiness. The teachings are studied and devotees then move onto awareness practice of how one separates oneself from happiness. Other practices include chanting, study, work and prayer.

Gurdjieff Ouspensky School
Now acknowledged as one of the spiritual masters of the twentieth century, Gurdjieff brough a system of methods and ideas from the east to he west called The Fourth Way, or the Work. This ancient teaching is for ordinary, normal men and women who wish to work to achieve higher states of consciousness while staying in the circumstances of their everyday life. Ouspensky organised these ideas into a form which he though would be especially suitable for the western intellect. The Fourth Way requies personal verification, unerstanding and efforts from everyone using it. Although very difficult, it aims to provids a short cut for modern men and women on the way of inner self development.

SPIRIT

Lucis Trust SW1

Established by Alice A Bailey, an author and lecturer in the first half of this century who pioneered the idea of a New Age of global co-operation and wholeness. She wrote 24 books presenting an esoteric perspective on psychology, occult meditation and the evolution of humanity, which aim to help individuals be more effective in serving humanity and the Plan of Light and Love during what is seen as a time of transition into the Age of Aquarius. She founded the Lucis Trust as an international agency in the raising of human consciousness, and it now has consultative status with the United Nations. The Lucis trust administers a number of programmes: The Arcane School, a meditation school run by correspondence; Triangles, which is a global network of individuals from different spiritual paths who use prayer and meditation to spread goodwill in the world; World Goodwill, which publishes material presenting a global spiritual perspectives on the issues facing humanity; and Lucis Press which publishes Alice Bailey's books.

Movement of Spiritual Inner Awareness SW1

Founded in California in 1963 by John Roger. See their work as being to awaken people to the awareness of spirit, and of their own true, divine essence. The focus of MSIA is 'soul transcendence'. They believe that soul consciousness can be attained through the practice of spiritual exercises and active study of the 'soul awareness discourses' which are the MSI teachings in book form.

Teilhard Centre W8

The Teilhard Centre works to extend understanding of the cosmic evolutionary thought of Pierre Teilhard de Chardin (1881-1955), a Jesuit priest and paleontologist. He believed that human evolution had not stopped but is continuing in the spiritual more than the physical aspect, effecting a gradual growth of the human community

66 The first retreat I went on was held in a boys' prep school in Sussex. I hadn't had any experience of anything like it before. We had to sleep in dormatories on lumpy mattresses on beds which were too short for anyone over 11. Then we had to get up at 6.30 am to meditate. I was thoroughly miserable the whole time because I was becoming more aware of how unhappy I was with the way I was living, and I spent a lot of the time wishing I could leave. However, when the 5 days I had booked for were up, to my own surprise I decided to stay on for another 5 days to the end of the retreat. Behind my decision to stay was the realisation that I was more in touch with what I really felt than I had probably ever been before, and this was in some way liberating. I also had a lot of support and a tremendous sense of community with the other people on the retreat. When I left and went back to my 'old life' I felt like a visitor from another planet - it was as if I was looking with new eyes. I felt much more centred in myself, my awareness of the environment and people seemed heightened, and some of the structures I had lived in seemed too small and badly fitting for me. It eventually led me to the decision to move and to change my job. 99

Imogen Fox

toward a highly differentiated, highly complex state of union.

The Teilhard Centre is a non-sectarian, educational charity with a diverse membership drawn together by interests in science, philosophy and religion, spirituality, personal growth and th desire to build a future where human beings love and respect not only one another but our fellow creatures and our planetary, galactic and cosmic home.

White Eagle Lodge W8

Founded in 1936 on the teachings of the spirit guide and teacher, White Eagle, who chanelled his message through Grace Cooke. The purpose of the teaching is to enable each individual to develop the light of Christ spirit which is believed to be in every human heart, so that it can radiate into the world. The teaching says that the basic law which controls life is love, expressed through love for God, humanity and nature, and this love is seen as leading people, through the experience of many lives, back to total awareness of the God within them.

OTHER GROUPS

3HO Kundalini Yoga Foundation   NW4

3HO stands for the healthy, happy, holy organisation. They practice Kundalini Yoga, the ancient, tantric technique which seeks to awaken the dormant cosmic energy in human beings and refine it by drawing it up through the seven chakras, or centres of consciousness and energy. The practices include adopting particular positions and movement, breathing techniques, meditation, chanting of mantras and use of mudras (symbolic gestures).

Baha'i Faith   SW7

According to the *Enclyclopaedia Brittannica* this is the 'most widely spread independent religion in the world after Christianity'. Central to the Baha'i Faith is the belief in the oneness of mankind and of all religions. It originated in Persia through a succession of three teachers, a 'Forerunner' who prepared the way for the 'Founder', Baha'u'llah, who died in 1892. The 'Interpreter' then explained the teachings further. There are no priests or clergy, but there are local Baha'i communities practising together through prayer, meditation, service to humanity and worship through work. They have their own scriptures, holy places and parliament.

Beshara Trust   OXON

The Beshara Trust was set up to provide an environment where any person who wishes to establish a spiritual dimension in their life can come together with others to study and work towards this. It seeks to do this without the restrictions of dogma or religion.

a course in miracles

weekly study groups · seminars · individual counselling
contact - heather moran · michael parfitt
centre for a course in miracles
56b sotheby road london n5 2ur 071 704 6197

A Course in Miracles

'A Course in Miracles' is a 'self-study course in spiritual development'. The book was heard as a kind of 'inner dictation' over seven years by a professor of medical psychology at Columbia University, Dr Helen Schucman. The teachings posit that there are only two emotions: love and fear. Love is seen to unite us in our original unity with each other and God. Fear is seen as coming from the ego, and as separative. According to the Course, rather than holding onto emotions such as aggression, resentment and guilt, if perception is shifted towards forgiveness it is possible to recontact this love. It is structured as a text, a workbook of 365 lessons for students and a manual for teachers.

Centre for 'A Course In Miracles'   N5

Centre For Healing Through Forgiveness   N15

Inner Miracle Partnership

College of Psychic Studies   SW7

The College of Psychic Studies runs courses, workshops and hosts lectures on a range of subjects which include healing, psychic phenomena, psychology of past lives, channelling etc. Training in healing and psychic unfoldment given. They believe that at the human level there is no single truth, but that truth can be found in all the great spiritual traditions, and also outside them.

Findhorn Foundation   SCOTLAND

Residential community founded in 1962 by Eileen and Peter Caddy and Dorothy Maclean on the principles that God, or the source of all life, is accessible to each of us at all times, and that nature, including the planet, has intelligence and is part of a much larger plan. Findhorn has no formal doctrine or creed, recognising that all major world religions share the same underlying principles. They subscribe to the 'New Age' belief that an evolutionary expansion of consciousness is taking place in the world, which will infuse humanity with spiritual values. Work, sacred dance and meditation are practised, however it is daily life which is seen as the 'spiritual classroom' with an emphasis on living and working in community with others and developing a responsive relationship to the earth. A range of courses is run (see 'Residential Workshops').

Friends of Shanti Nilaya UK
Founded by Elisabeth Kubler-Ross who has become renowed for her work with the dying. Holds workshops and seminars on aspects of death and dying. Non-sectarian.

Graigian Society   NW5
The Graigian Society grew out of the first green party, and at its core is the 'first Green monstery', a spiritual community in a house full of the creative works of its occupants. They aim to 'bring about a caring and sensitive society'. Workshops and groups are held to facilitate self development through 'natural psychology' which stresses relating to others, creativity , the arts and has elements of the philosophy of Jung and Gurdjieff. They believe that human growth is as important as environmental measures to save the earth. Conduct local environmental campaigns and run groups on 'Being in a Group' and art therapy. Members of the community are easy to spot because of their green striped habits, friendliness and gentleness. They have a leaning towards the Celtic and medieval, and strong links with Wales. 'Graigian' comes from 'Y-Graig' which is Welsh for 'The Rock'.

International School of the Golden Rosycross Surrey
A group in the tradition of the Rosicrucians, who seek to work in the world to enable people to become receptive to Divine Truth, Wisdom and Love. The seem to penetrate every more deeply into perfect knowledge, which they see as having been expressed by different seers at different times, and as part of an eternal process of universal development.

Open Gate London
Open Gate are not a group, but run workshops on aspects of psychology, spirituality and the arts, and longer programmes in East/West studies, process-oriented pscyhology, Buddhist and Shamanic studies. They hold residentials and retreats, some with well-known spiritual teachers.

Order of Bards Ovates and Druids   Surrey
Druidism is one of the old traditions of British paganism (see above). Worship and working in harmony with nature expresses itself in ecological activity and veneration of natural elements: plants, stones, trees, sun, moon and stars. Druids celebrate eight festivals during the year which consist of the equinoxes and solstices, and the four 'fire' festivals. Traditional to druidry is the bardic tradition - story telling, poetry, music and song, which is seen as another form of worship and spiritual celebration.

Subud Central London W9

Founded by Muhammad Subuh, (known to his followers as 'Bapak') an Indonesian who died in 1987. It is not a religion or teaching it itself - members are from all faiths - but aims to be a way of understanding and following the inner messages of religious teachings. This guidance is given through the 'latihan' or inner training, where an inner vibration is transmitted from person to person and causes illumination.

Theosophical Society W1

This is one of the longest established of the non-denominational spiritual groups. Theosophical belief is that man is essentially a part of the all pervading spirit which energises all matter. It sees a common essence in all religion, and seeks to study the truth of these without dogma. The society encourages the study of comparative religion, philosophy and science and to promote the development of the latent powers in man.

Wrekin Trust (some events in London)

Educational charity concerned with the spiritual nature of humanity and the universe. It does not subscribe to any particular doctrine or dogma, but aims to help people find the paths most suited to them. Conferences with distinguished speakers from different traditions both spiritual and scientific, and workshops on a variety of themes.

The Wrekin Trust is an educational charity concerned with promoting awareness and study of the spiritual principles that operate through us and the universe. It is not affiliated to any particular doctrine or dogma, does not offer any one way to the 'truth', and helps people to find the disciplines most suited to them. For further details of our workshops, conferences, summer schools, journey and pilgrimages contact:

THE WREKIN TRUST, RUNNINGS PARK, CROFT BANK, WEST MALVERN, WORCS. WR14 4BP. (0684 892898)

The White Eagle Lodge

The White Eagle Lodge was founded in 1936 on the teachings of the spirit guide and teacher White Eagle; since then many thousands of people have joined in the work, which is one of healing, meditation and the quiet radiation of the Christ light.

An information pack and book list are available. For details of our activities please write to New Lands, Liss, Hampshire, GU33 7HY, or contact our London centre, 9 St Mary Abbots Place, W8 6LS (071-603 7914).

Q: What *other* London guide tells you . . ?

Housing
Women
Good Deals
Sex
Drugs
Communications
Environment
Law
Arts
Media
Groups
Printing
Publishing
Surviving
Minorities
Health
Green Issues
Contacts
Agitation
Computers
Alternative
Technology
Kids
Travel
Food
Alternative
Medicine
Transsexuals
Groups
Squatting

● How to get housed
● How to recycle your household waste
● How to tell a magic mushroom
   from a deadly toadstool
● How to get educated
 - instead of going to school
● How to have safer sex
● What your rights on arrest are and the truth
   about what it's really like 'inside'
● How to get an arts grant
● Where to complain about racial harassment
● How to develop your inner potential
● How to squat
● How to get a women only lift home at night
● Who can give you the advice you need
● Which computer to buy
   and what all the jargon means
● Where to get free food
● How to start a community project
● Where to get cheap
   overnight accommodation
● The effectiveness of different contraceptives
● How to publish your own book
● How to escape into the country
● Where to 'get' religion
● How to sue in a small claims court
● Where to see pig racing in the inner city
● How to set up your own business
● and (almost) everything you ever wanted to
   know about the big city but were afraid to ask.

Advice
Centres
Disabilities
Networks
House DIY
Jobs
Foreigners
Bargains
Martial
Arts
Lesbians
& Gays
Community
Networks
Dole
Thriving
Self
Discovery
Libraries
Politics
Information
Men
Growth
Transport
Transvestites
Spirituality
Phone
Rights
Markets
Help

A: Survivors London.
The *other* London guide

ONLY £6.95

Survivors' London is 304 pages crammed with invaluable information to help you make your way in the big city. Whether you're an old hand, a new arrival or just passing through, **Survivors' London** tells you a different story about how to survive and thrive.

Survivors' London gives hints, tips, know-how, explanations and advice on virtually every relevant subject you can think of. And in case you need further help, you'll find more than 2,500 organisations listed as well as up-to-date details of what they do.

Available now from bookshops or order direct by filling in the slip below

■■

Name _____

Address _____

Please send me _____ copies of *Survivors'*
London at £6.95 + £1 p&p each (total £7.95 each).
I enclose a cheque for _____

Please make cheques payable to Brainwave and send to BCM Raft, London WC1N 3XX.

COMMUNICATION

Bookshops

The bookshops below are specialists in some aspects of the areas covered by this book. Some may be general bookshops, but because they stock a largish supply of books in these fields we have included them.

BOOKSHOPS EAST

Wisdom Publications

402 Hoe Street, London E17 9AA (081) 520 5588.

Mon-Sat 10-6, shop located on first floor. Probably the largest selection of in Europe of books on Buddhism and related art and culture. Publish the fabulous Tibetan art calendar (£13.95 for 1990), videos of Tibetan teachers, and audio cassettes on various subjects. Mail order, £2.50 for catalogue.

Genesis Books

188 Old Street, London EC1V 9BP (071) 250 1868.

Mon-Fri 11.30-7, Sat 11-3 (sometimes till 5pm if busy). Small bookshop situated in a therapy complex, with macrobiotic cafe located in building (the East West restaurant). They specialize in alternative medicine and macrobiotics books. Massage, psychology, herbalism, religion, Buddhism, green issues etc. Also sell crystals, 'new age' cassettes and videos.

BOOKSHOPS NORTH

East Asia Company

101 - 103 Camden High Street, Camden, London . (071) 388 5783 or 388 6704.

Wide range of books on Alternative Medicine as well as books on general health, symptom alleviation, natural living, oriental philosophy and lifestyle. They do charts (such as reflexology charts) on health for practitioners as well as for the public.

Sister Write

190 Upper Street, Islington, London N1 1RQ (071) 226 9782.

Mon-Sat 10-6, Thurs 10-7. Large section on women's spirituality and health, child care, also sections on black women,

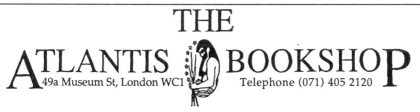

lesbians, fiction and a big children's section. Crafts made by women. Mail order.

Sunpower Books

198 Blackstock Road, London N4 (071) 704 0247.

10-6 Mon to Sat. This co-operatively run bookshop has sections on health and natural healing, spirituality, mysticism, wholefood, cookery and nutrition, women's health, pregnancy and child-care. Also sell aromatherapy oils, homoeopathic remedies and herbs.

Compendium Bookshop

234 Camden High St., Camden, London NW1 8QS (071) 267 1525 / 485 8944. Mon-Sat 10-6, Sun 12-6. Has an extensive range of books on self help, psychology, astrology, new science, healing and related subjects. There is also a large range of books dealing with recovery, co-dependency and the subject of adult children of alcoholics. Large range of imported material and a selection of self-help audio cassettes. Mail order.

Friends Book Centre

Friends House, Euston Road, London NW1 2BJ 387 3601x23.
Mon-Fri 9.30-5.30, except Tues opens 10.30. Open occasionally on Sats). This is a bookshop run by the Quaker Society of Friends and covers religion, including comparative religion, peace studies, north south issues, Quakerism, psychology, health, women, green issues and vegetarian cookery. Postcards. Mail order.

Rudolph Steiner Bookshop (1)

35 Park Road, London NW1 6XT (071) 723 4400.
Mon-Fri 10-2 & 3-5.30, Sat 10-2 & 3-5). Books on anthroposophy, Waldorf education, Goethean science, bio-dynamic agriculture, Anthroposophic medicine, the arts, children's books, arts, prints, wooden and soft toys, hauschka toiletries.

Karnac (Books) Ltd.

118 Finchley Road, London NW3 431 1075.
Mon-Sat 9-6. Stock a comprehensive range of books on psychoanalysis, psychotherapy, analytical psychology (Jung). Small section on women's studies and philosophy. Appropriately situated just round the corner from the Freud Museum, and close to the Tavistock Clinic. They also publish books in the psychoanalytic and psychotherapy field. Mail order from Gloucester Road Branch.

Changes Bookshop

242 Belsize Road, Kilburn, London NW6 4BT (071) 328 5161.
Mon-Fri 10-6, Sat 10-5. Specialists in books on psychology, psychotherapy, counselling and personal growth. Friendly - may offer you a cup of tea while you browse. Very efficient mail order service. You can phone and pay by credit card. It's a small bookshop but they are big on enthusiasm and are knowledgeable about the subjects. They are eager to talk about psychological theories and the latest psychotherapies. Brian Wade at Changes did the book reviews for the 'Psychotherapy' section of this book. They provide useful lists of books on particular psychotherapies e.g. NLP, Jungian together with reviews of those books. Produce a newsheet four times a year of new titles. Shouldn't all bookshops be like this?

Housmans Bookshop

5 Caledonian Road, London N1 9DX (071) 837 4473.
Stock selection of green issues and alternative books. Open Mon-Fri 10am- 6.00 pm Sat, 10.00am- 5.00pm

BOOKSHOPS SOUTH

Passage Bookshop

5 Canning Cross, Grove Lane, Camberwell, London SE5 8Bh (071) 274 7606.
General bookshop, but because it is next to the Maudsley Hospital carries tiles on psychiatry mostly, but also books on psychotherapy and psychology.

Spiritualist Association of Great Britain

33 Belgrave Square, London SW1X 8Ql (071) 235 3351.
Bookshop on the premises with titles on spiritualism, psychism etc.

BOOKSHOPS

Karnac (Books) Ltd.
58 Gloucester Road, South Kensington, London SW7 4QY (071) 584 3303.
Mon-Sat 9am-6pm. Specialise in books on psychoanalysis, analytical psychology and psychotherapy. Branch at Finchley Road. Mail order available.

Waterstones (1)
99 Old Brompton Road, Kensington, London SW7 3LE (071) 581 8522.
Mon-Sat 9.30-9, Sun 12-7. General bookshop with good sections on holistic health, psychology and self help, diet, religion, mysticism, psychism.

BOOKSHOPS - W1 & WC1 & WC2

AtoZ Martial Arts Centre
Ground Floor, 11 Kenway Rd, London SW5 ORP (071) 370 0236.
Sell books on martial arts and supplies.

Family Planning Association
27-35 Mortimer Street, London W1N 7RJ (071) 636 7866.
Mon-Thur 9-5, Fri 9-4.30. Books on birth control, conception, sexuality.

Wholefood Books
24 Paddington Street, London W1M 4DR (071) 935 3924.
Mon 8.30-6, Tues-Thurs 8.30-6.60, Sat 8.30-1.30. Specialises in nutrition and health, alternative therapies, natural childbirth and child rearing, organic gardening and farming, wholefood cookery. There also a wholefood shop on the premises.

Atlantis Bookshop
49A Museum Street, London WC1A 1LY (071) 405 2120.
Mon, Tues, Wed, Fri 10-5.30, Thurs 10-8, Sat 11-5. Atlantis bookshop was closed for a while, but is now back in business and expanded into the basement. It's the world's oldest occult bookshop, established in 1922. It covers all areas of occult, spiritualism, psychism, paganism, wicca and spirituality along with lighter subjects such as dowsing, ley lines and mythology.

Dillons Bookstore
82 Gower St, London WC1E 6EQ (071) 636 1577.
Very large bookshop which is easy to browse round, the books being mostly in subject order. They have a comprehensive stock of alternative medicine, psychology, psychotherapy and spiritual books.

Odyssey Books Ltd
30 Lamb's Conduit Street, London WC1N 3LE (071) 405 6735.
Mon-Fri 10.30-6, Sat 12.30-3.30. Holistic books for mind, body and spirit. Small, friendly, atmospheric bookshop. Established six years. Wheelchair access. The clinic for homoeopathy is within the shop. Mail order welcome.

Quest Bookshop
12 Bury Place, London WC1A 2LE (071) 405 2309.
Mon-Fri 10-6, Sat 10-4. Linked to the Theosophical Society and publishing house, Quest is a large bookshop stocking books from other publishers, covering theosophy, astrology, eastern religions, meditation, yoga, depth psychology, hermetic philosophy, alternative medicine, parapsychology etc.

Skoob
15 Sicilian Avenue, Southampton Row, Holborn, London WC1A 2QH (071) 404 3063.

10.30-6.30 Mon. Second hand books, many on psychology.

Skoob 2

19 Bury Place, Bloomsbury, London WC1A 2JH (071) 405 0030.
10.30 - 6.30 Mon to Sat. General second-hand bookshop with sections covering magic, eastern philosophy, general religions, shamanism, alternative health, mysticism, mythology, astrology and tarot. Two floors.

Books For A Change

52 Charing Cross Road, London WC2H 0BB (071) 836 2315.
Jointly organised by CND, Friends of the Earth, the United Nations Association and War on Want. A 'green' bookshop with books on practical and political aspects of ecology, recycled stationery, periodicals and some very nice postcards. Send SAE for comprehensive catalogue.

Books Etc

120 Charing Cross Road, London WC2 (071) 379 6838.
General bookshop which has a good selection of books on Mind Body Spirit, psychology, psychotherapy, alternative medicine.

Mysteries

9 Monmouth Street, Covent Garden, London WC2H 9DA (071) 240 3688.
Mainly a bookshop but they also sell pendulums, ritual magic candles, dakinis, pentagram rings, runes - you can make contact with the etheric just around the corner from John Le Carre's fictional home of MI5 at Cambridge Circus. It doesn't seem possible that anything else could be crammed into this lilac-coloured shop - and indeed it's often so full of people it can be difficult to get inside. Though primarily a bookshop (esoteric, self help, spiritual, natural health), there are also music and self help tapes and videos, jewellery, tarot decks and crystals. Tarot and palm readings are also carried out on the premises. Mail order.

Neal Street East

5 Neal Street, London WC2H 9UP (071) 240 0135/6.
The bookshop on the first floor of this shop selling oriental arts and crafts specialises in books on all things oriental. This includes eastern religions, meditation and oriental mythology; oriental astrology and divination; health from

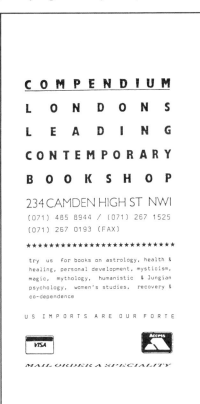

COMPENDIUM LONDONS LEADING CONTEMPORARY BOOKSHOP

234 CAMDEN HIGH ST NW1
(071) 485 8944 / (071) 267 1525
(071) 267 0193 (FAX)

try us for books on astrology, health & healing, personal development, mysticism, magic, mythology, humanistic & Jungian psychology, women's studies, recovery & co-dependence

US IMPORTS ARE OUR FORTE

MAIL ORDER A SPECIALITY

chinese herbs, kiatsu to macrobiotics; martial arts and yoga; oriental customs, arts and culture. They also stock calligraphic inks and brushes and can show you how to use them in their Chinese brush painting workshops. Other events hosted by the bookshop are ikebana and cookery demonstrations, and Chinese New Year Celebrations.

Silver Moon
68 Charing Cross Road, London WC2H OBB (071) 836 7906.
Mon-Sat 10.30-6.30. Women's health, spirituality, religion, self help, healing. Tarot cards and jewellery in matriarchal symbols. Fiction is all women authors and there is a lesbian, black and political section.

W. & G. Foyle Ltd
113-119 Charing Cross Road, London WC2H OEB (071) 437 5660.
Very large general bookshop. Covers the 'mind body spirit' field. Books are sorted by publisher so it's often difficult to browse.

Waterstones (2)
121-125 Charing Cross Road, London WC2H OEA (071) 434 4291.

DRAGON BOOKS
Mail Order

Eastern and Western mysticism, philosophy, occult, psychology and natural health, new and secondhand out-of-print books. Send 4 x 15p stamps for latest catalogues to **Dragon Books (L)**, 36 Chescombe Road, Yatton, Bristol BS19 4EN

Mon-Fri 9.30-7.30, Sat 10-7. Good general bookshop with sections on psychology and psychotherapy, self help, mystical, spirituality, divination.

Watkins Books Ltd
19-21 Cecil Court, Covent Garden, London WC2N 4HB 836 2182/836 3778.
Mon-Sat 10-6 except Weds when they open at 10.30. Refurbished a year ago and expanded into the basement, Watkins is known for the breadth and depth of its selection of books on natural therapies, personal development, astrology, mysticism etc. One of the best sections in London on spirituality and religion including eastern and western approaches, and the works of spiritual teachers. Bargains are to be had in the second hand section downstairs. If you need advice on which book to buy you'll be in good hands, because David Redstone and his staff at Watkins did the book reviews for the sections on complementary medicine, body approaches and spirituality in this book.

BOOKSHOPS WEST

Books for Cooks
4 Blenheim Crescent, London W11 2EE (071) 221 1992.
9.30-6 Mon-Sat.
Comprehensive range of cook books. Vegetarian, vegan, macrobiotics, holistic. Secondhand section.

Waterstone's Booksellers
193 Kensington High Street, Kensington, London W8 6SH (071) 937 8432.
Largish bookshop with a substantial 'mind body and spirit' section in the basement.

Inspiration

28 Devonshire Road, Chiswick, London W4 2HD (081) 994 0074.
Mon-Sat 10-6. New Age centre selling crystals, tarot cards and books, runes, relaxation, meditation and new age music tapes and jewellery. Astrological birth charts done.

Libraries

Before 1985 certain libraries specialised in particular subjects, but this is unfortunately no longer the case. Although the libraries below have not been able to keep up their specialist sections and buy new books, they still have the remains of specialist collections which were in existence before 1985.

If you want a particular book, and you know its title, you may be able to borrow it through the inter-library lending scheme. Ask at you local library about this.

There are also specialist collections in university libraries, but these can be difficult to get access to if you are not a student or member of staff.

Newham Bibliographical Services Department

62A Pond Road, Stratford, London E15 (071) 511 1332.
Section on Eastern Religion.

Medical Library

Marylebone Library, Marylebone Road, London NW1 5PS (071) 798 1039.
Large collection of material on medicine, health and related topics. They are happy to answer telephone, written or personal enquiries.

Swiss Cottage Library

88 Avenue Road, London NW3 3HA (071) 586 5989.
Large section on psychology.

Church Street Library

Church Street, Kensington, London NW8 (071) 798 1480.
Section on religion.

Westhill Library

Westhill, Wandsworth, London SW18 1RZ (081) 871 6386.
Specialist sections on eastern religion including Hinduism and Jainism.

Fulham Library

598 Fulham Road, London SW6 5NX (081) 748 3020.
Christian religious collection.

Westminster Central Reference Library

St Martin's Street, London WC2 (071) 798 2036.
Reference library with largish section on religion.

Publishers and Distributors

The publishers listed below have recently published books in the holistic field. Some are large, general publishers who may have a small number of titles on health, self improvement or related subjects.

Ashgrove Distribution

4 Brassmill Centre, Brassmill Lane, Bath BA1 3JN (0225) 425539.
Promote and distribute books of various publishers. Subjects include new age, health and healing, earth mysteries, religion and myth, psychology.

PUBLISHERS

Wisebuy Publications
25 Rest Cottages, London NW6 1RJ (071) 433 1121.
Publish three titles on food allergy, healthy eating and massage and relaxation.

Unwin & Hyman
15-17 Broadwick Street, London W1V 1FP (071) 439 3126.
Publish the large 'Mandala' series — personal growth, spirituality, healing etc.

Arlington Books
Kingsbury House, 15-17 King Street, London SW1Y 6QU (071) 930 0097.
Publish some books on health and self-help.

Arrow Books
Random Century House, 20 Vauxhall Bridge Rd, London SW1V 2SA (071) 973 9700 ex 217.
A publisher of general titles, with some New Age, health and self help titles.

Wellspring
46 Cyril Mansions, Prince of Wales Drive, London SW11 4HW (071) 720 3541.
Books and tapes on self discovery and the psychology of vision.

Grafton Books
8 Grafton Street, London W1 (071) 493 7070.
General, some green issues books.

Angus & Robertson
16 Golden Square, London W1R 4BN (071) 437 9602.
General; some titles on health/self help.

Fontana Paperbacks
8 Grafton Street, London W1X3LA (071) 493 7070.
General;some titles on health and green issues.

Shanti Sadan
29 Chepstow Villas, Notting Hill Gate, London W11 3DR 727 7846.
Books on yoga, Vedanta, poetry and the mysticism of the far east. Translations of Sanskrit classics. Publish 'Self Knowledge', a yoga quarterly journal devoted to spiritual thought and practice. Single copy including postage £1.50

Faber & Faber
3 Queens Square, London WC1 (071) 465 0045.
Titles on religion, philosophy, health, medicine, nursing, midwifery and psychology.

Dorling Kindersley
9 Henrietta Street, Covent Garden, London WC2E 8PS (071) 836 5411.
Range of books strong on visuals covering health (including a series from the British Holistic Medical Association on common problems), yoga and massage, childcare, vegetarian cooking.

Rider & Co
Century Hutchinson, Brookmount House, 62-65 Chandos Place, Covent Garden, London WC2N 4NW (071) 240 3411.
Publish books on ancient mysteries, divination, health and healing, martial arts, mysticism and religion, occult and personal growth.

Arkana (Penguin)
27 Wrights Lane, London W8 5TZ (071) 938 2200.
Publish New Age books for Mind, Body and Spirit. Psychology, transformation, health, science and mysticism, women's spirituality and astrology.

Bantam Books

Transworld Publishers, 61-63 Uxbridge Rd, W5 5SA, 579 2652/3.
General publishers with small range of self-help, popular psychology titles.

C W Daniel Comp Ltd

1 Church Path, Saffron Walden, Essex, CB10 1JP (0799) 21909.
Publishers of books on natural healing, and the metaphysical and spiritual.

Element Books

Longmead, Shaftesbury, Dorset SP7 8PL (0747) 51448.
One of the largest publishers and distributers of books on eastern and western religious traditions, spiritual teachers, psychology, modern spirituality, healing etc.

Foulsham

Yeovil Road, Slough, Berks SL1 4JH (0753) 26769.
Publish various self help and health titles, and have just started a new imprint, Quantum, for 'the exploration of inner space and its practical application'.

Fowler & Co Ltd

1201 High Road, Chadwell Heath, Romford, Essex RM6 4DH (081) 597 2491.
Small shop open Mon-Fri 9-5. Astrology specialists and mind, body, spirit titles. Also carry cassette tapes. Mail order.

Free Association Books

26 Freegrove Road, London N7 9RQ (071) 609 5646/0507.
Interesting range of books on psychoanalysis. There are titles exploring the work of theorists, as well some attempting the worthy task of bringing psychology and social/political/cultural issues together. Their journal, Free Associations, attempts to take this further by making psychoanalysis more relevant to urgent social issues and to contribute to a more socially conscious profession. Includes scholarly articles on women, race, power, group dynamics in institutions etc. £20 for 4 issues.

GAIA Books Ltd

Umbrella Studios, 12 Trundle St, London SE1 1QT 403 5124/407 9003.
Titles on natural health and living, self development and ecology, including The Gaia Atlas of Planet Management. Independently owned company.

Hamish Hamilton

27 Wrights Lane, London W8 5TZ (071) 938 3388.
General; some publications on green and alternative issues.

Macdonalds

3rd Floor, Greater London House, Hampstead Road, London NW1 (071) 377 4600.
General publishers; natural medicine, self help and green guides (including John Button's *Green Pages*).

Thorsons Publishing Group

Dennington Estate, Wellingborough, Northants NN8 2RQ (0933) 440033.
Large selection of titles in the Thorsons, Aquarian and Crucible range; health, self-help, spirituality, psychology, healing, psychism. Thorsons have cornered the health food shop market, where their bookstands are to be seen on display.

University Associates International

45-47 Victoria Street, Mansfield, Notts NG18 5SU 0623 640203.

Distribution centre of books on management training, organisation development, effective leadership etc.

White Eagle Publishing Trust
New Lands, Brewells Lane, Liss, Hampshire GU33 7HY (0730) 893300.
Publishing wing of White Eagle Lodge (q.v.). Publish the work of White Eagle, a spirit guide, and others. Audio cassettes.

Films

British Association for Counselling
37a Sheep Street, Rugby, Warwickshire CV21 3BX (0788) 78328/9.
Catalogue can be purchased for £1 (including p&p) describing videos and films for hire.

Concord Video and Film Council
201 Felixstowe Road, Ipswich, Suffolk IP3 9BJ (0473) 726012/715754.
Wide range of videos and films available for hire or purchase covering psychotherapy and counselling, alternative medicine, relationships, peace, social/global issues, the arts etc. Psychotherapy videos include famous therapists in action, coverage of issues such as death and bereavement, child abuse, eating disorders, drug addiction, group psychotherapy, counselling techniques etc. A real treat is the fly-on-the-wall's view of a Californian encounter group - get all the action without taking any of the risks! Hire charges range from £1 to £20, and sale from £20 to £200. Send £1 for video catalogue (includes updates).

Magazines and Publications

Attitudes
Mathew Manning Centre, 39 Abbeygate St, Bury St Edmunds, Suffolk IP33 1LW, IP33 1LN 02847 69502/752364.
General interest magazine which covers alternative thinking, health music, relationships, psychology, self awareness, green and topical issues. Produced by the Matthew Manning centre. Quarterly, subscriptions £5.50 per year, £10 abroad.

Caduceus
38 Russell Terrace, Royal Leamington Spa, Warks CV31 1HE (0926) 451897.
Articles on holistic healing, natural health, spirituality and the connection between body, mind and spirit aimed at healers, health care professionals and members of the general public with an interest in exploring holistic health. Quarterly, £2.50 per issue, 38pp.

Directory of Occult Resources (DOOR)
Spiral Publications, 8 King Street, Glastonbury, Somerset BA6 9JY.
Everything for the would-be Wiccan in here: groups, contacts and an impressive number of occult/pagan magazines and publications. £2.95 (UK) per year. Spiral also publish a journal, Starcraft, for £2 per issue.

Electromagnetic News
PO Box 25, Liphook, Hants GU30 7SE (042) 877430.
Charts electromagnetic fields research, the effects of powerlines, VDUs and

FILMS/MAGAZINES

microwaves, and looks at safety guidelines and medical uses. Bi-monthly, subs £15 per annum..

Group Relations
152 Park St Lane, Park St, St Albans AL2 2AU (0727) 72010.
A journal for people working in groups and teams. Published three times a year. £1.85 per issue. Sub £6.

Health Today
Queensway House, 2 Queensway, Redhill, Surrey, RH1 1QS (0737) 768611.
Free magazine for shoppers in health food shops. Reports on health and green issues. Their special feature is 'The Green Hand Gang Pages' for kids.

Here's Health
Victory House, 14 Leicester Place, London WC2H 7NB (071) 437 9011.
Glossy monthly magazine available in newsagents with articles on natural medicine, nutrition, vegetarian cookery, holistic health, news, interviews and reviews.

Homoeopathy International
243 The Broadway, Southall, Middlesex UB1 3AN (081) 574 4281.
The journal comes out three times per year. Subs £3 pa. which includes p/p.

Homoeopathy Today
Humane Education Centre, Avenue Lodge, Bounds Green Road, London N22 4EU (081) 889 1595.
Articles about homoeopathy, research, history, institutions and uses and treatment of particular conditions. Published by the Hahnemann Society. Quarterly, subscription £8 per annum. Apply for specimen copy.

Human Potential Magazine
5 Layton Road, London N1 0PX (071) 354 5792.
The who, what, where, when and why not of the 'growth' movement. Articles cover humanistic psychology, Jungian psychotherapy, sexuality, spirituality, controversy etc. with interviews and news, book reviews, and an extensive calendar of events with all the workshops and groups you could ever want to go to in the following three months. For subscription phone (081) 291 6254. Quarterly, £5 per year.

Journal Of Complementary Medicine
21 Portland Place, London W1N 3AF (071) 636 9543.
An academic publication which focuses on research and hopes to promote complementary medicine to other fields of science. £3.95 per issue. Twice a year.

Journal of Alternative and Complementary Medicine
Mariner House, 53a High St, Bagshot, Surrey GU19 5AH (0276) 51522.
Independent magazine devoted to alternative and complementary medicine. Excellent round up of recent research papers on complementary medicine, and thoroughgoing articles on issues of concern to those in the field. Letters and lighter features include 'A day in the life' of practitioners. Published monthly £1.95 each issue. £25 sub.

Kindred Spirit
P O Box 29, Warminster, Wiltshire BA12 9YD (0985) 217772 or (09853) 775.
A 'New Age' magazine covering earth energies, meditation, healing, death,

219

MAGAZINES/NETWORKS

spiritual experiences, crystals, scientific breakthroughs, psychology, esoterica, complementary medicine, alternative therapies, environmental issues. Interviews with innovative thinkers, environmentalists, spiritual teachers and therapists, plus news, book reviews, a resource directory and mail order catalogue. Quarterly £1.75 per issue, or subscriptions £8 per annum.

Link Up
51 Northwick Business Centre, Blockley, Glos GL56 9RF (0386) 701091.
Magazine with global perspective with articles on personal growth, spirituality etc. Nationwide/international focus. Qtly £1.85.

New Humanity
51A York Mansions, Prince of Wales Drive, London SW11 4BP (071) 622 4013.
Envisages integrating the disciplines of science, philosophy, politics, the arts, religion and the humanities to promote closer co-operation and understanding among them. 'Endeavours to 'clarify a direction in which humanity might evolve towards harmony and integration through diversity of knowledge.' Bi-monthly, £1.50 per issue.

One Earth
The Findhorn Press, The Park, Forres IV36 0TZ (0309) 30582.
In-depth articles on aspects of modern spirituality. Quarterly.

Open Mind
22 Harley St, London W1N 2ED (071) 637 0741.
Is published bi-monthly by MIND, the National Association for Mental Health magazine. Now in its eighth year of

publication the magazine has covered topics such as psychotherapy for troubled young people, complementary medicine, the politics of poverty, who should pick up the therapy bill. It has encouraged debate among health care professionals, patients and their relatives. Open Mind provides a regular 'benefits' column, an update on research in mental health publications, international developments and full listings of coming events. Yearly rates for six issues: £8 individuals, £10 organisations and institutions.

Psychic News
2 Tavistock Chambers, Bloomsbury Way, London WC1A 2SE (071) 405 3340 and 3345.
Established 1932. The world's only independent weekly Spiritualist paper containing news, reviews, events and comment. Price 24p. Obtainable from newsagents or direct subscription.

Resurgence
Ford House, Bideford, Devon EX39 6EE 02374 293.
Perhaps the most 'literary' of magazines devoted to holistic topics, Resurgence can boast contributors such as Kathleen Raine and James Hillman. A high standard of photography featured recently by the addition of colour pages. Subjects covered are ecology and its spiritual roots, cultural values, holistic education, world issues, religion, the countryside etc. Substantial book reviews section and a poetry section. Bi-monthly.

Self and Society
Gale Centre Publications, Whitakers Way, Loughton, Essex IG10 1SQ (081) 508 9344.

220

The European journal of Humanistic Psychology. Official Journal of the Association for Humanistic Psychology in Britain. Articles focus on a different subject of relevance in the field each issue. Bi-monthly - £1.95. Individual sub £10pa (UK).

Transformer
New Life Designs Ltd, 170 Campden Hill Road, London W8 7AS (071) 938 3788.
Free resource guide of events, practitioners, products and services. Quarterly. Spring issue is also programme for Festival of Mind, Body, Spirit.

Vegan
33-35 George Street, Oxford OX1 2AY (0865) 722166.
Journal of the Vegan Society. 36 pages, quarterly. Single issue £1, subs £5 pa. News, articles, health and nutrition, recipes, young vegans pages, book and product reviews. Also publish books on aspects of veganism, including The Cruelty Free Shopper (£3.99 from them) which contains comprehensive listings of products made and tested without cruelty to animals.

Vegetarian
ESG Publishing, 3rd Floor, 58 High Street, Sutton, Surrey 770 7337.
Magazine of the Vegetarian Society, attractive format and articles on nutrition, environmental issues, news and as you might expect, lots of vegetarian recipes and mouth-watering pictures. Bi-monthly, £1.00

Whole Life Magazine
P O Box 12, Wallsend, Tyne and Wear NE28 6AN (091) 234 0259.
Health, complementary medicine, thera-

pies, food, community, personal growth incorporated in an integrated way. Bi-monthly, on distribution in newsagents, healthfood shops and by subscription £1.50.

Yoga and Health
21 Cadburn Crescent, Lewes, East Sussex BN7 1NR (0273) 473495.
Monthly magazine covering all aspects of yoga and its health aspects, alternative therapies, book reviews, reviews of new products. £1.50.

Networks
Networks can range from highly structured organisations with strict membership criteria, to loose, informal contact groups. Some are simply information services, while others aim to help members exchange skills and resources.

Business Network
18 Well Walk, Hampstead, London NW3 1LD (071) 435 5000.
For the subscription of £35 per year, you get a register of members with whom to network, a monthly meeting with guest speakers and time for discussion and socialising, members' announcements or for browsing the networking tables, as well as a newsletter (bi- or tri-annually). Entry to meetings is £5 to members, £8 to non-members.

Breakthrough Centre
7 Poplar Mews, Uxbridge Road, Shepherds Bush, London W12 7JS (081) 749 8525.
Centre and network serving those who wish to combine personal growth, the sane, humane, ecological (SHE) economy and practical commercial ap-

proaches. Support for owner-managed small businesses, transforming large organisations, and career development courses and advice. Workshops on personal development in a commercial context. Open house time Tuesday to Saturday 5-7pm for contacts. Sunday evening meditation and sharing (second Sunday of the month, except August). Breakthrough club for owner managers. Noticeboards.

Ixia Ltd

PO Box 1255, London W4 3PX 994 3010.

Ixia produce a monthly diary of events in the areas of personal growth, ecology, complementary medicine, earth mysteries, higher awareness and other related subjects, in date order. Events include lectures, seminars, weekends, workshops etc. Inclusion is free, and it costs £12 for you to subscribe to a year's posted bulletins, which come in booklet form with descriptions of each event. Also keep data-base of organisations dedicated to providing information or education on a sustainable basis (though counselling and treatments on their own are not included at present).

Natural Health Network

Arnica House, 170 Campden Hill Road, London W8 7AS (071) 938 3788.

For practitioners of natural therapies and all those who are interested. Newsletter, annual conference.

Ace of Rods

Acca and Adda, BCM Akademia, London WC1N 3XX.

Contacts magazine for Wiccans/Pagans and for those who seek their vision. Contacts ads free to subscribers. 8 issues

VISION INTO ACTION

The Breakthrough Centre is a focus for Enterprise, committed to bringing new consciousness into the world of work.

Our clients are mostly self-employed, working for themselves and working on themselves. We relieve the isolation of working by yourself, with solid practical guidance from an imaginative, creative perspective - all for the price of a monthly massage.

To turn your vision into action, contact
Andrew Ferguson or Fiona Graham at
The Breakthrough Centre,
7 Poplar Mews, Uxbridge Road,
London W12 7JS.
Call us on 081-749 8525

£8.50 pa.

Acorn Centre

Spindlewood, Watery Lane, Lower Westholme, Shepton Mallet, Somerset (074 989) 338.

Events and conferences, meditation adventures around the British Isles. Also books mail order.

Association for Therapeutic Healers

c/o Celia Weller, Derbyshire House, Crank Road, Kings Moss, Merseyside (071) 240 0176.

A meeting point for the 'new' healers - support groups, courses, seminars workshops open days, talks and a regular newsletter. Register of practitioners. Membership £15 per year for newsletter, reduced fees for seminars, inclusion on register etc. Must be proposed and seconded by existing members.

First Editions
PO Box 2578, Sedona AZ 86336, United States 602/282 9574.
New marketing opportunities -international directory of 9,000 listings and newsletter. Co-operative mailings to the USA, metaphysical retailers. Mailing lists and workshops.

GAIA
2-4 High Street, Glastonbury, Somerset BA6 9DU (0458) 34131.
They provide 'alternative information' on vegetarian Bed and Breakfasts, guides and tours, rooms for hire, festivals in the Glastonbury area. They have 30 healers and therapists registered with them.

Networking Market
86 Wavertree Road, London NW3 5JY.
Exchange network for services where people can 'trade' various skills with each other, such as counselling, gardening, computer know-how, babysitting etc. Only £3 to register.

Scientific and Medical Network
The Old School House, Hampnett, North-leach, Glos GL54 3NN (0451) 60869.
Informal international group whose 600 strong membership consists mainly of qualified scientists and doctors, with some psychologists, engineers and philosophers. It aims to extend contemporary scientific and medical thinking beyond its current materialistic way of looking at the world, and include 'non -

physical possibilities'. Its main concerns include the nature of consciousness; brain/mind interface, parapsychology, causality; healing, psychoneuro-immunology; science, ecology and spirituality; values in education and training. Publishes newsletter 3 times yearly. Associate membership open to those sympathetic with aims (£7.50 pa). Full membership by invitation only to scientists. Members receive members lists, and can participate in local groups, working groups and special seminars and lectures. Mail order tapes of lectures.

Therip
5 Upper Wimpole Street, London W1.
Circulates information about teaching, training and research in psychoanalysis in institutions in Britain. Aims to be a forum for the exchange of views across disciplinary boundaries in the context of plurality of interests in psychoanalysis. Organises annual conference, public lecture series and is planning a series of workshops at the Freud Museum (see 'Museums' section).

Whole Health Institute
Mickleton House, Mickleton, Chipping Campden, Glos GL55 6RY (0386) 438727.
Aims to provide a focus and meeting

ground for professionals and lay people interested in the cause of health, and promote a new spirit in the healing arts, from both a traditional and non-traditional standpoint. Headquarters are in the USA.

EDUCATION

Recognised Academic Courses

The courses below are run by academic institutions and are recognised as educational qualifiations. Please refer to alphabetica list of centres at the back of the book for addresses.

Polytechnic of East London

School for Independent Study, Polytechnic of East London, Holbrook Centre, London E15 3EA (081) 590 7722.
Title (1) BA/BSc by Independent Study, (2) MA/MSc by Independent Study. *Duration* (1) 3 years full-time, 5 years part-time. (2) Minimum: full-time 1 year, part-time 2 years. *Entry requirements* (1) 2 'A' levels required, or comparable

qualifications. (2) Honours degree, or equivalent. Apply to course administrator for details of fees.

Regents College - Psychology Dept.

Inner Circle, Regents Park, London NW1 4NS (071) 487 7406.
Title MA in the Psychology of Therapy and Counselling. *Duration* 27 months with the possibility of 12 months extension in special cases. *Entry Requirements* Combination of a Bachelor's degree or appropriate equivalent, some professional experience and experience of groups, self-exploration, own therapy or counselling. Candidates will be considered individually in terms of experience and may be accepted without all the formal entry requirements. *Fees* £200 deposit plus six payments of £850 for the whole course. *Comments* Course consists of academic seminars on Humanistic and Integrative Psychotherapy and Existential, Psychoanalytic and Transpersonal approaches plus a range of second year options. Training seminars. Supervised

CERTIFICATE IN THE FUNDAMENTALS OF COUNSELLING
Part-time course. Training in counselling skills, combining academic, practical and experiential learning.

M.A. IN THE PSYCHOLOGY OF THERAPY AND COUNSELLING
(awarded by Antioch University, U.S.A.)
This two-year part-time M.A. consists of both theoretical and practical learning in psychotherapy and counselling, covering a wide range of approaches.

CONTACT: **Psychology Department, Regent's College,**
Inner Circle, Regent's Park, London NW1 4NS.
Tel. (071) 487 7406

six month part-time placement and writing a thesis. Degree awarded by Antioch University and additional British validation sought.

British School of Osteopathy
1-4 Suffolk Street, London SW1Y 4HG (071) 930 9254.
Title BSc in Osteopathy, 4 years part time. See 'Osteopathy' section for further details.

Roehampton Institute of Higher Education
Roehampton Lane, London SW15 5PS (081) 878 5751.
Title (1) Diploma in Psychological Counselling (2) MSc in Psychological Counselling. Duration (1) 1 year part-time (2) 2 year part-time. *Entry requirements* (1) Appropriate academic qualifications or experience in helping professions and counselling. (2) Candidates must be 25 years old and have a degree with a pass at 2.2 level or above. Special entry may be given to those with appropriate professional qualification. *Fees* Refer to organisers. *Comments* also run Diploma in Counselling and Supervision Course and Certificate in Counselling in Formal and Informal Settings (mainly for those in youth or social work).

Centre for Complementary Health Studies
University of Exeter, Streatham Court, Rennes Drive, Exeter EX4 4PU (0392) 433828.
Title (1) BPhil and (2) MPhil in Complementary Health Studies. Duration (1) 2 years part-time. (2) 1 year full-time or two years part-time, although applicants are advised to allow at least

50% longer than these minimum requirement. Entry requirements (1) Applicants should be those working in complementary and orthodox medicine or other caring professions with day-to-day responsibility for patients. (2) Substantial academic study in the arts, sciences or social sciences. Fees (1) £1,500 per annum, (2) £1,900, overseas students £5,000. *Comments* The centre also runs a research programme, and offers some information services.

Adult Education Classes
London has a wealth of further education classes. These classes are still relatively cheap and cover subjects such as psychotherapy, counselling, health, alternative therapies, religion or philosophy. The departments listed below offer a good selection of courses in this field. Prospectuses are free and can be obtained from:

University of London Department of Extra-Mural Studies
26 Russell Square, London WC1B 5DQ (071) 636 8000 ext 3850/3833
Lots of interesting day and evening adult education classes on psychology, psychotherapy, religion, myth etc. Ring or write for prospectus which is published yearly in June.

City University
Northampton Square, London EC1 (071) 253 4399.
They run evening classes in psychology, psychotherapy and counselling.

Humanistic Psychology at LSE

David Jones, S364, Psychology Dept, London School of Economics, Houghton Street, London WC2A 2AE. (071) 405 7686 ext 3313.

Courses in Humanistic Psychology from one day to one year. Includes various humanistic approaches, Transpersonal, Psychosynthesis, Gestalt, Counselling, Meditation, Diary keeping etc.

Chequer Centre

Chequer Street, London EC1.

Adult education courses covering such subjects as Alexander technique, aro-matherapy, compulsive eating support group, healing, herbal medicine, homoeopathy, massage, reflexology, shiatsu, confidence building for women and counselling.

PRODUCTS

Air Purifiers

Air Improvement Centre

23 Denbigh Street, London SW1V 2HF. (071) 834 2834.

Mon-Fri 9.30-5.30. Sat 10-1. Showroom stocking and supplying a wide range of air improvement products by different manufacturers. As well as air purifiers and ionisers, also stock humidifiers, dehumidifiers and mobile air conditioners. Also have stands in the electrical departments of Harrods and Selfidges.

Amcor Appliances Ltd

19 Woodfield Road, Paddington, London W9 2BA. (071) 289 4433.

Aromatherapy Oils

Aromatherapy oils or 'essential' oils are extracted from plants, flowers or trees and used in aromatherapy (see relevant entry in 'Body' section). Aromatherapy has recently become extremely popular and essential oils have started appearing even in some high street chains stores, often accompanied by leaflets about self-help use. However, while food and herbal medicine are regulated to a certain extent in terms of contents, standards and quality, at present there is no official standard by which

---

BIRKBECK COLLEGE
University of London
CENTRE FOR EXTRA-MURAL STUDIES

APPROACHES TO PSYCHOTHERAPY

The Centre for Extra-Mural Studies offers a range of short courses on various aspects of psychotherapy such as:

Gestalt Therapy
Transference
Melanie Klein
Jungian Psychotherapy
and others

Courses are usually held in the evenings over 10 or 20 weeks in Central London.

For further details of the current programme, contact:
Executive Officer Psychology
Centre for Extra-Mural Studies
26 Russell Square
London WC1B 5DQ
Tel 071-636 8000 ext 3869

the purity of essential oils can be measured, though some reputable essential oils manufucturers are now looking at this problem. The quality of the plants used and the conditions they have been grown in also affect the therapeutic potency of the oils. For instance, if artificial fertilizers or pesticides have been used, the oils could be adulterated with toxins. The best means of extracting the oils is through distillation, but adulteration can also take place in this process of extraction. Furthermore, the oils are suspended in vegetable oils and some manufacturers may dilute their oils much more than others, so it is difficult to tell which oils are good value for money. Some products called aromatherapy oils may not even contain the plant essence they are named after, because synthetic oils can be produced which contain the same active substances and smell the same as the original oil.

Perhaps the best way to ensure the quality of oils is to buy from a supplier with a background in aromatherapy, or those who work closely with consultant trained aromatherapists. Get informa-tion from them about their oils, how they ensure quality and ask about dilution ratios.

Hermitage Oils
East Morton, Keighley BD20 5UQ. (0274) 565957.
Retail and wholesale. Extensive range of oils of different qualities. Rapid turn round on orders. Telephone above number or send SAE for list and order form.

Fleur
8 Baden Rd, London N8. (081) 340 4097.
Can visit by appointment. They supply new age shops, health food shops and they do mail order.

Acumedic Centre
101-103 Camden High Street, Camden, London NW1. (071) 388 5783 or 388 6704.
Shop on the main Camden High St. They sell books on acupuncture and Chinese medicine, with an assortment of alternative medicine aids such as ionisers, massage equipment, tapes and biofeedback machines.

PRODUCTS

Baldwin and Co
173 Walworth Road, Camberwell, London SE17 1RW. (071) 703 5550.

Institute of Clinical Aromatherapy
22 Bromley Road, Catford, London SE6 2TP. (081) 690 2149.
Mail order essential oils and vegetable oils.

Micheline Arcier Aromatherapy
7 William Street , Knightsbridge , London SW1X 9Hl. (071) 235 3545.
The shop sells face oils, body oils and bath oils made from essential oils.

Cosmos Herbs
129 Chiswick High Road, London W4 4HS. (081) 995 7239.
11am-6pm Mon-Sat. Medicinal herbs and remedies sold, as well as occult ritual supplies and an intruiging range of incense and oils (from Luv Luv Luv oil to Graveyard dust). Member of British Herbal Medicine Association. Mail order available.

Neal's Yard Apothecary
2 Neil's Yard, off Shorts Gardens, London WC2H 9DP. (071) 379 7222.

Mon, Tues, Thurs 10-6, Wed, Sat 10-5.30. Also at Chelsea Farmers Market, Sydney Street, London SW3 (which is also open Sun 11-4) and 68 Chalk Farm Road, London NW1. (071) 284 2039. Cosmetics and toiletries, nutritional supplements, essential oils, herbal tinctures (including Chinese), medicinal herbs and powders, gifts. Nice line in naturally scented vegetable oil soaps, and toiletries and preprations packed in cute blue bottled..

Aromatique
Sarnett House, Repton Drive, Gidea Park, Essex RM2 5LP. (0708) 720289.
Mail order. Cosmetics and toiletries containing essential oils for different skin and hair conditions.

Ionisers (UK)
3 Gordon Cresent, Broad Meddows, South Normanton, DE55 3AJ. (0773) 863034.
Ionisers range between £39-£495. They also sell a range of about 20 of differnt Aromatherapy oils which are infused with Homoeopathic remedies.

Quinessence
3a Birch Avenue, Whitwick, Leicestershire LE6 3GB. (0530) 38358/180779.
Affiliated to the International Federation of Aromatherapists, mail order essential oils and essential oil remedies, ready mixed lotions and massage oils, vaporisers and mood enhancers - from 'wild passion' to 'celestial dream' ! Free advice service from qualified aromatherapist.

Verde
4a at No 11 Long St, London E2 8HJ. (071) 739 3612.
Mail order toiletries, bath treatment milks and ozone friendly room fragrance sprays made with essential oils. Stocked by shops.

Back Products

Anatomia
21 Hampstead Road, Euston Centre, London NW1 3JA. (071) 387 5700.

Back Shop
24 New Cavendish Street, London W1M 7LH. (071) 935 9120.
10am-6pm Mon-Sat. All manner of things for the back are here including chairs, pillows, beds, shoes, exercise equipment and meditation stools which give correct support to the back, and even a 'massage pillow' — a cushion which vibrates to give you your own portable massage. Also books, videos, mail order

Back Store Ltd
330 King Street, Hammersmith, London W6. (081) 741 5022.
Mon-Fri 10-6, Sats 10-4. Everything for the back is here. Allow yourself some time to choose.

Alternative Sitting
PO Box 19, Chipping Norton, Oxford OX7 6NY. (060871) 8875.
Specialists in work and domestic ergonomic problems. Sell ergonomic furniture.

Pelvic Support Chairs
New Mill Lane, Eversley, Hants RG27 0RA. (0734) 732365.
Pelvic support chairs, car accessories and the Nada chair - not really a chair but a portable back support sling.

Spine Design
21 Mona St, Beeston, Nottingham NG9 2BY. (0602) 420833.
Sell the 'banana chair'. A revolutionary version of a rocking chair, but designed to be easy on the back.

Wholistic Research Company
Bright Haven, Robin's Lane, Lolworth, Cambridge CB3 8HH. (0954) 781074.
Enormous range of mail order holistic health equipment also includes grain mills, pulsors, biomagnetic therapy equipment, herbal tablet makers, reflex foot rollers, humane mouse traps, enema/douche kits, iridology equipment, and mail order books. They also publish a handy booklet which explains the use of each product, and gives instructions on benefits, and how to use them.

Biofeedback Machines

Biofeedback machines are electrical equipment which give information about mood and state of mind through either measuring brain wave patterns or muscle tension. The machine has to be in contact in some way with the body and measures physical changes which reflect emotional or mental changes. The so-called lie detector is an example of the biofeedback machine, as is equipment used to measure the brain wave frequency of, for instance, people meditating.

John Bell and Croyden
Medical Dept., 54 Wigmore Street, London W1. (071) 935 5555.
Biofeedback machines that also have instruction tapes. attached to them. They also have a wide range of aids for disabled people.

Audio Limited
26-28 Wendell Road, London W12. (081) 743 1518 or 743 4352.
Several machines designed to measure brainwave frequencies and monitor

states of mind. Also manufacture the therapeutic strobe to alter mood.

First Harmonic
10 Mortlock Avenue, Cambridge CB4 1TE. (0223) 424931.
Biofeedback machine which uses a BBC computer and the Dodman system. The system monitors brainwaves.

Healthwatch UK
18b Parrin Lane, Monton, Eccles, Manchester M30 8BD. 061 789 1057.
Make a watch which monitors stress using biofeedback - it displays a number between 0 and 99 to let you know how stressed you are. Comes with book and costs £59.95 plus £1.25 p&p.

Biorhythm Charts

Dr Wilhelm Fliess, who was a friend of Freud's, first suggested that the behaviour and functioning of human beings is governed by regular cycles. There are three cycles in modern biorhythms which are set in motion from the day of birth. The physical cycle is 23 days long, the emotional cycle is 28 days long, and the mental cycle is 33 days long. During the length of each cycle the biorhythm is seen as curve which goes through a 'high' and a 'low'. It is when an individual's biorhythm wave crosses the mid point between the high and low points that it is claimed there is more danger of illness, accident or general fuctioning below par. If more than one biorhythm is passing through this stage, it is even more likely.

London Biorhythm Co Ltd
PO Box 413, South Kensington, London SW7 2PT..
Biorythm charts and the 'bio display unit',
230

a do-it-yourself biorhythm kit. Also do research into biorhythms and their effects and publish newsletter (£9 per year for 6 issues).

Birthing Pools

These are (usually circular or oval) pools filled with water in which women can give birth. Giving birth in water is said to ease the pain of contractions and provide an enviroment in which women can relax in the favoured position for active birth, crouching or kneeling. The agencies listed below provide pools for hire or sale.

Active Birth Centre
55 Dartmouth Park Road, Kentish Town, London NW5 1SL. (071) 267 3006,
Hire out portable water birth pools. £125 for four weeks. Call 267 6745 for free catalogue of their products.

Birthworks
Hill House Community, Folleight Lane, Long Ashton, Bristol BS18 9JB. (0272) 394202.
Available for sale or hire at £35 per week. Two types available: circular one which can be dismantled, and fixed rectangular one for hospitals.

Splashdown Birth Pools
17 Wellington Terrace, Harrow-on-the-Hill, Middlesex HA1 3EP. (081) 422 9308.
Water birth pools for hire or sale, with a choice of round and oval. Pools measure 5ft in diameter by 26 ins deep. £125 plus £20 for sterilised liner for four weeks standby hire. Door -to-door delivery anywhere in the UK. Free advice and information packs on water birth to enquirers, free water birth workshops. Sell and loan books and cassettes.

Clothes and Shoes

Natural Shoe Store (1)
325 King's Road, London SW3. (071) 351 3721.
Range of shoes both British and American designed to be kind and easy on the feet. Branch at Neal Street.

Natural Shoe Store (2)
21 Neal Street, London WC2. (071) 836 5254.

Back Shop
24 New Cavendish Street, London W1M 7LH. (071) 935 9120.
10am-6pm Mon-Sat. Sell shoes to help the back.

Green Farm Nutrition Centre
Burwash Common, East Sussex TN19 7LX. (0435) 882482/883457.

Crystals

Crystals and gems are sold both for healing and for their decorative beauty. A number of shops have opened up in London:

SHOPS

Natural Art Gallery
Unit Q14/15, Antiquarius Antique Centre, 131/141 Kings Road, Chelsea, London SW3. (071) 351 6548.
Mon-Sat 10-6. Retail shop which specialises in selling spectacular crystals and mineral specimens. Also importers and wholesalers of minerals and crystals, specialising in unusual and decorative pieces.

Snapdragon
12 South Park, Sevenoaks, Kent, TN13 1AN. (0732) 740252.
Mystical cards, tarot cards, crystal balls, special incense, healing pendants, pendulums. Keep a list of alternative medicine practitioners in the area. Tapes for healing.

Crystal Connection
23 Camden Lock, London NW1 8AF. (071) 267 4325.
Open seven days a week. 11.30-7.30. Crystals, balls, pyramids, gems, books, pictures, jewellery.

Rainbow Gems
The Railway Arches, 1st Rainbow Arch, Camden Lock Market, (off Chalk Farm Road) NW1.
Rainbow gems trades on Saturday and Sunday from 9.30-6 at Camden Lock market, and as well as a selection of crystals and minerals both polished and natural sells pyramids, spheres, eggs and wands. Also do gem elixiers.

Crystallize
347 Portobello Road, London W10 5SA. (081) 969 5665.
Tues-Sat 10-6. Stock a selection of crystals from around the world, jewellery, crystal gardens, singing bowls, American Indian power pieces, wands, craystal balls and sculpture.

New World Aurora
16A Neal's Yard, Covent Garden, London WC2. (071) 379 0818.
Open Mon-Sat 10-6. A wide range of natural quartz crystals, dowsing pendulums, rainbow crystal jewellery and balls, cards and posters, 'New Age' music and videos. Also mail order.

PRODUCTS

THE NATURAL ART GALLERY
Antiquarius Antique Centre
Unit Q14-15, 131/141 Kings Road
Chelsea, London SW3
071 351 6548

Open Monday to Saturday, 10am - 6pm

CRYSTALS formed over millions of years, created by the Planet are now available from **THE NATURAL ART GALLERY**, who specialise in offering a wide range of unusual and spectacular crystals imported from all over the world.

Imported by: **EVERLASTING GEMS** - Tel: 081 949 8126

MAIL ORDER

British Lapidary and Mineral Dealers Association

Glenjoy, 19/21 Sun Lane, Wakefield WR1 1JD. (0924) 373786.

One of the oldest established importers of crystals in the UK for wholesale and retail. As well as all the usual crystals and gems, supply aqua aura crustals which are coated with a transparent layer of gold, giving them a blue aura and appearance similar to aquamarine. Also arrange gem and mineral fairs - next one in London in October 1990.

Crystal Research Foundation

37 Bromley Road, St Annes-on-Sea, Lancs FY8 1PQ. (0253) 723735.

Also crystal light torches for colour crystal healing and crystal light boxes.

Delta Minerals

168 Fernhead Road, London W9 3EL. 968 8496.

Crystals, minerals and gems; pyramids and other geometric dynamics, magical and healing wands. Mail order or phone for appointment.

Kernowcraft

Bolingey, Perranporth, Cornwall TR6 0DH. (0872) 573888

Mail order supplier, retail and wholesale. Precious and semi-precious stones, crystals, avaialble also in bead form. Mounts, chains and fastenings for jewellery making, as well as silversmithing equipment. Pyramids, spheres, obselisks, wands, standing points etc. - ask for the crystal list when applying for information.

Wessex Impex Ltd

c/o Stonebridge Farmhouse, Breadsell Lane, St Leonards on Sea, East Sussex TN38 8EB. 042 483 659 .

Visitors by appointment only please. Importers of rough crystals, manufacturers of crystal jewellery, gemmologists, lapidaries, wholesale and retail. sues', Yoga, astrology, psychology etc.

Daylight Bulbs

Otherwise known as full spectrum lighting, this is used to treat seasonal affective disorder (shortened to 'SAD') which is a form of depression caused by lack of sunlight, and which some people get in the winter. The lack of sunlight affects the pineal gland, which starts to secrete too much of a hormone called melatonin, which causes depression.

DNA

PO Box 77, West Kensington, W14 0QQ. (071) 603 0687.

Full Spectrum Lighting

Unit 5 Wye Industrial Estate, London Road, High Wycombe, Bucks HP11 1LH. (0494) 26051.

Bulbs fitted with full spectrum light.

PRODUCTS

Hygeia Studios
Brook House, Tetbury, Glos GL8 8NS. (045383) 2150.
Health-oriented illumination: lamps, true-lite tubes. Also colour therapy instruments from this business run by a training college in colour therapy.

Wholistic Research Company
Bright Haven, Robin's Lane, Lolworth, Cambridge CB3 8HH. (0954) 781074.
Dalight bulbs are just one of the products on offer from this extensive mail order catalogue. See 'Ionisers' section for full details.

Home Acupuncture
Acuhealth
32 Maple St, London W1P 5GD. (071) 580 0242.
Market the Acuhealth 900 No Needles Home Acupuncture Unit which stimulates acupuncture points with mild electronic impulses. Comes with instruction manual. Costs £149 with a 30 day, money back guarantee.

Float Tanks
South London Natural Health Centre
7A Clapham Common South Side, Clapham Common, London SW4 7AA. (071) 720 8817.
Phone 720 9506 for Gracemill Ltd who are manufacturers and installers of the 'ocean float room'.

Floatarium Ltd
21 Bond Street, Brighton BN1 1RD. (0273) 679555.
Sphinx floatation tank sold, a deluxe size

in which two people can float at the same time! Back-up information service for purchasers. Also available is the 'Dream Machine', which provides programmes of light and sound to promote different moods and mental states.

Futons
Futon Factory
192 Balls Pond Road, London N1 4AA. (071) 226 4477.
Pure cotton futons with stylish patterned covers, and the 'Floaton' - a futon on a special waterbed which distributes pressure evenly.

Futon Express
23-27 Pancras Road, London NW1 2QB. (071) 833 3945.
10-6pm Mon-Sat. Hand made, 100% cotton filled futons and futon sofa beds as well as the 'Party Paker' portable futon for those who don't want to risk a night on their host's camp bed. Branches at 56 Chalk Farm Road, NW1 (485 1000) and 149 St Johns Hill, SW11 (924 2517).

Woodman & Woolfe
23-27 Pancras Road, London NW1. (071) 833 3945.

Futon Company
654A Fulham Road, London SW6 5RU. (071) 736 9190.

Games
Trading Centre
Findhorn Foundation, The Park, Forres, Scotland IV36 0TZ. (0309) 31074.
Produce the Transformation Game: "a playful yet substantial way of understanding and transforming the way you

233

play your life. Just as life is filled with insights, setbacks, pain and miracles, so is the Transformation Game. It mirrors players lives, highlighting strenghts, identifying blind spots and bringing fresh perspectives to current challenges". Also sell Angel cards, nature and tree calendar, tree diary,

Herbs/Herbal Remedies

SHOPS

Baldwin and Co

173 Walworth Road, Camberwell, London SE17 1RW. (071) 703 5550.
Long established herbalists.

Hong Ning Co

15 Little Newport Street, London WC2. (071) 437 4910.
Chinese herbalist shop

Nutribiotics

35 Highview Avenue , Edgware , Middlesex HA8 9TX. (081) 958 7553.
Supply specially potentised homoeopathic and herbal remedies, and also stock aloe vera gel products. Sell a first aid homoeopathic kit.

Herbalists

74 Lee High Road, London SE13. (081) 852 9792.
Open between 8.30 am-5.15pm.
They have been established since 1926 . Can give advice to those wondering which herb to choose.

Cosmos Herbs

129 Chiswick High Road, London W4 4HS. (081) 995 7239.
11am-6pm Mon-Sat. Medicinal herbs and

remedies sold, as well as occult ritual supplies and an intruiging range of incense and oils (from Luv Luv Luv oil to Graveyard dust). Member of British Herbal Medicine Association. Mail order available.

Culpeper Herbalists

8 The Market, Covent Garden Piazza, WC2. (071) 379 6698.
Mon-Sat 10-8, Sun 11.30-7. Range of herbs, also cruelty free toiletries.

Neal's Yard Apothecary

2 Neil's Yard, off Shorts Gardens, London WC2H 9DP. (071) 379 7222.
Mon, Tues, Thurs 10-6, Wed, Sat 10-5.30.
Also at Chelsea Farmers Market, Sydney Street, London SW3 (which is also open Sun 11-4) and 68 Chalk Farm Road, London NW1. (071) 284 2039. Cosmetics and toiletries, nutritional supplements, essential oils, herbal tinctures (including Chinese), medicinal herbs and powders, gifts. Nice line in naturally scented vegetable oil soaps, and toiletries and preprations packed in cute blue bottles..

East Asia Company

101 - 103 Camden High Street, Camden, London . (071) 388 5783 or 388 6704.
Sell herbal and homoeopathic remedies.

MAIL ORDER

Green Farm Nutrition Centre

Burwash Common, East Sussex TN19 7LX. (0435) 882482/883457.
Large mail order catalogue with lambswool bedding, VDU screens also available. Large range of dietry supplements, and skin and hair care products.

PRODUCTS

Homoeopathic Pharmacies

E Gould and Son
14 Crowndale Road, London NW1 1TT.
(071) 388 4752.
Mon-Fri 9-5.45. Closed Sats. Open Sun am.

Ainsworths Homoeopathic Pharmacy
38 New Cavendish Street, London W1M 7LH. (071) 935 5330/(08833) 40332.
Same day postal supply of all traditional homoeopathic medicines including many novel remedies. Vetinary remedies as well.

Nelson & Co
73 Duke Street, London W1. (071) 629 3118.

East Asia Company
101 - 103 Camden High Street, Camden, London . (071) 388 5783 or 388 6704.
Sell herbal and homoeopathic remedies.

Ionisers

Ions are gas molecules present in the air which carry a positive or negative charge. Research has shown that positive ions have the effect of making people more irritable, tired and perform less well, and that negative ions in the air tend to make people more alert and perform better. Negative ions are produced by such things as plants, the breaking of water into droplets and by ultra-violet light from the sun. Positive ions are produced, among other things, by fluorescent lighting, electronic equipment, air conditioning and man-made fabrics - though humankind isn't to blame for all positive ions, because there are certain winds which blow in certain parts of the world, and are known to contain a high proportion of positive ions. When such winds blow, legend and experience show that crime and traffic accidents increase.

Ionisers increase the amount of negative ions in the air. They are usually small and fairly inexpensive, and are often used by people who work in office conditions to counteract the effect of the synthetic environment.

SHOPS

Air Improvement Centre
23 Denbigh Street, London SW1V 2HF. (071) 834 2834.
Mon-Fri 9.30-5.30. Sat10-1. Showroom stocking and supplying a wide range of air improvement products by different manufacturers. As well as air purifiers and ionisers, also stock humidifiers, dehumidifiers and mobile air conditioners. Also have stands in the electrical departments of Harrods and Selfidges.

The London Ioniser Centre
65 Endell St., Covent Garden, WC2H 9AJ. (071) 836 0251.
10-6 Mon- Fri. Sat 10-4. Full range of ionisers. They will give advice to you on all aspects of ioniser usage. Will also visit offices to give advice. Ionisers range from £25 to £400. They have sold recently to lots of dentists - though they say that alternative medicine practitioners feature strongly in their clientel.

PRODUCTS

MAIL ORDER

Green Farm Nutrition Centre
Burwash Common, East Sussex TN19 7LX. (0435) 882482/883457.
Mail order ioniers.

Ionisers (UK)
3 Gordon Cresent, Broad Meddows, South Normanton, DE55 3AJ. (0773) 863034.
Ionisers range between £39-£495. They also sell a range of about 20 of different aromatherapy oils which are infused with homoeopathic remedies.

Mountain Breeze Air Ionizers
6 Priorswood Place , Skelmersdale, Lancashire WN8 9QB. (0695) 21155.
Room and car ionisers, air filters and an aromatherapy oil diffuser.

Wholistic Research Company
Bright Haven, Robin's Lane, Lolworth, Cambridge CB3 8HH. (0954) 781074.
Enormous range of mail order holistic health equipment also includes grain mills, pulsors, biomagnetic therapy equipment, herbal tablet makers, reflex foot rollers, humane mouse traps, enema/douche kits, iridology equipment, and mail order books. They also publish a handy booklet which explains the use of each product, and gives instructions on benefits, and how to use them.

Jewellery

Crystal Connection
23 Camden Lock, London NW1 8AF. (071) 267 4325.
Open seven days a week. 11.30-7.30.
Crustals, balls, pyramids, gems, books, pictures, jewellery.

Rainbow Gems
The Railway Arches, 1st Rainbow Arch, Camden Lock Market, (off Chalk Farm Road) NW1 .
Rainbow gems trades on Saturday and Sunday from 9.30-6 at Camden Lock market, and a selection of crystals and minerals both polished and natural sells pyramids, spheres, eggs and wands.

New World Aurora
16A Neal's Yard, Covent Garden, London WC2. (071) 379 0818.
Open Mon-Sat 10-6. Crystals and crystal jewellery.

Celtia Ltd
Celtia House, Longrock, Penzance, Cornwall TR20 8HX. (0736) 51680.
Celtic design jewellery, belts, purses, bags, ornaments, cards and celtic inspired compositions on tape.

Wessex Impex Ltd
c/o Stonebridge Farmhouse, Breadsell Lane, St Leonards on Sea, East Sussex TN38 8EB. 042 483 659 .
Visitors by appointment only please. As well as being importers of rough crystals, they manufacture crystal jewellery.

Juicers
Juicers extract the juices of fruit, vegetables and sometimes of herbs and plants. Consuming fresh juice is a way of ingesting high doses of nurtrients for therapeutic purposes - for instance in the Gerson cancer therapy diet which features fresh juice as part of the detoxification process. Many healthy people also like to drink juice, because they feel it helps to maintain good health.

There are different types of juicer. Centrifugal juicers grate the fruit or vegetable and then spin the pulp, forcing the juice out by centrifugal force. These are the cheapest juicers, but they tend not to extract such a high level of nutrients as other models. Nose cone pressure juicers break down the material with a cutter or masticator. This is then forced into a cone under high pressure, and the juice is forced out. This method produces juice which is rich in nutrients, but is more expensive than the centrifugal juicer. In juice presses the material is first pulped, then put into a strong nylon cloth which retains the pulp when the juice is squeezed out by a press.

Green Farm Nutrition Centre
Burwash Common, East Sussex TN19 7LX. (0435) 882482/883457.
Large mail order catalogue with lambswool bedding, VDU screens also available. Large range of dietry supplements, and skin and hair care products.

Wholistic Research Company
Bright Haven, Robin's Lane, Lolworth, Cambridge CB3 8HH. (0954) 781074.
As well as selling juicers, Wholistic Research Company produce a useful booklet explaining the uses of their wide range of products, gives advice on which juicer to choose. See 'Ionisers' for more details about their range.

Martial Arts Suppliers

Dragon Martial Arts
128 Myddleton Road, London N22 4NQ. (081) 889 0965.
Weds, Thurs, Sats 9.30-5.30. Books, equipment, suits and martial arts weaponry.

Shaolin Way
10 Little Newport Street, London WC2. (071) 734 6391.
A shop which sells martial arts supplies of different designs.11-7pm seven days a week.

Massage Aids

Europa Distribution Co
2a Milner St, London SW3. (071) 589 8158.
They sell a 'thumper' automatic massager - all the joys of massage without any of the arm strain.

Back Shop
24 New Cavendish Street, London W1M 7LH. (071) 935 9120.
10am-6pm Mon-Sat. Among their many other items, the Back Shop stocks a 'massage pillow' — a cushion which vibrates to give you your own portable massage.

Green Farm Nutrition Centre
Burwash Common, East Sussex TN19 7LX. (0435) 882482/883457.
Large mail order catalogue.

Marshcouch
36 Glebe Close, Hemel Hempstead, Herts HP3 9PA. (0442) 63199.
5 different models of treatment couch, can be custom built for individual's height with choice of fabric or vinyl covering at no extra charge. From £34 - £260 excluding VAT and small delivery charge.

Miscellaneous

ABC Corporation

PRODUCTS

90 Hainault Rd, Chigwell , Essex, IG7 5DH. (081) 501 1178.
Sell an 'Advanced Body Clock'.

Applied Technology Alternative Medicine Ltd
42 Ospringe Road, Faversham, Kent ME13 7LJ. (0795) 535143.
ATAM supply computer systems for homoeopathic prescribing for practitioners, but are now bringing out a system for self-diagnosis which can be used by non-professionals.

Lois Mary Blackburn
53 St John's Priory Park, Farringdon Road, Lechlade, Gloucestershire GL7 3EZ.

Stained glass artist with interest in the healing aspects of colour and symbolic images. Small or large pieces to commission..

Natural Birth Control

Wholistic Research Company
Bright Haven, Robin's Lane, Lolworth, Cambridge CB3 8HH. (0954) 781074.
Mail order. Mini computer available for use with natural birth control methods, to help you compute more accurately your most fertile times.

Organic Wines

Organic wine is made from grapes grown without chemical fertilisers or weedkillers, and which have not been sprayed with insecticide. To earn the name of organic, no synthetic additives should be used to preserve or flavour the wine. Farmers and producers of organic wine should use only ecologically sound techniques. Wine-producing countries have their own bodies which lay down guidelines for organic wine and monitor its production. Bottles of organic wine will diplay the symbol of approval by such a body as proof of their integrity.

Available now in addition to wine, are organic beers and spirits. Enthusiasts claim that drinks grown organically are less likely to cause hangovers because they don't contain harmful additives. However, this is a claim which hasn't as yet been put to clinical trials!

Organics
290 Fulham Palace Road, London SW6 6HP. (071) 381 9924.
Mail order.

Vinceremos Wines
Unit 10, Ashley Industrial Estate, Wakefield Road, Ossett , West Yorkshire WF5 9JD. (0924) 276393.
Range of organic wines, beers and spirits from around the world including rum from Cuba, Armenian brandy and sparkling white wine from India. Prices start from £2.85 per bottle.

Vintage Roots
25 Manchester Road, Reading, Berks RG1 3QE. (0734) 662569.
Range of organic wines mostly from France and include the French 'classics'. They are planning to stock organic beer and vinegar in the near future. Also able to provide wines that are suitable for vegtarians, and some wines that are also bio-dynamic.

238

Pollution Control

Life Reharmonics
24 Chapel Market, Islington, London N1. (071) 278 4610.
Makers of 'Reharmoniser', which they claim helps to neutralise 'negative energy' (electromagnetic fields, geomagnetic energy, radiation etc)..

Future Concepts
198 High Road, London N22 4HH. (081) 883 0767.
Various subtle energy devices.

Green Farm Nutrition Centre
Burwash Common, East Sussex TN19 7LX. (0435) 882482/883457.
VDU filter screens available.

Mountain Breeze Air Ionizers
6 Priorswood Place , Skelmersdale , Lancashire WN8 9QB. (0695) 21155.
Mail order air filters.

Posters

Tantra Designs
48 Kensington Park Rd, Bristol, BS4 3HU. (0272 724 708.
Phone for illustrated colour catalogue of

tantra posters, cards, brooches, prints, statues, handicrafts and window prints. Enclose SAE. Also sell aromatic oils and incense.

Tapes - Personal Development

The tapes listed below are very different in their approach to personal development, and techniques range from subliminal messages to lectures and talks by renowned healers or teachers.

Lifeskills
3 Brighton Road, Finchley, London N2 8JU. (081) 346 9646 or 580 4972.
Mail order and telephone order only. Established 12 years. Typical prices £8 per tape (incl VAT).

Airlift Books
26-28 Eden Grove, London N7 8EF. 607 5792/5798.
Distributors of tapes including Louise Hay on healing, Derek Gale on guided fantasy and relaxation, Shakti Gawain, Stuart Wilde, Mantak Chia etc.

Triangle Truth Ltd
PO Box 89, London SE3 7JN. (081) 305 2317.
Series of tapes on on subjects such as forgiveness, weight loss, confidence, prosperity, relationships. £8.95 per tape.

New World Aurora
16A Neal's Yard, Covent Garden, London WC2. (071) 379 0818.
Open Mon-Sat 10-6. Stock some personal development tapes.

Dharmachakra Tapes
PO Box 50, Cambridge, CB1 3BG. .
Taped lectures by Ven. Sangharakshita,

founder of Friends of the Western Buddhist Order on many aspects of Buddhism.

Matthew Manning Centre
39 Abbeygate Street, Bury St Edmunds, Suffolk IP33 1BR. 0284 752364/145965.
Personal Development tapes and relaxation tapes to promote well being by perhaps the most famous healer in Britain today.

SCWL
3rd Floor, 8 Holyrood Street, London SE1 2EL. 630 7732/403 3884.
These tapes use subliminal messages for the eradication of problem behaviour, the development of mental powers and well-being, and even to help you improve your golf or ten-pin bowling.

Tapewise
23 New Road, Brighton BN1 1WZ. (0273) 680281.
Tapes on the problems of teenage life for worried parents, produced by the Trust for the Study of Adolescence.

Gale Centre for Creative Therapy
Stable Cottage, Whitakers Way, Loughton, Essex IG10 1SJ. (081) 508 9344.
Personal development and psychology tapes.

Snapdragon
12 South Park, Sevenoaks, Kent, TN13 1AN. (0732) 740252.
This 'New Age' shop sells tapes for healing, among many other things.

Tapes - Music

Seventh Wave Music
15 Broughton Rd, Thornton Heath, Croydon CR4 6AG. (081) 689 8721.
Atmospheric music, creating landscapes using sound and rhythm composed by Nigel Shaw. Four albums available.

New World Aurora
16A Neal's Yard, Covent Garden, London WC2. (071) 379 0818.
Open Mon-Sat 10-6. Large selection of 'New Age' music and videos. Also mail order.

PRODUCTS

Celtia Ltd
Celtia House, Longrock, Penzance, Cornwall TR20 8HX. (0736) 51680.
Celtic inspired compositions on tape.

Dawn Awakening
PO Box 15, Newton Abbot, Devon TQ12 6XE. (080426) 336.
Distributors of New Age and relaxing music, and some relaxation tapes. Mail order catalogue available.

Earthly Delights
Manor Farmhouse, Blackwell, Nr Buxton, Derbyshire SK17 9QT. .
'Sounds' by Earthly Delights and Noctural Emissions. Truly alternative, not to say arcane - 'X' rated stuff.

Earthsounds Music
Old Mill, Skeeby, Richmond, North Yorks DL10 5EB. (0748) 5959.
Series include 'Fire of Ritual', 'Seed Thoughts' and 'World Musics'.

Elfington Cassettes
The Old Forge Studio, Back Road, Wenhaston, Halesworth, Suffolk IP19 9EP. 050 270 678.
The music of Mike Rowland composer of The Fairy Ring, gentle music for relaxation and meditation.

Free Flow Music
The Cabin, Dorstone, Hereford HR3 6BL. (0981) 550786.
Distribute tapes from Voices of Silence group.

Inner Harmonies
3 Crail View, Northleach, Glos GL54 3QH. (0451) 60155.
Relaxing music from four composers, including "Living Earth' by Annie Locke, copies of which has been presented by a US peace delegation to the Soviet Union.

Music Suite Ltd
Cenarth Newcastle Emlyn Dyfed SA38 9JN . (0239) 710594 .
Original compositions by Adrian Wagner, Francis Monkman (ex of 'Curved Air' - remember them?), Prana, and various story tapes.Bulk cassette and video duplicating service, CD and record manufacturing and electronic music studio.

Private Music
1 Bedford Avenue, Londn WC1B 3DT. .
Independent label formed by Peter Baumann, founding member of the electronic music group, Tangerine Dream. Artists include Ravi Shankar, Jerry Goodman, Nona Hendryx, Yanni, and Tangerine Dream.

Tapes - Relaxation

Shapetapes & Planet Tree Music
31 Redington Road, Hampstead, London NW3 7QY. (071) 435 9847.
Series of tapes which correlate to particular shapes (square, triangle etc) which aim to have a particular 'toning' effect on the body.

Dawn Awakening
PO Box 15, Newton Abbot, Devon TQ12 6XE. (080426) 336.
Music to relax with.

Matthew Manning Centre
39 Abbeygate Street, Bury St Edmunds, Suffolk IP33 1BR. 0284 752364/145965.
Relaxation tapes by this famous healer.

Videos

Yoga Dham
67 Pinner Park Ave, North Harrow, Middlesex HA2 6JY. (081) 428 6691.

Yoga video, mail order.

Airlift Books

26-28 Eden Grove, London N7 8EF. 607 5792/5798.

Martial Arts videos. Mail order available.

New World Aurora

16A Neal's Yard, Covent Garden, London WC2. (071) 379 0818.

'New Age' videos. Mail order.

Namaste Films

PO Box 351, Swindon, Wilts. (0793) 763666.

42 minutes relaxation video of the ocean and coast of Australia.

Water Filters

If you want to find out what your water contains, apply to your local water authority for a report on its chemical and bacterial composition and compare these levels of metals and chemicals with permitted EEC levels. Information on permitted EEC levels can be obtained from your local water authority or by sending an SAE to **Friends of the Earth**, 26-28 Underwood Street, London N1 7JQ (01 490 1555). If there are greater levels of impurity than the EEC recommendations, then complain to the EEC.

Water filters come in jug form, or can be fitted to the tap, or can be plumbed into the water supply pipe. They vary enormously in cost and effectiveness. The cheapest are jug filters which use charcoal to remove unpleasant tastes and smells, especially cholorine. The charcoal must be replaced regularly - usually at least once a month. Though they are cheap tests show that they are not as effective in removing a whole

range of toxic pollutants as plumbed-in filters.

Plumbed in filters can use a variety of methods to extract pollutants and bacteria from the water. Granular silver activated carbon filters remove some chemicals, including chlorine. The silver in this type of filter helps to remove bacteria, though only after the water has been left from 2 to 24 hours. Ultraviolet radiation is used in some filters to kill bacteria, though this is less effective if there is a lot of iron in the water. Microstraining puri-

fiers are the most effective in cleaning water, and only they can really be called 'purifiers' rather than just 'filters'. They work using highly refined filtration and absorbtion to remove bacteria and chemicals. These systems also use electrokinetic attraction which draws the dissolved impurities to it. Since this then becomes clogged, the filtration unit must be replaced every 1 to 2 years with cartridges available from the supplier.

Green Farm Nutrition Centre
Burwash Common, East Sussex TN19 7LX. (0435) 882482/883457.

Wholistic Research Company
Bright Haven, Robin's Lane, Lolworth, Cambridge CB3 8HH. (0954) 781074.

General Ecology (UK) Ltd
3rd Floor, Suffolk House, George Street, Croydon CR0 1SQ. (081) 760 0522.
Market the Seagull range of non-chemical water purifiers, as used by many ailine companies. Portable device also available.

S Hetman & Co
Unit 15, Bunning House, Chambers Road, London N7 0NX. (071) 609 8340.
Supply water filters using reverse osmosis.

Well Waters, Ltd.
Unit 8, Trojan Industrial Estate, Cobbold Rd., London NW10 9ST . (081) 452 3479.
Silverstar water filtration unit, composed of activated carbon impregnated with metallic silver £230.

SERVICES

Ethically Sound Investments

A number of ethical investment funds have sprung up over the last few years, just as 'green' products have become much more common. However, what is becoming evident is that one person's 'green' is another person's 'grey' area.

Different ethical investment funds have different criteria - some for instance are very clear on not investing in the tobacco industry, others have no investment at all in nuclear weapons or energy. It's best to check out what criteria is used, and make sure it is in agreement with your own. In unit trusts your money is spread across a number companies to minimise risk. Because it is the nature of modern business to be mostly about large multi-nationals which have many subsidiary companies doing different things, it's very difficult to invest in the mainstream without including some investment in questionable areas, especially if your criteria are very tight. It can also be difficult to find out all the interests of a large company with many subsidiary companies.

If you decide to invest with a unit trust scheme, in addition to the sensible financial questions such as what degree of risk is involved, what charges are made and what the premium is, you can ask about what ethical criteria are used, how rigorously they are applied and whether the fund has an independent vetting committee and if so how it works. If the fund claims to be 'green', do they look only at the finished product, or do they take into account the processes of production, and even the company's general record on the environment?

Another way of researching your ethical investment is to apply to **EIRIS**, the Ethical Investment Research Service. They research companies' interests in several areas of concern, and cover all companies in the Financial Times All-Share index. Their address is *EIRIS, 401 Bondway Business Centre, 71 Bondway, London SW8 1SQ. (071) 735 1351.* Send SAE with enquiries.

If you don't want to take your chances with the multi-nationals, then you can invest in small schemes which loan money for small project. This has the advantage of being very ethical, though the premium may not be as good.

Merlin Jupiter Ecology Fund

Knightsbridge House 197 Knightsbridge SW7 1RB (071) 581 8015.
Investment in companies which are environmentally concerned, have 'social commitment'. Avoids those with direct links with South Africa, armaments, nuclear power or tobacco.

Ethical Investment Fund

10 Queen Street, Mayfair, London W1X 7PF (071) 491 0558.
Unit Investment underwritten by Royal Heritage Life Assurance.

Allchurch's Investment Management Service

19-21 Billiter Street, London EC3N 2RY (01) 528 7364.
Set up originally as the Ecclesiastical Insurance group to serve the church and clergy. Now run Amity fund for ethical investment.

Ecology Building Society

18 Station Road, Cross Hills, Keighley, West Yorkshire, BD20 8TB (0535) 35933.
Lends money for property or projects which are likley 'to lead to the saving of non-renewable resources, the promotion of self-sufficiency in individuals or communities, or the most ecologically efficient use of land'. Examples are: small-scale workshops, back-to-back houses, homes for people running ecological businesses, organic farms, houses with special energy saving or energy efficient features, properties which will help to promote the life of small communities etc.

Friends Provident Unit Trust

Pixham End, Dorking, Surrey RH4 1QA (0306) 740123.
Run the stewardship trust: includes unit trust, income trust, the north American stewardship trust, personal equity plan.

ICOF (Industrial Common Ownership Finance)

12-14 Gold Street, Northampton, NN1 1RS 0604 37563.
Lend money to co-operatives.

RECRUITMENT / CONTACTS

Mercury Provident

3 Orlingbury House, Lewes Road, Forest Row, Sussex RH18 5AA (034282) 3739. Founded on the principles of Rudolph Steiner (see Anthroposophical Society), supports projects which are of benefit to the community, have community support and are in some form of social ownership.

Tilt Ltd

Birdwood House, 44 High St, Totnes, Devon 0803 867099. A community company using local money to invest in local projects. Money is used to create ecologically and socially sustainable projects.

TSB Trust Company Ltd

Charlton Place, Andover, Hampshire SP10 1RE (0264) 56789. Among the unit trust schemes they offer is the TSB Environmental Investor Fund. The investments are vetted by an independent committee set up under the auspices of the Conservation Foundation.

Recruitment

Exchange Resources

28 Milsom Street, Bath BA1 1DP. (0225) 469671. Recruitment and consultancy in computing, communications, electronics, engineering and science. Try to avoid clients with strong militaristic, nuclear power or white South Africa

Friendship Agencies

London can be a lonely place - the agencies listed below cater for those interested in growth, holistic health, vegetarianism and 'green' lifestyle to meet friends and partners or to make contact internationally.

Contact Centre

BCM Cuddle, London WC1V 6XX. . British and international contact service for vegans/vegetarians, and international contact service open to non vegetarian/vegans. £12.75 for life membership, plus small fee if you wish to advertise in broadsheets.

CONTACT CENTRE

Contact Centre is a friendship agency, quite different from all others catering for vegetarians and vegans both in Britain and abroad, for any purposes.

Contact Centre is inexpensive and enables you to choose your friend(s) from detailed advertisements and/or to write an advertisement yourself without disclosing your name and address.

Contact Centre gives you full scope, you don't even have to complete a form. Instead a friendly ear is lent to every member.

Contact Centre operates the British Vegetarian/ Vegan Service and the International Vegetarian/ Vegan Service comprising various divisions to meet individual requirements.

If you are vegetarian or vegan, please ask for membership details.

• • • • • • • • • • • • •

Separately, there is the *International Contact Promotion Service*, which is open to non-vegetarians as well, for any harmless purposes. This is operated through a network of young agents enrolling members and earning good money.

If you are aged 15-19 and reliable, perhaps you can join this worldwide network of young agents. You will receive full training. But hurry up, as the number of agents is increasing fast. If we have to disappoint you, you can join at half the fee.

Contact Centre, BCM Cuddle, London WC1V 6XX

245

Vegetarian Matchmakers

Johnson House, Coronation Road, London NW10 7QE. (081) 348 5229.
Provides a comprehensive service for unattached vegetarians, vegans, macrobiotics and those of similar mind nationwide. Introductions, friendship, get-togethers, weekend breaks/holidays etc. Hundreds of participating members, from teenage to sunset years. Has been bringing veggies happily together since 1980, and is a member of the Association of British Introduction Agencies.

Alternative Register

12 Woodside Road, London N22 5HU. (081) 889 1608.
Register for those seeking friends or partners. Also keep a professional register for therapists etc. seeking useful business contacts. Membership £25 per annum, includes Register of Members and regular updates.

Friendships

Apperley Court, Apperley, Gloucestershire GL19 4QD.
Is a nationwide friendship agency. For those people interested in meeting people involved in holistic medicine, new age, meditation, 'green issues', Yoga, astrology, psychology etc.

Rooms For Hire

Sound Health

261 Grove Street, Deptford, London SE8 3PZ (081) 691 7519.
Consulting rooms and space for workshops in SW18.

Living Centre

12a Durham Road, Raynes Park, London SW20 (081) 946 2331.

Large group room (up to about 40 sitting) available weekends and evenings. (£10 per hour). Carpeted. Kitchen.

Gaunts House

Wimborne, Dorset, BH21 4JQ (0202) 841522.
Large conference, seminar and retreat centre available for hire (can accommodate up to 200 people) by community wishing to promote 'individual growth and fulfilment from a non-sectarian basis'. Facilities include gym and heated pool.

FOOD

Macrobiotics

Macrobiotics is familiar to most people as a kind of diet. But it is also a whole theory of health and well being based on the balancing of the opposite and complementary energies of Yin and Yang. Literally the word Macrobiotics means 'large life'.

Macrobiotic theory is based in the Oriental belief that good health is based on the balance of life energy. Yin energy is feminine, receptive, damp, cold and is symbolised by the moon. Yang energy is masculine, active, dry, hot and symbolised by the sun. Everything that exists partakes more or less of the qualities of these elemental energies. As in acupuncture, illness is seen as an imbalance of these forces in the body. Since food can be classified as Yin or Yang, a Macrobiotic diet is a way or restoring this balance through eating the right foods.

Cereals and brown rice form the basis of the Macrobiotic diet because they contain the best balance of Yin and Yang. Yin foods are those which contain a lot of water, grow above the ground and tend to be hot, sour or sweet in taste. They tend to be blue, green or purple. Yang foods tend to be hard, dense, dry, grow below ground and are often red or yellow in colour. Different methods of cooking can also increase the tendency towards Yin or Yang: quick cooking increases Yin, and slow cooking, Yang. Foods that will promote this balance depend on the temperament of the eater and his or her environment. It is better to eat local foods too, because there is a natural affinity between the food of a region and its people. But it is important to stress that each individual is unique and has his or her own requirements for healthy eating.

Although Macrobiotics is a good way of healing oneself, at first it is important to consult a trained macrobiotic dietitian, especially if you have a particular complaint. Diagnosis is carried out by observation of the colour and shape of the patient's body, an assessment of their temperament, and by taking the 'pulses' (see Acupuncture section for an explanation of the pulses). Emphasis is not only placed on eating healthily, but also on lifestyle. Disease can also be a result of not looking after the body properly, of having a negative attitude to life or of being in the wrong environment.

Though it can be hard to keep to a macrobiotic diet - if you like eating out then you may find it harder - many people have found it can help in treatment of very stubborn conditions, as well as promoting increased vitality and better digestion.

Macrobiotic Counselling

Community Health Foundation EC1

Shops and Restaurants

East West Restaurant
(see below under Vegetarian Restaurants East) is a long-established macrobiotic restaurant and snack bar. Clearspring is a

wholefood shop which is in the same building as the East West restaurant, and sells macrobiotic supplies and a range of delicious macrobiotic snacks.

Bushwacker
59 Goldhawk Road, London W12 (081) 743 2359.
Wholefood shop sells range of wholefood, organic fruit and vegetables, medicines, books and also macrobiotic specialities.

Vegetarianism and Veganism

A vegetarian diet is one which excludes all meat. A vegan diet excludes not only meat but also all animal products, such as milk, eggs and sometimes honey. Most vegans also prefer not to use or wear leather.

The past few years has seen an increasing number of people becoming vegetarian or vegan. A number of different factors have contributed to this change in eating habits. Recent publicity about the possible harmful effects of meat and dairy products has added to the argument that a vegetarian diet is healthier and has offset the popular and unfounded fear that unless your diet includes a lot of meat you will become undernourished in some way. The saturated fats present in animal products have been found to be contributory to the development of heart disease, and links between high meat consumption and low fibre intake have been found with breast and bowel cancer. Much research shows that a high fibre, vegetable and fruit based diet is also less

fattening and promotes healthy functioning of the digestive system.

However, most people who adopt a vegan or vegetarian diet do so for ethical reasons. Since the consumption of meat and dairy products is no longer necessary for our survival, it is argued that the suffering inflicted upon animals in the food creating process is also unnecessary. Factory farming and mass production of meat means that in the modern world animals are subjected to greater suffering that in the days of the smallholding. The publicity which has been given to the way in which meat is produced has left many people feeling that since they cannot condone the process,

they cannot eat the product either.

Ecological awareness too has played its part in the change in eating habits. Animal farming tends to use up more resources than plant farming and requires more acres of land for less food production. Forests throughout the world have been cleared for animal grazing and this has led to further ecological problems.

In the 1990s it is far easier to be a vegan or vegetarian than it was 20 years ago. Health food shops have sprung up all over the country, and vegetarian restaurants have become commonplace, at least in the big cities. Many restaurants offer special vegetarian dishes or a vegetarian menu. The growth of high quality vegetarian cuisine means that fewer people are cracking the old nut rissole and lentil jokes, and vegetarians are not seen as 'cranks' any more. Life can still be difficult for the vegan who wants to eat out, though milk substitute products such as soya milk are available even in some local supermarkets in London.

Some people who would like to exclude meat from their diet still feel unsure about what they would eat instead, or still feel anxious about the prospect of a vegetarian coming for dinner. For further information on this and on other aspects of vegetarianism and veganism, contact the centres below.

Vegetarian Society

Parkdale, Dunham Road, Altrincham, Cheshire WA14 4QG (061 928) 0793.
Campaigns to promote vegetarianism, gives information and advice, publishes books, leaflets and Vegetarian magazine, produces range of merchandise, sup-

ports non-animal research into the benefits of vegetarianism. Also runs cookery courses (see Vegetarian Society Cookery School in Residential Workshops section).

Vegan Society

33-35 George Street, Oxford OX1 2AY (0865) 722166.
Publishes info pac (SAE); a good recipe book 'The Caring Cook' (£1.99); 'The Cruelty Free Shopper' (£2.50); publications on child nutrition, infant feeding and veganism; Membs £10, concs.

Vegetarian Resaurants

EAST

Cherry Orchard

241 Globe Road, Bethnal Green, London E2 0JD (081) 980 6678.
Tues-Fri 12-3 and 6.30-10.30, Sat 12-10.30, Sun & Mon closed. Vegan and vegetarian dishes at reasonable prices, canteen service at lunchtime changes to waitress service at night. Very pleasant garden in the Summer. Run by women members of the Buddhist centre next door..

East West Restaurant

188 Old Street, London EC1 (071) 608 0300.
Mon-Fri 11am-10pm. The only macrobiotic restaurant in town.

Slenders

41 Cathedral Place, St. Paul's, London EC4 (071) 236 5974.
Wholefood, 8.30-6.15 Mon to Fri, vegan.

VEGETARIAN   RESTAURANTS

VEGETARIAN RESTAURANTS

NORTH

Fallen Angel
*65 Graham Street, Islington, London N1
(071) 253 3996.*
Mon-Sat 12-12, Sun 12-11.30. Wine bar/
Cafe.

Something Else
*49 Cross Street, Islington, London N1
(071) 226 6579.*
6.30-11 Mon to Thur, 6.30-11.30 Fri and
Sat, Sun 7-10.30. Vegan.

Milward's
*97 Stoke Newington Church St., Stoke
Newington, London N16 (071) 254 1025.*
Mon-Fri 6-12, Sat and Sun 12-12. Vegan/
Wholefood.)

Spices
*30 Stoke Newington Church St., Stoke
Newington, London N16 (071) 254 1025.*
2-3 and 6-12 Mon-Thur, Fri 12-3 and 6-1,
Sat 12-1am, Sun 12-12. Vegan/Whole-
food.

Diwana Bhelpoori House (1)
*121 Drummond Street, Euston, London
NW1 (071) 387 5556.*
12-11.45 daily. Indian. Cheap.

Ravi Shankar
*133 Drummond Street, Euston, London
NW1 (071) 388 6458.*
12-11 daily. Indian food.

Sabras
*263 High Road, Willesden, London NW10
(081) 459 0340.*
1-3 and 5-10 Tues to Fri, 1-10 Sat and Sun.
Indian.

Manna
*4 Erskine Road, Chalk Farm, London
NW3 (071) 722 8028.*
6.30-12 daily. Wholefood, sometimes
vegan.).

SOUTH

Dining Room
*Winchester Walk, London Bridge,
London SE1 (071) 407 0337.*
Tues-Fri 7-10. Vegan/wholefood.

Well Bean
*10 Old Dover Road, Blackheath, London
SE3 (081) 858 1319.*
Mon-Fri 9-6, Sat 9-5.30. Wholefood: main
dish and soup every day, pies, pizzas,
salads. Bring your own bottle.

Full of Beans
*127 Rushey Green, Catford, London SE6
(081) 698 3283.*
9.30-5.30 Mon-Sat. Wholefood, hot
meals, snacks, cakes. Vegan dishes
sometimes avaialable.

Health Place Cafe
*17 Strutton Ground, London SW1 (071)
222 4588.*
Mon-Fre 9-9. Home made vegtarian food
and organic wines and beers. Healthfood
shop two doors up.

Wilkins Natural Foods
*61 Marsham Street, Victoria, London
SW1 (071) 222 4038.*
Mon-Fri 8-6. Wholefood cafe, mainly
lunctime trade. Some vegan dishes.

Wholemeal Cafe
*1 Shrubbery Road, Streatham, London
SW16 (081) 769 2423.*
Midday to 10pm, 7 days a week. Open
Sat and Sun 9-11.30am for breakfast.
Wholemeal. Fully licensed. No smoking.

De Las Casas

153 Clapham High Street, London SW4.
Vegetarian and vegan dishes. 48 seats and small health food shop at the front. Open evenings except Sundays. All food is cooked with filtered water, and is made with organically grown ingredients wherever possible. Licensed applied for, so bring your own bottle.

Windmill Wholefoods

486 Fulham Road, London SW6 6NH (071) 385 1570.
Mon-Sat 12-11pm. Sun 7pm-11pm. Licensed. 60 seater vegetarian restaurant. Vegetarian and vegan dishes, organic vegetables used. Organic wines and beers available. Wholefood shop at the same address specialises in organic vegetables. Starters average £1.20, main meals £3.40.

Hockney's

98 High Street, Croydon, Surrey (081) 688 2899.
Purely vegetarian, vega meals available too. Tue - Sat 12 noon-5.30pm counter lunch, 5.30 - 9.00 supper served by a waiter

VEGETARIAN RESTAURANTS WEST

Baba Bhelpoori House

118 Westbourne Grove, Bayswater, London W2 (071) 221 7502.
Closed Mon. Open 12-3, 6-10.45.

Diwana Bhelpoori House (2)

50 Westbourne Grove, Bayswater, London W2 (071) 221 0721.
12-3 and 6-10.30 daily. Indian. Cheap.

Angel Gate

51 Queen Caroline Street, Hammersmith, London W6 (081) 748 8388.
Vegan, wholefood and vegetarian.

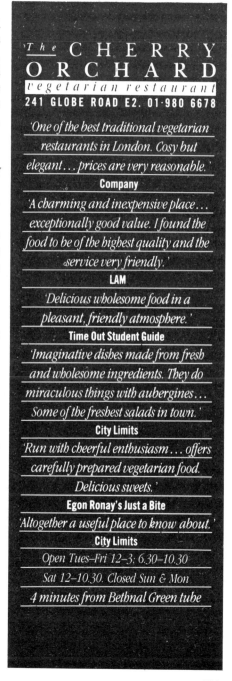

The CHERRY ORCHARD
vegetarian restaurant
241 GLOBE ROAD E2. 01·980 6678

'One of the best traditional vegetarian restaurants in London. Cosy but elegant... prices are very reasonable.'
Company

'A charming and inexpensive place... exceptionally good value. I found the food to be of the highest quality and the service very friendly.'
LAM

'Delicious wholesome food in a pleasant, friendly atmosphere.'
Time Out Student Guide

'Imaginative dishes made from fresh and wholesome ingredients. They do miraculous things with aubergines... Some of the freshest salads in town.'
City Limits

'Run with cheerful enthusiasm... offers carefully prepared vegetarian food. Delicious sweets.'
Egon Ronay's Just a Bite

'Altogether a useful place to know about.'
City Limits

*Open Tues–Fri 12–3; 6.30–10.30
Sat 12–10.30. Closed Sun & Mon
4 minutes from Bethnal Green tube*

251

Gate Vegetarian Restaurant
51 Queen Caroline Street, Hammersmith, London W6 (081) 748 6932.
12 noon-11.30pm Mon-Fri, 12 noon-12 midnight Sats. Licensed (organic and non-organic wines). Private parties catered for. Linked to the Rudolph Steiner inspired Christian Community.

Hearth Cafe At Earthworks
132 Kings Street, Hammersmith, London W6 OQU (081) 846 9357.
Wholefood, Mon-Wed 11am-6pm. Fri & Sat 11am-10.30 pm.

Woodlands Restaurant (1)
402 High Road, Wembley, Middlesex (081) 902 9869.
12-2.45 and 6-10.30 daily, Indian food.

VEGETARIAN RESTAURANTS W1

Country Life
1 Heddon Street, London W1 (071) 434 2922.
11.30-3.00, Fri 11.30-2.00. Closed Sat and Sun. Vegan/wholefood. Buffet. Cheap.

Cranks Health Foods (2)
17-18 Great Newport Street, London W1, Leicester Square,
Wholefood, 8 - 10.30 Mon to Fri, vegan.

Cranks Health Foods (3)
8 Marshal Street, London W1 (071) 437 9431.
Mon to Fri. 8-10.30 Vegan/wholefood.

Cranks Health Foods (4)
9-11 Tottenham Street, London W1 (071) 631 3912.
8-8 Mon-Fri, 9-8pm Sat, closed Sun. Vegan/wholefood.

Govinda's
9 Soho Street, Soho, London W1 (071) 437 3662.
Purely vegetarian restaurant

Hare Krishna Curry House
1 Hanway Street, London W1 (071) 636 5262.
10.30-11pm all week. Has just re-opened and seats 50. Gujerati vegetarian dishes and wholefood. Licensed.

Mandeer
21 Hanway Place, London W1 (071) 323 0660.
10.30 Mon-Sat, closed Sun. Tasty Indian. (Cheap.).

Nuthouse
26 Kingley Street, London W1 (071) 437 9471.
10.30-7.00 Mon-Fri, 10.30-6 Sat, closed Sun. Vegan/wholefood. Cheap.

Raw Deal
65 York Street, London W1 (071) 262 4841.
10-10 Mon to Fri, Baker Street, Wholefood.

Woodlands Restaurant (2)
77 Marylebone Lane, London W1 (071) 486 3862.
12-2.45 and 6 - 10.30 daily, Indian food.

Woodlands Restaurant (3)
37 Panton Street Off, Haymarket, London W1 (071) 839 7258.
12-2.45 and 6-10.30 daily, Indian food.

VEGETARIAN RESTAURANTS WC1 & WC2

Greenhouse
16 Chenies Street, London WC1 (071) 637 8038.

Goodge Street tube. Mon 10-6, Tues-Fri 10-10, Sat 1-8.30. Reasonable prices, vegan dishes available.

Bunjie's Coffee House
27 Litchfield Street, London WC2 (071) 240 1796.
12-11 every day. Sunday 5-11. Wholefood. Cheap, folk music some nights.

Cranks Health Foods (1)
1 Central Avenue, Covent Garden Plaza, London WC2 (071) 379 6508.
9.30-8.00, Sun 9.30-7. Covent Garden tube.

Food for Thought (1)
31 Neal Street, Covent Garden, London WC2 (071) 836 0239.
Covent Garden, Wholefood/ Vegan, 12-8, Sat 12-8 closed Sun.

London Ecology Centre
45 Shelton Street, Covent Garden, London WC2 (071) 379 4324.
10.30am-10.30pm, closed 10. Covent Garden, Wholefood and vegan. Licensed.

Neal's Yard Bakery and Tea Room
6 Neal's Yard, Covent Garden, London WC2 (071) 836 5199.
10.30-8 Mon Tue Thur Fr, Covent Garden, Wholefood, vegan dishes available and as many different types of tea as you could wish.

Shan
200 Shaftesbury Avenue, Soho, London WC2 (071) 240 3348.
12-10 Mon-Sat, closed Sun.

LONDON GETAWAY

Residential Workshops

A residential is a workshop which takes place over a weekend or longer, and in which the participants stay together in accommodation provided, usually because the venue is in the country. This builds up a more intensive atmosphere, and can enable people to enter more fully into the workshop. See also 'Residential Communities' in this section.

Arbour Low Spiritual Healing Centre
Sinclairs Hill, Duns, Berwickshire TD11 3LU (0361) 82866.
As well as spiritual healing, they also run courses in relaxation and meditation. All activities are on a contribution basis. Residence is available at reasonable full or part board basis. Vegetarian non-smokers only, no pets. Physically and mentally handicapped people can be catered for.

Ashtanga Centre
22 Fairwood Road, Westbury, Wilts, BA13 4ED (0373) 822074.
Residential centre running residential weekend courses on yoga, massage (ITEC), meditation, touch for health. £70-£80 for weekend inclusive of food accommodation and tuition.

Aura Soma
Dev Aura, Little London Tetford, Nr Horncastle, Lincs LN9 6QL (065 883) 781.
Colour therapy and its healing adjuncts 6-day residential courses, cost £325.

Bartragh
Bartragh Island, Lillala Bay, County Mayo, Eire 010 353 9632285/32514.

Beacon Centre for Harmony and Health
Cutteridge Farm, Whitestone, Exeter, Devon EX4 2HE (039281) 203.
Courses on self enlightenment and transformation, yoga, meditation, tai chi circle dancing, crystal healing and psychotherapy. Fully centrally heated with sauna and olympic size trampoline for those who are feeling 'bouncy'. Situated within 20 mins drive of Dartmoor, the sea and Exeter city centre. Working organic farm. Long weekend is £75, plus £4 (+ VAT) per night for shared accommodation - includes hire of self catering kitchen. Bed and breakfast also available. Write for programme. Available for hire for groups.

CAER (Centre For Alternative Education And Research)
Rosemerryn, Lamorna, Penzance, Cornwall TR19 6BN (0736) 810530.
Wide range of workshops including Alexander technique, gestalt, massage, rebirthing, resonance therapy, stress management, yoga, shamanism, women's and men's groups and body-oriented approaches, groupwork, RSA certified courses in groupwork and

counselling etc. One of the longest established centres for residential workshops in personal and professional development in Europe. It is situated in seven acres of woods and gardens, near the sea in an area of Outstanding Natural Beauty. The house itself is an old Cornish manor house. When there are no groups there, you can stay on a nightly basis. Wheelchair access. Dinner, bed and breakfast £20. Average price of a 5 day group £250 (includes residential costs), 3 day group £90. Concessions for low waged and unwaged.

Eden Centre for Holistic Health and Creative Development
Eden House, 38 Lee Road, Lyton, Devon EX35 6BS (0598) 53440.
Holiday retreats £56 per week, accommodation only. £112 including food. Minimum booking is for one week. Offer a wide range of therapies - massage, aromatherapy, relaxation, meditation, Alexander technique, stress management.

Findhorn Foundation
The Park, Forres IV36 0TZ, Scotland (0309) 73655.
Courses include Learning to Love, Letting Go - Unfolding Your Inner Self, Massage, Deep Ecology, Primal Painting, Towards Sexual Wholeness, Myths we Live By, Gestalt to name but a few. Participants live and work in the Findhorn Community in the 'Experience Week', completion of which is a requirement for participation in most courses longer than a weekend. For prices see under List of Centres section. For details of the philosophy of Findhorn see Other Groups in Spirit section.

Gablecroft College of Natural Therapy

Church Street, Whittington, Shropshire SY11 4DT (0691) 659631.
Residential training in massage, reflexology, aromatherapy, sports injury treatment, healing and dowsing. ITEC recognised. Finnish sauna and vegetarian, organic meals.

Hazelwood

Loddiswell, Nr Kingsbridge, S Devon TQ7 4EB (0548) 82232 / 883 2124.
Workshops on voice work, and music weekends with classical performers in concert (£175 per weekend for the latter).

Holwell Centre for Psychodrama and Sociodrama

East Down, Barnstaple, Devon EX31 3NZ 0271 850 267/597.
Weekend and week long courses covering Living Without the Hurt Child, Learn to Love the Devil in You, Couples, Dreams, Journal Process, Cancer/AIDS and Psychodrama and How Do Psychotherapists Handle Their Own Anxiety? and more. £120 per residential week-end, £315 per week. Centre also available for hire. No wheelchair access at present, but changes are being made. Creche facilities by arrangement.

Hourne Farm

Steel Cross, Crowborough, Sussex (0892) 661093.
Set in the Sussex countryside, they offer a programme of weekend workshops, courses, open weekends and summer schools. Study of leylines, divination, yoga, holistic therapies, crystals. Approx £45 per weekend workshop.

Le Plan Seminars

10 Irene Road, London SW6 4AL (071) 736 2460.
Weekend courses in Provence, France, on aspects of healing and spirituality both individual and global. Also run 4-part diploma course in healing (cost £525 for each part).

Maitri

Little Abshot Road, Titchfield, Hants PO14 4LN (0489) 572451.
'Maitri' means 'friend to oneself' and here they run self development courses including stress management, regression

This figure is a God of Healing found in an underground passage on the site of an Iron Age fort. The two thousand year old granite carving is unique in the United Kingdom.

Since 1978 this has been the home of CAER, a centre for personal development and training secluded in a magical landscape near the sea. There, in a relaxed setting with delicious food, you'll find residential groups throughout the year with some of the finest leaders anywhere.

For a colour brochure and programme contact:

CAER,   Rosemerryn,
Lamorna,   Penzance,
Cornwall, TR19 6BN.
Tel: 0736 810530

and discover what makes it so special.

therapy, polarity therapy, synergetics, meditation and channelling. Centre used to be the stables of the old Abshot Manor, which were converted 6 years ago. Swimming pool, vegetarian food, special diets catered for with prior notice. Training centre for the International School of Polarity Therapy. £65 per weekend, £90 for a four day course.

Pegasus

Running Park, Croft Bank, West Malvern, Worcs WR14 8BR (06845) 65253.
Weekends about aspects of healing such as counselling skills, developing healing potential, healing relationships. Residential fees £92-£100.

Pellin Centre

43 Killyon Road, Clapham, London SW8 2XS (071) 622 0148.
Intensive residential personal growth programme in Italy (in 1990 will take place in Moio, 100 kilometres south of Naples) described by the organisers as 'arduous and challenging' in a safe and nourishing environment. Morning and evening group for individual gestalt work. £230 per programme week, excluding air fares.

Silver Crescent Seminars

6 Palace Gate, London W8 5NF (071) 584 3889.
Esoteric traditions from east and west given a psychological understanding, including astrology, numerology, tarot, Kabbalah, subtle healing etc. £99 per weekend.

Studio 8

10 Wycliffe Row, Totterdown, Bristol BS3 4RU (0272) 713488.
Open arts workshops, tutorial groups,

Art Synthesis course exploring creativity, imagination and adventure through drawing, painting and other visual arts - 'awareness through art'. Venues are London, Wales, Kent and Italy. £43.50 for non-residential London weekends, £190 for a week in Wales or Kent inclusive.

Tighnabruaich

Tigh na bruaich, Struy, by Beauly, Inverness-shire IV4 7JU, Scotland (0463) 76254.
Healing centre in Scotland. Run 'The Watershed', a course exploring the self through nature. Can take up to 4 people to stay combining holiday with daily two-three hour therapy session. Vegetarian organic food. Watershed £350, stay £305 per week.

Vegetarian Society Cookery School

Co-ordinator Parkdale, Dunham Road, Altrincham, Cheshire WA14 4QG (061 928) 0793.
Courses at various levels on how to cook vegetarian food for vegetarians and non-vegetarian participants. Weekends, weeks and the 'Cordon Vert' Diploma course.

Yoga for Health Foundation

Ickwell Bury, Ickwell Green, Nr Biggleswade, Bedfordshire SG18 9EF (0767) 27271.
Residential, generally short stay (one/two weeks) yoga centre. Day and overnight guests also welcome. Please notify in advance of day visits.. Also run special courses for the disabled. £33 per day, £60 per weekend.

One of Britains leading centres for holistic education offers reasonably priced weekends workshops.

• Dreamwork • Tai Chi • Shamanism • Art of Loving
• Women's groups • Men's groups • + much more.

Send SAE to Dept B

Monkton Wyld Court, Charmouth,
Bridport, Dorset DT6 6DQ
Tel: Charmouth (0297) 60342

BARTRAGH ISLAND

A magnificent island and smaller islands off the West Coast of Ireland in Co. Mayo (approx. 30 minutes from Knock International Airport).

Nearly 400 acres, half sand-dunes (with miles of golden beaches, a shipwreck and buried treasure) and half natural agricultural farmland with fields surrounded by the Atlantic Ocean and Killala Bay.

Come and visit **BARTRAGH HOUSE**, a large stately home built around two courtyards and with extensive walled gardens, outbuildings and orchards, the only dwelling on the island, which is a natural habitat for all species of plants, birds and marine life.

Residential courses, seminars and workshops in Biodynamic Psychology will be available from June, 1991.

If you are interested to book the whole, or part of its facilities, to attend courses, or offer workshops, please contact Mary Molloy, The Biodynamic Clinic, 23 High Street, The Green, Ealing, London W5 4DF, telephone 081 579 1904 or in Ireland (096) 32285 or 32514.

Holidays

The centres listed below provide the opportunity for residential workshops or healthy activities coupled with a holiday location. For more information about wholesome breaks, try **The Complete Healthy Holiday Guide** by *Catherine Mooney, Headway Books £6.95* which lists over 300 places to stay where healthy food is served and healthy activities are on offer.

Churchill Centre
22 Montagu Street, Marble Arch, London W1H 1TB (071) 402 9475.
Massage learning holidays in Lanzarote.

Cortijo Romero
72 Meadowsweet Road, Creekmoor, Poole, Dorset BH17 7XT (0202) 699581.
Self development holidays in this well-established centre situated in the foothills of the Sierra Nevada, Spain. Groupwork, meditation, music, healing, yoga and mountain walks. Vegetarian cuisine and swimming pool.

Fasting Walks
C/o Christoph Michl, Pratjeweg 1, D-2152 Horneburg, Germany.
Arrange walks and holidays throughout Europe where participants fast while enjoying the scenery and each other's company. Participants usually cover 25 kilometres a day after a 7am start, and find accommodation in the evening for the whole group. They are based in Germany and mainly German-speaker oriented, but are keen to have British people on the walks and are looking for a person in Britain who could act as a contact.

Gateway

c/o 76 Nelson Road Central, Great Yarmouth (0493) 844458.
Centre in South West France offering limited accommodation in tranquil setting. There's a swimming pool and a resident psychic adviser and dream counsellor is always on hand.

Health Management

31 Rosslyn Hill, London NW3 5UJ (071) 431 0760.
Mediteranean Holidays and country weekend breaks include yoga, meditation, massage etc. Vegetarian cuisine.

Living Planet Travel Ltd

PO Box 922, London N10 3UZ (0582) 429365.
Adventure holidays to Peru, India, Mexico and Nepal. Will arrange individual itineraries - for instance will introduce you to the Buddhist kingdom of Zanskar and Ladakh and their traditional Tibetan culture (£1600 for a 34 day holiday).

Millennium Institute

PO Box 935, Palo Alto, CA 94301, USA (415) 321 2169.
Residential courses on personal growth and spirituality in Bali in a purpose built local-style complex. Two weeks in this idyllic setting will set you back $2974 including flight. Also run journeys and expeditions to the ancient power places of Peru, the Inca trail, Egypt and Greece, India and Nepal etc.

Mother Nature

Mother's Office 2 Park Terrace Carmarthen SA31 3DG .
Accommodation here is in Tipis and thatched huts - chop your own firewood and meet around the cauldron for dinner. Being close to nature is part of the education here, with workshops on the medicine wheel teachings of the Native American Indians, natural magic of the European tradition, hypnosis, healing and green friendship camps. £120 for a week, £50 weekends

New Spirit Quests

Dove Cottage, Henton Wells, Somerset BA5 1PD (0749) 74604\181429.
Offer advice, information and support to those wishing to visit sacred sites in the South West of Britain. Can suggest itineraries or escort you to the site, and even lead you through a guided meditation when you get there if you want. They can give telephone advice, or you can visit and stay taking advantage of their bed and breakfast facilities and meditation room. If you want they can give you meditation/yoga instruction or book you up with a local alternative medical practitioner. West Country Invitation Package £6. Advice/services charged by the hour.

Oak Dragon Camps

PO Box 5, Castle Cary, Somerset BA7 7YQ (0269) 844272.
Run a yearly series of outdoor, educational camps centred around various subjects such as spirituality, myth, creative arts, healing and green issues for both adults and children. Camp facilities include vegetarian food, children's funspace, hot showers, etc. Each day there is a camp pow-wow, workshops in marquees, ongoing practical projects, celebrations and spontaneously arising events. Numbers limited to 70-100 people. £60 for 8 days adults, £15 children.

Skyros Centre

92 Prince of Wales Road, London NW5 2NE (071) 267 4424 / 431 0867 (24 hr answerphone).
There are three centres on the island of Skyros in Greece - Atsitsa, Skyros Centre and the Skyros Institute. Atsitsa offers holistic health holidays where participants can join in a programme of yoga, massage, meditation etc. £395-£495 (depending on season), includes courses, accommodation and full board, flight not included. Skyros Centre offers personal development courses such as psychodrama, gestalt, bioenergectics etc. £385-£450, includes courses accommodation and half board, flight not included. Skyros Institute offers training courses in personal development and holistic health (£415-£515, includes courses, accommodation and half board, flight not included. Prices given are for two weeks.

Sunra

26 Balham Hill, Clapham South, London SW12 9EB (081) 675 9224.
Health holidays in the sun. £520 including flight for two week holiday. Yoga and meditation and massage.

Vegi Ventures

17 Lilian Road, Burnham-on-Crouch, Essex CM0 8DS (0621) 784285.
Activity and sightseeing holidays in Britain and abroad for people who prefer a vegetarian diet. Samples of what is on offer are a Scottish Highland adventure on the Isle of Rasaay (£198 inclusive of board and lodging and tuition), canal cruising in France and Austrian ski parties.

Residential Communities

Lauriston Hall

Castle Douglas, South West Scotland .
Though no longer a 'commune', the 20 adults and 11 children on Lauriston Hall live together as individual members of a housing co-op, some in families, some by themselves, and others in small, non-family 'living groups' and share some aspects of their work. Hold visitors weeks when people can come and experience first hand what goes on. Run a number of residential workshops as well such as gay men's weeks, Reichian weeks, tai

RESIDENTIAL HEALTH CENTRES

chi, music, alchemy and taoist weeks, and 'maximising our immunity' workshop. Sliding scale from £8.50 per day up to £15, depending on income, workshops may cost more.

Lower Shaw Farm

Old Shaw Lane, Shaw, Nr Swindon, Wilts SN5.

Community with no collectively stated religious or party political base. Workshops and holidays, as well as working weekends etc. Prices are cheap - £40-£45 per weekend workshops which includes food and accommodation. Some of the weekend workshops they do are Shiatsu, fools' weekend, yoga, massage, death exploration, pottery, women and crafts (such as photography), rug making etc.

Monkton Wyld Court

Nr. Charmouth, Bridport, Dorset (0297) 60342.

Holistic education centre and the home of 10 adults, 2 teenagers, 5 young children plus 2 or 3 short term volunteers. They work co-operatively, taking care of a wide range of groups involved in therapy, healing, yoga, tai-chi, dance, theatre and the arts as well as children's groups youth groups, mentally handicapped and other community groups. They maintain their own land and grow their own food. Weekend workshops range from 'Drums, Rhythm and Voices' to 'Dreamwork and Psychosynthesis'. Appetising vegetarian dishes cooked in a big communal pot. The all-in prices make it good value.

Residential Health Centres

Bethany Vegetarian and Vegan Nursing Homes

7/9 Oak Park Villas, Dawlish, Devon EX7 0DE (0626) 862794.

Run on Christian principles, it offers care to all vegetarians and vegans, and is registered with the local health authority as a nursing home and rest home with 23 beds. Special diets such as diabetes, wholefood, Gerson type cancer therapy, gluten free are catered for. Visiting chiropodist, hairdresser, masseuse, occupational therapist, homoeopath and acupuncturist. Aim to give residents holistic health care with a choice of naturopathic or allopathic therapy. Non smoking environment. Nursing bed £250 per week, rest home bed £175 per week. Also accept DHS patients.

Breakspear Hospital

For Allergy and Environmental Medicine, High Street, Abbots Langley, Herts WD5 0PU (0923) 261333.

Private Hospital opened March 1988 with in-patient, day-patient and out-patient facilities. Patients seen by appointment only. Monthly seminars, lectures. Sale of books and vitamins. Prices £85 for initial consultation with doctor, thereafter prices individually ascertained. No concessions. Register of practitioners. Wheelchair access.

Park Attwood Therapeutic Centre

Trimpley, Bewdley, Worcs DY12 1RE (02997) 444.

Nursing home run by qualified doctors using Anthroposophical Medicine - 'a therapeutic community in a clinical setting'. Have treated people for conditions both physical and mental. Also run in-service training for nurses, and are open to visits from interested health professionals.

Raphael Medical Centre

Hollanden Park, Coldharbour Lane, Hildenborough, Kent (0732) 833924.
In- and out-patient facilities for Anthroposophical therapies.

Tyringham Naturopathic Clinic

Newport Pagnell, Bucks MK16 9ER (0908) 610450.
Osteopathy, acupuncture, massage, indoor pool with sauna and jacuzzi, gymnasium, hydrotherapy. Outdoor sports facilities. £188 -£434 per week.

Retreats

A retreat is an intensive period of meditation, study or other religious practices which is residential. They almost always take place in the country. All retreats have a programme of activities. There are usually set times for meditation or prayer, and this structure provides a framework within which the retreatant can let go of having to organise his or her life and concentrate on inner spiritual experience.

Retreats can vary enormously in terms of what the programme is and whether the organisers expect you to participate fully in all activities, or whether you can just be there and join in as you wish. It is as well to decide beforehand what you do want and to check with the organisers about the programme.

Some retreats have an intensive pro-

gramme with a great deal of meditation or prayer, and some may be silent some, or all of the time. Others have a looser programme. There may be an early start, as early as 4am for some, and accommodation may be in dormitories or occasionally in smaller rooms. You may be ked to bring a sleeping bag. Sometimes participants are expected to work on the retreat, sometimes all the work is done for them. Food is usually vegetarian.

A good publication for finding a place for a retreat, even in central London is **The Vision**, the Journal of the National Retreat Association *(24 South Audley Street, London W1 (071) 493 3534)*, which costs £1 plus post and packing. This lists all the Christian retreat houses in Britain and group and individual retreat facilities.

Please refer to List of Centres section at the back of this book for addresses.

Gaia House

Woodland Road, Denbury, Nr. Newton Abbot, Devon TQ12 6DY (0803) 813188.
Buddhist vipassana (insight) meditation retreats, as well as working retreats, yoga, reiki, zen etc. Facilities for solitary retreats also available. Weekend £35, £77 for a week.

Four Winds Centre

High Thicket Rd, Temple Hill, Dockenfield, Farnham, Surrey GU10 4HB (025125) 4480/3990.
Directed by Frank Kevlin, a Sufi leader, Four Winds runs a 'Summer Experience', a series of workshops on spiritual and psychotherapeutic themes. Programmes in 1989 included Nirtan: Music, Meditation and Dance, Communicating Using

NLP, Spiritual Retreat, Love, Anger and Conflict etc. The centre is also available for hire, and for individual retreats.

Creative and Healing Arts
222 Westbourne Park Road, London W11 1EP (071) 229 9400.
Mainly weekend retreats in the country with yoga, shaitsu, dance and music.

London Buddhist Centre,
51 Roman Road, E2. (081) 981 1225.
Retreat centre in Suffolk with weekend or longer retreats for meditation, Buddhism, yoga, tai chi and other themes.

EVENTS

Discos and Dances

Barefoot Boogie
Jacksons Lane Community Centre, Archway Rd and Jacksons Lane, London N6 (081) 444 7356 / 883 2966.
No smoking, barefoot boogie perrier drinking folks only. Great place to let your hair hang down on a Friday night. Large hall, world music and rock. Bring an instrument if you wish.7.30 -11pm. £4.

Hold Back The Night
The Feathers Club, Dalgarno Way, Ladbroke Grove, London W10. Information (081) 208 1983.
New venue, last Saturday of every month 9pm-2am. Multi-event club: dance floor with 'world grooves' (Latin, African, jazz and soul music), acoustic live sounds room, cabaret (featuring the likes of John Hegley and Josie Lawrence), chill-out room, trampolines and inflatables, juice bar (for those wanting something a bit

stronger, bring your own), vegetarian and vegan cuisine. For those who can't stand the strain, masseur and reflexologist will be in attendance for foot first aid. Creche from 9-12. £4.50 entrance, £3.50 concessions.

Whirl-Y-Gig
(081) 864 6760.
Wednesday nights and alternate Saturdays. The original alternative disco. A place to dance to world music and refresh yourself at the cafe selling Norfolk Punch and a range of health drinks. While Whirl-y-Gig used to take place in Notre Dame Hall in Leicester Square, this venue has been temporarily closed, so ring for details of venue - Old Hampstead Town Hall is now usually used.

Circle Dance
Old Hall Community, East Bergholt, Colchester, Essex CO7 6TG (0206) 298294.
Celebrate the seasons with dances and songs of unity from many lands. Stefan Freedman choreographs dances and accompanies on the accordion, flute and guitar. Holidays, weekends and day workshops. Write for details.

Lectures

Alternatives
St James's Church, 197 Piccadilly, London W1V 9LF (071) 287 6711.
This is a project dedicated to providing a platform for New Age ideas - creative and spiritual alternatives to currently accepted Western thought. It does this through a regular lecture series, workshops, meditations and sacred dance. It also provides a counselling service for

other New Age groups, advising them how to start their own projects or helping them with any group dynamics problems.

Turning Points

Office: 120 The Vale, London W3 7JT (081) 749 1065.
Tuesdays 7-10pm. Established in 1982, originally at St James's, Piccadilly, then branching out to include other venues in central London, Wales and Greece.Topics include personal and planetary change, healing, creativity, men and women, etc. Light refreshments are served and there is time for socialising. Workshops and conferences. Sell tapes and books. Wheelchair access sometimes. £3 per evening, £25-£30 per day workshop. Concessions.

New Connexions

c/o Finchley Reform Synagogue, Fallow Court Avenue, London N12 (081) 441 5416.
Lectures on 'New Age' spirituality, self development etc.

Exhibitions

New Life Designs

170 Campden Hill Road, London W8 7AS (071) 938 3788.
Organise three festivals:
Festival for Mind, Body, Spirit (May bank holiday weekend)- the original 'New Age' festival which has been going for 13 years. Covers natural health, personal growth, spiritual/philosophical organisations, psychic arts, ecology, crafts and products. As well as the stalls, there's an ongoing programme of lectures, demonstrations and workshops.

The Healing Arts (8th-11th November, 1990). Alternative medicine and complementary therapies exhibition - therapies, products, training bodies etc. Lectures and workshops, and a physical therapy room where a team of body workers will give you a taste of the technique of your choice.
Green Consumer Exhibition (May bank holiday weekend). Environmentally friendly products, information on green issues.

Swan House Special Events

Holly Road, Hampton Hill, Middlesex TW12 1PZ (081) 783 0055.
Organise **The Health Show** (formerly Here's Health Exhibition) 5-8th July 1990. Now covers green living (who doesn't these days), fitness, beauty and healthy eating as well as natural remedies and therapies.

Galleries and Museums

Freud Museum

20 Maresfield Gardens, Hampstead, London NW3 435 2002/5167.
Weds-Sun 12-5. Admission £2 adults, £1 concessions (children under 12 free). Freud lived here for the last year of his life after fleeing Nazi-occupied Vienna with his family in 1938. His library and study house his collection of Greek, Egyptian, Oriental and Roman antiquities and here you can also see the famous analytic couch. The museum also runs exhibitions, lectures and seminars and shows videos based on Freud's own home movies.

263

Radio Counselling

Counselling Programme

London Broadcasting Company, Communications House, Gough Square, London EC4P 4LP (071) 353 1991.
Counselling programme on the radio (LBC) run by either Phillip Hodson or Anne Hooper. It's on Crown FM 97.3mHz (FM only) every weekday from 1pm - 3pm. It is a call-in counselling programme where personal, emotional, sexual and marital problems are discussed on air. Some counselling is actually done on air, and where appropriate follow-up agencies are suggested. Every Wednesday at 2.00pm they have a Noticeboard section where they read out the latest counselling and training courses available to the general public. The first hour of the programme always includes a guest and they will discuss a particular topic like drug addiction, stress management, miscarriage, PMT, etc. Counselling phone number is *(071) 819 8111* to take part in the phone-in.

Other Events

Urasenke Foundation

4 Langton Way, London SE3 (081) 853 2595.
Traditional Japanese tea ceremony - sessions are £10 and you have to be a member of the society.

Glastonbury Earth Link

2-4 High Street, Glastonbury, Somerset BA6 9DU (0458) 31960.
Week of events, lectures, discussions, stalls, exhibitions and celebrations to explore the topic of how personal and community responsibility can further the evolutions of strategies supporting planetary recovery..

Tibet Foundation

43 New Oxford Street, London WC1A 1BH (071) 379 0634.
Organise Tibetan cultural events, such as the World Tour of Sacred Music and Sacred Dance by the Tibetan monks of Gaden Shartse Monastery. Send SAE for details of other events.

HELP

Organisations for Specific Problems

New Approaches To Cancer

C\O The Seekers Trust, Addington Park, Maidstone, Kent ME19 5BL (0732) 848336.
Charity which promotes the positive benefits of holistic and self-help methods of healing to cancer patients, which they see as complementing hospital treatment. Has national referral network linking support groups and individuals.

Wandsworth Cancer Support Centre

PO Box 17, Battersea Central Mission, 14/28 York Rd, London SW11 3QE (071) 924 3924.
Offer a holistic approach to those with cancer, their relatives, friends and health professionals. Run courses in relaxation and visualisation, workshops, on-going groups, counselling service, offer healing and massage, also workshops for health professionals. There are also books, tapes, periodicals and videos about cancer available on loan to mem-

bers. Membership £5 per annum for individuals (£2 concessions).

Alternative Centre
The White House, Roxby Place, Fulham, London SW6 1RS (071) 381 2298.
Specialise in the treatment of psoriasis and eczema.

Clinics Health International
Riverbank House, Putney Bridge Approach, London SW6 3JD 371 9717/371 9590.
Clinic specialising in the treatment of eczema, acne, psoriasis, dermatitis and other skin conditions through Chinese herbal medicine. Consultants are two Professors from China..

London Headache and Migraine Clinic
7 Park Crescent, London W1N 3HE (071) 637 1491.
Offers a range of safe and natural therapies for the treatment and relief of headaches, migraines and related conditions. Use acupuncture, herbal medicine, osteopathy and counselling as well as stress management, exercise and dietry advice if appropriate.

St James Centre for Health and Healing
197 Piccadilly, London W1V 9LF (071) 437 7118.
As well as offering a range of therapies and counselling, St James centre also runs free cancer support groups.

Recovery Tools
31 Craven Street, London WC2 5NP (071) 839 8868.
Groups for recovering alcoholics, their families, adult children of alcoholics and recovering drug users.

Cancer Help Centre
Grove House, Cornwallis Grove, Clifton, Bristol BS8 4PG (0272) 743216.
Provides a complementary/holistic approach to cancer, which can be used alongside orthodox medical treatment. Programme includes counselling, dietry advice, relaxation and meditation, healing by touch. Patients can make day visits or stay over a longer period and participate in both one-to-one and groups sessions, and are put in touch with local support group.

Fellowship of Sports Masseurs and Therapists
B M Soigneur, London WC1N 3XX (081) 886 3120.
Run training courses for those wishing to become masseurs for sports people.

Useful Organisations

Action Against Allergy
23/24 George Street, Richmond, Surrey TW9 1JY.
Information centre (by mail only) and also charity headquarters for AAA membership and fund raising for research. Receive approximately 100 letters a week from allergic people needing advice of various kinds. They are not a medical body, but they try to indicate where and how they might get medical help. Annual meeting with prominent speaker. Mail order sales of books. Membership £10 per year, members get magazine 3 times per year and access to postal lending library.

Appropriate Health Resources and Technologies Action Group

1 London Bridge Street, London SE1 9FG (071) 378 1403.

AHRTAG supports and provides information on the primary health care approach (PHC) around the world. The aim of PHC is to provide comprehensive health care for everyone with an emphasis on preventive care, co-operation between different sectors of society, community participation and a fair distribution of resources..

Association for Dance Movement Therapy

99 South Hill Park, Hampstead, NW3.

This is a professional body, providing support for Dance/Movement therapists, and those interested in the subjects. No public workshops on a regular basis. Established 1982. Approx 100 member in the UK. They regret that because they are a voluntary body they cannot provide literature or specialised information in response to individual requests. Publications. Seminars for practitioners. Conferences/workshops/visiting speakers. Register of professional members. Code of ethics.

Association for Humanistic Psychology

c/o 26 Huddlestone Road, London E7 OAN (081) 555 3077.

AHP is an organisation for people from all walks of life interested in the values of humanistic psychology. There are workshops, lectures and social events regularly. Has its own journal 'Self and Society' and a separate section for practitioners e.g. therapists, counsellors etc.

Association of General Practitioners of Natural Medicine

The Hon Secretary, 38 Nigel House, Portpool Lane, London EC1N 7UR (071) 405 2781.

The association controls the standard of teaching and practice of a GP of Natural Medicine. Membership £20pa. Conferences and training sessions. Fund raising activities: sponsored walks, annual gatherings etc. Concs.

Association of Humanistic Psychology Practitioners (AHPP)

87 Whippscross Rd, Leytonstone, London E11 1NJ 455 8737/530 3283.

Is a professional organisation existing to promote the highest standards of excellence among humanistic psychology practitioners. Practitioners have to satisfy strict criteria of training and professional competence and are required to adhere to high standards of practice and ethics. They produce a membership directory (free) listing practitioners who are members.

Balint Society

The Tollgate Centre, Tollgate Rd, Beckton (071) 474 5656.

The Society promotes learning and research into the understanding of the doctor-patient relationship. Meetings and lectures. Trainees and young practitioners welcome. Journal to members free. £20 membership

British Association for the Person-Centred Approach

BAPCA, London WC1N 3XX.

Is a newly formed organisation whose aims include bringing together all people, groups and organisations who work in the tradition of the person-centred approach based on the work of Carl Rogers. It is part of a European wide organisation - there are similar associations in France, Germany, Italy and Hungary.1990 will see the first international Women's Forum to be held in September. Details of this and other events can be obtained from the above address.

British Association of Art Therapists Ltd

11a Richmond Road, Brighton BN2 3RL. Supply information about courses and training available in art therapy. Publish journal £7 subs (individual), £14 subs (organisation). Provide a folder of information on Art Therapy as a profession in Great Britain £5.

British Herbal Medicine Association

Field House, Lye Hole Lane, Redhill, Avon BS18 7TB (0934) 862994. Association for herbal practitioners, manufacturers and retailers of herbal medicines set up to promote and monitor herbal remedies and their sale. Publish British Herbal Pharmacopoeia (2 volumes at £35 each, less for members).

British Nutrition Foundation

15 Belgrave Square, London SW1X 8PS (071) 235 4904. Leaflets and briefing papers on various aspects of nutrition, send SAE for list. Seminars on nutrition..

British Society of Dowsers

Sycamore Cottage, Hastingleigh, Ashford, Kent TN25 5HW (0233) 75253. Seminars and residentials on dowsing for beginners and old hands. Also lec-

tures in London. Disseminates information on dowsing, network of local groups, lending library, journal to members, books and dowsing equipment for sale. Membership £16.50 per annum (UK), £19.65.

College of Health

18 Victoria Park Square, London E2 9PF (081) 980 6263. Was set up in 1983 to represent the interests of users of the health service. The college keeps a register of over 1200 self help groups and voluntary organisations for people who suffer from particular diseases, disabilities and handicaps. Campaign. Publish 'Guide to Hospital Waiting Lists', 'Guide to Homes for the Elderly', 'Guide to Going into Hospital'.

Council for Complementary and Alternative Medicine

Suite 1, 19A Cavendish Square, London W1M 9AD (071) 409 1440. Set up to provide a forum for communication and co-operation between professional associations of complementary practitioners.

Dulwich Health Society

130 Gypsy Hill, London SE19 1PL (081) 670 5883. Promotes information and action on geopathic stress and magnetic therapy. According to the theory of geopathic stress, illness is caused by sleeping long term in an area of harmful 'earth radiation'.

Emerson College

Forest Row, Sussex RH18 5JX (0342) 822238. Training in Waldorf education, educational eurythmy, biodynamic agriculture, rural development, social development, sculpture, voice development, speech and drama - all are applications of Rudolph Steiner's anthroposophy (qv). Also run some residential workshops.

Floatation Tank Association (UK)
3A Elms Crescent, London SW4 .
Is a professional body for people offering float tank facilities for public use. It sets professional standards and disseminates information. Membership subscription: £75 professional membership, £30 individual membership. Information and literature about floating. Workshops.

Green Paths Centre
13 Croftdown Road, London NW5 1EL 485 9981/4870.
Programme of workshops, discussions, lectures, meetings for people 'greening' their lives, lifestyles and businesses. Aims to facilitate personal growth and social renewal from a green perspective.

Health Practitioners' Association
181 Erith Road, Bexley Health, Kent DA7 6HS.
Advice on training in complementary therapies. Register of practitioners. Postgraduate training seminars in London.

Identity Counselling Service
2 Warwick Crescent, London W2 6NE (071) 289 6175.
Specialise in counselling for personal and relationship issues, and those confused about their sexual identity and orientation.

Inform
London School of Economics and Political Science, Houghton St, Aldwych, *London WC2A 2AE (071) 405 7686.*
Monitor religious movements and 'cults'. Information for those involved and those close to them.

International Psychoanalytic Association
Broomhills, Woodside Lane, London N12 (081) 446 8324.
Keep a register of trained psychoanalysts throughout the world.

London Convivium for Archetypal Studies
PO Box 417, London NW3 6YE.
Registered charity. Disseminate new ideas on archetypal psychology (Jung) and the arts. Yearly conference, usually in June. Produce an annual book called 'Sphinx' £10.

London Food Commission
88 Old Street, London EC1V 9AR (071) 253 9513.
Researches the state of food in the capital, information on what goes in and out of food. Campaigns against harmful practices in production. Publications available mail order cover fast food, food adulteration, additives, food irradiation etc. Also publishes quarterly 'Food Magazine'.

Marylebone Centre
17 Marylebone Road, London NW1 5LT (071) 935 6328.
This is an ordinary GP practice which employs an acupuncturist, osteopath, homoeopath and masseur to treat patients when appropriate. While they usually only treat patients registered with them from their catchment areas, they will take referrals from other GPs for those who need an assessment of which

complementary therapy could help them. Would that all GP surgeries were like this.

Medical Information Service

Boston Spa Wetherby, W Yorks LS23 7BQ (0937) 843434\210926.
Research articles from specialist journals in their Complementary Medicine Index - part of their Current Awareness Topics Services. £29 per year membership plus fee for search.

Pagan Funeral Trust

BM Box 3337, London WC1N 3XX.
Information and advice about arranging a pagan funeral. Newsletter.

Pathways Bulletin

12 Southcote Road, London N19 5BJ (071) 607 7852.
Regular bulletin of events and resources for growth and healing. £3 pa. membs.Information on individual therapy, group work, training courses, organisations and journals. Introductory booklets and videos. Brochure design and distribution service offered to practitioners. Send SAE to above address.

Society for Existential Analysis

Antioch University, Regents College, Inner Circle, Regents Park, London NW1 4NS (071) 487 7556.
Provides a forum for the expression of views and the exchange of ideas amongst those interested in the analysis of existence from philosophical and psychological perspectives. Its aim is to be a professional association which will seek to develop and expand existential-phenomenological approaches to psychotherapy and counselling. Membership is open to anyone interested in this field and includes psychotherapists, psychiatrists, psychoanalysts, counsellors and students.

Topaz Line

BM Topaz, London WC1N 3XX.
Counselling by post - send letter or tape outlining the situation. Free service which supports itself by donations.

United Kingdom Standing Conference for Psychotherapy

167 Sumartra Road, London NW6 1PN (071) 431 4379.
A federation of psychotherapy organisations seeking to accredit trainings in psychotherapy.

Q: What *other* London guide tells you . . ?

Housing
Women
Good Deals
Sex
Drugs
Communications
Environment
Law
Arts
Media
Groups
Printing
Publishing
Surviving
Minorities
Health
Green Issues
Contacts
Agitation
Computers
Alternative
Technology
Kids
Travel
Food
Alternative
Medicine
Transsexuals
Groups
Squatting

● How to get housed
● How to recycle your household waste
● How to tell a magic mushroom
   from a deadly toadstool
● How to get educated
- instead of going to school
● How to have safer sex
● What your rights on arrest are and the truth
   about what it's really like 'inside'
● How to get an arts grant
● Where to complain about racial harassment
● How to develop your inner potential
● How to squat
● How to get a women only lift home at night
● Who can give you the advice you need
● Which computer to buy
   and what all the jargon means
● Where to get free food
● How to start a community project
● Where to get cheap
   overnight accommodation
● The effectiveness of different contraceptives
● How to publish your own book
● How to escape into the country
● Where to 'get' religion
● How to sue in a small claims court
● Where to see pig racing in the inner city
● How to set up your own business
● and (almost) everything you ever wanted to
   know about the big city but were afraid to ask.

Advice
Centres
Disabilities
Networks
House DIY
Jobs
Foreigners
Bargains
Martial
Arts
Lesbians
& Gays
Community
Networks
Dole
Thriving
Self
Discovery
Libraries
Politics
Information
Men
Growth
Transport
Transvestites
Spirituality
Phone
Rights
Markets
Help

A: Survivors London.
The *other* London guide

ONLY
£6.95

Survivors' London is 304 pages crammed with invaluable information to help you make your way in the big city. Whether you're an old hand, a new arrival or just passing through, **Survivors' London** tells you a different story about how to survive and thrive.

Survivors' London gives hints, tips, know-how, explanations and advice on virtually every relevant subject you can think of. And in case you need further help, you'll find more than 2,500 organisations listed as well as up-to-date details of what they do.

Available now from bookshops or order direct by filling in the slip below

Name _____   Please send me _____ copies of *Survivors'*
                                         London at £6.95 + £1 p&p each (total £7.95 each).
Address_____
                                         I enclose a cheque for _____
_____

Please make cheques payable to Brainwave and send to BCM Raft, London WC1N 3XX.

Alphabetical List of Centres

Prices are correct at the time of going to press. We have included when possible, information on what each organisation offers and a breakdown of costs, including concessionary rates

3HO Kundalini Yoga Foundation

55 Sunny Gardens Road, London NW4 1SJ. (081) 203 7302.
Spiritual teacher is Yogi Bhajan who is resident in Europe and teaches around the world. Many members of 3HO are practising Sikhs. Run evening, weekend courses, seminar, residentials and retreats in France and the USA. Have residential communities and some people involved are natural healing practitioners. They also run a health food business and sell 'Yogi Tea', a healthy tea drink.

5 to Midnight

5 Bittaford Terrace, Bittaford, South Devon PL21 0DX. (0752) 894675.
Dance Therapy, Ritual Theatre, Photo Therapy. Residential workshops at various locations, some in London. Weekend workshops £40-50.

Abraxas

27 Bathurst Mews, London W2 2SB. (071) 402 0290.
Jungian Psychotherapy. Run seminars and workshops on dreams. On-going evening and weekend workshops. Broadly Jungian but gestalt, art therapy and music is embraced. £100 for 10 evenings or £100 for two weekends.

Academy and Professional Hypnotherapy Association

181 Cat Hill, Cockfosters, East Barnet, Herts EN4 8HS. (081) 441 9685.
Hypnotherapy. Treat various problems such as smoking, lack of confidence and overweight. £42 per session.

Acca and Adda

BCM Akademia, London WC1N 3XX. (081) 677 5837.
Paganism. Workshops, tuition in esoteric subjects, magic and Wicca. Consultations in tarot, runes, palmistry, geomancy, I-Ching etc. Also publish O Fortuna, journal of spiritual, magickal and ecological progress. Esoteric subjects, beliefs and philosophies (of all kinds). Challenging (and impossible) big prize crossword every time. Quarterly. Sample issue £1.50 plus stamp, or £6 subscription . Day workshop £20 includes full vegetarian lunch and refreshments. No concessions, but may accept work (e.g. gardening, filing etc) in lieu.

Action Against Allergy

23/24 George Street, Richmond, Surrey TW9 1JY.
Allergy Therapy. A self help for people with allergic illness. Newsletter. £5 subs. SAE to above address.

Active Birth Centre

55 Dartmouth Park Road, Kentish Town, London NW5 1SL. (071) 267 3006.
Active Birth. Provides an educational service for expectant parents which centres around yoga in pregnancy and preparation for an active birth. Full programme of workshops and seminars. Programme for mums and babies such as baby gymnastics and baby massage. Free national information and networking service by post or telephone. Sell books, pregnancy clothes, natural pregnancy and baby care products. Catalogues on request. £7.50 per person per evening on average. £5 Yoga class. Concessions. They offer a training in Active Birth.

Actors Institute

137 Goswell Road, Barbican, London EC1V 7ET. (071) 251 8178.
Courses on self expression and self management for professional actors, including the Samuri And Mastery Course.

Acumedic Centre

101-103 Camden High Street, Camden, London NW1. (071) 388 5783 or 388 6704.
Acupuncture, Biofeedback, Herbalism, Homoeopathy, Shiatsu, Stress Management. Specialist supplies and health products sold in shop on the premises. Bookshop. Chinese acupuncture. Professional supply showroom for equipment and products. See East Asia Company in the 'Products' of this book. £20 per session typical.

Acupuncture and Osteopathy Clinic

34 Alderney Street, Pimlico, London SW1. (071) 834 6229.

Acupuncture, Hypnotherapy, Osteopathy, Shiatsu. £30 initial consultation, £20 thereafter.

Acupuncture Clinic of North London
Winchester Court, 237 Green Lanes, London N13. (081) 886 9494.
Acupuncture.

Acupuncture Clinic
538 Forest Road, Walthamstow, London E17 4NB. (081) 520 3811.
Acupuncture, Aromatherapy, Herbalism, Homoeopathy, Naturopathy, Osteopathy. £13-£15 per session with remedies included.

Adlerian Society for Individual Psychology
161 Charlton Church Lane, London SE7 7AA. (081) 858 1767.
Adlerian Psychotherapy. They are a UK association of practitioners and associate members interested in Alfred Adler and the movement based upon his work which he called 'Individual Psychology'. They hold a programme of public lectures, a conference in Oxford and one day sessions in various parts of the country. Typically £18 per one day workshop. Concessions. Wheelchair access to public meetings and counselling centre in Swiss Cottage. They offer a training in Adlerian Psychotherapy.

Aetherius Society
757 Fulham Road, London SW6 5UD. (071) 736 4187/ (071) 731 1094.
Colour Therapy, Healing, Homoeopathy. Open to public Mon-Sat 9am-10pm. Centre where lectures/healing services and personal instructional courses are held, and they have a health food shop nearby. They

also have a northern headquarters and groups throughout the country. Sell books and have a mail order service. Manufacture and sell radionic pendulums and holy stone shapes. Give spiritual counselling. Run a 'UFO hotline' on 071 731 1094. Hold conferences and seminars. Wheelchair access. Services/ healing free, donations welcome. Lectures £2. Courses £20-50 (one-two day).

African Herbs Ltd
104 Kingsley Road, Hounslow East, Middlesex TW3 4AH. (081) 570 5795.
Herbalism. astrology, spiritualism.

Alexander Teaching Centre
188 Old Street, London EC1V 9BP. (071) 250 3038.
Alexander Technique. Established since 1983. Register of practitioners. Bookshop in the main building. £15 - £16 an individual lesson. Workshops from £45. Introductory evening classes £45. Concessions.

All Healing Clinic
39 Gilden Crescent, Gospel Oak, London NW5 4QA. (071) 485 9669.
Acupuncture, Colour Therapy, Massage, Reflexology. Will visit your home to carry out treatment, as long as you don't live too far away from the above address. £15 per session.

Alternative and Orthodox Medicine Clinic
P.O. Box 598, Marylebone Road, Marylebone, London NW1 5HW. (071) 486 7490.
Allergy Therapy. African nations skin problems. Scarring treated.

Anerley Natural Health Clinic
23 Genoa Road, Anerley, London SE20 8ES. (081) 778 6394.
Acupuncture, Herbalism, Homoeopathy, Hypnotherapy, Osteopathy.

Anna Freud Centre
21 Maresfield Gdns, Hampstead, London NW3 5SH.
Child psychotherapy and training in Child Psychotherapy.

Anthroposophical Association
Rudolph Steiner House, 35 Park Road, Regents Park, London NW1. (071) 723 4400.
Office open 10-1, 2-6. Lectures, performances, classes in eurythmy, painting, drawing, creative speech, groups, workshops and courses exploring Rudolf Steiner's Anthroposophy and its implications. Opened in 1926, bookshop, library open to public. Information about Steiner schools, homes and other activities. Weekend seminars for teachers in Steiner schools. Wheelchair access. Lectures and evening workshops £2.50 (£1.50 concs). Day workshops £5 (£3 concs).

Anthroposophical Medical Association
Rudolph Steiner House, 35 Park Road, London NW1 6XT. (071) 723 4400.
Anthroposophical Medicine. Professional body of doctors who practise or have an interest in Anthroposophical medicine. Information on Anthroposophical medicine, anthroposophical doctors, training courses, literature and conferences.

LIST OF CENTRES

Arbours Consultation Service
6 Church Lane, London N8.
(081) 340 8125.
Psychoanalytic Therapy. £Neg with individual therapist. Concessions.

Argo Human Resource Consultants
171 Highbury Hill, London N5 1TB. (071) 359 4330/989 5793.
Consultative service for individuals and groups/organisations/business teams to address issues of increased satisfaction, enthusiasm, competence and balance to develop new strategies and tactics.

Aromatherapy Associates
68 Maltings Place, Bagleys Lane, Fulham, London SW6 2BY. (071) 371 9878/(071) 731 8129.
Aromatherapy. Nine practitioners and three treatment rooms. All associates are fully qualified, insured members of the International Federation of Aromatherapists. Mail order - body and bath and face oils. £37 initial consultation, £32 subsequent treatment. They offer a training in Aromatherapy.

Aromatherapy Training Centre
56a Riggindale Road, Streatham, London SW16 1QJ. (081) 677 1293.
Aromatherapy, Reflexology. Wheelchair access. £15-£30 per session.

Art from Within
119 Grosvenor Avenue, Highbury, London N5 2NL. (071) 354 1603.
Art Therapy, Psychosynthesis. Groups held at the Highbury Centre at above address. Booking necessary. Groups are maximum of 10 people and are not drop-in. Individual sessions are usually six initial sessions after which it is open ended. Short term and long term in-depth work. £20-£25 for individual sessions. £80 for six evenings for groups, or £50 per weekend.

Arts Psychology Consultants
38 Earls Court Square, Earls Court, London SW5 9DQ. (071) 602 2707.
An eclectic, humanistic, arts based psychology and counselling service to anyone working in the performing or creative arts. Established in 1988, it has a full time staff of three, and an associate staff of more than 50. Also offer training, career guidance, psychometric testing and psychiatric assessment. Register. Concessions. Individual sessions £25 per hour, one day training group £300.

Asatru Folk Runic Workshop
43 St Georges Avenue, London N7. (071) 607 9695.
Paganism. Northern mysteries study group. Courses in runecraft, lectures, consultations.

Association for Analytic and Bodymind Therapy and Training
8 Princes Avenue, Muswell Hill, London N10 3LR. (081) 883 5418.
Couple Therapy, Diet Therapy Therapy, Gestalt, Hypnotherapy, Primal Therapy, Cranio-Sacral Therapy and 'S-therapy'. The centre is small, personal, friendly and supportive. There are three men and three women therapists, each with a distinctive style and expertise. It has been established for 20 years. There are also talks on the principles and methods therapists use. £15 - £35 for individual sessions. Approx £5 per session for group therapy. They offer a training in psychotherapy.

Association for Marriage Enrichment
c/o Westminster Pastoral Foundation, 23 Kensington Square, London W8 5HN.
Couple Therapy. Hold residentials through the UK for couples in 'marriage enrichment'. Non-residential activities can be arranged for suitable groups. Small selection of books from USA available. £100 per couple per weekend. Concessions.

Association for Neuro-Linguistic Programming
100b Carysfort Road, London N16. (071) 241 3664.
Neuro-linguistic Programming. Register of practitioners of NLP. Contact and information point for general public and practitioners. Introductory and applications seminars on NLP. Two conferences a year. Prices vary.

Association for Systematic Kinesiology
39 Browns Road, Surbiton, Surrey KT5 8ST. (081) 399 3215.
Acupuncture, Massage, Touch For Health. Register. Clinic with one treatment room and two offices, established in the area for 13 years. Wheelchair access. First visits: kinesiologist £30, kinesiologist + consultant £40, acupuncturist £30. Subsequent visits: kinesiologist £20, acupuncturist £25.

Association of Ayurvedic Practitioners
7 Ravenscroft Avenue, Golders Green, London NW11 0SA. (081) 455 3909.
Ayurvedic Medicine.

LIST OF CENTRES

Association of Biodynamic Psychotherapists
153 Goldhurst Terrace, London NW6 3EU. (071) 328 3868.
Professional body, referral list for Biodynamic Psychotherapy. Professional newsletter, discussion with other psychotherapists. £15-20 per session.

Association of Colour Therapists
c/o ICM, 21 Portland Place, London W1 3AS. 636 9543.
Colour Therapy.

Association of Jungian Analysts
3-7 Eton Avenue, South Hampstead, London NW3. (071) 794 8711.
Training and referral list for Jungian Psychotherapy.

Association of Natural Medicines
27 Braintree Road, Witham, Essex, CM8 2DD. (0376) 511069.
Training courses in Acupuncture, Homoeopathy, Naturopathy, Hypnotherapy, Massage and Reflexology.

Association of Reflexologists
27 Old Gloucester Street, London WC1N 3XX. (081) 445 0154.
Professional association for reflexologists. Iinformation in general public, and on schools for those wishing to train. Instructional meetings on other therapies and quarterly newsletter to members. Meetings arranged at various venues. Register. Workshops £20.

Astro-Psychotherapeutic Practice
1 Grafton Road, Acton,

London W3 6PB. (081) 992 9514.
Astrological Psychotherapy, Jungian Psychotherapy, Men's Therapy. Established 5 years. Ring for appointment. They also do mail order tape horoscope readings. Psychotherapy session from £20. Horoscope readings from £45. Workshops from £65.

Audio Limited
26-28 Wendell Road, London W12. (081) 743 1518 or 743 4352.
Biofeedback, Meditation, Relaxation Training. Day and evening courses. Also individual biofeedback training, massage. £25 for a day workshop.

Awakenings
18 Marylands Road, London W9 2DY. (071) 289 8306.
Healing. Also use astrology, graphology and psychic intuition in treatment, with other therapies if required. Workshops, courses, meetings on natural healing. Noticeboard for information. SAE for further information. 45 minute appointment: £25 first session, £15 subsequent; UB40/OAP/Students £20 first session, £10 subsequent.

B

Baha'i Faith
27 Rutland Gate, Knightsbridge, London SW7 1PD. (071) 584 2566.
Contact for details of local meetings.

Barbican Natural Health Centre
105 Whitecross Street, Barbican, London EC1Y 8JD. (071) 628 6139.
Acupuncture, Allergy Therapy,

Aromatherapy, Hypnotherapy, Naturopathy, Osteopathy.

Barnes Physiotherapy Clinic
2a Elm Bank Gardens, Barnes, London SW13 0NT. (081) 876 5690.
Counselling, Physiotherapy, Psychotherapy. Established 1983. Sessions £20.

Barry Long Foundation
BCM Box 876, London WC1N 3XX. (081) 341 3850.
Mail order books and tapes of Barry Long. No callers or activities on site.

Bates Association of Great Britain
11 Tarmount Lane, Shoreham-by-Sea, West Sussex. (0273) 452623.
Bates Eyesight Training. Professional body for teachers of the Bates method. Can put you in touch with practitioners (send SAE) - there are six practising in London at the time of going to press. Can give general information on the method and supply booklist. Visiting lectures and workshops can be arranged. £15-25 per session. Workshops vary. Most teachers work with children at reduced fees. Low cost training clinics.

Bates Eyesight Training
128 Merton Road, London SW18 5SP. (081) 874 7337.

Bayswater Allergy Clinic
25B Clanricarde Gardens, Bayswater, London W2 4JL. (071) 229 9078.
Allergy, Diet Therapy. Biochemical testing for food and chemical allergies, nutrition and treatment of candidosis. Correction of diet and dietary counselling. .

Bennet and Luck Natural Health Centre

54 Islington Park Street, Islington, London N1 1PX. (071) 226 3422.
Acupuncture, Aromatherapy, Bach Flower Remedies, Counselling, Diet Therapy Therapy, Homoeopathy, Massage, Naturopathy, Osteopathy, Reflexology, Shiatsu. Established for 3 years, this centre is also a health food shop selling books and a range of organic produce. Can refer if necessary. Wheelchair access to building but not to toilets. Prices range between £16- 25 per session.

Beshara Trust

Frilford Grange, Frilford, Near Abingdon, Oxon OX13 5NX. (0865) 391 344.
Runs seminars with visiting leaders.

Better Health Centre

15-17 South End Road, Hampstead Heath, London NW3. (071) 794 0848.
Acupuncture, Diet Therapy, Healing, Homoeopathy, Homoeopathy, Osteopathy, Reflexology. Homoeopathic chiropody. Run courses in homoeopathy and chiropody, and homoeopathy and nutrition. Run research institute into homoeopathic medicine. See also other centre at 129 Kentish Town Road, NW1. Practitioners have many years experience and some are qualified doctors as well as complementary practitioners. £20-25 per session.

Better Health Centre

129 Kentish Town Road, London NW1. (071) 485 7493.
See Better Health Centre, South End Road, Hampstead branch for details of therapies etc. Wheelchair access.

Bexleyheath Natural Health Clinic

6 Sandford Road, Bexleyheath, Kent DA7 4AX. (081) 303 9571.
Acupuncture, Allergy, Aromatherapy, Bach, Cranial Osteopathy, Diet Therapy, Homoeopathy, Homoeopathy, Hypnotherapy, Regression, Biomobility. Established for 4 years, there are four practice rooms and waiting area. Consultations are by appointment only, but they are open to visitors. Sell books, tapes, cosmetics, dietry supplements and a selection of health foods. Homoeopathy £20/£30 for initial consultation, subsequently £11/£15. Osteopathy £20.50 initially, then £17.50, Hypnotherapy £25, Acupuncture £18 initial consultation, then £14.50, Regression £50, Massage £20-£18.

Bharatiya Vidya Bhavan (Institute of Indian Culture)

4a Castletown Road, West Kensington, London W14 9HQ. (071) 381 3086.
Hinduism, Meditation, Yoga. The philosophy of the Bharatiya Vidya Bhavan is summed up in their mottos: "Let noble thoughts come to us from all sides', and "The world is one family'. Spiritual director is Mathoor Krishnamurti. Every weekend, hold gatherings of people to sing bhajans (religious songs) and celebrate with music, prayer and sacred dance. Also host discourses and seminars by well-known scholars and swamis. Hindu religious festivals are observed with prayers and offerings. Meditation hall for those of all religions, bookshop with sections on various religions and philosophy. Sell tapes, records and CDs of religious songs.

Biodynamic Clinic

23 High St, The Green, Ealing, London W5 5DF. 579 1904.
Biodynamic Massage. and work with the bio-energy field. Mon-Sat 9-9. Pleasant reception and large treatment area. Drop-in or by appointment. Established December 1989. Mother and baby clinic and children's clinic. Monthly talks given at local town hall. Wheelchair access. Sessions cost £20 per hour pro rata, or £12 per hour for the apprentice clinic, or £30 per hour with senior practitioners. Weekend workshops £60.

Biodynamic Psychotherapy and Teaching

13 Mansell Road, London W3 7QH. (081) 749 4388.
Biodynamic Massage, Jungian Psychotherapy. Two psychotherapists with 10 and 15 years of clinical experience offering Jungian psychotherapy which includes the body-dimension. Work with individuals, couples and groups; supervision available, especially for body therapists who want more analytical input: hypnotic trance work (past-life regression) available. Foreign languages available: German, some French and Spanish spoken. Sale of publications/video by A B and G Heuer. £23 per session; group prices depending on size of group, average £10 per 3 hour session.

Bioenergetic Training Association for Great Britain/Bioenergetic Associates.

22 Fitzjohn's Avenue, Swiss Cottage, London NW3. (071) 435 1079.
Bioenergetics. Bioenergetic Analysis as developed by Dr Alexander Lowen and his trainers. They offer an on-going

evening group, weekly, subject to initial interview. Open to all. Individual on-going bioenergetic therapy offered. Workshops £15 evening, £30 day. Individual therapy £25 - £35 by negotiation. They offer a training in Bioenergetics.

Bloomsbury Alexander Centre

Bristol House, 80a Southampton Row, Bloomsbury, London WC1. (071) 404 5348.
Alexander Technique. Lessons are on a one to one basis, so appointments have to be made. A course of lessons can be from 10 to infinity! People are welcome to drop in for information or to book appointments, and teachers are at the centre from 8am-8pm. There are three rooms, with about a dozen teachers using the centre, which has been established for two and a half years. The longest qualified teacher has been teaching for 12 years, and the centre provides a home for two senior teachers who have been teaching since the 1930s. Occasional introductory courses, courses for those with some experience, and for qualified teachers. Speakers on request. Books. Training starting in 1993 approximately. Access: ground floor, 2 steps to manage, slightly awkward door. £17 per session, ranging down to £12 according to experience of teacher. Concessions.

Bluestone Clinic

16 Harley House, Marylebone Road, Marylebone, London NW1. (071) 935 7933 or 935 8958.
Aromatherapy, Diet Therapy, Massage, Miscellaneous Body, Osteopathy, plus Pulsed Electro-Magnetic Energy (PEME) which it is claimed speeds up healing in the body by 50%. Cold

beam laser treatment and remedial beauty treatments. Visiting spiritual healers. 2 hour treatment £52 (includes remedial massage £20, plus osteopathy £20, and treatment on PEME which is charged at £20 per hour). Subsequently if you don't require osteopathy treatment is £40. Aromatherapy massage is £42 per hour.

Body Clinic

32 The Market Place, Falloden Way, Hampstead Garden Suburbs, London NW11 6JJ. (081) 458 9412.
Acupuncture, Aromatherapy, Chiropody, Hypnotherapy, Laser Therapy, Massage, Naturopathy, Osteopathy. Also electrolysis, neuro-muscular massage, feradic therapy, G5 massage, facials, leg waxing, paraffin wax therapy, manicures, steam cabinet, sunbed, specialists in sports injuries and back problems. Has been established since January 1987. It is open 7 days a week and has late evenings Tues, Weds and Thurs till 9pm. There are 5 therapy rooms and 8 practitioners. Clients can usually pop in without an appointment, but this is not so on the late evenings or Sunday as these tend to get booked up in advance. Sell range of vitamins, essential oils, sports aids, therapeutic bath salts and books. Wheelchair access. One hour full body massage would cost £19.50. If you book a course of 5 therapies you get one free. Special rates for students. Concessions.

Body-Mind Centring

Flat 5, 64 Sinclair Road, London W14 . (071) 602 8637/(0223) 894041.
Body-mind centring uses the movements of infancy, individual rhythms and expressive qualities of the body to release patterns and correct imbalances

in the body. Methods used include touch, anatomical imagery and guided and improvised movements to bring about a more harmonious, responsive and expressive ways of moving and being. It can help with conditions such as low back pain if it is due to chronic misuse, and can promote grace and co-ordination. Individual sessions and group workshops in London and Cambridge. Workshops can be arranged for special interest groups. Individual session £18.

Body-Mind Health Private Clinic

631 Green Lanes, Hornsey, London N8. (081) 340 0509.
Acupuncture, Diet Therapy Therapy, Homoeopathy, Hypnotherapy. The centre has been established 10 years ago they also treat people with spiritual difficulties and personality disorders. Between £22-£30 for consultation and treatment, depending on the type of treatment and consultation

Bodyspace

Guy Gladstone, The Open Centre, 188 Old St. London EC1. (071) 254 8047.
Bioenergetics, Psychodrama. and Pulsing. £25/one hour session. One day workshop £25. Drop-in evening talks on bioenergetics.

Bodywise

119 Roman Road, Bethnal Green, London E2 0QN. (081) 981 6938.
Acupuncture, Alexander Technique, Counselling, Feldenkrais, Homoeopathy, Martial Arts, Massage, Naturopathy, Osteopathy, Reflexology, Shiatsu, Yoga, Courses in Tai Chi, Aikido, Yoga, Alexander Technique and Massage. Small or large rooms available for rent. Yoga class £2 (1 hour). Alexander Technique:

LIST OF CENTRES

lesson £14, 5 week course £45, 1 day introductory course £38. Feldenkrais method: £30 six week course or lesson. Tai chi: £5 (two hours), Aikido: £4. Individual session in massage and reflexology: £20. Homoeopathy and acupuncture: £30 first session, £18 follow ups. Concessions available.

Bodyworks Natural Therapies
Greyhound House, 23-24 George Street, Richmond, Surrey TW9 1JY. (081) 332 1751.
Aromatherapy, Massage, Osteopathy, Reflexology, Shiatsu. Acupuncture, kinesiology, diet therapy and shen tao can be arranged with advanced notice. Launched March '89, Bodyworks provides a home visiting complementary practitioner service covering central and greater London. Treatments are given either in clients homes, or their places of work. 1 hour £28, one and a half hour £35. A small fee may be added for visits outside London.

Brackenbury Natural Health Centre
30 Brackenbury Road, Hammersmith, London W6 OBA. (081) 741 9264.
Acupuncture, Alexander Technique, Allergy Therapy, Aromatherapy, Bach, Bach Flower Remedies, Bates Eyesight Training, Biodynamic Massage, Colonic Irrigation, Colour Therapy, Counselling, Diet Therapy Therapy, Herbalism, Homoeopathy, Homoeopathy, Massage, Naturopathy, Osteopathy, Polarity Therapy, Reflexology, Shiatsu. 9am-9pm Mon-Fri, 9am-1pm Sat. Established in 1983, this is a large centre with over 25 qualified therapists and seven treatment rooms with cane

furniture and indoor plants. Offer free advice to anyone unsure about treatment. Some natural products sold, give talks and Qi Gong sessions in local church hall, hold workshops and occasional open days. Register. Creche. No access. £18-£30. Concs available for students, OAPs, UB40s, low income.

Brahma Kumaris World Spiritual University
98 Tennyson Road, London NW6 7SB. (071) 328 2478.
Meditation. They will give free instruction in meditation on a one-to-one basis. Practice Raja Yoga.

Breakspear Hospital
For Allergy and Environmental Medicine, High Street, Abbots Langley, Herts WD5 0PU. (0923) 261333.
Allergy Therapy.

Bretforton Hall
Bretforton, Vale of Evesham, Worcs WR11 5JH. 0386 830537.
Residential clinic offering Aromatherapy, Colour Therapy, Massage, Cymatics (treatment by sound). £16 per session.

British Acupuncture Association and Register
34 Alderney Street, London SW1V 4EU. (071) 834 1012.
Professional body for acupuncture. Handbook of registered practitioners costs £1.50.

British and European Osteopathic Association
6 Adele Road, Teddington, Middlesex. (081) 977 8532.
Osteopathy. They keep a register of members.

British Association for Counselling (North London Branch)
72 Great North Road, London N2 0NL. (081) 340 3924.
Counselling. They have a local resource list of personal counsellors in private practice in North London, available at no charge by post. The branch has been established 5 years. They have an ethical code of practice. They also publish information about counselling for the general public. This branch of the BAC offers a support network for counsellors: monthly meetings with speakers on counselling topics and access to the decision making of the BAC. £5-£30 per session, often negotiable according to the individual practitioner.

British Association for Counselling (South London Branch)
33 Crantock Rd, London SE6 2QS. (081) 698 3205.
Hold a monthly support group for counsellors.

British Association for Counselling
37a Sheep Street, Rugby, Warwickshire CV21 3BX. (0788) 78328/9.
Send £12 plus £2 postage for book listing counsellors throughout the UK, with details of their training, orientation and specialist areas. Produce journal 'Counselling' (£15 subs, £4 individual copies), and publications on counselling such as 'Careers in Counselling' and 'Guide to Training Courses in Counselling'. They sell cassettes and videos (also for hire) on counselling. They produce a useful resource pack for those involved in AIDS counselling. In London there is a North London Branch and a South London

277

LIST OF CENTRES

branch (listed above). You can become a member - phone or write for details. Prices are determined by the counsellor who is recommended to you, but the fees are usually very reasonable.

British Association for Social Psychiatry
112A Harley Street, London W1. (081) 555 2603.
Art Therapy, Bereavement Counselling, Family Therapy.

British Association of Psychotherapists
121 Hendon Lane, Hendon, London N3 3PR. (081) 346 1747.
Individual psycho-analytic psychotherapy for adults and children. The BAP was founded in 1951 and in 1981 became a charity. The Clinical Service offers advice and information through consultation to adults and adolescents and children suffering from emotional and psychological problems. Those seeking help can discuss with an experienced psychotherapist whether psychotherapy would be an appropriate form of help and treatment. There are some external courses for people wanting to understand more about working in a psychodynamically orientated way. Consultation fee £30. On-going therapy between £18-£22. A few places are available in the Reduced Fee Scheme with trainee psychotherapists. They offer a training in Psychoanalytic Therapy and Jungian Psychotherapy.

British Buddhist Association
11 Biddulph Road, Maida Vale, London W9 1JA. (071) 286 5575.
Buddhism, Meditation. Nonsectarian Buddhist group under direction of A Haviland-Nye

Dhammacariya. Teach meditation, and run part-time study courses for various levels of experience and knowledge. Shrineroom for meditation, bookshop. Open by appointment.

British Chiropractic Association
Premier House, 10 Greycoat Place, London SW1P 1SB. (071) 222 8866.
Chiropractic. Will provide a range of leaflets on the treatments of different symptoms. Comprehensive list of practitioners.

British College of Acupuncture
8 Hunter Street, London WC1N 1BN. (071) 833 8164.
Acupuncture. Have clinic where students work. Register of practitioners. They offer a training in Acupuncture.

British College of Naturopathy and Osteopathy
6 Netherhall Gardens, Hampstead, London NW3 5RR. (071) 435 7830 (clinic), 435 6464 (college).
Naturopathy, Osteopathy. Founded in 1935, this is a private training college with clinic open to general public. Register. Wheelchair access. £10 initial consultation, £5 each subsequent consultation. They offer a training in Naturopathy and Osteopathy.

British Homoeopathic Association
27A Devonshire Street, London W1N 1RJ. (071) 935 2163.
Homoeopathy. Register of qualified medical doctors trained in homoeopathy, and homoeopathic vets and chemists. Send SAE for list.

British Hypnosis Research
8 Paston Place, Brighton BN2 1HA. (0273) 693622.
Hypnotherapy, Neuro-linguistic Programming. Centre at St Ann's Hospital, London (appointments through Brighton centre). Training in Eriksonian hypnosis, psychotherapy and NLP. Register. Training videos and books available. Therapy with director £50, with trainees free of charge. Training in Hypnotherapy and Neuro-linguistic Programming.

British Hypnotherapy Association
1 Wythburn Place, London W1H 5WL. (071) 723 4443.
Hypnotherapy. Emotional and psychosexual difficulties, migraine and anxieties. Write giving details and a brief indication of your problem, stating area in London where you work or study and enclose £2. You will receive a list of practitioners and a pamphlet. Produce publications and give talks. £20 per 50 minute hour.

British Ki Aikido Association
c/o The Secretary, 48 Oakshott Court, Polygon Road, London NW1 1ST. (071) 281 0877.
Aikido. Classes mainly in north London.

British Naturopathic and Osteopathic Association
Frazer House, 6 Netherall Gardens, London NW3 5RR. (071) 435 8728.
Naturopathy, Osteopathy. They have a register of practitioner members available: send large SAE for 24p and £1.50 for list plus leaflets.

LIST OF CENTRES

British Osteopathic Association
8-10 Boston Place, Marylebone, London NW1 6QH. (071) 262 5250.
Osteopathy. Run clinic (see London College of Osteopathic Medicine) which specialises in offering low-cost treatment to those with low income. Register.

British Psycho-Analytical Society and The Institute of Psychoanalysis
63 New Cavendish Street, London W1. (071) 580 4952 or (071) 636 2322.
Psychoanalysis, Psychoanalytic Therapy. This establishment was founded by Ernest Jones, the biographer of Freud. They also offer a training in Psychoanalysis.

British Reflexology Centre
Monks Orchard, Whitbourne, Worcs WR6 5RB. (0886) 21207.
Reflexology. Register. Newsletter, books and charts. Details of Reflexology trainings and courses on related subjects.

British School of Osteopathy
1-4 Suffolk Street, London SW1Y 4HG.(071) 930 9254.
Osteopathy. Out-patients clinic, children's clinic, expectant mothers' clinic and sports injury clinic. Training in ostepathy.

British School - Reflex Zone Therapy of the Feet (Ann Lett Ltd)
87 Oakington Avenue, Wembley Park, London HA9 8HY. (081) 908 2201.
Reflexology. Established in 1980 to train nurses, physiotherapists, midwives and doctors in reflex zone therapy. Affiliated to European schools in Holland, Scandinavia, Belgium, Spain, France, Italy, Israel, Switzerland and East and West Germany with the same training programme. 20,000 practising therapists, most of whom use their training in hospitals, clinics, and some in private practice. Register.Wheelchair access. They offer a training in Reflexology.

British School of Iridology
Dolfin House, 6 Gold Street, Saffron Walden, Essex CB10 1EJ.
Training in Iridology and register of practitioners.

British School of Oriental Therapy and Movement
46 Whitton Rd, Twickenham, Middx TW1 1BS. (081) 744 1974.
Shiatsu. Drop in classes in Kitaiso, Tues (advanced) and Thurs (beginners). Training in Shiatsu. Register of practitioners.

British School of Reflexology
The Holistic Healing Centre, 92 Sheering Road, Old Harlow, Essex CM17 0JW. (0279) 29060.
Register. Clinic and training school for 18 students, established 15 years. Wheelchair access. Sessions cost £13 for 45 minutes. They offer a training in Reflexology.

British School of Shiatsu-Do
188 Old Street, London EC1V 9BP. (071) 251 0831.
Shiatsu. Treatments by appointment. Send SAE to their office for full details of courses. Established 1983. Hold open evenings for lectures. Sell books, futons and neck rolls. Talks and demonstrations by arrangement. Treatments: £18 for students of BSS. £25 for prospective students. Concessions. They offer a training in Shiatsu.

British Shingon Buddhist Association
'Kongosatta', 12 Finchley Park, London N12 9JN.
Buddhism. Linked with the British Cheirological Society (q.v.).

British Society of Hypnotherapists (1950)
37 Orbane Road, Fulham, London SW6 7JZ . (071) 385 1166.
Hypnotherapy. Established 1950. Register of practitioners. Training for treatment of neurotic behavioural problems, traumas and psychosomatic illness.

British T'ai Chi Association
7 Upper Wimpole Street, Marylebone, London W1M 7TD. (071) 935 8444.
Tai Chi. Original Yang and Cheng forms. For health, meditation and self defence. £80 for a course of ten two hour classes.

British Touch for Health Association
8 Railey Mews, Kentish Town, London NW5 2PA. (071) 482 0698.
Touch for Health (Kinesiology). A national network of independent instructors and consultants in all aspects of kinesiology. Anyone can take a touch for health class with a qualified instructor. They have no centre as such, each instructor operates from own premises. The association was formed in 1980. The association works on a subscription basis and publishes a quarterly journal 'In Touch'. There is a mail order book service and regular meetings and

LIST OF CENTRES

conferences. £40-£100 per course, depending on size and venue. An individual consultation costs £10-£30.

Brothers
207 Waller Road, London SE14 5LX. (071) 639 9732.
Men's Therapy, Psychosynthesis. Growth programme for men using psychosynthesis, education and analytic techniques. Established for 5 years, Brothers runs introductory and on-going workshops. Admission is based on written application. Also offer individual sessions for men. Annual conference 'Embodying the Masculine'. £60 per weekend.

Brunel Management Programme
Brunel University, Uxbridge, Middlesex UB8 3PH. (0895) 56461 x 215.
Assertion, Management, Stress Management Training. Courses on self knowledge and self development for managers. Stress at work. Courses on interpersonal effectiveness in management. plus other short courses. £150 - £200 per day for the management courses.

Buddhapadipa Temple
14 Calonne Road, Wimbledon, London SW19. (081) 946 1357.
Meditation, Retreats. This is a Thai Buddhist temple, where you can learn traditional Vipassana meditation free. You can also do a meditation retreat here for a minimal charge.

Buddhist Society
58 Eccleston Square, Victoria, London SW1V 1PH. (071) 834 5858.
Buddhism, Retreats. Introducing Buddhism course open to public - a series of 8 lectures running continuously through-

out the year. Library open to public to browse, but not to borrow. Members may attend courses on Zen, Theravadin and Tibetan Buddhism. Residential summer school. Correspondence course in basic Buddhism, cassettes and bookstall. Seminars and lectures. Quarterly journal, 'The Middle Way', free to members . Basic Buddhism course free. Membership £16 per annum in London, £11.50 for those outside a 50 mile radius. Summer school £175 per week.

C

CAER (Centre For Alternative Education And Research)
Rosemerryn, Lamorna, Penzance, Cornwall TR19 6BN. (0736) 810530.
Alexander Technique, Feminist Therapy, Gestalt Therapy, Massage, Men's Therapy, Rebirthing, Resonance Therapy, Shamanism, Stress Management, Yoga. Body-oriented approaches, Groupwork, RSA certified courses in Groupwork and Counselling etc. One of the longest established centres for residential workshops in personal and professional development in Europe. They offer a training in Counselling and Psychotherapy.

Camden Osteopathic and Natural Health Practice
96 Malden Rd., Camden Town, London NW5 4DA. (071) 482 1248.
Acupuncture, Homoeopathy, Naturopathy, Osteopathy.

Camden Psychotherapy Unit
25/31 Tavistock Place, London WC1H 9SE. (071) 837 5628.
Family Therapy, Psychoanalytic Therapy. Offers therapy to Camden residents experiencing psychological and emotional difficulties. Free

Capital Hypnotherapy Centre
Temple Lodge, 51 Queen Caroline Street, Hammersmith, London W6 9QL. (071) 737 1929.
Anti-smoking Therapy, Hypnotherapy, Counselling, Primary Cause Analysis. Sessions cost approximately £35.

Centre For Healing Through Forgiveness
22 Conway Road, Harringay, London N15 3BD. (081) 802 1455.
Centre for study, prayer, meditation, interactive group exercises, song and sacred dance based around 'A Course in Miracles'. Director is Simon Christopher who runs some events. Evening, weekend groups, courses and seminars. Run regular retreats in South Devon. Counselling also available. Beginners study group £4, weekend £50.

Centre for 'A Course In Miracles'
56b Sotheby Road, London N5 2UR, . (071) 704 6197.
Study, prayer, meditation and group sharing around 'A Course In Miracles'. Evening courses and seminars.

Centre for Autogenic Training
Positive Health Centre, 101 Harley Street, London W1. (071) 935 1811.
Autogenic Training. Individual or group session, also in-house

programmes for groups from one company or area can be arranged. £40 for pre-course assessment, £140 for the course.

Centre for Counselling and Psychotherapy Education
21 Lancaster Road, Notting Hill, London W11 1QL. (071) 221 3215.
Professional training and sessions: individual, couple and group therapy. Centre established 1983; comprising two houses (130 students). Holistic approach which includes the spiritual dimension. Weekend workshops (£50 and short-term groups). £6-£25 per session (average £15, sliding scale). Concessions.

Centre for Massage and Movement Studies
17 Beechdale Road, London SW2 2BN. (0903) 204893.
Massage. Weekend workshops as well as training in the Eyerman technique and Massage.

Centre for Pagan Studies
Flat b, 5 Trinity Rise, Tulse Hill, London SW2 2QP. (081) 671 6372.
Paganism. Established for educational, therapeutic and spiritual purposes to provide academic classes and experiential workshops in north European shamanism, wicca and ritual mythic drama. Also aims to act as a guide to seekers through the labyrinth of competing wares in the esoteric marketplace. Classes, workshops, apprenticeship training. Practice through ritual drama, mythic re-enactment, ecstatic dance, path-working, chanting, making music etc.

Centre for Past Life Therapy and Research
95 Prospect Road, Woodford

Green, Essex IG8 7MD. (081) 505 8720.
Hypnotherapy, Relaxation, Pastoral Counselling, Stress Control, Past Life Regression Therapy, Divine/Metaphysical Healing, Reincarnation. By appointment only. Quiet residence in East London. Clients can be visited. One hour consultation plus one hour relaxation therapy £25. Two hours of hypnotherapy/regression £32.

Centre for Personal Construct Psychology
132 Warwick Way, Pimlico, London SW1V 4JD. (071) 834 8875.
Personal Construct Therapy. Approximately £92 per weekend workshop. Training in Personal Construct Therapy.

Centre for Psychological Astrology
PO Box 890, London NW3 2JZ. (071) 223 2478.
Astrological Psychotherapy

Centre for Release and Integration
62 Twickenham Road, Teddington, Middx TW11 8AW
(081) 892 1121
Postural Integration.

Centre for Stress Management
156 Westcombe Hill, Blackheath, London SE3 7DH. (081) 293 4114.
Assertion Therapy, Biofeedback, Counselling, Hypnotherapy, Stress Management, Cognitive/Behavioural Therapy, Anxiety Management, Psychodynamic Counselling. Established 1987, included training room and two counselling rooms. Training in cognitive/behavioural approaches to psychotherapy, and counselling and stress management. Mail order, books, relaxation tapes, hypno-

sis tapes, videos on health, daily logs, biofeedback machines, biodots. In-house workshops for organisations. Free leaflets on health (send SAE). Lectures, workshops. Management consultancy for industrial stress. Sliding scale £10-£50 per session. Various prices for workshops.

Centre for Transpersonal Psychology
7 Pembridge Place, Bayswater, London W2 4XB.

Centre of Integral Psychoanalysis
6 Colville Road, London W11 2BP. (071) 727 4404.
Psychoanalytic treatment for adults, children and adolescents; individual analysis and group therapy. Founded in San Paulo, Brazil, branches throughout the world. Lectures every Monday 7.30pm, admission free - please drop-in. The first interview is free. £15 per half hour individual therapy. £10 group therapy per session.

Chalice Foundation
PO Box 684, London E17 3JP. (0803) 834406 .
Healing, Massage. Courses on healing development, self healing, massage (ITEC). Small friendly informal groups. Appointment needed. Courses are held at Regent's College in NW1. Two-weekend healing development course costs £115. Holistic massage weekend £55. Five day massage £165.

Chantraine School of Dance
47 Compayne Gardens, West Hampstead, London NW6 3DB. (071) 624 5881.
They teach the dance of contemporary expression, an approach to dance and movement

LIST OF CENTRES

created by Francoise and Alain Chantraine. Established in France in 1958 and in England in 1977. Emphasis is on the development of the person as the dancer and towards a unity of mind, body and spirit. There is no one building; classes are held at adult education institutes mostly in North London, but also in South Kensington. Currently set at ILEA Adult Education rates (i.e. very reasonable).

Cheirological Society
18 Southerton Road, Hammersmith, London W6.
Cheirology. Teaches cheirology (hand analysis) in the fields of psychological diagnosis, emotional integration, vocational and medical analysis and spiritual evolution. Founded in 1889. Use Chinese Buddhist methods of analysis in its training programme within a western tradition and holistic perspective. Runs regular courses at introductory, intermediate and advanced levels. Publishes newsletter, journal, research papers and text books. Register of practitioners and consultants. Also centres in east London (Dagenham), Ealing, Finchley, Surbiton and Hammersmith.

Chelsea Pastoral Foundation
155A Kings Road, Chelsea, London SW3 5TX. (071) 351 0839.
Counselling. Young persons' counselling service, for those aged between 17 to 24.

Chessington Hypnotherapy Clinic
130 Guilders Road, Chessington, Surrey. (081) 397 3146.
Aromatherapy, Diet Therapy Therapy, Hypnotherapy. Psychologist. Wheelchair access, one step on entry. £35 per ses-

sion (1 hour). Free consultation.

Children's Hours Trust
28 Wallace House, 410 Caledonian Road, London N7 8TL. (071) 609 5568.
Child psychotherapy. They listen to children and their play. Client-centred approach based on Rachel Pinney's theories of 'creative listening' - full attention and no interpretation. Small centre. Registered charity formed in 1983. You can visit by appointment. Workshops twice a month in London and by arrangement elsewhere, children welcome. Creche. Wheelchair access. Register of practitioners. Mail order. Library. Volunteers welcomed. £15 per session (negotiable). £25 for unit of two. Concessions.

Chinese Clinic
12 Bateman Street, London W1V 5TD. (071) 494 3593.
Acupuncture, Herbalism. Chinese herbalism and western orthodox medicine practised by two doctors. £15 for one session. Concessions.

Chinese Yoga Federation
44 Albany Mansions, Albert Bridge Road, London SW11.
Yoga.

Chiron
26 Eaton Rise, Ealing, London W5 2ER. (081) 997 5219.
Biodynamic Massage, Bioenergetics, Couple Therapy, Gestalt Therapy, Massage. Offers body psychotherapy drawing on the work of Lowen (bioenergetics), biodynamic psychology (Boyesen), gestalt body therapy (Rosenberg) and core energetics (Pierrakas). Ongoing evening psychotherapy groups. Weekend workshops. Member of UK standing conference for psychotherapy. They offer a training in

psychotherapy.

Chiropractic Advancement Association
56 Barnes Crescent, Wimborne, Dorset BH21 2AZ.
Chiropractic. Register of members of the British Chiropractic Association. Publish newsletter for members 'Back Chat'.

Chiropractic Clinic
8 Sunningdale Gardens, Stratford Road, Kensington W8 6PX. (071) 937 4836.
Chiropractic. £25 per session.

Christian Community
Temple Lodge, 51 Queen Caroline Street, London W6 9QL. (081) 748 8388.
Set up by Rudolph Steiner in 1922 to practice the spirit of Christianity rather than merely to uphold the traditional forms. Celebrate the sacraments, Christian festivals, hold study groups, services, workshops. Counselling is available, and a homoeopathic doctor visits on Thursday (phone (081) 458 4304 for appointment). Bookshop and vegetarian restaurant. Donations for services, talks.

Chung San Acupuncture School
15 Porchester Gardens, Maida Vale, London W2 4DB. (071) 727 6778/ (071) 229 0136.
Acupuncture. Clinic on Sunday with students of school. Treatment also available from qualified practitioners. Treatment by student £10, by qualified practitioner £20. They offer a training in Acupuncture.

Churchill Centre
22 Montagu Street, Marble Arch, London W1H 1TB. (071) 402 9475.
Massage, Reflexology. Supplies treatment couches. Training for

ITEC certificate given. Massage £16-£20. They offer a training in Massage and Reflexology.

City Health Centre
36-37 Featherstone Street, London EC1Y 8QX. (071) 251 4429.
Acupuncture, Alexander Technique, Counselling, Herbalism, Homoeopathy, Iridology, Massage, Neuro-linguistic Programming, Osteopathy, Shiatsu. Western and Chinese herbal pharmacy, Iris Photography/ consultation service, Vega Diagnosis. 6 treatment rooms, consultations by appointment. Practitioners available for short free consultations to help people decide the best form of treatment or therapy. Mail order herbal pharmacy. Treatment fees £18-25 (half to one hour), consultation fee (one to one-and-a-half hours) £30-£35.

Clapham Common Clinic
1st Floor, 151/153 Clapham High Street, Clapham Common, London SW4 7SS. (071) 627 8890 or 622 4382.
Acupuncture, Alexander Technique, Aromatherapy, Counselling, Homoeopathy, Massage, Osteopathy,Psychotherapy. Est. 3 years. Open Mon-Fri 9-9pm. Sat 10-6. £18-£28 per session.

Clare Maxwell Hudson
87 Dartmouth Road, London NW2 4ER. (081) 450 6494.
All forms of massage, including shiatsu. Clinic for members of the public. Home visiting service for London. Sessions from £25. Training in Massage and Reflexology and Shiatsu.

Clinic of Alternative Therapies
18 The Drive, South Woodford, London E18 2BL. (081) 989 2216.

Acupuncture, Homoeopathy, Vega Testing. Treatment for arthritis, rheumatism, migraine. £15 initial consultation.

Clinic of Herbal Medicine
8 Whitgift Street, Croydon, Surrey CRO 1DH. (081) 681 0924.
Herbal medicine. Member of National Institute of Medical Herbalists. £20 first visit, £12 subsequent visits. Concessions.

Clinic of Herbal Medicine
61 Fernside Road, Balham, London SW12. (081) 675 6405.
Herbalism. Open Tue-Sat inclusive with one practitioner and a variable number of students in attendance. Appointment only for sessions but you are welcome to drop in to get the feel of the place. First consultation waged £9, unwaged £5. Subsequent consultations waged £5, unwaged £3 (excluding the cost of medicines). Creche. Wheelchair access.

Clinics Health International
Riverbank House, Putney Bridge Approach, London SW6 3JD. 371 9717/371 9590.
Allergy Therapy, Herbalism, Stress Management. They offer traditional Chinese medicine and will treat all skin conditions including eczema and psoriasis. Two resident dermatologists and 3 practitioners from China. Psychotherapy is also available alongside herbal treatment if needed.

Clissold Park Natural Health Centre
154 Stoke Newington Church Street, Stoke Newington, London N16 0JU. (071) 249 2990.

Acupuncture, Aromatherapy, Counselling, Herbalism, Homoeopathy, Osteopathy. Have been established in Stoke Newington for 6 years and have 5 treatment rooms where patients may be seen by appointment. Offer an acute 'homoeopathic drop-in' 3 evenings a week on Monday, Wednesday and Friday at 5pm where patients can be seen without an appointment. Also offer various evening and weekend courses on different aspects of health. Sell homoeopathic first aid kits and books. £20 average per session.

College of Healing
Runnings Park, Croft Bank, West Malvern, Worcs. WR14 4DU. (0684) 565253.
Residential courss on aspects of healing, and training in healing.

College of Natural Therapies
22 Bromley Road, Catford, London SE6 2TP. (081) 690 2149.
Aromatherapy.

College of Osteopaths Education Trust
Administrative Services, 110 Thorkill Road, Thames Ditton, Surrey KT7 0UW. (081) 398 3308.
Osteopathy. Run teaching Clinic at Neal's Yard Therapy Rooms - the above address is the administrative office only. They offer a training in Osteopathy.

College of Psychic Studies
16 Queensberry Place, London SW7 2EB. (071) 589 3292.
Healing. Training for mediumship, healing; consultations with sensitives. Send A5 SAE for complete programme. Publish 'Light' three times yearly, £1.50 each. Membership £7.50, £12 or £18 per year depending on level.

283

LIST OF CENTRES

Colon Health
(071) 286 1572.
Colonic Irrigation, Diet
Therapy. Telephone for
appointment.

Colonic International Association
*26 Sea Road, Boscombe,
Bournemouth, Dorset BH5
1DF. (0202) 36354 / 736
3367.*
Training in Colonic Irrigation.

Communication and Counselling Foundation
*Haflodas, Tregoran, Dyfed,
Wales SY25 6UG . (0974)
298998/(0570) 470831.*
Feminist Therapy, Psychosyn-
thesis. Programme of workshops
and residentials, including The
Psychology of Transition and
Envisioning the Future retreat.
Run 'Women, Earth and Spirit', a
series of workshops/retreats for
women. Wheelchair access.
Training in Psychosynthesis.

Community Health Foundation
*188-194 Old Street, London
EC1V 9BP. (071) 251 4076.*
Diet Therapy, Iridology, Macrobiotics, Martial Arts, Massage,
Reflexology, Shiatsu. Established in 1976, this is one of the
largest natural health centres in
London. They run a wide range
of courses dedicated to natural
health care. There is a clinic for
individual advice on macrobiotics, shiatsu, massage, iridolgy
and reflexology. Also have
rooms to rent for workshops/
courses. There is a macrobiotic/
vegan restaurant on the premises as well as a book and food
shop. They hold open days and
free introductory evenings. £60
for a weekend course. £20 per
shiatsu massage. £25 for a macrobiotic consultation. Concessions. Course fees: Shiatsu, 12
Monday evenings or three week-

ends or a six day intensive costs
£135; Macrobiotic cooking, six
Tuesday evenings or one weekend £60; Yoga and Meditation,
six evenings or one weekend,
£40; Tai Chi, evening classes, £4
per class; Swedish Massage, 12
Monday evenings, £220, graduates receive an ITEC certificate.
Training in Macrobiotics.

Confederation of Healing Organisations
*Brundenell House, Quaniton,
Aylesbury, Bucks . 029675
250.*
Body set up to promote professional standards in healing, to
which many healing organisations belong.

Constructive Teaching Centre
*18 Landsdowne Road,
Holland Park, London W11.
(071) 727 7222.*
Alexander Technique.

Cortijo Romero
*72 Meadowsweet Road,
Creekmoor, Poole, Dorset
BH17 7XT. (0202) 699581.*
Holidays in the foothill of the
Sierra Nevada mountains in
Spain, including Creativity,
Meditation, Psychosynthesis,
Rebirthing

Counselling in North London
*c/o 2 Hemington Ave, Friern
Barnet, London N11 3LR.
(081) 368 2144.*
Counselling, Psychodynamic,
Humanistic and Existential Psychotherapy. Appointments avail
able day and evening, week-
days and weekends. £12-25 neg.

Cranial Osteopathic Association
*478 Baker Street, Enfield,
Middlesex EN1 3QS. (081) 367
5561.*
Cranial Osteopathy. Register of

members, who charge on average £20-£25 per session. Training in Cranial Osteopathy.

Cranial Osteopathy and Structural Therapy
*Primrose Hill, 28 Oppidans
Road, Chalk Farm, London
NW3. (071) 379 7662.*
Osteopathy.

Creation-Centred Spirituality
*St. James Church, 197
Piccadilly, London W1V.
(071) 734 4511.*
Christianity. Experiential workshops on Creation Centred Spirituality, including women's spirituality, creativity, dreams etc.,
using various media to explore
christian themes. Talks, ongoing courses, celebrations. £14-
20 for a day workshop (Concessions £14, £7). £3 talks (concessions £1.50).

Creative and Healing Arts
*222 Westbourne Park Road,
London W11 1EP. (071) 229
9400.*
Osteopathy, Shiatsu, Yoga. Individual sessions, classes and
workshops. Weekend retreats
with shiatsu, yoga, dance, music. Treatments £20 for an hour.
Classes vary from £2 for group
class and £20 for one to one
tuition. Workshops vary, £45
average per weekend. Concs.

Creative Arts and Therapy Consultants
*Margot Sunderland,
'Terpsichore', 70 Cranwich
Road, London N16 5JD. (081)
809 5866.*
Therapy and the arts combined,
also training course.

Creative Arts Workshops
*1 Ravenstone Road, London
N8 0JT. (081) 888 4259.*

284

Art Therapy, Creativity. Workshop on various themes to do with self-development and spirituality, inspiring new ideas from creative art images. £30 per day.

Croydon Buddhist Centre
98 High St, Croydon CRO 1ND. (081) 688 8624.
Buddhism, Meditation, Yoga. A centre of the Friends of the Western Buddhist Order (see London Buddhist centre for details), with an emphasis on meditation, study, devotional ceremonies. Evenings, weekends, retreats at their centre in Sussex. Run Hockney's (a vegetarian restaurant), a wholefood shop and a bookshop. Six week meditation evening course £30 (£15 concessions).

Crystal Connection
23 Camden Lock, London NW1 8AF. (071) 267 4325.
Crystal Therapy. Electro-crystal healing and light touch healing. Wheelchair access. Workshops. Monday to Friday. £15 upwards.

Crystal Research Foundation
37 Bromley Road, St Annes-on-Sea, Lancs FY8 1PQ. (0253) 723735.
Crystal Therapy. Run crystal healing training, also correspondence courses. Publish 'Crystal News' (£1.25).

D

Dancing on the Path
39A Glengarry Road, London SE22. (081) 693 6953.
Counselling, Dance Therapy. Individual sessions and sha-

manic dance workshops by psychotherapist trained in the Dancing Path by Gabrielle Roth. £35 day workshop.

Dick-Read School for Natural Birth
14 Pitt Street, London W8. (071) 937 4140.
Active Birth. Natural childbirth procedures according to the Dick-Read approach. Individual tuition given. Visiting speakers to groups. Book and teaching cassette also available. Sliding scale, average £10 per 2 hour session.

Dietary Therapy Society
33 Priory Gardens, London N6 5QU. (081) 341 7260.
Organisation of professional dietary therapists. Register. £15-25.

DMA UK Technologies for Creating
1/12 Belgravia Workshops, 157-161 Marlborough Rd, London N19 4NF. (071) 281 7496.
Creativity. They do not offer a therapy - are affiliated with the arts rather than the human potential movement. They offer a variety of courses for learning the skill of creating. The organisation was formed in 1985. Hold regular introductory evenings. Varies from course to course. 'Path of Least Resistance' available for £7.50 + £1.50 p&p.

Dr Edward Bach Centre
Mount Vernon, Sotwell, Wallingford, Oxon OX10 0PZ. (0491) 34678.
Bach Flower Remedies available by post, books, free advice service, consultations by appointment. Are planning seminars which are scheduled to start 1990.

Druid Order
161 Auckland Road, London SE19 2RH.
Public meetings at London Ecology centre fortnightly on Fridays at 7.15. Public ceremonies on Tower Hill at Spring equinox (12 noon GMT), at Stonehenge at Summer solstice, on Primrose Hill at Autumn equinox (12 noon GMT). Teaching and training given to companions in Groves and classes, available to those who wish to be initiated into the Druid order. Collection at evening meeting.

Eagle's Wing Centre for Contemporary Shamanism
58 Westbere Road, West Hampstead, London NW2 3RU . (071) 435 8174.
Shamanism. Established in 1986. One year course 'Elements of Shamanism', weekends and residentials on teachings of Native American Indians. Native American smudge sticks for sale £4 each. Typical weekend £45/50, residential £65. One year course (mainly residential) £625.

Ealing Holistic Centre for Homoeopath and Autogenic Training
55 Mattock Lane, West Ealing, London W13 9LA. (081) 579 0068.
Autogenic Training, Bach Flower Remedies, Counselling, Homoeopathy, Hypnotherapy. Established for 7 years. Appointments only. First consultation (1 and a half - 2 hours) £45 including one item of homoeopathic medicine if needed. Follow up

LIST OF CENTRES

consultations £25-£30 including one item of homoeopathic medicine if needed.

Ealing Psychotherapy Centre

St Martin's Rooms, Hale Gardens, Acton, London W3. (081) 993 5185.
Psychoanalytic Therapy. Individual and group analytic psychotherapy. Established for ten years with around twenty psychotherapists. Appointments need to be made in advance by letter or telephone to the general administrator. Therapists at the centre are available for teaching, lecturing, staff group consultancy etc. Wheelchair access. Individual sessions £17 - £22. Group psychotherapy around £10 per session. Limited concessions.

East-West Clinic of Natural Healing

46 Whitton Rd, Twickenham, Middlesex TW1 1BS. (081) 744 1974.
Acupuncture, Herbalism, Shiatsu. also Chinese Herbalism. Small clinic established one and a half years. Movement classes and meditation classes. £18 first consultation, £15 subsequent consultations. Herbs individually priced. Concessions.

Eckankar

8 Godolphin Road, Shepherds Bush, London W12 8JE. (081) 746 0131.
Contact only for local group. Classes/courses by donation.

Edgware Centre for Natural Health

128 High Street, Edgware HA8. (081) 952 9566.
Acupuncture, Alexander Technique, Herbalism, Hypnotherapy, Massage, Naturopathy, Osteopathy. Average £17 per session.

Edmonton Acupuncture Clinic

322 Fore Street, Edmonton, London N9 0PN. (081) 803 8102.
Acupuncture. Established 8 years. £20 per session. £16 OAP. £15 students. Home visits £25 (within 20 min drive).

Eigenwelt London

12 Howitt Rd, London NW3 3LL. (071) 586 3254.
Client-centered Therapy, Counselling, Existential Psychotherapy, Psychodrama. Weekend courses in London run by nationwide organisation based in Newcastle. Run courses in Edinburgh, Cumbria, Ilkeston, Worcester etc. Also offer in-service training. £45 per weekend for self funding; £52 if sponsored.

Equilibrium Therapy Centre

117 Granville Road, Southfields, London SW18 5SF. (081) 870 8761.
Acupuncture, Counselling, Couple Therapy, Eating Problem, Hypnotherapy, Osteopathy, Relaxation Training. Dietry advice. Hypnotherapy workshops. Counselling and hypnotherapy: daytime £18, evenings £25. Assessment session £25. Acupuncture and osteopathy £20. Concessions.

European Shiatsu School

6 Palace Gate, Kensington, London W8 5NF. 067 286 459.
Acupuncture, Aromatherapy, Herbalism, Homoeopathy, Osteopathy, Shiatsu. Formerly called the Shiatsu School of Natural Therapy. Clinics around London, this address mailing only, no clinic. Appointments only. Books sold. They supply teachers to give talks/workshops

anywhere in the UK or Europe. Wheelchair access. Cost £25 per 45mins- 1 hour session. Frequent free taster evenings for prospective students. Introductory workshops (one day) £24. Concessions. They offer a training in Shiatsu.

European Shiatsu School

7 Heath Villas, Vale of Health, Hampstead, London NW3. (071) 435 8787.
Herbalism, Homoeopathy, Shiatsu. Wonderful view. £25 approx per treatment

European Shiatsu School

13 North Common Road, Ealing, London W5. 067 286 459.
Herbalism, Shiatsu. and deep tissue bodywork, physiotherapy. Wheelchair access. £25 approx per treatment.

European Shiatsu School

163 Cromwell Road, London SW5 0SQ. (071) 370 6772.
Iridology, Shiatsu. £25 per treatment approx.

European Shiatsu School

222 Westbourne Park Road, London W11. (071) 229 9400.
Osteopathy, Shiatsu. £15 - £25 approx per treatment

Faculty of Homoeopathy

2 Powis Place, Great Ormond Street, Bloomsbury, London WC1N 2HR. (071) 837 8833 ext 85/72.

LIST OF CENTRES

Homoeopathy. Must be referred by your GP because it is a national health hospital. Treatment is free. They offer a training in Homoeopathy.

Faculty of Traditional Chinese Medicine of the UK

13 Gunnesbury Avenue, London W5. (081) 993 2549.
Acupuncture, training.

Falcons

25 Kite House, Grant Road, London SW11 2NJ. (071) 585 3445.
Aromatherapy, Diet Therapy Therapy, Hypnotherapy, Reflexology, Stress Management. Consultation and facilities for small groups. Use of leisure complex: swimming, jacuzzi, sauna by arrangement. Initial session £30, subsequent £25.

Family Planning Association

27-35 Mortimer Street, London W1N 7RJ. (071) 636 7866.
They can put you in touch with your local family planning clinic. Will answer all queries about contraception, sexuality and health over the phone. Leaflets.

Feldenkrais Method

28a Hampstead High St, London NW3 1QA. (071) 794 4066.
Feldenkrais. £30 per session. Weekend course £50.

Feldenkrais Method

188 Old Street, London EC1V 9BP. (081) 549 8145.
Feldenkrais. Can refer you to a practitioner. They offer a training in Feldenkrais.

Finchley Alternative Medicine Centre

253 Ballards Lane, Finchley, London N3 1NG. (081) 445 2631.

Practice Bioresonance which is a combination of homoeopathy and acupuncture. £40 per session.

Findhorn Foundation

The Park, Forres IV36 OTZ, Scotland. (0309) 73655.
Very large community in northeast Scotland, situated in and around the seaside village of Findhorn. Courses attract up to 4,000 visitors per year. Residents of the 200 strong 'open' community run various businesses, including solar panel making, a computer consultancy, a Steiner school and Meadowlark nursing home. 'Experience Week' £180-240, Weekend workshop £50-£110, week course £200-290, retreat weeks from £80-210.

Float Centre

20 Blenheim Terrace, St Johns Wood, London NW8 OEB. (071) 328 7276.
Flotation Tank Therapy. Float tanks (8ft x 7 ft x 4ft wide) in secluded rooms. Open 10-7, seven days a week. Sessions must be booked at least two days in advance. One week introductory course (3 x 1 hour sessions) £48. Each one hour session costs £22, but discounts apply if you book more than one.

Float Experience

Battersea. (071) 350 1001.
Flotation Tank Therapy, Jungian Psychotherapy. One tank, an 'ocean floatroom'. Small private centre established four years ago. Information about floating available. By appointment only. £20 per session.

Food and Chemical Allergy Clinic

149 Primrose Lane, Shirley Oaks, Croydon, Surrey CR0 8YP. 081 654 1700.

Allergy Therapy, Massage, Reflexology. Established 8 years. Testing for allergies, desensitisation. Also treat asthma, eczema, ME, candida, multiple sclerosis, hayfever. Ring for appointment. Wheelchair access. £15 per 45 minute session.

Fook Sang Acupuncture and Chinese Herbal Practitioners Training College UK

1037B Finchley Road, Golders Green, London NW11 7ES. (081) 455 5508 or 0734/ 665454.
Acupuncture, Herbalism. Chinese osteopathy. The clinic has recently moved from Gloucester Place to Golders Green. Acupuncture treatments last from 1-3 hours, depending on the severity of the condition. Associated clinic in Reading, and affiliated training college. Initial consultation and acupuncture £25, subsequent acupuncture treatments £20, herbal prescriptions plus consultation £25. They offer a training in Acupuncture and Herbalism.

Forty Hill Natural Therapy Centre

478 Baker Street, Enfield, Middlesex. (081) 367 5561.
Acupuncture, Cranial Osteopathy, Naturopathy, Reflexology. Relaxation and Bee Venom Therapy (in which the patient is stung by a bee - widely used on the continent to relieve arthritis). Also supervised fasts. Wheelchair access. £20-£25. Concessions.

Foundation for International Spiritual Unfoldment

71 Trumpington Road, Forest Gate, London E7 9EH. (081) 555 4643.
Meditation. Courses by appoint-

LIST OF CENTRES

ment. Residential courses bi-annually. Open evening Wednesdays 8pm, except first week of month when held on Friday at 8pm. Donation.

Free Daist Communion
32 Church Crescent, London N10 3NE. (081) 444 5292.
Teacher is Heart-Master Da Love-Ananda who sometimes visits the UK. Evenings, weekends, courses and regular retreats at home (London, Kent, Hampshire) and abroad (USA, Canada, New Zealand, Australia, Holland, Fiji, Hawaii). Co-operatively run businesses worldwide. Centre has meeting rooms, video rooms, meditation halls, bookshop, retreat rooms. Bimonthly newsletter (free).

Friends of Shanti Nilaya UK
10 Archery Field House, Wharton Street, London WC1X 9PN.
Workshops on death. Founded by Elisabeth Kubler-Ross.

Fulham Clinic
56 New King's Road, London SW6 4LF. (071) 731 5015.
Acupuncture, Aromatherapy, Cranial Osteopathy, Homoeopathy, Massage, Neuro-linguistic Programming, Touch for Health (Kinesiology). A group of six practitioners work at this centre. £30 approx per session depending on the practitioner.

G

Gaia House
Woodland Road, Denbury, Nr. Newton Abbot, Devon TQ12 6DY. (0803) 813188.
Buddhism, Meditation, Retreats.

Founded by Christopher Titmuss and Christina Feldman, Buddhist Vipassana (insight) meditation is taught here on retreat. There is a residential community here too, and facilities for solitary retreats £11 per day, decreasing for stays of longer than 30 days. Working retreats at a reduced rate, and for those with skills to offer are free. Some concessions.

Gale Centre for Creative Therapy
Stable Cottage, Whitakers Way, Loughton, Essex IG10 1SJ. (081) 508 9344.
Family Therapy, Group Oriented Therapy, Psychodrama. Voice therapy, individual therapy, short courses for members of the helping professions. Mail order books and tapes. Low cost concessions available.

General Council and Register of Consultant Herbalists
Marlborough House, Swanpool, Falmouth, Cornwall TR11 4HW. (0326) 317321.
Herbalism. Register of practitioners.

General Council and Register of Osteopaths
56 London Street, Reading. 0734 576585.
Naturopathy, Osteopathy. Professional association linked with British College of Naturopathy and Osteopathy. Register.

Gerda Boyesen Centre for Biodynamic Psychology and Psychotherapy
Acacia House, Centre Avenue, Acton Park, London W3 7JX. (081) 743 2437.
Biodynamic Massage, Massage. Evening, weekends and long courses. ITEC Diploma courses. Psycho-peristaltic massage.

Prices vary. Low cost massage given by trainees. Concessions. They offer a training in Biodynamic Massage.

Gestalt Centre London
64 Warwick Road, St Albans, Herts AL1 4DL. (0727) 64806.
Established in 1983 the centre's initial focus was on Gestalt Therapy and training. With a growing number of graduates the associate programme now offers a wide range of workshops from peace building to encounter marathons within a variety of formats i.e. one day events to week long residentials. The centre is an association of accredited therapists working throughout London and the home counties with an administrative base at St. Albans. Individual therapy £10 - £30. Weekend workshop £50 average. A 'low cost' course £80 (usually £130). Concessions. They offer a training in Gestalt.

Gestalt Studio
49 Croftdown Road, London NW5 . 485 2316.
Feminist Therapy, Gestalt Therapy. Offer weekly beginners and advanced mixed groups, and beginners and advanced women's groups. Individual therapy, advanced events, including training and supervision events. Women's weekends, mixed weekends. Contact for brochure. Subsidised therapy for those in financial difficulties.

Gestalt Therapy in West London
36 Newburgh Road, Acton, London W3 6DQ. (081) 993 0868.
Gestalt. Group, individual and family therapy. Up to £25, concessions negotiable.

Graigian Society
10 Lady Somerset Road,

LIST OF CENTRES

Kentish Town, London NW5 1UP. (071) 485 1646 (after 12 noon and before 6pm). Beautiful house open to visitors on Sundays. Activities include 'Being in a Group' group (Sundays 4-6pm), art therapy, tarot and pottery tuition. Telephone or write before visiting. Members get 4 newsletters per year, access to regular Sunday group, access to art and pottery tuition, discounts on booklets and pottery, and are entitled to attend communal holidays in Wales after a year's membership. Members are expected to help support the society's environmental campaigning. Cost for groups: first visit a contribution (e.g. milk, fruit juice or vegetarian biscuits); on second visit people are expected to become members for a year. Membership: £3 per annum (concessions), £5 per annum (waged). Couples (of any kind) £7 per annum. Communities, companies and societies £12 per annum.

Group Relations Training Association
7 Stanley Rd, Oxford OX4 1QY. (0865) 724141.
Group Oriented Therapy. They do an annual 5 day group relations training laboratory using the T group method. This residential, includes food and accommodation. They also hold an annual conference, normally held over 4 days late September, early October. The conference gives the opportunity to join in a range of activities, including the latest in personal growth and therapeutic techniques. £300 (organisations), £200 (individual) for the group laboratory training workshop. £Varies for the conference.

Guild of Aromatherapy Practitioners
59 Murray Road, London SW19.
Aromatherapy.

Guild of Pastoral Psychology
5/36 Arterberry Road, London SW20 8AQ. (081) 946 3172.
Jungian Psychotherapy. Explores relationship between religion and depth psychology, particularly the work of Jung and his followers. No qualifications necessary for membership. Lectures, conferences. Library for members. Lecture pamphlets. Membership £16.50 for Londoners, £13 for ministers of religion and the retired.

Gurdjieff Ouspensky School
Box 1531, London NW3 6RW.
Practical Fourth Way work for normal men and women in everyday life taught by word of mouth. Provides methods, tools and exercises for work to achieve higher states of consciousness and inner development. Strong emphasis on personal verification, understanding and efforts. Welcomes people from all backgrounds, nationalities and cultures who wish to work on themselves.

Haelen Centre
41 The Broadway, Crouch End, London N8. (081) 340 1518.
Acupuncture, Herbalism, Homoeopathy, Massage, Osteopathy, Shiatsu. Clinic above wholefood shop. £15-£30 depending on practitioner sessions between half an hour- one and a half hours.

Hahnemann College of Homoeopathy
243 The Broadway, Southhall, Middlesex UB1 1NF. (081) 843 9200.
Homoeopathy. They offer a training in Homoeopathy.

Hahnemann College of Homoeopathy
342 Barking Road, Plaistow, London E13 8HI. (071) 476 7263.
Homoeopathy. Treatment by students of the college.

Hakomi Institute
61 Grantham Rd, Chiswick, London W4 2RT. (081) 994 8544.
Teach Hakomi method, a body-mind therapy which emphasises gentleness and letting go. £85 for a weekend (including Friday evening). Rolfing also available.

Hale Clinic
7 Park Crescent, Regents Park, London W1N 3HE. (071) 631 0156.
Acupuncture, Alexander Technique, Chiropody, Chiropractic, Herbalism, Homoeopathy, Massage, Naturopathy, Osteopathy. Also offer chiropody. £Vary.

Hampstead Healing Centre
9 Cannon Place, London NW3 1EH. (071) 435 5432.
Bach Flower Remedies, Couple Therapy, Healing, Massage, Reflexology. Ring for appointment. Established 10 years. £25 per session. £10 concessions. Workshops £25 per day.

Hampton Healing Centre
2a Belgrade Road, Hampton, Middlesex. (081) 979 6234.

289

LIST OF CENTRES

Acupuncture, Autogenic Training, Bach, Chiropractic, Colonic Irrigation, Homoeopathy, Stress Management, McTimoney Chiropractic. Occasional workshops at the centre e.g. crystal healing, massage, preventative medicine. Some books available. From £16-30. Concessions.

Hampton Holistic Centre for Homoeopath and Autogenic Training
12 Wolsey Road, Hampton Hill, Middlesex TW12 1QW. (081) 579 0068.
Autogenic Training, Bach Flower Remedies, Counselling, Diet Therapy, Homoeopathy, Hypnotherapy. Established for 7 years. Appointments only. First consultation (1 and a half hour - 2 hours) £45 including one item of homoeopathic medicine if needed. Follow up consultations £25-£30 including one item of homoeopathic medicine if needed.

Harry Edwards Spiritual Healing Sanctuary
Burrows Lea, Shere, Guildford, Surrey GU5 9QG. (048641) 2054.
Healing. Established in 1946, the Sanctuary covers 14 acres. Main work is distant or absent healing. Some books and cassettes available. No charge for services.

Hayes Hypnotherapy Centre
Suite 6, Grange Chambers, 503 Uxbridge Road, Hayes, Middx UB4 8RL. (081) 561 5282.
Hypnotherapy. By appointment only. Free initial consultation, apply for fees. Concessions.

Healing Centre
Garden Flat, 49 Cavenish St, London NW6 7XS.
Healing.

Healing Fields Practice
Garden Flat, 65 Anson Road, London N7 OAS. (071) 607 1823.
Astrological Psychotherapy, Bach. and Californian flower remedies. Holistic approach to therapy. Available for talks and presentations on flower remedies - fees negotiable. £20 per session and consultation. £60 astrological chart and reading. Concessions.

Healing Workshops
111 Queens Crescent, Chalk Farm, London NW5 4EY. (071) 482 4049.
Counselling, Healing, Meditation, Guided Visualisation, Attitudinal Healing and Positive Thought Techniques. Courses include study groups based on the best-selling book, You Can Heal Your Life by Louise Hay. Venues vary, but one to one healing sessions and weekly healing circle takes place in NW5. Currently producing a range of books and audio tapes for mail order. Desk top publishing service available. Healing circle - entrance by donation. Individual sessions £23 (one and a half hours). Study groups £69 for 6 weeks. No concessions, but occasional bursaries at their discretion.

Health Connection
7 Hereward Rd, London SW17 7EY. (081) 767 2935.
Their eclectic approach to psychotherapy includes humanistic therapy, gestalt, transpersonal psychology with an awareness of psychodymanic principles. £20-£25. Concessions available.

Health Management
31 Rosslyn Hill, London NW3 5UJ. (071) 431 0760.
Massage, Stress Management, Yoga. Courses and holidays. Private lessons also given. 6

week course £40, workshop £15-25.

Herb Society
PO Box 415, London SW1P 2HE. (0803) 867823.
Herbalism. Disseminates information on herbs for all those interested. Members include professional growers, medical herbalists, beauticians, cooks and the merely curious, and they receive quarterly 'Herbal Review', and can use library. Also information on herb sources and local herb groups. Lectures for general public. Membership £12, £8 senior citizens, students and under 18s, £16 overseas.

Heron Training Workshops
152 Park Street Lane, Park Street, St. Albans AL2 2AE. (0727) 72010.
Management, Transactional Analysis. Public courses for both men and women held in hotels. They also run Transactional Analysis in education for teachers and others working with young people. £125 per session. Individuals sponsoring themselves £35. Education programmes are £18 per day (weekends only).

Hidden Strengths
97 Warren Rd, Whitton, Middlesex TW2 7DG. (081) 755 0353.
Biodynamic Massage, Feminist Therapy. Biodynamic psychotherapy workshops for women. Introductory days, weekend workshops and ongoing groups. Have been running groups for 4 years. £50 for a weekend workshop. Free initial consultation if interested in the groups. Concs.

Highbury Centre
137 Grosvenor Avenue, Highbury, London N5 2NH. (071) 226 5805.

LIST OF CENTRES

Active Birth, Alexander Technique, Art Therapy, Biodynamic Massage, Counselling, Dream Therapy, Hypnotherapy, Massage, Polarity Therapy, Psychosynthesis, Voice Therapy. Also self-presentation work. A small centre established for 6 years. Rooms to let to qualified therapists for groups and individual work. Residential Alexander Technique courses run outside London. Individual sessions average around £10-20, weekend workshops £40-80. Concessions may be given by individual therapists.

Hillside Practice
One Hillside, Highgate Road, Dartmouth Park, London NW5. (071) 482 3293.
Biodynamic Massage, Counselling, Couple Therapy, Gestalt Therapy, Homoeopathy, Jungian Psychotherapy, Primal Therapy, Shiatsu, Yoga. The centre comprises three houses close together. Established 5 years. Overlooks the heath. Receptionist available for phone calls mornings 9-1. Wheelchair access by prior arrangement. £Vary depending on the practitioner. Concessions.

Hocroft Clinic
3 Hocroft Road, West Hampstead, London NW2 2BN. (071) 435 9506.
Naturopathy, Osteopathy, Ayurvedic Medicine. First appointment one and a half hour; £25. Subsequent treatment (40 minutes) £18.

Holistic Health Consultancy
94 Grosvenor Road, London SW1V 3LF. (071) 834 3579.
Allergy Therapy, Bach Flower Remedies, Diet Therapy Therapy, Herbalism, Homoeopathy, Iridology, Naturopathy. Spagyrik practitioners. Established in

1983, the consulting room of this centre has a panoramic river view. Telephone consultations are offered to established patients, who can also order medicines mail order. Wheelchair access. First consultation (2 hours) £48.80 includes typed analysis, full explanation of findings, nutritional and naturopathic instructions and homoeopathic medication. Homoeopathic consultation £35 (one and a half hours inclusive of medication). Follow up £27 (1 hour). Herbal medications extra. Concessions available.

Holistic Yoga Centre
The Old Manor House, The Green, Hanslope, MK19 7LS. (0908) 510548.
Couple Therapy, Enlightenment Intensive, Mind Clearing. The centre is a private house, strictly by appointment only. The centre runs 4-5 Enlightenment Intensives a year and residential couple therapy and mind clearing intensives. Established since 1987. Fully residential with a capacity for 24 people. Cost: Enlightenment Intensives: three day fully residential £95. Two week residentia: £295. Sessions for mind clearing and couple therap: £25 per hour. Concs. They offer a training in Mind Clearing and Enlightenment Intensives.

Holwell Centre for Psychodrama and Sociodrama
East Down, Barnstaple, Devon EX31 3NZ. 0271 850 267/597.
Gestalt, Psychodrama, Sociodrama, Playback Theatre, Journal Process and Dream Workshops. Some workshops in the Greater London area, but see 'Residential Workshops' for bulk of programme. Holwell is a farm, dating back to 1244, with pond, lawns and developing

woodland. £120 per residential weekend, £315 per week. Concessions.

Homoeopathic Development Foundation Ltd
73 Duke Street, London W1. (071) 629 3205.
Homoeopathy. Register of doctors practising in London. Information on Homoeopathy. they have a selection of books which are available on mail order free no charge, donation are welcome as they are a charitable organization.

Homoeopathic Health Centre
342 Barking Road, Plaistow, London E13 8HL. (071) 476 7263.
Homoeopathy.

Homoeopathic Health Clinic
29 Streatfield Road, Kenton, Middlesex HA3 9BP. (081) 907 4885.
Counselling, Homoeopathy. Well baby clinic, well women's clinic, special dermatological, asthmatic and bronchial clinic. Established for 10 years. Medically qualified doctor. Four room centre with easy access. Easy access to public transport. Parking facilities. They also offer telephone or postal consultation for patients at a long distance. Cervical smear tests are carried out by a woman doctor in a friendly environment with 24-36 hour results. Creche facilities and wheelchair access. Full medical consultation lasting one and half hour for £25 (£20 for children). Follow up sessions cost £15 (£12 for children).

Homoeopathic Trust
Hahneman House, Great Ormond Street, Bloomsbury, WC1N 2HR (071) 837 2495.

Located next to the Great Ormond St Hospital, the Trust will supply you with a list of GPs who practice homoeopathy. This list is contained within an info pack which costs £1.50.

Hong Tao Acupuncture and Natural Health Clinic

21 St Thomas Drive, Hatch End, Pinner, Middlesex HA5 4SX. (081) 421 2668.
Acupuncture. Allergy testing. Consultation and first treatment £24, follow up £18. Allergy test £38. Concessions for OAPs at discretion of doctor.

House of the Goddess

33 Oldridge Road, London SW12 8PN. (081) 673 6370.
Paganism. Support, learning and celebration for the pagan community. For free contact list send SAE. Also counselling service, training courses (including initiation). Most important events are the Pagan Moon and Halloween. Most festivals and meetings cost between £1.50-£2.50. Counselling is £15 per hour session. Birth, death, weddings cost £25, funeral is free.

Human Potential Resource Group

Dept of Educational Studies University of Surrey, Guildford, Surrey GU2 5XH. (0483) 509191.
Assertion, Bioenergetics, Co-counselling, Counselling, Couples, Creativity, Encounter, Feminist Therapy, Gestalt, Group Oriented Therapy, Jungian Psychotherapy, Management, Neuro-linguistic Programming, Stress Management. Also Intensive Journal workshops, life work planning, exercises in expanding intelligence. Most workshops are held at the University of Surrey. Some are

in London. Broad range of courses, often over the weekend, so it's possible if you're a Londoner for you to commute. They run a number of short (one week) training courses in gestalt, NLP, counselling, group work, stress management and birth trauma issues. Approx £60 per weekend workshop. The short (one week) trainings cost approx £250. They offer a training in Group Oriented Therapy.

Humanistic Psychology at LSE

David Jones, S364,, Psychology Dept, London School of Economics, Houghton St, London WC2A 2AE. 405 7686x3313.
Co-counselling, Gestalt Therapy, Meditation, Psychosynthesis, Transpersonal psychology. They offer a training in Humanistic Psychology.

Hygeia Studios

Brook House, Tetbury, Glos GL8 8NS. (045383) 2150.
Colour Therapy. Large 14 bedroomed house, 29 rooms in all standing in 4 acres with pond and stream, orchard and field. £95-50 residential weekend (nine and a half hours tuition with free hand-outs). They offer a training in Colour Therapy.

Hypnoanalysis Centre

The Hale Centre, 7 Park Crescent, London W1.
Hypnotherapy, Touch for Health (Kinesiology). The centre has a number of practitioners. Phone to make an appointment. Wheelchair access. First session £45. Subsequent sessions £40. Anti-smoking sessions £70.

Hypnocare

Flat 5, 138 Sutherland Avenue, London W9 1HP. (071) 286 2003.
Healing, Hypnotherapy. Gestalt

and counselling. £30-45 sliding scale.

Hypnotherapy Training Centre

9 Avocet Mews, Plumstead, London SE28 0DA.
Hypnotherapy. They offer a training in Hypnotherapy.

Hypnotherapy/ Psychotherapy Practice

37 Orbain Road, Fulham, London SW6 7J2. (071) 385 1166.
Counselling, Hypnotherapy. Large therapy room. £15 on average per session. Concessions.

I

Identity Counselling Service

2 Warwick Crescent, London W2 6NE. (071) 289 6175.
Counselling. Specialise in counselling for personal and relationship issues, and those confused about their sexual identity and orientation. Training workshops for counsellors (£20 per day). Assessment session £25 (neg). Counselling sessions £16-£20. Limited number of sessions at reduced fees.

Imprint

377 Wimbledon Park Road, London SW19 6PE. (081) 788 1500.
Art Therapy, Dream, Jungian Psychotherapy. Based in the top floor of a private house with darkroom (photography), art and printing facilities. Established 10 years. Appointment required. £20 for two and half hours of art therapy. £18 for a psychotherapy session. Concs.

LIST OF CENTRES

Independent Register of Manipulative Therapists
32 Lodge Drive, Palmers Green, London N13 5JZ. (081) 886 3120.
Osteopathy. Register of both osteopaths and neuro-muscular manipulators.

Inner Abilities
2 Langton St, London SW10 OJH. (071) 351 1811.
Focusing (a psychological method for self-help, creativity, psychotherapy and counselling) is offered at this centre. Weekend workshops, open evening groups and individual counselling as well as training others in focusing. Has been established for three years. Tapes and articles on focusing are available. Wheelchair access. Typically £60 for a weekend workshop, £20 for an individual session. Concessions.

Inner Miracle Partnership
5 Galgate, Barnard Castle, Co Durham DL12 8EQ. (0833) 31236.
Run courses in A Course In Miracles. Mail order books, tapes and videos. Correspondence course.

Inner Sound and Voice Workshops
C/O Gillian McGregor, Garden Flat, 9 Yonge Park, Highbury N4 3MU, London N4 3NU. (071) 607 5819.
Voice Therapy. Jill Purce has been inspired by the sonic yogas of India and Tibet, the use of mantra and shamanic use of sound and rhythm. Week long workshop, introductory weekends and one day 'Voice of Shamanism'. Workshops exploring sound for healing and transformation of consciousness us-

ing breathing. £265 for week. Introductory weekends £65, one day £45.

Inner Track Learning
Forge House, Limes Road, Kemble, Glos. GL7 6AD. (0285) 770635.
Courses on accelerated learning skills. The inner track method is derived from Suggestopedia, accelerated learning, neuro-linguistic programming and Yoga. It also incorporates study skills developed by Tony Buzan. Its aim is to help you develop your full learning potential. Books and cassettes available. Weekend workshops £68.

Insight Care Complementary Health Clinic
24 Chapel Market, Islington, N1 9EZ. (071) 278 1212.
Acupuncture, Homoeopathy, Iridology, Laser Therapy. Open Mon-Sat 8am-5pm. Established for five years. Linked to the College of Opthalmic Somatology. £15 + VAT per consultation, exclusive of medications. Register. No concessions. Wheelchair access.

Insight Seminars
9 Spring Street, London W2 3RA. (071) 706 2021.
Personal development seminars which aim to be gentle, nurturing and give participants an experience of their own value. Has been operating in London for 11 years. Address given is a small office, but visitors are very welcome. £300 per person for a six day course, but often special offers available for more than one person. Concessions.

Institute for Complementary Medicine
21 Portland Place, London W1N 3AF. (071) 636 9543.

Allergy, Diet Therapy, Homoeopathy. Runs a referral service for the general public to complementary practitioners. Provides information on complementary medicine, campaigns and researches, and can give advice on trainings. Network of public information points around country run by people who are not practitioners (so that they can be independent). Library. Supporters' Club (£12 per year for membership) which meets and receives newsletter. Scientific journal. A very helpful and useful organisation . Membership £12 per annum.

Institute for Optimum Nutrition
5 Jerden Place, Fulham, London SW6 1BE. (071) 385 7984.
Diet Therapy, Diet Therapy Therapy. ION was established in 1984, and the building spans 1,500 square feet. Members can drop in a use library. Clinic and training. Register. Wheelchair access. Sell books, have space to hire, run annual conference and produce a quarterly magazine, 'Optimum Nutrition'. £59 for consultation, including hair analysis. £39 for one-day workshop. They offer a training in Diet Therapy.

Institute of Allergy Therapists
Ffynnonwen Natural Therapy Centre, Llanguyryfon, Aberystwyth, Dyfed SY23 4EY .
Allergy Therapy. Register

Institute of Biodynamic Psychology and Psychotherapy
Lamerton House, 23 High St, The Green, Ealing, London W5 5DF. 567 6677.
They offer a training in Biodynamic Massage and Biodynamic Psychotherapy.

293

LIST OF CENTRES

Institute of Clinical Aromatherapy
22 Bromley Road, Catford, London SE6 2TP. (081) 690 2149.
Aromatherapy. Register of practitioners. They offer a training in Aromatherapy.

Institute of Emotio-Somatic Therapy
52 Bishopthorpe Rd., SE26 43PA . (081) 659 0021.
This mixing of osteopathy and psychotherapy is a combination of simple body technique and an eclectic counselling approach. 4 term course. .

Institute of Family Therapy
43 New Cavendish St, Marylebone, London W1M 7RG. (071) 935 1651.
Family Therapy. Charity formed in 1977. They offer a clinical service to families with a wide range of behavioural and relationship problems. These problems may include difficulties with young children and adolescents or they may relate to marriage, bereavement or the care of elderly parents. They practice a systems framework of Family Therapy. Some therapists work with couples and individuals. Conciliation service. They hire out training videos, hold day workshops and organise conferences. Wheelchair access to some rooms. Fees on a sliding scale depending on income of client. They offer a training in Family Therapy.

Institute of Group Analysis
1 Daleham Gardens, Swiss Cottage, London NW3 5BY. (071) 431 2693.
Group Oriented Therapy. Training course only, they do not practice at the above address,
but will refer you to one of their practitioners. They offer a training in Group Oriented Therapy.

Institute of Holistic Therapies
486 Fulham Road, London SW6 5NH. (081) 540 1743.
Alexander Technique, Iridology, Massage, Reflexology, Shiatsu, Touch For Health, Relaxation and Natural Healing. £60 per weekend workshop. Full-time students and unemployed £50.

Institute of Psychosynthesis
The Barn, Nan Clarks Lane, Mill Hill, London NW7 4HH. (081) 959 2330.
Psychosynthesis. Established 17 years, psychosynthesis psychotherapy for individuals, couples and groups. Group leaders will offer workshops and seminars. Counselling service with interview procedure. Mail order books. Wheelchair access. Prices as arranged with individual therapists. Mail order books and articles. Concessions. They offer a training in Psychosynthesis.

Institute of Psychotherapy and Social Studies
18 Laurier Road, London NW5.
Miscellaneous Mind, Psychoanalytic Therapy. Psychoanalytic and Humanistic psychotherapy practiced here. Sliding scale; students provide low cost therapy. They offer a training in psychotherapy.

Institute of Pure Chiropractic
14 Park End Street, Oxford ONX 1HH. (0865) 246687.
Chiropractic. They are a registered professional body for McTimony Chiropractic. Send SAE for list.

Institute of Structural Bodywork
Hyatt Carlton Tower, C/O Roger Golten, The Peak, Cadogan Place, London SW1X 9PY. (071) 235 5411.
Aston Patterning, Hellerwork, Rebalancing, Rolfing, Cranio-Sacral Therapy and Traeger work is also available. ISB is an information service for the above therapies. Maintains and up-to-date database of therapists, courses and events and networks information world-wide. Established in 1986. They advise on ergonomic products and sell books and products on on related topics such as tensional integrity models and books by Buckmaster Fuller. Air and water pollution control devices also available. Talks and demonstrations can be arranged. £25-£60 per session depending on therapy experience of therapist. Concessions.

Institute of Traditional Herbal Medicine and Aromatherapy
6 Palace Gate, London W8 5NF.
Aromatherapy.

International Association of Colour Healers
33 St Leonards Court, East Sheen, London SW14 7NG.
Colour Therapy.

International Colon Hydrotherapy Foundation
27 Warwick Avenue, London W9 2PS. (071) 289 7000.
Allergy Therapy, Colonic Irrigation, Diet Therapy Therapy. Colonic irrigation to help with many disorders such as skin and heavy toxic conditions. £35 per session.

International Federation for Radionics
21 Portland Place, London W1N 3AF.
Radionics.

International Federation of Aromatherapists
4 Eastmearn Road, West Dulwich, London SE21 8HA.
Professional body for Aromatherapists. Register and list of accredited courses - send SAE. Newsletter and insurance service to full members (qualified aromatherapists only). Membership also open to general public.

International NLP Training
48 Ferme Park Rd, London N4 4ED. (081) 348 5949.
Hypnotherapy, Neuro-linguistic Programming. Eriksonian Hypnosis practised. Seminars on neuro-linguistic Programming. The centre is an office, the workshops take place at other locations. Average size of workshops is 50 people. Associated centres in France, Belgium, Luxemburg and Germany. £95 for a two day introductory course including a fire walk!

International Order of Kabbalists
25 Circle Gardens, London SW19 3JX.
Lodge meetings once a month, and corresponding members work on a monthly basis. Information on Kabbalistic astrology available at the same address. Quarterly magazine, 'The Kabbalist' £1.25 per copy plus 20p postage, or £3.50 for a year's subscription post free. Send letter with SAE.

International Primal Association
79 Pembroke Road, London E17. (081) 521 4764.
Primal Integration. Will refer you to primal integration practitioners in the UK. £Vary depending on the practitioner.

International School of the Golden Rosycross (Lectorium Rosicrucianum)
45 Woodlands Road, Earlswood, Redhill, Surrey.
Headquarters of Lectorium Rosicrucianum

International Society for Krishna Consciousness (ISKON)
10 Soho Street, London W1. (071) 437 3662.
Hinduism. Founded by Bhaktivendanta Swami Prabhupada, ISKON adheres closely to the Veda Scriptures, and devotees chant the Hare Krisha Mantra. Practice Bhakti Yoga (the Yoga of devotion or love). They are *Vaishnavas* or worshippers of Vishnu, a Hindu deity. There's a residential community at centre and a vegetarian restaurant. They have a college for Vedic studies in Herts, 'Bhaktivedanta Manor'. The monastic followers wear the traditional saffron coloured robe and shaven head of Indian holy men, and lay followers wear white.

Isis Centre for Holistic Health
5 Clonmell Road, London N17 6SY, . (081) 801 4406.
Acupuncture, Counselling, Cranial Osteopathy, Healing, Massage, Osteopathy. Practice established 1978, centre opened 1983. Approx £18-25 depending on therapy. Donations for spiritual healing.

Iyengar Yoga Institute
223a Randolph Avenue, London W9 1NL. (071) 624 3080.
Yoga. The Institute runs classes for children and adults from beginners to teaching level. Remedial classes for people with problems are also held. Students can drop in any time. Daytime, weekend and evening classes, with small groups. Qualified teachers only. They also sell books, videos and yoga mats. Information is available about classes round the country. Yoga days, exhibitions, seminars and lectures. £3. Concessions. They offer a training in Yoga.

J

Jeyrani Health Centre
4-6 Glebelands Avenue, South Woodford, London E18 2AL. (081) 530 1146.
Acupuncture, Aromatherapy, Gestalt Therapy, Hypnotherapy, Metamorphic Technique, Osteopathy, Polarity Therapy, Reflexology, Stress Management, Yoga, Vega Testing. Courses for fertility and gynaecological counselling. People are more than welcome to drop in or call for further information and an informal chat. The centre has five consulting rooms and a large reception area. Open six days a week, 9.30-9 and out of hours appointments are possible. Established for two and half years. General evenings are on Tuesdays 7-9. Blended essential oils are sold. Creche facilities on Tuesdays. Prices range from £3.50 for general classes to £150 for more specialised courses. Usual price is £50 for an initial

LIST OF CENTRES

consultation and £15 - £25 for a one hour therapy session. They offer a training in Active Birth and Aromatherapy.

K

Karma Kagyu Cho Khor Ling
Unit 21F Perseverance Works, 38 Kingsland Road, London E2. (071) 739 9430.
Buddhism, Meditation. The Venerable Lama Chime Rinpoche is the director and teacher of this Tibetan Buddhist centre, and he gives some lectures here. Chanting and meditation are the practices here, and there are evenings, weekends courses.

Keith Mason School of Radionics
21 Portland Place, London W1N 3AF. (0425) 53677.
Radionics. Also available holistic animal clinic in Salisbury. They offer a training in Radionics.

Keys College of Radionics
21 Portland Place, London W1N 3AF.
Radionics.

Ki Kai Shiatsu Centre
8 Willow Road, Hampstead, London NW3. (081) 368 9050.
Flotation Tank Therapy, Meditation, Shiatsu, Qi Gong and Postural Re-alignment (Sotai). Warm inviting workshop room overlooking Hampstead Heath. Classes are kept small (14) for maximum student-teacher contact. They offer a range of treatments, practice sessions and Qi

Gong classes. There is also a floatation tank which can be used in conjunction with shiatsu treatments, to enhance the treatment process. Lending library on Chinese medicine/shiatsu related subjects. Weekend introductory classes cost £30. Average treatment price £18. Concessions. They offer a training in Shiatsu.

Kushi Institute
188 Old St, London EC1V 9BP. (071) 251 4076.
Macrobiotics. Upstairs from the East-West centre macrobiotic restaurant, the Kushi institute runs courses on macrobiotic cooking and nutrition.

L

Lavender Hill Homoeopathic Centre
33 Illminster Gardens, London SW11 1PJ. (071) 978 4519.
Homoeopathy.

Lever Clinic
10 Harley St, London W1. (071) 580 4280.
Acupuncture, Osteopathy. physiotherapy and electrolysis. Five treatment rooms. Wheelchair access. £18 per session.

Lever Clinic
25 Fyfield Road, Enfield, Middx EN1 3TT. (081) 366 0666.
Acupuncture, Osteopathy.

Lewisham Homoeopathic Clinic
7a Gilmore Road, Lewisham, London SE13 5AD. (081) 852 0573.
Homoeopathy. Established for 10 years, nine homoeopaths

practice at this clinic. Consultations by appointment, weekend and evening appointments available. Drop-in 'Acutes' clinic on Saturdays from 10am-5pm for those suffering from common complaints and injuries or for urgent cases. Mail order books. Sell Neal's Yard Apothecary creams etc. Visiting speakers available for groups. Register. Concessions. First consultation: £25 (adult), £20 (child); follow-up appointments £15 (adult), £10 (child) includes medicines etc. 'Acutes' clinic £5 for 15-20 min consultation.

Lewisham Homoeopathic Clinic
26 Clarendon Rise, London SE13 5EY. (081) 852 0573.
Homoeopathy.

Life Directions
9 Cork St, Mayfair, London W1X 1PD. (071) 439 3806.
Assertion Therapy, Management Training, Stress Management. Based in Cambridge, but some courses in London. Also in-house training for companies. Wheelchair access. Three day weekend workshop £75. Concessions.

Life Training Centre
35a Chepstow Road, Notting Hill, London W2. (071) 727 0652.
Self Esteem Enhancement: 5 sessions in small groups normally evenings, including audio tapes, occasional weekend format also available. Life Training Weekend: 35 hour intensive training in self-awareness, including practical exercises which can be used for personal development work in daily life. Follow up groups take the form of self-led meetings once a week for support and continuation of the work of the courses. Training is available for teachers of

the Self Esteem course. Advanced focus courses include: relationships, communication, sexuality, effective parenting. Self Esteem course £60 (including 5 session tapes). Life Training weekend £150. Advanced courses (2 day) £95.

Lifecare
14 Lindeth Close, Old Church Lane, Stanmore, Middx. (081) 954 3545.
Aromatherapy, Hypnotherapy, Neuro-linguistic Programming, Reflexology, Stress Management. Workshops in aromatherapy and reflexology and personal growth. Run 'Breakthrough' course. Specialise in corporate stresses and commuter stress, claustrophobia and flight phobias. Cost varies: between £35-55 per day; one to one sessions £25 per hour.

Lifespace
21a Ospringe Rd, London NW5. (071) 584 8819.
Client-centered Therapy, Gestalt Therapy, Transactional Analysis. Bodywork, eating disorders. Training in groupwork, individual and group therapy, weekend workshops, professional consultancy and training and non-managerial supervision. Summer workshop in Italy. Individual sessions £20-£25. Workshops £20-£23 (with reductions for a series). Concessions.

Lifeworks
11 Southampton Road, London NW5. (071) 267 0269.
Acupuncture, Aromatherapy, Colonic Irrigation, Healing, Homoeopathy, Martial Arts, Massage, Naturopathy, Osteopathy, Reflexology, Reiki. First session £30-£45, subsequent sessions £20-£25 for an hour.

Lincoln Centre and Institute of Psychotherapy
19 Abbeville Mews, 88 Clapham Park, London SW4. (071) 978 1545.
Psychoanalytic Therapy. Referral required from GP (or other doctor) to clinical director. Founded and incorporated in 1967 as a registered charity. Fees: a) low fee scheme by trainees £8 per session, three times a week; b) otherwise typically £25 per session. They offer a training in psychotherapy.

Living Art Training
11 Stowe Road, Ravenscourt Park, London W12 8QB. (081) 749 0874.
Living Art has been running for 15 years. Personal and spiritual growth through painting and other creative work i.e. movement, chanting, music, meditation. Weekend workshops. Advance booking only. £86 + VAT for weekend workshops. Approx £260 + VAT for a week in the country, fully residential, materials supplied.

Living Centre
12a Durham Road, Raynes Park, London SW20. (081) 946 2331.
Alexander Technique, Allergy Therapy, Aromatherapy, Counselling, Diet Therapy Therapy, Homoeopathy, Hypnotherapy, Massage, Osteopathy, Reflexology, Shiatsu, Yoga Preventative Dentistry, Art Classes and Chi Kung. Meditation meetings led by monks and nuns from Chithurst Buddhist Monastery (free). The centre comprises fifteen rooms and large lecture room. Intensive courses on massage, yoga and shiatsu. Near to Raynes Park British Rail station and the A3. £10 - £50 per session.

Living Colour
33 Lancaster Grove Swiss Cottage London NW3. (071) 794 1371.
Colour Therapy. Run courses on body consciousness and the effects of colour. Individual therapy and courses from colour awareness to colour counselling. They perform colour analysis for clothes so that you can find the colour that suits you best. Cost: £30 per one hour session, thereafter £20 per session. They offer a training in Colour Therapy.

Living Qabalah
5 Hindmans Road, London SE22 9NF. (081) 693 9951.
Kabbalah, Psychosynthesis. Psychotherapy, teaching seminars in Qabalah, Tarot and Magick. Individual guidance and groupwork, public workshops that include dance, ritual, meditation, psychological exercises, visualisation etc. Public meetings in rented workshop spaces, individual work at centre. Sample price: £30 for a one day workshop.

London Aikido Club
4 Bath Street, London EC1. (071) 253 7434 /(081) 590 7722.
Courses and classes from basic to advanced in Takemusu Aikido. Also courses in weapons training.

London Association of Primal Psychotherapists
18A Laurier Road , Tufnel Park , London NW5 1SH. (071) 267 9616.
Primal therapy based on the work of Alice Miller and Arthur Janov. The centre has been established since 1986. They are five psychotherapists trained by Janov. Interviews on application. Therapy offered in Ger-

LIST OF CENTRES

man, French, Spanish, Italian and Norwegian. £32.50 per hour. Low cost therapy at £12 per hour available with training therapists. They offer a training in Primal Therapy.

London Buddhist Centre
51 Roman Road, Bethnal Green, London E2 OHU. (081) 981 1225.
Buddhism, Meditation, Retreats. Centre of the Friends of the Western Buddhist order, founded by the Venerable Sangharakshita, an Englishman who spent 20 years in India as a monk. Seek to synthesise elements from all Buddhist traditions. Day and evening classes, weekends in meditation and Buddhism. Own retreat centre in Suffolk, women's retreat centre in Shropshire and men's in Norfolk and Wales. Weds introductory evening £5, £3 concessions. Introductory Meditation course £60, £40 concessions. Residential weekend retreat £60, £40 all inclusive. Residential Mon-Fri retreat £150 all inclusive.

London Centre for Clinical Hypnotherapy
Red Lion Square, London WC1. (071) 499 2813.
Hypnotherapy. Individual consultations and workshops. Self improvement cassettes. £60 per session.

London Co-counselling Community
17 Lisburne Road, Hampstead, London NW3 2NS. (071) 485 0005.
Co-counselling. You must do the training to become a member. In London there are about 700 members and more in the UK and worldwide. They do a newsletter which is now more a journal on co-counselling. Various workshops.

London College of Classical Homoeopathy
Morley College, 61 Westminster Bridge Road, London SE1 7HT. (081) 540 6041.
Homoeopathy. Telephone or call for appointment for clinic. Fees by donation (are applying for charity status).

London College of Massage and Shiatsu
c/o Portland Place London W1N 3AF. (071) 978 8150
Aromatherapy, Massage, Reflexology, Shiatsu. Tuition from beginner to practitioner level. Weekend and/or part-time evening courses. Drop in evenings . Massage and shiatsu videos available. Weekends £60. 10 week course, one evening per week plus full day £204 including VAT.

London College of Osteopathic Medicine
8-10 Boston Place Marylebone London NW1 6QH. (071) 262 1128.
Osteopathic Association clinic, established 1927. Registered charity ostensibly to provide treatment for those who cannot afford usual private fees. Appointments always necessary. Payment by voluntary contribution. Target cost price of first treatment £10, follow up £8. Training in Osteopathy.

London Dharmadhatu
27 Belmont Close, Clapham, London SW4. (071) 720 3207.
Buddhism, Meditation, Retreats. Part of Vajradhatu, an international Buddhist organisation founded by the Tibetan teacher the Ven Chogyam Trungpa Rinpoche of the Kagyu School. His books such as *Cutting Through Spiritual Materialism*, and *Shambhala* are an excel-

lent guide to the spirit of Buddhism framed in western terms. Provide Shambhala Training, a secular meditation programme. Retreats in Ireland. Events, classes include study and meditation practice.

London Group
BM Vixack, London WC1N 3XX.
Paganism.

London Institute for the Study of Human Sexuality
Flat C, Langham Mansions, Earls Court Square, London SW5 9UH . (071) 373 0901.
Couple Therapy, Feminist Therapy, Sex Therapy. Run weekend workshops, talks, women's sexuality groups, AIDS counselling and sex education courses. Training in Sex Therapy.

London Kagyu Centre
Unit 21F Perseverance Works, 38 Kingsland Road, London E2. (071) 609 8591.
Buddhism, Meditation. Tibetan Buddhist group under the direction of Lama Chime Rinpoche. Meditation/puja Weds evening.

London Natural Health Clinic
Arnica House, 170 Campden Hill Road, Notting Hill Gate, London W8 7AS. (071) 938 3788.
Homoeopathy, Osteopathy, Acupuncture, Naturopathy, Medical Herbalism, Aromatherapy, Massage, Reflexology, Kirlian Photographic Diagnosis, Natural Trihology for the Skin, Scalp and Hairloss.

London School of T'Ai Chi Chuan
45 Blenheim Road, Bedford Park, London W4 1ET. (071) 400 6580.

Tai Chi. Teaches Yang family style short form. Runs beginners and advanced classes. The beginners' form is taught in 3 thirds, each third being offered in 10 hours of weekly class, 3 times a year. As in an academic year, if a student starts in the Autumn season, the he/she can expect to learn the entire form by the end of the Spring season. It's best to do an introductory class, which are offered at the beginning of each season. Residential trainings in Europe and America. £40 per course, £20 per extra course in the same season. Concessions.

London Society for Ericksonian Psychotherapy and Hypnosis

1 Mill Lane, Stedham, Midhurst, West Sussex GU29 ORS. 083 081 5613.
Hypnotherapy. Provides workshop education in Ericksonian psychotherapy for those with a qualification in one off the recognised helping professions (psychology, nursing, medicine, social work etc) and to full-time students on courses leading to such a qualification.

London Soto Zen Group

23 Westbere Road, Cricklewood, London NW2. (071) 794 3109.
Buddhism, Meditation. Affiliated to Throssel Hole Priory (see 'Retreats' section), practice Soto Zen Buddhism as taught by the Order of Buddhist Contemplatives. Evenings, weekends and courses on meditation and Buddhist ceremony.

London Sufi Centre

21 Lancaster Road, Notting Hill, London W11 1QL. (071) 221 3215.
Meditation, Retreats, Sufism. The Centre was founded to offer genuine spiritual training for those interested in the Sufi path, and aims to be non-sectarian. Founded by Hazrat Inayar Khan. Present Head of Order Pir Vilayat Kahn, who visits the UK. Holds classes on their teachings and on traditional Sufi practices including meditation, dance, prayers, breath and sound, visualisation etc. Healing course and service. Individual retreats at the London Centre, group retreats (meditation, sacred dance, chanting, etc.) and residential UK Sufi Summer Camp, both at Hourne Farm, Essex. £3 per evening.

London Zen Society

10 Belmont Street, Camden, London NW1 8HH. (071) 485 9576.
Buddhism, Meditation, Retreats. Rinzai sect Zen group, offshoot of Ryutaku-Jai monastery in Mishima, Japan, whose abbot is Kyudo Nakagawa Roshi. Sitting every day: Monday-Friday 6-8pm, Weds 7-9pm and Thurs 6-8am. 7 day retreats at centre, day sesshins. Basic instruction given to beginners. Resident monk at centre. No charge for classes.

Lucis Trust

Suite 54, 3 Whitehall Court, Victoria, London SW1 2EF. (071) 839 4512.
The Lucis trust administers a number of programmes: The Arcane School, a meditation school run by correspondence; Triangles, which is a global network of individuals from different spiritual paths who use prayer and meditation to spread goodwill in the world; World Goodwill, which publishes material presenting a global spiritual perspectives on the issues facing humanity; and Lucis Press which publishes Alice Bailey's books. Free lending library of esoteric books available in London. Meetings fortnightly in the Charing Cross Hotel. Meditation meetings at the time of the full moon, and lectures on healing, ecology, development, metaphysics etc at the time of the new moon .Bimonthly journal, 'The Beacon', and quarterly, World Goodwill newsletter.

M

Maitri

Little Abshott Road, Titchfield, Hants PO14 4LN. (0489) 572451.
Assertion, Bioenergetics, Enlightenment Intensives, Massage, Meditation, Polarity Therapy, Resonance Therapy, Shiatsu. Run a variety of residential growth workshops in Hants.

Man To Man

17 Mackeson Road, London NW3 2LU. (071) 482 3588.
Men's Therapy, and individual therapy. Evening and weekend personal growth groups for men. Admission to evening groups by interview only. Open to men of any sexual orientation. £8 per evening session. £50 per weekend, £70 per residential weekend.

Manjushri London Centre

10 Finsbury Park Road, Finsbury, London N4 2JZ. (071) 359 1394.
Buddhism, Meditation, Retreats. Group following Gelug school of the Tibetan Buddhist tradition. Resident teachers are Geshe Namgyal Wangchen (who is resident in the UK) and Lama Thubten Zopa Rinpoche (who

visits). Run evening and week-end groups on meditation and Buddhist philosophy. Have residential communities where members live. Occasional retreats in the UK. Gompa (shrine room for meditation), book-shop, tea-room and library. Open for drop-in visits every day except Tues from 2pm. Puja Sunday morning. Large retreat centre/monastery in Cumbria. 3 evening (£1.50 concessions).

Marigold Treatment Centre
134 Montrose Avenue, Edgware, Middlesex HA8 0DR. (081) 959 5421.
Herbalism. Approximately £25 per session plus remedies.

Martial Arts Commission
First Floor, Broadway House, 15-16 Deptford Broadway, London SE8. (081) 691 8711.
Contact for details of approved martial arts clubs in London.

McCarthy Westwood Consultants
25 Kite House, The Falklands, Grant Road, London SW11 2NJ. (071) 585 3445.
Aromatherapy, Bach, Diet Therapy, Hypnotherapy, Stress Management. Management Courses in stress management and aromatherapy.

Mehta Method of Therapeutic Head Massage
14 Stranraer Way, Freeling Street, Off Caledonian Road, London N1 0DR .
Massage, Osteopathy. Indian head, neck and scalp massage which has been practiced in India for over 1,000 years. Also offer weekend training courses in head massage. Prices available on request.

Melissa Morant Centre
7 Heath Villas, The Vale Of Health, London NW3 1AW. (071) 435 8787.
Homoeopathy, Shiatsu. Individual Shiatsu sessions as well as workshops - £36 per weekend .

Meridians Clinic
40 Weymouth Street, London W1. (071) 935 5136.
Acupuncture, Massage, Reflexology. Physiotherapy, manipulative therapy. Established for 9 years, with three treatment rooms. Appointment only. Tea, chat and music on offer. All practitioners are registered or chartered. Initial session £30, £23 subsequent sessions. £16 students and unwaged FREE.

Metamorphic Association
67 Ritherdon Road, London SW17 8QE. (081) 672 5951.
Metamorphic Technique. Established 7 years. Meeting/session room, office and display for books and other material. Mail order, sell books, cassettes and other products. Open day twice a month. Offer home visits for the disabled in the Greater London Area. Wheelchair access. Journal 'Metamorphosis' 3 times a year, £1.50 each.£18 per 1 hour session. £50 for a 12 hour weekend workshop. Home visits: cost of transport for practitioner and donations.

Metanoia
13 North Common Road, Ealing Common, London W5. (081) 579 2505 .
Couple Therapy, Family Therapy, Gestalt Therapy, Transactional Analysis. Training in Gestalt and Transactional Analysis.

Micheline Arcier Aromatherapy
7 William Street , London SW1X 9Hl. (071) 235 3545 .
Aromatherapy. Established 9 years. Mail order. Initial consultation half hour £14. One hour treatment £28. They offer a training in Aromatherapy.

Mill Hill Health Care
3 Hankins Lane, Mill Hill, London NW7 3AA. (081) 959 1752.
Bach, Counselling, Diet Therapy, Radiathesia, Reflexology. Small centre (private house). Established 10 years, no drop-in. £12-£15. Concessions.

Minster Centre
57 Minster Road , Cricklewood, London NW2 3SH. (071) 435 9200 .
Assertion Therapy, Biosynthesis, Couple Therapy, Feminist Therapy, Gestalt Therapy, Group Oriented Therapy, Psychodrama, Stress Management, Transactional Analysis. Work in groups and individual sessions. Also run professional programme of specialist workshops for those in the helping professions. Cost varies for groups and weekends. Individual sessions £6 minimum. They offer a training in psychotherapy.

Movement of Spiritual Inner Awareness
1 Harcourt Street, London W1H 1D. (071) 262 0623.
Retreats.

Moving Line Counselling and Therapy
c/o 13 Oldfield Mews, London N6 . North London: (081) 341 4413; South-East London (081) 656 9209, East London (071) 790 8146, South-West London (071) 733 7883.
Counselling, Psychosynthesis. Londonwide counselling and therapy network using the methods and perspective of psychosynthesis. Individual ses-

LIST OF CENTRES

sions, couples, workshops. £13-20 per session.

Mu Sum Ba
93 Percy Road, London W12 9QH. (081) 743 7246.
Music therapy. Self development through rhythm awareness in group format only. Ring for details of workshops.

Mushindokai
12 Finchley Park, North Finchley, London N12 9JN .
Buddhist martial art.

Nafsiyat Inter-Cultural Therapy Centre
278 Seven Sisters Road, Finsbury Park, London N4. (071) 263 4130.
Specialises in offering psychotherapy to people from ethnic and cultural minorities. Runs workshops and seminars for people in the helping professions to enable them to work across other cultures, including the Diploma in Intercultural Therapy (run in association with University College, London). Also in-service training for organisations. Individual sessions free to Islington residents, otherwise sliding scale. Workshops usually £50 for two days.

Napier Chiropractic Clinic
141 Golders Green Road, London NW11 8HG . (081) 458 3311.
Chiropody, Chiropractic, Massage. Established 4 years. By appointment only. Two treatment rooms and two chiropractors, masseuse and chiropodist. Concessions. Wheelchair ac-

cess. Consultation £35, Chiropodist treatment £22. X-ray if necessary £40. Massage £25/hr.

Natale Institute London
118 Peckham Park Road, London SE15 5U2. (071) 732 8792.
Offers personal development and experiential educational courses in self esteem, effective communication, channelling, mastering relationships and sexuality. London branch of The Natale Institute, which is an international organisation. Organise and promote individual therapists or lecturers. Wheelchair access for courses held in Kensington Town Hall. £160 for one weekend (two and a half days), £350 for 2 weekends plus three days.

National Council and Register of Iridologists
80 Portland Road, Bournemouth BH9 1NQ.
Iridology. Register of trained iridologists available with SAE.

National Federation of Spiritual Healers
Old Manor Farm Studio, Church Street, Sunbury-On-Thames, Middlesex TW16 6RG. (0932) 783164/5.
Healing. The head office of NFSH has been here for 12 years, looking after the needs of members and running a national referral register for those seeking a healer. Sell books and tapes, and publish 'Healing Review' quarterly (£1, free to members). Courses and training in healing and its aspects. Approximately £110-£125 per training weekend.

National Institute of Medical Herbalists
41 Hatherley Road, Winchester, Hants SO22 6RR. (071) 228 4417.

Herbalism. Established in 1864, this is the oldest body of professional practitioners in the world. They have an annual conference for members. Maintain a register of qualified members, who must adhere to a code of ethics and practice. Members train on a four year course at School of Herbal Medicine in Sussex. Typically practitioners charge £15 - £20 plus remedies for initial consultation, £10 - £15 thereafter.

Natural Family Planning Teachers
c/o Mrs Rosalind Byrne, 51 Ditton Road, Surbiton, Surrey KT6 6RF. (081) 399 4789.
London co-ordinator for Natural family planning teachers.

Natural Healing Centre
1A New Pond Parade, West End Road, Ruislip Gardens, Middlesex HA4 6LR. (0895) 675464.
Acupuncture, Allergy, Allergy Therapy, Bach, Counselling, Herbalism, Homoeopathy, Radionics, Reflexology. This small centre has been established for eight years. £18 for initial consultation, £15 subsequent except acupuncture which is £25 for initial consultation, and psychotherapy and hypnotherapy which is £18 per session.

Natural Healing Centre
165 Capel Rd, London E7 0JT. (081) 478 3942.
Acupuncture, Alexander Technique, Allergy Therapy, Aromatherapy, Chiropody, Counselling, Homoeopathy, Hypnotherapy, Laser Therapy, Magnetic Therapy, Massage, Osteopathy, Polarity Therapy, Reflexology, Beauty Therapy and slimming clinic, Hellerwork, Cranio-Sacral Therapy. Established in 1972, there are eleven therapists working at this centre. Books and products are sold.

Wheelchair access. Creche facilities. Prices vary from £27-55.

Natural Health Clinic
286 Preston Road, Harrow, Middlesex. (081) 908 4272.
Allergy Therapy, Diet Therapy Therapy, Homoeopathy, Shiatsu. This clinic has been established since 1984 and people can drop in. Mail order: vitamins, minerals, essential oils and homoeopathic medicines. Initial consultation £12 plus cost of medicines.

Natural Medicine Centre
87 Beckenham Lane, Shortlands, Bromley BR2 0DN. (081) 460 1117.
Acupuncture, Aromatherapy, Gestalt Therapy, Herbalism, Homoeopathy, Homoeopathy, Hypnotherapy, Massage, Reflexology, Shiatsu. Biomobility offered. Two therapy rooms. 9-9pm Mon-Sat. Two steps for wheelchair. £16-30 for first session. Concessions.

Nature Cure Clinic
15 Oldbury Place, Marylebone, London W1M 3AL. (071) 935 6213.
Acupuncture, Diet Therapy, Diet Therapy Therapy, Massage, Naturopathy, Osteopathy, Physiotherapy. Registered charity for those unable to afford private treatment. All patients see a qualified doctor on their first visit. Consultations by appointment only. Founded in 1928. Occasional lectures. Mailing list sent on request. Wheelchair access. £15 for first consultation. £7.50 for subsequent visits. Register of practitioners. Concessions.

Naturemed Partnership
Silver Birches, Private Road, Rodborough Common, Stroud, Gloucs GL5 5BT. (045387)
3446.
Major centre in UK for Spagyrik therapy, also offer herbalism, AK, reflexology and Flyborg therapy. Register. Car parking facilities. Wheelchair access. £20 per session.

Natureworks
16 Balderton Street, London W1. (071) 355 4036.
Acupuncture, Allergy Therapy, Aromatherapy, Colour Therapy, Counselling, Crystal Therapy, Healing, Herbalism, Homoeopathy, Hypnotherapy, Naturopathy, Neuro-linguistic Programming, Osteopathy, Reflexology, Relaxation Training, Shiatsu, Stress Management, Qigong, Chinese physiotherapy, clinic for those coming off tranquillisers. Types of massage available are: Eyerman technique, foot pressure massage, Indian head and neck massage, remedial massage. Also available at this centre are acuflex reflexology, fitness assessments, diet counselling, lifestyle management. Based in a dance centre, also dance and movement classes, body conditioning clinic (pilates). Prices range from £15-35.

Neal's Yard Therapy Rooms
2 Neal's Yard, Covent Garden, London WC2 H9D. (071) 379 7662.
Acupuncture, Alexander Technique, Aromatherapy, Autogenic Training, Bach, Biodynamic Massage, Biofeedback, Chiropractic, Colour Therapy, Cranial Osteopathy, Diet Therapy, Diet Therapy Therapy, Healing, Herbalism, Homoeopathy, Hypnotherapy, Iridology, Massage, Naturopathy, Osteopathy, Polarity Therapy, Reflexology, Sex Therapy, Shiatsu, Touch For Health, Psychic Counselling and Clairvoyance.
Established 1982. People can drop in for a chat, information, guidance on which therapy to choose. Toy box available for children. Information pack can be sent countrywide. Advice freely given even to non residents of South East. £20-35 for first consultation, from £15-25 for follow-ups.

New Cross Natural Therapy Centre
394 New Cross Road, London SE14. (081) 469 0858.
Acupuncture, Alexander Technique, Cranial Osteopathy, Diet Therapy Therapy, Gestalt Therapy, Herbalism, Homoeopathy, Massage, Metamorphic Technique, Neuro-linguistic Programming, Osteopathy, Polarity Therapy, Postural Integration, Psychoanalytic Therapy, Reflexology, Reiki, Touch for Health (Kinesiology), Yoga. Next to New Cross tube. Limited access. Creche by arrangement. Limited parking. Established 1985. Mostly run by women. Women practitioner available for all but Shiatsu. £24 initial consultation, thereafter £18. Concessions. Informal, collectively run, transport.

New Life Lodge
60 Gloucester Road, Brownswood, London N4 2LN. (081) 800 3831.
Biodynamic Massage, Hypnotherapy, Massage. Mid life career counselling

Nichirin Shoshu of the United Kingdom
1 The Green, Richmond, Surrey. (081) 948 0381/2.
Buddhism. Founded on the teaching of Nichiren Daishonin who lived in 13th century Japan. Main practice is mantra chanting.

Nimatullahi
41 Chepstow Place, Notting Hill Gate, London W2 4TS. (071) 229 0769.
Sufism. Centre of traditional Sufi order under the direction of the Master Dr Javad Hurbakush who is in residence. Order established in 1400, London centres since 1976. Meditation takes place twice a week. Call or write for appointment. Books and journals about Sufism are available in English, French and Persian. Wheelchair access. Events free.

Nine Needles Health Care Centre
121 Sheen road, Richmond upon Thames, Surrey TW9 1YJ. (081) 940 8892.
Acupuncture, Shiatsu. Established in the UK since 1987, appointments only Monday to Saturday. Practitioner trained in Japan, where he operated his own clinic for 7 years. Holds Japanese licence. First acupuncture session £25, thereafter £20. Shiatsu £22. Concessions. They offer a training in Acupuncture and Shiatsu.

Nordoff-Robbins Music Therapy Centre
6 Queensdale Walk, London W11 4QQ.
Music therapy. Music therapy for children with special needs, normally one half-hour session per week. Established 1981 when 14 children attended weekly for their sessions. Now between 70-80 children come weekly, some in small groups. Two conferences annually. Discussions, illustrated with video material of the work are arranged for individuals and small groups. One termly parents meetings. Scale of costs is confidential, according to parents' means. They offer a training in Music therapy.

North London Centre for Group Therapy
138 Bramley Rd, Oakwood, Southgate, London N14 4HU. (081) 440 1451.
Couple Therapy, Family Therapy, Group Oriented Therapy and Individual Psychotherapy. Established 12 years. Referrals are usually made through a GP. Other professionals in related fields may also refer, and individuals seeking psychotherapy can contact the centre direct. Individuals, couples and families are offered an initial consultation, at which the appropriate form of therapy is considered. They offer services to mental health professionals such as individual supervision, group supervision, consultations to professionals and staff groups and work discussion groups. Lunch time seminars and an annual group-analytic workshop (with residential facility). Group fees - £52 p.c.m. (one and half hour session per week). Concessions. Other fees are available on request.

North London Counselling Practice
11 Abbey View, Mill Hill, London NW7 4PB. (081) 959 7322.
Counselling, Couple Therapy, Sex Therapy. They are a group of trained counsellors and therapists, each working from home. Established three years. £25 per session. Willing to negotiate price.

North London Counselling Service
28 Northolme Road, Highbury, London N5 2UU. (071) 359 2356 .
A network of psychosynthesis counsellors and therapists working in the North London area. Individuals, couples, courses and workshops for groups. No access. £15-£20 per hour for individual sessions. Concessions.

Nutribiotics
35 Highview Avenue, Edgware, Middlesex HA8 9TX. (081) 958 7553.
Bach Flower Remedies, Counselling, Crystal Therapy, Diet Therapy Therapy, Herbalism, Homoeopathy. Strictly by prior appointment. Established 1986.

Oasis
72 Great North Road, East Finchley, London N2 ONL. (081) 340 3924.
Allergy, Gestalt, Relaxation Training, Touch For Health. Basic listening and counselling skills, Gestalt Therapy one-to-one, for couples, families and groups. Huna and Shamanistic Healing. Individual sessions £25 hour, groups £10 for a 2 and a half hour session.

Open Centre
188 Old Street, London EC1V 9BP. (081) 549 9583.
Bioenergetics, Encounter, Feldenkrais, Massage, Postural Integration, Psychodrama, Transactional Analysis. pulsing. Runs wide range of workshops using different therapeutic approaches. On-going groups and weekend workshops. The centre is situated in a complex housing a bookshop (Genesis) and the East West Restaurant. Weekend workshops from £50. On going groups from £8 - £12 per evening.

LIST OF CENTRES

Open Gate
6 Goldney Road, Clifton, Bristol. (0272) 7345952.
Run a variety of workshops and residentials on aspects of psychology and spirituality including Buddhism, dancing path workshops, myth, shamanism, creativity often with well known or distinguished speakers, group leaders and spiritual practitioners.

Order of Bards Ovates and Druids
260 Kew Road, Richmond, Surrey, TW9 3EG.

Orpheus Centre
PO Box 77, West Kensington, London W14 0QQ. (071) 603 0687.
Bach Flower Remedies, Colour Therapy, Crystal Therapy, Absent Healing, Inner Self Therapy, Relaxation Techniques, Colour Crystal Therapy. Nonpredictive astrology, tarot and dream interpretation. Advice on healing for animals. Workshops and courses. Sessions of one particular therapy approx £15, typical treatment which would include colour and crystal treatment, counselling and a foot massage (duration 2 hours) - £20.

P

Pagan Link
c/o 4 Caznove Road, London N16 6BD . (071) 263 5966.
Paganism. Pagan-Link meetings are held at the White Lion of Mortimer pub at Stroud Green Road, London N4, on alternate Thursday evenings. The meetings are friendly and informal and are open to people of all paths who are involved or simply interested in Paganism or the Occult and wish to exchange views and ideas. Contact Ray on the above number (eves) for details.

Pellin Centre
43 Killyon Road, Clapham, SW8 2XS. (071) 622 0148.
Feminist Therapy, Gestalt Therapy. Training in Gestalt.

Person-Centred Art Therapy Centre
17 Cranbourne Gardens , London NW11 0HN . (081) 455 8570.
Art Therapy, Person-Centred counselling, using art therapy and gestalt therapy when appropriate. Mainly one to one. Supervision. Individual plus group consultancy. House in residential area. £22 per hour. Workshops £28 per day per person in groups of 9.

Philadelphia Association
4 Marty's Yard, 17 Hampstead High Street, London NW3 1PX. (071) 794 2652.
Existential Psychotherapy, Psychoanalytic Therapy. No therapy practised at the centre but:1) network of private psychotherapist working from own homes or practices. Some group therapy possible. 2) Low cost residential therapeutic community households. Started 1965. No drop-in. Monthly lectures. Individual therapy £10-£25 per session. The houses are according to local DHSS board and lodging (not expensive).They offer a training in psychotherapy.

Playspace
Short Course Unit, Polytechnic Of Central London, 35 Marylebone Road, Marylebone, London NW1 5LS. (071) 486 5811 ext 465.
Art Therapy, Assertion, Dance Therapy, Dream, Feldenkrais, Gestalt, Group Oriented Therapy, Psychodrama, Voice Therapy. Runs a variety of part time courses in counselling and psychotherapy. Weekend workshop typically £38.

Playworld
2 Melrose Gardens, New Malden, Surrey . (081) 949 5498.
Workshops and events around the theme of finding oneself: creativity, mask-making, movement and rhythm etc. Various venues in London. £12 per whole day workshop. Concessions.

Polarity Therapy Association
33 Dudley Court, Upper Berkley Street, Marble Arch, London W1H 7PH.
Polarity Therapy. List of qualified practitioners.

Primrose Healing Centre
9 St George's Mews, Primrose Hill, London NW1 8XE. (071) 586 0148.
Acupuncture, Alexander Technique, Aromatherapy, Bach, Bach Flower Remedies, Counselling, Diet Therapy, Diet Therapy, Healing, Herbalism, Homoeopathy, Hypnotherapy, Massage, Naturopathy, Osteopathy, Polarity Therapy, Rebirthing, Reflexology, Reiki, Shiatsu, Stress Management, Voice Therapy.

Private Health Centre
37 Green Street, Forest Gate, London E7 8DA. (081) 472 0170.
Acupuncture, Chiropody, Homoeopathy, Massage, Osteopathy, Reflexology. Herbal teas, remedies and herbal shampoos are also sold here. Prices

LIST OF CENTRES

vary between £12- 35 depending on the practitioner and the treatment.

Private Polyclinic
142 Green Street, Forest Gate, London E7. (081) 472 0170.
Acupuncture, Ayurevedic Medicine, Chiropody, Herbalism, Homoeopathy, Massage, Osteopathy, Yoga. plus specialist for consultants in orthodox medicine, X-ray dept, path. lab. There is health shop at the centre where remedies, minerals, vitamins, books, joint and back supports etc are sold. Monthly talks for doctors where local GPs are invited. Wheelchair access. £16-23 initial consultation, £12-18 thereafter.

Psychosynthesis and Education Trust
48 Guildford Road, Stockwell, London SW8 2BU . (071) 633 8295.
Psychosynthesis. Run public programme of courses on various topics from a psychosynthesis perspective (e.g. dreams, woman's identity, relationship with money, body etc). Also ongoing interpersonal groups, lectures. Course on psychosynthesis and education, and a young adults group for those between the ages of 15 and 20. Counselling service. Professional training in psychosynthesis. Mail order books and publications. Sliding scale for one to one counselling, public weekends £50.

Psychotherapy Centre
1 Wythburn Place, London W1H 5WL. (071) 723 6173.
Wholistic investigative psychotherapy for emotional problems, relationship difficulties etc. Established 1959. Quiet accessible building. To get 16 page brochure write stating your problem and enclose £2. Practitio-

ners available in the south of London too. Extensive range of publications. Training prospectus available. From £36 per 50 minute session, depending on which practitioner you see. Advanced trainees under supervision charge less.

Psychotherapy for Individuals, Couples & Groups
110 The Avenue, London N10. (081) 365 3951.
Assertion Therapy, Bereavement Counselling, Gestalt Therapy. Use other approaches where appropriate, such as visualisation, family sculpting, sensitivity awareness. They belong to the Spectrum incest intervention project, working with survivors and perpetrators. Established eight years. Work in North and South London. £25-£30 for individual work. £30-£60 for couples work. £65 for weekends. Concessions.

Psychotherapy Workshops for Women
97 Warren Road, Whitton, Middlesex. (081) 755 0353.
Biodynamic Massage, Feminist Therapy. Groups for women: ongoing, weekend workshops, individual sessions in London and Brighton. Weekend workshops £50 including Friday evenings. Concessions.

Putney Natural Therapy Clinic
11 Monserat Road, Putney, London SW15. (081) 789 2548.
Acupuncture, Aromatherapy, Chiropody, Diet Therapy Therapy, Herbalism, Homoeopathy, Massage, Naturopathy, Osteopathy, Reflexology, Shiatsu. Small friendly centre. Professional and confidential consultation. You can drop in (best between 9.30-3) for information.

Leaflet available or ring for advice. Occasional workshops. Wheelchair access. Prices between £20-30 per session. Chiropody £13 a session. Concessions.

R

Radiance Education Unlimited
24 Duncan House, 7 Fellows Road, London NW3 3LS. (071) 586 2980.
Reiki. Established in England for 6 years. Introductory talks and seminars, books and tapes. Register. Reiki Session £25, seminar £110. Concessions available.

Radix
90 Viceroy Close, Edgbaston, Birmingham B5 7UU. (021) 440 6129.
Radix is a form of neo-Reichian bodywork which aims to help students learn to increase awareness of their emotions, and reduce blocking of life energy as it flows through the body. Occasional workshops in London, and can refer you to local London practitioners.

Raphael Clinic
211 Sumatra Road, West Hampstead, London NW6 1PF. (071) 794 0321.
Healing, Massage, Meditation. Holistic healing centre. Also weekend courses including meditation, massage, dance, personal mythology, healing etc. Weekend courses £69 plus VAT.

Raworth Centre
"Smallburgh', Beare Green, Dorking, Surrey RH5 4QA. (0306) 712623.

LIST OF CENTRES

Aromatheapy, Diet Therapy, Kinesiology, Massage, Reflexology. Full and part-time study training courses.

Re-Vision
8 Chatsworth Road, London NW2 4BN. (081) 451 2165.
Psychosynthesis. Re-Vision is a small organisation started in 1988 offering psychosynthesis training courses to practising counsellors, therapists and others in the caring professions who are wanting to widen their perspective of work. In addition, run self-development workshops in psychosynthesis, and some other therapies (e.g. gestalt, Jungian etc). Open evenings, network of therapists available for individual, couple or family therapy, supervision for professionals, in-service consultancy or training offered to organisations within the caring professions.

Rebirthing Centre
Flat B, 2 Wandsworth Common West Side, Wandsworth, London SW18 2EL. (081) 870 9284.
Rebirthing. also dreamwork, the inner child, goal setting, balancing, the masculine/feminine polarities. Phone to make an appointment for a free introductory talk. Established for five years. Register of practitioners kept. £40 for an individual session which can last for two hours. Concessions.

Redwood Women's Training Association
Invergary, Kitlings Lane, Walton-on-the-Hill, Stafford ST17 0LE . 0785 662823.
Anti-smoking Therapy, Assertion Therapy, Feminist Therapy, Sex Therapy, Voice Therapy. Founded in 1980 by Anne Dickson, this is the administrative office for a network of train-

ers all over the country. Can help individuals, groups or organisations find trainer, send £3 for one year's subscription to bi-annual programme.

Refuah Shelaymah Natural Health Centre
42c Braydon Road, London N16 6QB, . (081) 800 2200.
Colonic Irrigation, Counselling, Diet Therapy Therapy, Herbalism, Osteopathy, Polarity Therapy. Established for 2 years, this is a centre with 3 rooms, two of which are fully wheelchair accessible. Telephone advice line of the Natural Health Network. Creche facilities a possibility. First half hour consultation is free. Full fee £25 first session, £18 subsequently. Concessions down to £5 for some therapies. Colon hydrotherapy £36.

Register of Traditional Chinese Medicine
19 Trinity Road, London N2 8JJ. (081) 883 8431.
Professional association for acupuncturists whose training and practice embody techniques of diagnosis and treatment used in the People's Republic of China. Directory of Practitioners £1.50.

Reiki Centre
12b Steels Road, Chalk Farm, London NW3 4SE. (071) 586 3363.
Aston Patterning, Astrological Psychotherapy, Reiki. Aston Patterning.

Resonance
18 Station Terrace, Great Linford, Milton Keynes, Bucks MK14 5AP. (0908) 605931.
Encounter, Gestalt Therapy, Group Oriented Therapy and courses on humanistic psychotherapy. This is not a drop-in centre. Established 12 years in the UK. Telephone or write for

appointments in individual psychotherapy. Programme available (send SAE). They do training groups and talks etc for groups of people working together. Consultancy service available. Supervision for practising counsellors/therapists. Wheelchair access. £20 per hour for individual sessions. £25 per day for non residential groups. £8 per evening for ongoing encounter group.

Resonance
102 Ritherton Rd , London SW17 8QQ. (081) 673 1353 .
Aromatherapy, Art Therapy, Counselling, Couple Therapy, Creativity, Flotation Tank Therapy, Gestalt Therapy, Kirlian Diagnosis, Massage, Rebirthing, Reflexology, Tarot. Established two years. Best to ring for appointment, but you can drop in. They run courses in DMA(technologies for Creating); Tarot for beginners; Video evenings; a support group (Tuesday evenings; Dolphin workshops. One year apprenticeship in Shamanic Healing. Sell Oasis water filters, smudge sticks, books, crystals, essential oils, medicine bags, sacred crafts from all over the world. One large group room for hire (20'x16') plus three individual therapy rooms. Wheelchair access. Creche can be arranged. Individual sessions £18-25 per hour; Support group £7 per session; Video evening, £3; Weekend groups £50-70. Concs.

Richmond Natural Health Centre
New Road, Ham Common, Richmond,, Surrey TW10 7HYH. (081) 332 1751/2.
Various therapies on offer. Above address is not a business address. Telephone referral service only here, and therapist goes to the clients home.

306

LIST OF CENTRES

RIGPA Fellowship
44 St Paul's Crescent, Camden Town, London NW1 9TN. (071) 485 4342.
Buddhism, Meditation, Retreats. Tibetan Buddhist group under the direction of Ven. Lama Sogyal Rinpoche who visits the centre and gives lectures and seminars and leads retreats in Britain, France and Germany. Courses are led by the Lama and eminent teachers of different traditions on topics such as meditation, developing compassion, healing, care for the dying and Buddhist view and philosophy. Bookshop. Centre open for meetings and by appointment. £3 evening class. Concessions.

Royal London Homoeopathic Hospital
Gt. Ormond St, Bloomsbury, London WC1. (071) 837 3091 x 72.
Homoeopathy. NHS Hospital.

S

Satyananda Yoga Centre
70 Thurleigh Road, Wandsworth, London SW12. (081) 673 4869.
Hinduism, Meditation, Yoga. Guru is Swami Satyananda Saraswati of who set up the Bihar School of Yoga in 1963 and has now gone into seclusion. Director is Swami Pragyamurti Saraswati who teaches at the centre, all over the UK, Eire and France, and organises the yearly visit to ashram in India. Practice through yoga and teach asanas (postures), breathing practices, relaxation, meditation and yo-

gic cleansing practices. Classes, courses and seminars. Children's yoga classes. Concessions.

Sayer Clinic Covent Garden
12/13 Henrietta Street, London WC2E 8LH. 497 2741.
See Sayer Clinic Marble Arch clinic for details.

Sayer Clinic Kensington
8 Sunningdale Gardens, Stratford Road, London W8 6PX. 937 8978.
See Sayer Clinic Marble Arch for details.

Sayer Clinic
Marble Arch, 22 Seymour Street, London W1. 723 2725.
Acupuncture, Chiropody, Chiropractic, Homoeopathy, Massage, Osteopathy, Reflexology. Sports/dance injury clinic, gynaecology clinic, physiotherapy.

School of Complementary Medicine
9 Sharpleshall Street, Primrose Hill, London NW1 8YN. (071) 586 1263.
Training course to become a general practitioner in the field of Complementary Medicine which includes Chinese acupuncture, shiatsu, acupressure, massage, reflexology, touch for health, kineosiotherapy, herbalism, bach flower remedies, nutrition, psychosomatic medicine, counselling skills, TA techniques, NLP, Chi Kung exercises, anatomy and physiology — one training course includes all of these, plus the general principles of complementary medicine.

School of Electro-Crystal Therapy
117 Long Drive, South Ruislip, Middlesex HA4 0HL. (081) 841 1716.
Crystal Therapy. Electro-crystal

therapy only. Established for 9 years. Lectures throughout UK and abroad. Books. Wheelchair access. £15 per hour for treatments. Concessions available.

School of Hypnosis and Advanced Psychotherapy
28 Finsbury Park Road, N4 2JX. (071) 359 6991.
Hypnotherapy, Neuro-linguistic Programming, Ericksonian hypnosis. Register of graduates from the school. They offer a training in Hypnotherapy.

School of Meditation
158 Holland Park Avenue, London W11 4UH. (071) 603 6116.
Meditation. Frequent public meetings. Ring office for details and they will send you a booklet. Public meetings are 60p. To learn the meditation it costs one week's wages, though they will look at each case individually and are likely to make concessions.

School of T'ai-chi Ch'uan - Centre for Healing
5 Tavistock Place, St. Pancras, London WC1H 9HH. (081) 459 0764.
Healing, Martial Arts, Meditation, Intuitive Foot Massage. Personal guidance, talks, workshops. Founded by Beverley Milne, director Ghislaine Picchio. Lending library of books and cassettes. Sell monographs, lecture cassettes, study papers. Workshops and lectures. Day workshop £22, evenings/afternoons £3. Some concessions available.

School of the Dancing Dragon
115 Manor Road, London N16 5PB. (081) 800 0471.
Counselling, Healing, Massage, Psychic Development. Massage

LIST OF CENTRES

is based on a combination of Swedish and intuitive massage and energy balancing. It is taught as a dance-like form. £15 - £30 per massage session. They offer a training in Massage and Healing.

School of Yoga
22 Old Farleigh Road, Selsdon, Surrey CR2 9PB.
Yoga.

Serpent Institute
18 Mark Mansions, Westville Rd, London W12 9PS. (081) 743 8124.
Counselling, Feminist Therapy. Psychotherapy for individuals and couples. Some talks and workshops. Sliding scale. They offer a training in psychotherapy.

Shanti Sadan
29 Chepstow Villas, Notting Hill Gate, London W11 3DR. 727 7846.
Hinduism, Meditation, Yoga. 'Shanti Sadan' is Sanskrit for 'Temple of Inner Peace', and it was founded in 1933 by Dr Hari Prasad Shastri, who died in 1956. His teachings are carried on here by his followers. These are on the philosophy and practice of Adhyatma Yoga, the yoga of self-knowledge, as taught in the ancient Indian classical texts, the Upanishads and Bhagavad Gita, and adapted to modern life. Lectures on Weds and Fris at 8pm during term time. Publish over 30 books on yoga and related subjects. Also lectures at other venues in central London. Public lectures and meditation courses are free - there is a voluntary collection.

Sheila Revell Centre
49 Ellora Road, Streatham, SW16 6JG. (081) 677 4685.
Bach Flower Remedies, Hypnotherapy, and Self Hypnosis.

Relaxation tapes. £28 per session. Courses of treatment which works out cheaper.

Shiatsu Society
19 Langside Park, Kilbarchan, Renfrewshire PA10 2EP. (05057) 4657.
Shiatsu. Register of practitioners. Network organisation for everyone interested in Shiatsu. Quarterly newsletter.

Shirley Goldstein Holistic Therapies
30 Gloucester Crescent, Camden Town, London NW1. (071) 267 2552.
Aromatherapy, Bach Flower Remedies, Counselling, Healing, Massage, Polarity Therapy, American Essences Diagnosis. Also sell massage tables and angel cards. Various courses. £25 per treatment. £200-£400 for courses. They offer a training in Massage.

Sivananda Yoga Vedanta Centre
50 Chepstow Villas, Notting Hill, London W11 2QY. (071) 229 7970.
Hinduism, Massage, Meditation, Yoga. Spiritual teacher is Swami Vishnu Devananda who visits the UK. Practice includes meditation, asanas, pranayama, chanting, study and Karma Yoga (see Yoga section). Classical approach to Hatha and Raja Yoga in daily classes. Daily meditations open to public, evening and weekend courses. Retreats at their ashrams in the Bahamas, India, Quebec, New York State and California. London centre open for drop-in with bookshop on premises.

Skills with People
15 Liberia Road, Islington, London N5 1JP. (071) 359 2370 or 368 3605.
Assertion, Counselling, Creativ-

ity, Group Oriented Therapy, Stress Management. Specialises in providing in-company training, and a wide range of interpersonal skills training. £30 - £40 a day for workshops

Society for the Study of Holistic Health
160 Upper Fant Raod, Maidstone, Kent ME16 8DJ.
Courses on natural theapies,

Society of Analytical Psychology
1 Daleham Gardens, Swiss Cottage, London NW3 5BY. (071) 435 7696.
Jungian Psychotherapy. Register. They offer a training in Jungian Psychotherapy.

Society of Students of Holistic Health
160 Upper Fant Road, Maidstone, Kent ME16 8DJ. (0622) 29231.
Alexander Technique, Aromatherapy, Cranial Osteopathy, Homoeopathy, Osteopathy. £18 - £28 for first consultation. £12 £18 thereafter.

Sound Health
261 Grove Street, Deptford, London SE8 3PZ. (081) 691 7519.
Voice Therapy. Voice work and singing as a therapeutic process; counselling with a humanistic and psychodynamic approach. Workshops. Individual sessions £30. Concessions.

South Camden Women's Centre
90 Cromer St, London WC1. (071) 278 0120.
Alexander Technique, Aromatherapy, Assertion Therapy, Healing, Herbalism, Homoeopathy, Self Defence, addictive relationships therapy and photography. Drop-in Mon, Tue, Thur, Fri 10-5 and Wed 10-1. An advice centre

LIST OF CENTRES

which operates a natural health clinic that run courses and workshops. Sliding scale £7-£18 for an individual session.

South London Hypnotherapy Association
Oaklands House, 29 Oaklands Road, Bromley, Kent. (081) 460 7578.
Hypnotherapy. £20 anti-smoking session. (£2 extra at evening and weekends), £18 per session for lack of confidence, depression etc. Also do past life regression.

South London Natural Health Centre
7A Clapham Common South Side, Clapham Common, London SW4 7AA. (071) 720 8817.
Acupuncture, Alexander Technique, Allergy, Aromatherapy, Chiropractic, Colonic Irrigation, Colour Therapy, Counselling, Cranial Osteopathy, Diet Therapy, Diet Therapy Therapy, Feldenkrais, Flotation Tank Therapy, Herbalism, Homoeopathy, Hypnotherapy, Massage, Naturopathy, Osteopathy, Reflexology, Shiatsu, Touch for Health (Kinesiology), Yoga. Candida clinic. Very large centre, reception open to personal visits 9-9 Mon-Fri, 9.30-5.30 Sats. 4 years old. 30-35 practitioners. Drop in any time to browse, plenty of information on everything at the centre and other interesting connected local events, workshops etc. Half hour consultations available for people to find out about what it available and which therapy might be appropriate for them. Mail order super blue green algae, books, audio tapes, Bach flower remedies, aromatherapy oils, food supplements, floatation tanks also available. No

wheelchair access, but will carry people and chairs upstairs. £15-25 for a session. £42 for an introductory series of three floats. They offer a training in Massage.

South London Network for Counselling and Psychotherapy
51 Clyde Road, Wallington, Surrey SM6 8PZ. (081) 647 7659.
Existential Psychotherapy, Gestalt Therapy. A network of therapists working from home and the Pellin Centre. Pellin contribution training, a mixture of existential, gestalt and cognitive material psychotherapy. Individual £12-25, couples £18-£40, groups £100-£150 per ten session.

Spectrum
7 Endymion Road, London N4 1EE. (081) 341 2277.
Bioenergetics, Couple Therapy, Couples, Encounter, Feminist Therapy, Gestalt Therapy, Homoeopathy, Psychodrama, Sex Therapy. Established for 13 year, Spectrum offer a humanistic, eclectic approach to psychotherapy. There are 17 rooms and 25 therapists are involved. Drop-in evenings and seminars. Run an incest project which has charitable status, a sexual abuse and dysfunction programme. Run a standing conference on incest. Wheelchair access. Individual sessions £20-46, workshops approximately £15 per session. Concessions. They offer a training in psychotherapy and counselling.

Spira - Self Defence for Women
93 Percy Road, Shepherds Bush, London W12 9QH. (081) 743 7246.
Spira aims to empower the individual by applying the ancient arts of Chi Kung and Tai Chi,

using breathing and movement meditations. They also are intended to help you discover the source of your inner strength (Chi) and find ways to express and direct the unified power of body, mind and spirit. These methods can help deal with stress and increase assertiveness. All women are welcome regardless of age or abilities. Day workshops, intensives and six to twelve week courses. £Neg.

Spiritualist Association of Great Britain
33 Belgrave Square, London SW1X 8QL. (071) 235 3351.
Healing, Spiritualism. Seminars, workshops, lectures and demonstrations of clairvoyance. Individual sessions with mediums, which the SAGB state are 'to provide evidence of survival (after death) and NOT to predict the future'. £12 per day workshop (£10 members), individual sessions with mediums £19 per hour (£16 members). No charge for spiritual healing, but voluntary donations accepted from those who can afford it.

Splashdown Birth Pools
17 Wellington Terrace, Harrow-on-the-Hill, Middlesex HA1 3EP. (081) 422 9308.
Active Birth. Free information, advice and workshops on water birth.

Sri Aurobindo Circle
8 Sherwood Avenue, Streatham Vale, London SW16 5EW. (081) 679 0854.
Hinduism, Meditation, Yoga. Follow teachings of Sri Aurobindo and the Mother, and now under the direction of Sri M P Pandit. Central belief is in evolution of consciousness, which is seen as divine at its core. Evenings, weekends, study circle, work in groups, collective meditation.

309

LIST OF CENTRES

St James Centre for Health and Healing
197 Picadilly, London W1V 9LF. (071) 437 7118.
Acupuncture, Art Therapy, Counselling, Healing, Herbalism, Homoeopathy, Meditation, Osteopathy, Relaxation Training, Stress Management. Psychotherapy, self-care, therapies and support groups. Cancer support. Individual sessions approximately £20 per hour. Concessions. Cancer support group free. Free clinics twice a month.

St. Marylebone Healing and Counselling Centre
St. Marylebone Parish Church, 17 Marylebone Road, London NW1 5LT. (071) 935 6374.
Counselling. There is both a pastoral centre here and a medical centre. The pastoral centre was opened in 1987 and has a drop-in and referral system for counselling and befriending. It is situated in the restored crypt of St. Marylebone church and has six counselling rooms, a small hall and a teaching room. The medical centre is an NHS general practice which also provides osteopathy, acupuncture, massage, homoeopathy etc. for NHS patients registered with the practice. Sadly for those not living with the catchment area, this is only for locals. Let's hope however that this is the shape of things to come, and that more people will be able to be referred for complementary treatments on the premises by their GP. Free. Donation for counselling.

Studio 8
10 Wycliffe Row, Totterdown, Bristol BS3 4RU. (0272) 713488.
Not so much therapeutic in orientation, more an exploration of creativity and imagination through art in weekend and residential format. See 'Residential Workshops' section.

Studio E
49 The Avenue, London NW6 7NR. (081) 459 5442.
Martial Arts, Transpersonal Therapy. Weekend workshops on myth, expression painting, inner dance etc. Tai chi weekly classes. Individual psychotherapy sessions. £30-42 per weekend.

Subud Central London
50 Shirland Road, London W9.

Sunra
26 Balham Hill, Clapham South, London SW12 9EB. (081) 675 9224.
Acupuncture, Aromatherapy, Counselling, Homoeopathy, Martial Arts, Massage, Meditation, Mind Clearing, Osteopathy, Rebirthing, Reflexology, Shiatsu, Yoga, Chi Kung, Mind Clearing, Oriental Medicine, Chinese Medicine, Tarot, Compulsive Eating Therapy. Sauna and jacuzzi with electronically purified water. From £3.20 per yoga class. Treatments from £20. Full membership of centre is £200 which gives unlimited use of sauna and jacuzzi. Classes and therapy do not require membership. Day membership for sauna and jacuzzi. They offer a training in Massage.

T

Tavistock Clinic
120 Belsize Lane, Swiss Cottage, London NW3 5BA. (071) 435 7111.
Couples, Family Therapy, Group Oriented Therapy, Kleinian Analysis, Psychoanalytic Therapy. They offer a training in Family Therapy and Group Oriented Therapy and Psychoanalytic Therapy.

Teach Yourself Meditation
BCM ACT, London WC1N 3XX.
Two books to teach yourself meditation; beginners and advanced courses.

Teilhard Centre
23 Kensington Square, London W8 5HN. (071) 937 5372.
Small groups meet regularly, and annual weekend conference, annual lecture and occasional day conferences are held. Publish 'Teihard Review, Journal for Cosmic Convergence', three times yearly.

Teleos Clinic
3rd Floor, 9 Cavendish Square, Oxford Circus, London W1 9DD. (071) 637 3088.
Chiropractic, Homoeopathy. Mostly beauty treatment oriented: acne treatment, facelifts. £Vary.

Thames & Ganges Trading Co
36 Eastcastle Street, London W1. (071) 631 4106.
Herbalism. Treatment with herbs (mostly Indian and Pakistani herbs). Appointment necessary. Open 5-8pm Mon, Tue, Wed and Sat. Prices vary.

Theosophical Society
50 Gloucester Place, London W1H 3HJ. (071) 935 9261.
Public lectures on spirituality. Prices vary from free lectures with collection to £5-£12 for day events. Cheaper for members and low waged.

LIST OF CENTRES

Therapy Made Unique
21 Primrose Road, South Woodford, London E18 1DD . (081) 989 3510.
Aromatherapy, Bach Flower Remedies, Diet Therapy Therapy, Homoeopathy, Reflexology. Aromatherapy for arthritic ailments and sports injuries. Specialists in homoeopathy for children's illnesses. Workshops on how to use Bach flower remedies, nutrition, and (on the last Saturday of every month) pendulum dowsing to help maintain good health. £10-18 depending on status and treatment. Concessions for children and pensioners, £12 half massage, £18 reflexology and homoeopathy, £20 for full aromatherapy message.

Throssel Hole Priory
Carrshield, Hexham, Northumberland NE47 8AL. (0434) 345204 (9.30am-7pm).
Buddhism, Retreats. Soto Zen Buddhist retreat centre and monastery in Northumberland affiliated with Shasta Abbey whose spiritual director/abbess is Rev. Master Jiyu-Kennett. Throssel Hole Priory is run by Rev. Master Daishin Morgan, one of her senior disciples, who lectures regularly there. Bookshop, tour of monastery, meditation instruction by appointment. Donation requested for all retreats.

Tibbi-Naturopathic Medical Foundation
75 Falcon Road, Battersea, London SW11 2PF.
Naturopathy.

Tibet Foundation
43 New Oxford Street, London WC1A 1BH. (071) 379 0634.
Information on Tibetan Medicine. The Foundation runs seminars with visiting Tibetan physicians, with whom consultations are also available. Promotes Tibetan culture and events in the UK.

Transcendental Meditation Baker Street Centre
24 Linhope Street, Marylebone, London NW1 6TH. (071) 402 3451.
Meditation. Run courses on transcendental meditation. Free introductory presentations, phone for details. Cost of instruction is £180 per course fee. Concessions.

Transcendental Meditation National Office
Mentmore Towers, Mentmore, Leighton Buzzard LU7 0QH .
Meditation. Can put you in touch with your local TM centre.

UK Homoeopathic Medical Association
243 The Broadway, Southall, Middlesex UB1 3AN (081) 574 4281.
Mainly for practitioners who have qualified in homoeopathy, who go on to a register of practitioners, which is made available to the public. £40 pa. membs. You can ring up to find a local practitioner. They will send free a directory of members. Quicker response if you send SAE. Publish journal.

UK Training College of Hypnotherapy and Counselling
College House, 10 Alexander Street, Bayswater, London W2 5NT. (071) 221 1796/(071) 727 2006.
Hypnotherapy. Register of therapists; training.

Universal Training
35 Tempo House, 15 Falcon Road, London SW11 2PJ. (071) 351 7437.
Courses in personal development which include meditation, body language training, affirmations plus own brand of self exploration. Format for core course, Turning Points, is one weekend plus three evening. £250 plus VAT.

Video Therapy
BM 6994, London WC1N 3XX. (071) 821 9146.
Video therapy to improve self presentation, assertiveness and communication. Individual sessions lasting 2 hours.

Welbeck Counselling Service
5 Clarkes Mews, Marylebone, London W1N 1RR. (071) 935 3073.
Counselling, Sex Therapy, Stress Management. Humanistic counselling encompassing Rogerian, Egan, Gestalt and Transactional Analysis, as well as behavioural therapy and career counselling 2 consulting rooms. A number of the staff are chartered psychologists. Run open training

311

events programme. Space to rent occasionally. Personal counselling £38, couple £45 including VAT. Career counselling £75 per hour, stress management £65 per hour.

Wellspring Clinic

1 Coniger Road, Parsons Green, Fulham, London SW6 3TB. (071) 736 3367.
Acupuncture, Aromatherapy, Chiropractic, Colonic Irrigation, Counselling, Massage, Osteopathy, Radionics, Reflexology. Radionic hair analysis, vitamin assessments, detoxification programmes, skin treatments, energy medicine, herbal tonics. Established since 1987, 5 therapy rooms in a Victorian House. Sell vitamins, herbal remedies, skin care products. Colonics £40.25 or £201.15 for 6 sessions. Aromatherapy £30 for one and a half hours. Acupuncture £25. Hair analysis £34.50. Celluite treatments £300 plus VAT for 6. Counselling £30 for 1 hour.

West London Buddhist Centre

7 Colville Houses, Talbot Road, Westbourne Park, London W11 1JB. (071) 727 9382.
Alexander Technique, Buddhism, Massage, Meditation, Retreats, Yoga. A centre affiliated with the Friends of the Western Buddhist Order (see also London Buddhist Centre) founded by an Englishman, the Ven. Sangharakshita who spent 20 years in India studying Buddhism. Small centre which consists of two floors of a Georgian terrace staffed by volunteers. Evening classes, weekends, courses and retreats in Sussex and Suffolk. Residential communities (not at centre but nearby). Run wholefood shop, Friends Foods. Bookshop and practice rooms at centre, open

for drop-in. Weekly drop-in classes £3 per evening (£1.75 concessions). 6 week courses £28 (£18 concessions). Weekend retreats £35 (£25 concessions).

West London School of Therapeutic Massage and Reflexology

41 St. Lukes Road, Westbourne Park, London W11 1DD. (071) 229 7411.
Aromatherapy, Homoeopathy, Massage, Massage, Reflexology, Shiatsu. They offer a training in Massage and Reflexology.

Westminster Natural Health Centre

52 Rochester Row, Westminster, London SW1 1JU. (071) 834 0861 or 630 6686.
Acupuncture, Alexander Technique, Aromatherapy, Biodynamic Massage, Chiropractic, Counselling, Diet Therapy, Herbalism, Homoeopathy, Massage, Naturopathy, Osteopathy, Reflexology, Shiatsu, Yoga. Open for drop-in information 9.30-4.30. Established in 1987, this natural health centre won the Journal of Alternative and Complementary Medicine's 'Practice of the Year' award in 1988 and 1989. There are 7 consulting rooms and 25 qualified practitioners who are also insured. Small reading room. Access: one step up to ground floor. Range £18-£30. Concessions.

Westminster Pastoral Foundation

23 Kensington Square, Kensington, London W8 5HN. (071) 937 6956.
Assertion, Bereavement Counselling, Counselling, Couples, Family Therapy. Short courses on aspects of counselling and spirituality. Individual and group

sessions. They offer a training in Counselling and Group Oriented Therapy.

White Eagle Lodge

9 St. Mary Abbots Place, Kensington High Street, London W8 6LS. (071) 603 7914.
Healing, Meditation, Yoga. Services of worship, healing, meditation and prayer for 'sending out the light'. Meetings at above address, also open for drop in 2-5.30, Mon-Thurs. Bookshop, library, chapel for meditation.

Wholeness

26 Mulberry Way, South Woodford, London E18 1ED. (081) 530 8804.
Colonic Irrigation, Hypnotherapy, Neuro-linguistic Programming. This husband and wife team have been established for 2 years at this address. Mail order. Sell books and products. Wheelchair access. £25 for colonic irrigation, £20 for psychotherapy. Concessions available.

Wholistic Health and Life Extension

290 Hanworth Road, Hampton, Middlesex TW12 3EP. (081) 979 7841.
Crystal Therapy. Workshops on use of crystals and gems in healing. Also electronic gem therapy. 1 day workshop £30.

Wholistic Health Centre

1 Upland Road, South Croydon, Surrey CR2 6RD. (081) 681 8665.
Acupuncture, Aromatherapy, Bach Flower Remedies, Diet Therapy Therapy, Iridology, Laser Therapy, Macrobiotics, Osteopathy, Shiatsu. The centre has been established since 1983 and is based on the holistic approach to health. Three quarters of an hour from Victoria

station and they say it's a 'very dynamic' centre. They give talks, organise open days and participate in the local fairs. Sliding scale. A free fifteen minute 'chat' is available by appointment. First diagnosis around £22. First treatment between £15 and £20.

Will (Workshop Institute for Living Learning)

218 Randolph Avenue, London W9. (071) 328 8955.
Group Oriented Therapy. They practice 'theme-centred interaction' which is a group dynamic method based on the belief that thought and feeling should not be separated and that every group member has equal rights. £40 per weekend workshop.

Wilson Associates

174 Franciscan Road, London SW17 8HH. (081) 767 6756.
Run 'Being Brilliant' course which aims to uncover inner talent and ability. 6 sessions of 90 minutes each £175.

Wimbledon Clinic of Natural Medicine

1 Evelyn Road, London SW19 8NU. (081) 540 3389.
Acupuncture, Alexander Technique, Aromatherapy, Colonic Irrigation, Counselling, Homoeopathy, Hypnotherapy, Laser Therapy, Massage, Osteopathy, Reflexology, EAV Diagnosis, Allergy Testing and Desensitisation, Ozone Therapy, Bioenergetic Medicine, Sports Injury Clinic, Psychotherapy. Large centre with up-to-date equipment for diagnosis and treatment, which has been established for 10 years. Open days, mail order water filters, equipment. Wheelchair access. From £10-50.

Women Unlimited

79 Pathfield Road, London SW16 5PA. (081) 677 7503.
Assertion Therapy, Feminist Therapy. and Empowerment Training, Consultancy and Team Building Sessions. Consultancy work and group work offered to organisations who want their staff to get more out of their personal and working lives. Sliding scale according to income. Average 1 hour counselling (individual) session is £20.

Women's Natural Health Centre

1 Hillside, Highgate Road, London NW5 1QT. (071) 482 3293.
Acupuncture, Counselling, Healing, Herbalism, Homoeopathy, Massage, Osteopathy, Reflexology. Mon-Fri 9-6. Established 6 years. Appointment needed. For women and their children on a low income only. Access for wheelchairs limited though they can do home visits. £10 per session.

Women's Therapy Centre

6 Manor Gardens, Holloway, London N7 6LA. (071) 263 6200.
Art Therapy, Assertion, Assertion Therapy, Bioenergetics, Eating Problem, Feminist Therapy, Gestalt, Massage, Psychoanalytic Therapy, Sex Therapy, Stress Management. Workshops and therapy given by women for women. Also workshops for black women, women with disabilities, lesbians. Established for 14 years. Advice and information, referral to private therapy network. Sells books. The Women's Therapy Centre always needs volunteers, and is also currently looking for funding. Sliding scale for workshops and therapy. Very low fees avail-

able for unemployed. They offer a training in Feminist Therapy.

Wood Street Clinic

133 Wood Street, Barnet, Herts EN5 4BX . 441 0231/449 7656.
Acupuncture, Alexander Technique, Aromatherapy, Chiropractic, Counselling, Herbalism, Homoeopathy, Hypnotherapy, Massage, Osteopathy, Reflexology, Marriage Guidance, Psychotherapy, Chiropody. Owned and run by Mr Mervyn D Cole. Consultation service for those unsure of which therapy to choose (for a fee).

Workshops with a Difference

19 Fourth Cross Road, Twickenham, London TW2 5EL. (081) 894 5980/(0598) 53440.
Motivational workshops in groups, and one to one work with individuals wishing to move into their vision through accessing their higher consciousness. Workshops take place in different venues -health clubs and centres mostly. One to one work in Twickenham or the client's own homes. Lending library of Lazaris material for clients and rental service for the general public. Wheelchair access. Sample: 2 day workshop £75.

Wrekin Trust

Runnings Park, Croft Bank, West Malvern, Worcs WR14 4BP. (0684) 892898.
Varied programme of workshops on a variety of psychological, self developmental and spiritual issues such as Kabbalah, astrology, past life therapy, relationships, women and men, death and dying, myth, etc. Some are residential, and others take place in London. Also Summer

LIST OF CENTRES

schools, journeys and pilgrimages. Mail order lectures. Non residential weekend workshop £58, residential £110. Membership (from £12) entitles you to a reduction. Mailing list and newsletter £4 per year.

Yoga Culture and Therapy Foundation

Flat G, 22 Montague St, London WC1B 5BH. (081) 451 2783.

Practice Yoga Therapy, which, distinct from ordinary yoga, is specifically aimed at curing disease. This is done through postures, breathing, cleansing through exercises, diet, massage. Can put people in touch with yoga teachers. Yoga weekends. Will be starting a Yoga Therapy training course in 1991. Individual session costs vary depending on individual practitioners, £20 per session average.

Yoga Dham

67 Pinner Park Ave, North Harrow, Middlesex HA2 6JY. (081) 428 6691.

Yoga. Individual and group yoga classes, also weekends. Yoga videos. Residential weekends £62-£69.

Yoga for Health Foundation

Ickwell Bury, Ickwell Green, Nr Biggleswade, Bedfordshire SG18 9EF. (0767) 27271.

Yoga. Massage and reflexology also available. Established 1978, this is a primarily residential, generally short stay (one/two weeks) centre. Day and overnight guests also welcome.

Please notify in advance of day visits. Centre takes 25 guests residentially. Set in four acres of grounds. Books and tapes available by mail order. Special conferences and seminars during the year, as well as concerts. Family festival every August. Wheelchair access. Must be a member to stay. Per day (full board, yoga sessions and activities) £33. Weekends £59.50. Per week £210. Membership £10 per annum, £15 families.

Z

Ziva Belic Aromatherapy International School

20 Darwin Road, South Ealing, London W5 4BD. (081) 568 0415.

Aromatherapy. Established 5 years. Video available, aromatherapy and essential oils also sold. Register. Model clients often required for trainees, so phone early mornings for this free treatment. £20 for individual sessions. They offer a training in Aromatherapy.